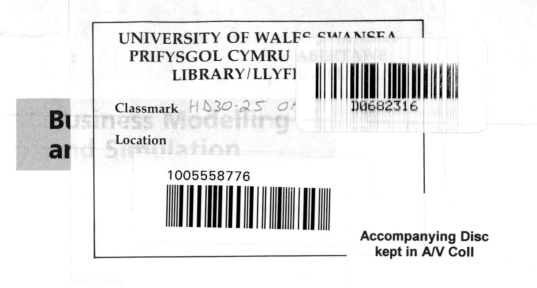

Business Modelling and Simulation

Les Oakshott Bsc (Hons), Msc, PGCE

Senior Lecturer in the Department of Mathematical Sciences,
University of the West of England, Bristol

An imprint of **Pearson Education**

Harlow, England · London · New York · Reading, Massachusetts · San Francisco · Toronto · Don Mills, Ontario · Sydney
Tokyo · Singapore · Hong Kong · Seoul · Taipei · Cape Town · Madrid · Mexico City · Amsterdam · Munich · Paris · Milan

Dedicated to Vicky, Andrew and Kim

Pearson Education Limited
Edinburgh Gate
Harlow
Essex CM20 2JE
England

And Associated Companies throughout the world

Visit us on the World Wide Web at:
http://www.pearsoneduc.com

First published in Great Britain in 1997

ISBN 0 273 61251 4

British Library Cataloguing in Publication Data
A CIP catalogue record for this book can be obtained from the British Library

10 9 8 7 6 5 4 3

Typeset by Florencetype Ltd, Stoodleigh, Devon
Printed and bound in Great Britain by Redwood Books, Trowbridge, Wiltshire

Contents

13 A review of simulation software 313

Les Oakshott

Preface

Business requires employees who are numerate and computer literate. The ability to use computer software, and to be able to make sensible recommendations based on the output from the software, is an essential prerequisite to the success of the individual employee, and ultimately the company itself. Many of these computer programs involve the use or the development of models, and an understanding of how these models work, as well as their strengths and weaknesses, is an important skill a graduate can take to his or her future employer.

This text looks at a number of different models, ranging from simple models that can be used to determine the best inventory control policy for a company, to models that can simulate the working of a complex procedure or system. Although some of these models can be used without the need for computer software, the emphasis in this text is the use of computers to help solve problems. To illustrate how models can be used to solve business problems, a number of scenarios and case studies have been incorporated into the text. The purpose of the scenarios is to illustrate particular models or modelling techniques. These scenarios will occur at regular intervals throughout most chapters, and can be used to reinforce a student's understanding of a particular topic. Case studies have been included in the text to exemplify how the technique of simulation is carried out in practice. They are drawn from different sectors of business and illustrate the wide variety of problems that can be solved using this modelling technique.

Students purchasing this text will have different backgrounds and different needs. Some will be following a general business course and will only require an overview of the subject. Other students will be following more quantitative courses, which might involve a substantial element of modelling. There are other courses that specialise in the technique of simulation, and students following these courses will require a much deeper understanding of the subject. This book attempts to satisfy all these different needs, although for some students, this text might be seen as an introduction to one particular aspect of modelling. For these students, there are a number of other more specialised texts that might be needed, and these are referred to at various stages in the text and in the further reading sections. For the general reader there are a number of self-contained chapters that will give an understanding of modelling techniques, while the student studying a more specialised course will need to follow certain chapters in sequence. The student's background in statistics is another issue addressed in this text. Modelling requires a knowledge of statistics and probability, which not all students will possess or will have forgotten. To help these students, a chapter has been included on statistics, which provides the statistical concepts necessary to underpin the material supplied in the text.

This text emphasises the practical issues connected with modelling, and makes use of computer software wherever possible. However, it does not attempt to teach a particular package, nor does the use of a package imply that this is the best package for a particular application. The choice of packages has been made mainly by what is generally available in the higher education sector. In all cases printouts from the packages are provided, and in some cases the calculations are performed manually as well. A disk is available at the back of the book which contains details of the data files used in the text. Most of these files are Excel based, but they should be able to be read by most spreadsheets.

How to use this book

Chapter	Content	Prerequisites
Chapter 1	Overview and an introduction to the scenarios and case studies.	None
Chapter 2	A brief outline of models and modelling. Useful to all students.	None
Chapter 3	A chapter on statistics for those students who need some revision on basic statistical and probability concepts.	None
Chapter 4	Discussion of a range of models that can be solved by analytical means. Useful for students studying modelling or operational research topics.	Chapter 3 for parts
Chapter 5	A general chapter on simulation modelling for all students, but particularly those who only want an overview of the technique. Case Study 1 is included here.	None
Chapter 6	Contains details of where simulation could be used. Case Study 2 is included here.	None
Chapter 7	A more technical chapter for those taking a specialised course that contains a substantial amount of simulation.	Chapter 3
Chapter 8	A description of spreadsheet modelling, that could be useful on many courses.	Chapters 5 and 7
Chapter 9	Gives an outline of the construction of simulation models.	Chapter 5
Chapter 10	This chapter looks at the practical issue of data collection.	Chapters 3 and 5
Chapter 11	Gives details of how to validate a simulation model. The third case study is given here.	Chapters 3 and 10
Chapter 12	This chapter explains how to use statistics to analyse the results from simulation experiments. The fourth case study is included here.	Chapters 3 and 11
Chapter 13	A chapter on simulation software that could be useful for any level of reader.	None

Acknowledgements

I would like to thank the Microsoft Corporation for permission to use material generated from Excel worksheets and to distribute data files in electronic form. I would also like to thank the Systems Modeling Corporation and SPSS Ltd for permission to include details of their software and MINITAB Ltd for providing material and software through their Author Assistance Programme. The Palisade Corporation have been most helpful in supplying software to help in the preparation of Chapter 8.

I would also like to thank the following people: Mr Skinner of Whiteladies Health Centre, Bristol, for giving me permission to use the health centre as a scenario in this text; Andrew Greasley and David Smith for co-authoring Chapters 6 and 11; Ruth Davies, Julian Flowers and the Operational Research Society for permission to reproduce their paper on the simulation of a health care problem; Mike Pool for his help in writing Case study 1; Irmgard Husinsky for allowing me to make reference to the EUROSIM software comparisons; staff at the University of the West of England, Bristol, who read the manuscript; students at the University of the West of England for help in collecting data for the scenarios; Penelope Woolf at Pitman Publishing for the patience she has shown through my many missed deadlines!

Les Oakshott
1996

1

Introduction and overview

Les Oakshott

As business becomes more complex, the decisions faced by management become more difficult to solve. Decisions can no longer be taken as a result of a 'hunch' or what was once called *experience*. Instead, managers and people who are paid to make decisions need to use an armoury of techniques to help them. Most of these techniques are quantitative in nature and so the decision maker needs to be numerate. Being numerate does not necessarily mean being a mathematician, but it does mean being comfortable with figures and appreciating that there are a number of numerate techniques that can be applied to business problems. Many of these techniques are essentially concerned with data manipulation. Data manipulation is the analysis of data in order to extract from it some information that will be of benefit to the company or organisation. So, we might want to analyse a company's sales in order to make comparisons with the previous year. However, we might also want to use the data to predict the sales for the next year, in which case we are attempting to develop a **model** of the sales data. Although statistical models are very useful, this text is concerned mainly with models of processes. These models attempt to replicate the structure of the process so that the effect of changes on the process can be estimated. They can be **physical** models or they can be **symbolic** models, and in this text we will be interested in the latter. We shall see in later chapters that this type of model is a very powerful tool in the decision maker's 'tool kit'.

The role of modelling in the decision-making process

The types of decisions we are concerned with in this text are generally of the 'What if?' variety. For example:

- What if the demand for this product increased?
- What if we changed the way that this process operates?
- What might happen if this machine failed?

- ■ What if we ordered a component in batches of 1000?
- ■ What if the profit on this item increased?
- ■ What if we obtained a larger quantity of this material?
- ■ What would happen if the labour hours available were increased?

However, we will also give examples of the use of models to answer more specific questions, such as:

- ■ How many of each product should we make to maximise profits?
- ■ How many machines do we need for this process?
- ■ How many staff do we need to give a certain level of service?
- ■ What is the optimum order quantity?
- ■ What is the best design for this warehouse?
- ■ What is the chance that this investment will fail?

Although these decisions can be – and often are – made using unscientific methods, this type of decision making is unlikely to lead to the best decision being made. The use of the word *best* is deliberate in that there is not always a *wrong* decision. The best decision may give the highest profit or the lowest cost, so that not using the best decision may incur a cost to the company. Since business is now fiercely competitive, and many companies are working at very slender profit margins, every process within a company needs to be working at optimum efficiency. To achieve an improvement in efficiency, a company may have to reduce its labour force, but it could equally mean that outdated methods are replaced with more efficient alternatives. If efficiency can be improved, the company will become more competitive, which will be of benefit to all the employees of a company.

In the following chapters, we will be looking at several types of models that can be of use to a wide variety of businesses. Some of these models are 'ready to use', while others will have to be built. An understanding of the model-building process is one of the key aims of this text.

The need for a text on modelling and simulation

A knowledge of modelling techniques is one of the most important assets a graduate can take to a business. This knowledge should be gained from courses studied at university level, but numerous studies have shown that graduates entering business do not have sufficient understanding of these techniques. This has been highlighted following a survey commissioned by the DTI (Simulation Study Group, 1991). The survey investigated the awareness of small- and medium-sized enterprises (SMEs) in the manufacturing sector to simulation modelling. Simulation modelling is the main emphasis in this text, and concerns the modelling of complex systems where other modelling techniques are not adequate. The survey team found that the awareness of simulation in this sector was low, preventing the realisation of savings of some £300m per annum. Part of the reason for the low awareness of this particular modelling technique is that it is not covered adequately at university level. The survey indicated that the amount of teaching of simulation varies greatly and is often at an awareness level only. The actual hours spent on simulation varied from as little as two hours up to a maximum of 72 hours. The distribution is skewed to the bottom of the range, with 62 per cent of the teaching being below twenty hours. The reason for the low number of hours taught on this modelling technique is often because so many other topics have to be fitted into the syllabus. Modelling is often taught as part (and often a small part) of a general quantitative methods module. It may also be taught by lecturers who have not had sufficient training in some of the modelling techniques and do not feel confident to teach it to any depth. There is also the problem that most modelling requires the use of computer software, which is not always available in university departments.

Design criteria for this text

In the preparation for this book, the author carried out his own (unpublished) survey. This survey was aimed at departments within universities and colleges of higher education where it was thought that courses on business modelling would take place. The survey was not as comprehensive as the one carried out by the DTI, but it was only intended as a guide as to the potential market for a new textbook on modelling and simulation. The main purpose of the survey was to discover what lecturers wanted from a book on modelling, but it also asked questions about the hours devoted to the teaching of modelling and simulation. Out of 100 questionnaires that were sent out, 30 replies were received. Of this 30, eleven were from the 'old' universities, fifteen from the 'new' universities, and four were from colleges of higher education. The awards that were covered ranged from Masters in Business Decision Making to an HND in Mathematics, Operational Research and Statistics. The majority had business or management in the title. The class contact varied from six to ninety hours, with the data skewed to the bottom of the range, as was shown in the DTI survey. The majority of the sample did not teach simulation as a separate subject, although four replies did not specify. This information is summarised in Table 1.1. The fact that the breakdown by the separate subject is identical to the breakdown by the type of institution is coincidental, although a higher proportion of older universities do tend to teach simulation as a separate subject.

Table 1.1 ■ Summary of the results from the survey carried out in 1994

Separate subject?	Number	Average contact hours	Average number of students
Yes	11	24	32
No	15	15	49
Not specified	4	29	40

The main conclusion was that little appeared to have changed in terms of the amount of teaching that was devoted to simulation since the DTI had conducted its survey in 1991. Simulation was still taught as a topic within a more general quantitative module, and little time was allocated to modelling and simulation. This conclusion helped influence the main aim of the text, which was to produce a book that would be suitable for a wide range of courses. It is hoped, therefore, that students following a module that has some modelling element to it will find at least part of the text useful.

In addition to providing information on the amount of teaching devoted to modelling and simulation, the survey helped prioritise the topics that a book of this nature should contain. The most important topic appeared to be a general description of models and modelling. Other topics that were considered to be important included principles of simulation, use of spreadsheets in modelling, basic probability and statistics, and simulation software. All of these topics have been allocated separate chapters in this book.

Other useful information that came from this survey was that a textbook on modelling and simulation should not be too theoretical, but should contain examples of *how* modelling and simulation is carried out in practice. This has been achieved through the use of real case studies and scenarios.

The treatment of statistics

Although there are a few models that can be used without a knowledge of statistics, this is the exception rather than the rule. A knowledge of statistics is necessary both to understand how to build a model, and to help analyse the output from a model. The results obtained from many models are *sample* results, and this means that we need to apply statistics in order to make inferences about the *population*. The survey findings suggested that a chapter on basic probability and statistics is necessary and this has been included. It is also recognised that most statistical analysis is carried out using computer software, and this has been reflected in the extensive use of statistical software in this text. The main statistical package used in this text is MINITAB, although SPSS is used as well. Most students will have used one or both of these packages, but it is not essential for an understanding of the principles involved. Most of the calculations have been carried out by hand as well as by computer, so the computer printouts can be ignored (or vice versa). The data and output from these packages have been saved on the computer disk that accompanies this text.

The use of computers and computer software

Most modelling is carried out by computer these days, and any text on modelling and simulation should reflect this fact. However, the intention was not to write a manual on using a particular package. Instead, the purpose is to give examples of how software can be used to aid the modelling process. In some cases an explanation is provided on how to use a spreadsheet for a particular task, but in general this is not provided as it was felt to be unnecessary and would distract from the main emphasis of the text.

The two main types of software used are spreadsheets and simulation packages. The spreadsheet used is Excel, although most modern spreadsheets would be equally as good. A spreadsheet is excellent for some types of modelling, and when combined with an 'add on' such as @RISK, can be a very powerful modelling device. However, spreadsheets cannot be used for all types of models, and for most simulation modelling a different type of software is required. There are a large number of products on the market that can be used for simulation modelling, and most are excellent. The main simulation package used in this text is ARENA, but this is not meant to imply that this is the best simulation package available. The range of simulation software is large, and Chapter 13 is provided to give some guidance when choosing. Not only has the variety of software multiplied, but the 'user friendliness' of the software has improved dramatically. The Windows environment of modern PCs has encouraged software designers to pay far more attention to the user aspect of computer programs, and very little training is required to use most software. This is in contrast to DOS programs, where it was often necessary for the user to be sent on a course to learn the package. Of course, ease of use does have its drawbacks. The major one is that a user does not need to know much about the technique being used. If a technique has certain limitations or the output from the package is difficult to interpret, then erroneous conclusions could be made, resulting in a poor decision. There is no easy solution to this problem, although it is clear that managers and other users of the software should have at some time been exposed to the principles behind the technique. Hopefully, this text will provide the necessary understanding so that these packages can be used with confidence.

Case studies and scenarios

This book contains a number of case studies and scenarios. The four case studies represent real problems that have been solved using a modelling approach. Case study 1 is drawn from the service sector and is concerned with modelling a process or system that does not currently exist. The design of a new system is always difficult as information relating to its operation is not always available. Models require data, so this lack of information can make the modelling process difficult. In this case study, the model was built using a combination of data from an existing system and the knowledge of people in the industry. This collaboration of consultants and client staff is an important ingredient in the successful outcome of any business project.

The second case study is concerned with the provision of a transport facility in a garden festival. Modelling of transport systems can be difficult, but the latest modelling software has made this task much easier. This case study illustrates the importance of **sensitivity analysis** in the modelling process.

The third case study is a manufacturing problem, and is a good example of the importance of **validation** in model building.

The final case study is taken from the health-care sector. This sector has undergone many changes in the past few years, and hospital managers have increasingly turned to quantitative modelling as a means of improving the effectiveness of health care.

The two scenarios used in this book are based on real situations. The Whiteladies Heath Centre is a doctors' surgery, while the Drive Thru Burger restaurant is a typical fast-food drive-in restaurant. One or both of these scenarios are used in most chapters to illustrate a part of the modelling process or a particular modelling technique. The Whiteladies scenario is used to demonstrate the stages in the development of a simulation model.

The Whiteladies Health Centre

The Whiteladies Health Centre is situated in the heart of Bristol, and the centre has fund-holding status. There is a combination of appointment and 'open' surgeries, although for the purpose of this scenario we only consider the open surgeries. There are two open surgeries each day, except Wednesdays; from 8 am to 10 am and from 4 pm to 6 pm, and up to six doctors can be on duty at any one time.

A patient requiring a consultation with a doctor will turn up at the surgery and be assigned a doctor by the receptionist. The patient can ask to see a specific doctor, but this may incur an additional wait. Once allocated to a doctor, the patient will take a seat in the surgery and wait to be seen. Although the surgery is open from 8 in the morning and 4 in the afternoon, the doctors do not generally start work until around 8.30 and 4.30 respectively, so early arrivals have to wait. Patients waiting at the end of the surgery period will always be seen.

The number of patients varies from day to day, with Monday having the largest number. The number of doctors on duty also varies, and all six will be on duty on Monday. The consultation time is another variable parameter, and this can vary both by patient and by doctor.

As with all doctors' surgeries, patients have to wait to be seen. To the patient this waiting time can at best be annoying and at worst reflect badly on the efficiency of the surgery in particular and health care in general. However, if there were no queues, it is likely that the doctors would be under-utilised. Since a doctor is an expensive and valuable resource, this would not be acceptable either. The purpose of this study was therefore to investigate the queuing problem at the health centre, and to offer solutions as to improvements that might be attempted.

The data collected for this scenario consists of information on arrival times and consultation times, for each day of the week during the week beginning 7 November 1994. This data is supplied in Appendix 1 and on the disk that accompanies this text.

Drive Thru Burger restaurant

This is typical of many fast-food restaurants in that the range of food supplied is fairly basic but relatively cheap. The difference with this system is that customers are served in their cars, so that the service point is a window where a car will stop and wait to be served. In this scenario, there are two service points. A car requiring a meal will arrive at the restaurant and drive to an ordering window, where the occupants will give their order. The car will then drive to the paying window, where the food will be collected and paid for. If the food is not ready when the customer arrives at the paying window, he is asked to park in the waiting area. This would represent a deterioration of service and does not happen very often. The restaurant is open for ten hours a day, although data was not collected for the whole of this period. The data collected on the arrival of cars to the system and the time taken to be served at the two service points are given in

Appendix 1 and on the disk that accompanies this text. The data was collected on the following days and times:

Wednesday 9 November 1994	1 pm to 2 pm
Thursday 10 November 1994	6 pm to 7 pm
Friday 11 November 1994	7 pm to 8 pm

The restaurant is typical of a system where the demand for its product is variable. Decisions have to be made regarding the quantities of raw material to purchase, the price charged for products and the number of staff employed. If poor decisions are made, custom may be lost or profits may be adversely affected. To help improve the decision-making process, there are various models that can be used, ranging from inventory control models to risk analysis using simulation. Models can also be used to evaluate the effects on the quality of customer service, by changes to the system or increases in the number of customers using the restaurant. Quality of service in this study was taken to be the time spent in the queue of cars waiting to be served. This could be improved either by improving the efficiency of the cooking process or an increase in the number of service points.

References and further reading

Hollocks, B. (1992) 'A well-kept secret? Simulation in manufacturing industry reviewed', *OR Insight*, Vol. 5, Issue 4, October–December.

Simulation Study Group Horrocks, R. (1991) (ed) *Simulation in UK Manufacturing Industry*, The Management Consulting Group, Barclays Venture Centre, University of Warwick Science Park, Coventry.

2

Models and modelling

Les Oakshott

Introduction

Although this book is primarily concerned with mathematical models in general and simulation models in particular, it is necessary for the reader to have a basic knowledge of models and modelling. This is for two reasons. First, the process of modelling is the same no matter what type of model is being developed. Second, and perhaps more important, it is necessary to know which models are suitable for particular purposes. This chapter therefore attempts to outline the different types of models and uses examples to illustrate when they are suitable.

What is a model?

The idea of a model has existed since the time man developed the ability to think and attempt to change and therefore control his surroundings. In order to change his environment, early man had to understand how he interacted with the outside world and this involved *abstracting* from the environment those features that were important to him. By thinking of parts of the environment while ignoring others, a simplified model of the environment was effectively created. So in the cultivation of plants, for example, man needed to understand changes in the seasons but not how the phases of the moon affected the tides.

Throughout this book we will refer to a model as a *simplified* representation of a *system*, where a system refers to any collection of objects or processes that interact in some way. How we model a system will depend on reasons for studying the system in the first place. Take a domestic heating system. To a heating engineer a heating system would mean the components of the system such as the boiler, pipes and valves and the interactions of these different components. The purpose of looking at this system might be to try and improve the heat output in different parts of the house. However, an expert in fluid dynamics might be more interested in the flow of water through the pipes. The purpose of such a study might be to research how this flow is affected by the material of the pipes or the pressure of the water.

Systems also vary in size and complexity. The stock-control procedure in a small company might consist of one or two items which are held in a warehouse or store before being sold or transferred elsewhere. An airport, on the other hand, is a very large and complex system which is made up of a number of smaller sub-systems. It may be possible to study these sub-systems separately if the interaction between them is minimal. So the disembarkation of passengers might be sufficiently independent for a model of this sub-system to be built. However, the crew rostering system is closely tied up with the timetable of flights and the two need to be considered together.

The task of defining the system and deciding its boundaries is the most important aspect of modelling, since everything else we do follows from this definition. This aspect of modelling is more of an art than a science and this skill can only be obtained through experience. However, there are general principles that can be adopted and these will be discussed later in this chapter.

■ **Whiteladies Health Centre**   *Scenario 2.1*

> The system of interest is from the time patients arrive at the surgery to when they leave. We are not interested in phone calls or whether the patients then join another system in the chemist shop. However, if it turns out that the number of doctors on duty depends on the number of home visits, we may need to extend our boundaries to include requests for these visits.

Simple models are best

As well as defining our boundaries, we also need to make suitable assumptions about the system. This is necessary because we are attempting to build a simplified representation of a system. It is tempting to include as much detail in our model as possible but this should be avoided for two reasons. First, a complex model is more difficult to build and will therefore take longer to develop, with a greater chance of errors. Second, and perhaps more important, a simple model may be quite adequate for the intended purpose. An over-complex model may be unnecessary and may even make *experimenting* on the model difficult. A model that is more general will be easier to change so that ideas for improving the system can be tested with greater ease. So how do we decide on what assumptions to make? To a large extent this again is achieved through experience. But as we shall see later, modelling is an iterative process and although we might start with a very simple model we will probably find that we have to relax our assumptions in order to improve accuracy. For the stock-control system, we might assume that the demand or usage of the product is constant, but if this turns out to be incorrect we may need to use a more complex model. For the airport model, we might initially assume that the flow of passengers disembarking from a plane is independent of the time of day, but if this turns out to be incorrect we may need to refine the model.

■ **Whiteladies Health Centre** *Scenario 2.2*

The initial assumptions made included the following:

■ All doctors work at the same rate, so we can treat all doctors the same.

■ The patients arrive at a constant rate: that is, arrival rate is not dependent on time of day or day of week.

■ All patients are seen provided they arrive before the end-of-surgery period.

■ Doctors do not have breaks or get called away once the surgery has started.

■ The receptionists also work continuously while the surgery is open.

■ Patients do not leave the surgery until seen by a doctor.

■ Patients will go to whichever doctor is free and do not have a preference for any particular doctor.

■ Patients are seen on a 'first come first served' basis.

Some of these assumptions should appear quite reasonable while others are immediately suspect. It is likely that more patients are likely to arrive on a Monday than a Tuesday and patients often have a preference for a particular doctor. However, it may be that these extra factors will not improve the model's accuracy significantly.

This section has provided some general explanation of what a model is. We now need to look at the process of modelling in more detail.

Model validation – the modelling cycle

We must not forget that a model is only a simplified representation of reality. If we have specified the boundaries of the system incorrectly or made erroneous assumptions then our results will not be accurate. The cliché 'garbage in, garbage out' is particularly true with model development. So how do we ensure that our models are accurate? The answer is that we must continually test our results against known facts. In practice this means that our model is continually being improved until the results are acceptable. Figure 2.1 illustrates the modelling cycle in diagrammatic form.

System definition

During the initial stages of modelling we must define the system and agree the aims of the study. We should also list the assumptions to be made since this will influence the data to be collected and determine the complexity of the model. In a stock-control system we might want to try and reduce the quantity of goods held in the warehouse. Since it costs money to hold goods in stock, the purpose of a stock-control model should be to minimise the cost of holding stock while

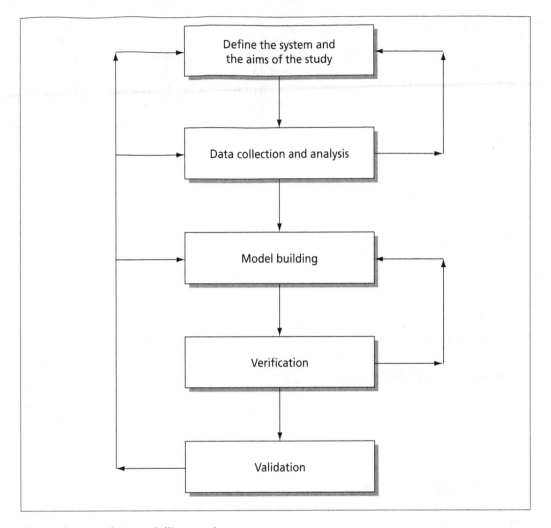

Figure 2.1 ■ **The modelling cycle**

achieving a specified level of service. Service in this context means supplying the customer with goods within an agreed time scale. For an airport we might want to reduce congestion in the luggage collection area. The model of the airport should allow ideas for improving the system to be tried out on the model rather than the real system.

Data collection

The next stage after formulating the aims of the study is to decide what data needs to be collected and how this collection is to be organised. Collection of data is a very important task and great care must be taken in the method or methods adopted. In the model of the airport, data will need to be collected on such things as arrival time of passengers and the time it takes to complete the different tasks. Questions will arise as to the quantity of data required to achieve an accurate model and when and how this data should be collected. The process of data collection often makes us reconsider the assumptions already made and this in turn may change the data required for the model. Following the successful collection of the data, it is necessary to analyse it. This analysis can often reveal problems with the data which can mean that further data needs to be collected.

Model building

The model-building phase will depend on the type of model that is to be built. Some models require experience in the formulation of complex mathematical equations while others simply require some knowledge of spreadsheets. Sometimes it is possible to approach a problem in a number of different ways and the model developed will depend on the approach taken. In many cases the use to which the model is to be put will be an important factor in deciding how the model should be built. A model that is to be used for strategic purposes may use different techniques to a model that is to be used for day-to-day planning, and this factor may override other considerations such as the cost of developing the model. The important point to remember when building any model is that it should initially be made as simple as possible.

Verification and validation

Once the model has been built it is necessary to verify that it is correct. **Verification** is different to **validation** which we will look at shortly. The process of verification will depend on the type of model, but essentially it involves checking that the model does what we expect. Validation is different in that it is a check to see if the model produces results that agree with what is observed in the real system. The task of validation is an essential part of model building and if we are unable to validate our model then any results that the model subsequently produces will not be reliable. It is unlikely that a model will validate the first time, and changes are likely to be required before a valid model is produced. Usually we would have had suspicions about some of the assumptions and the validation will merely confirm these suspicions. If this is the case, adjustments will need to be made to the model in order to allow for the change in assumptions. This will inevitably mean that the model becomes more complex. In some cases it will take many attempts to achieve a satisfactory model and even then the validation may not be perfect.

Validation will sometimes be difficult because the real system does not exist. An example could be the design of a new ferry terminal. Since the terminal does not yet exist, there will not be any data that can be used for comparison purposes. In these situations there are a number of alternative strategies, such as using similar installations or asking 'experts' to give their opinion on the results from the model. Even if a similar system does not exist it may be possible to find a system where part of the model can be tested. In the case of the ferry terminal, a system may exist where the off-loading facilities are similar so some data on this part of the system can be obtained. A view on whether the results look reasonable can also be obtained from people who are knowledgeable about the proposed system. Even where the system exists, the use of people not connected with the modelling can be extremely useful as they can provide a second opinion on the validity of the results.

Once the model has been validated it can be used to experiment with changes to the system or, in the case of a new system, it can allow different designs or ideas to be tried out.

▪ Whiteladies Health Centre   *Scenario 2.3*

> As with many surgeries, the problem appeared to be excessive queuing times by patients. Doctors are a scarce resource who need to be fully utilised, but it may be possible to alter the system in such a way that the time the patients spend in the surgery is reduced. However, before a model of this system can be used to test out any ideas it is necessary to validate the model. One possible validation check in this case is the patient queuing times. The average queuing times determined by the model should match those observed in real life.

Types of models

We often differentiate between **physical** models which look like the real thing and **symbolic** models which are designed to represent some aspect of reality. To differentiate between the two types of models, imagine that we have to design a housing estate. We could build a scale model of the estate with the houses, trees and other parts of the estate made from solid materials. Alternatively, we could draw the different components on paper. If all we wanted was to get a feel for the development, we might be happy to use a rectangle to represent a house and another symbol to represent a tree. Using this symbolic model we could experiment with different layouts or different road access points. Clearly this model is very limited in that it only represents the general layout and not such factors as roof styles or other more detailed aspects. However, it is very quick to produce and may be useful for certain purposes. It would of course be of no use in, say, comparing the insulation properties of different materials.

Symbolic models

There are many other types of symbolic model. These include graphs, circuit diagrams and even maps and charts. A road map is a simple but effective model of the road system and allows us to plan a route with confidence. Three-dimensional aspects of the terrain are represented on some maps by contour lines or by topographical effects. Charts of the sea allow us to visualise three-dimensional views of the seabed through the use of depth markings.

These symbolic models are examples of visual models and are non-mathematical. Non-mathematical models are particularly useful when we require a general understanding of a system. They can also give us ideas about how the system can be improved, but they cannot predict the outcome of any changes. For example, we could see what change in road distance would result in the building of a bypass but the map would not allow us to assess the effects of the bypass on traffic levels. In order to be able to obtain this amount of detail we would need to have a **mathematical** model of traffic flows.

Mathematical models

Mathematical models are far more useful but usually more difficult to build. A mathematical model is a set of mathematical and logical relationships between different elements of the system. If we wanted a model of a bypass that would allow traffic levels to be estimated, we would need to develop relationships between traffic densities and factors such as average speed of the vehicles. A mathematical model of a stock-control system would need to include the demand for the product as well as factors such as the cost of holding stock and any discounts for large orders. Mathematical models vary in complexity; a model of a simple stock-control system might be a single equation, while a model of the flow of a fluid through a pipe is much more complex and will involve second order differential equations. Because there are so many different types of mathematical models, we usually try to categorise the systems we are attempting to model.

System classification

Systems are either **static** or **dynamic**. A static system is either where time doesn't play any significant role or where we are only interested in the system at one particular instant in time. Many financial systems are static in that they give the financial state of a company or individual at a particular date.

A system that is changing over time is usually said to be a dynamic system. The flow of a fluid through a pipe is a dynamic system since the state of the system varies with time. The progress of an airline passenger as he moves through an airport is also dynamic since he will be in a different position at different times.

Systems can also be **discrete** or **continuous**. A discrete system is where the state of the system changes at discrete time intervals while a continuous system changes smoothly. The movement of an airline passenger through the airport is discrete since *events* happen (such as baggage collection) at particular times. The flow of a fluid through a pipe is continuous since there are no obvious points in time where events happen.

Deterministic and stochastic models

Models of systems are either **deterministic** or **stochastic**. A deterministic model is where an exact solution can be obtained; this is often called an analytic solution. We will look at analytical models in detail in Chapter 4, but essentially the solution to an analytical model will always be the same for the same set of input parameters. The EOQ stock-control model is a simple formula for stock-control systems, where the demand for a product is assumed to be known and constant.

This formula gives us the quantity of stock (Q) to order so as to minimise stock-holding costs. The formula is:

$$Q = \sqrt{\frac{2CD}{h}}$$

Where C is the cost of ordering, D is the expected demand and h is the cost of holding one unit in stock. All the variables in the right-hand side of the equation are known with certainty. By substituting these values into the equation, a value of Q is obtained. In practice, the demand for a product is rarely known with certainty and may vary. The use of an average in these circumstances may be adequate but if we require a more accurate model then a stochastic model is required. A stochastic model has parameters (or variables) that do not have fixed values. The values vary so that for the same set of conditions a different answer will result. Imagine repeated calculations of Q in the EOQ stock-control formula where the value for D changed for each calculation. We would not be able to give a single answer for Q although we could work out an average value. In many stochastic models the variability in a particular parameter closely follows a **probability distribution**. A probability distribution is a mathematical formula or table that gives the probability that a particular value will occur. In the rolling of a die the probability that any face will occur is ⅙ or 0.167 and the probability distribution in this case is:

Face	1	2	3	4	5	6
Probability	0.167	0.167	0.167	0.167	0.167	0.167

Of course, as we all know, it is possible to roll a die several times and never get a six! However, in the long run the frequency of occurrence of each face should be the same.

The distribution above is a very simple one and it is what we would call a discrete distribution since the values that can occur are all discrete values. An example of a discrete probability distribution is the Poisson distribution. This distribution fits the situation where events occur at random such as arrivals to a system. Where the variable can take on any value, we have a continuous distribution such as the exponential distribution or the normal distribution. These probability distributions will be discussed further in Chapters 3 and 10.

In some cases an analytical solution can be obtained for certain classes of stochastic models that involve queuing mechanisms. These models require many simplifying assumptions to be made but they do allow us to calculate certain *steady state* characteristics of the system, such as the average queuing time. In the simplest of these systems the arrival distribution is Poisson, the distribution for the service time is exponential, and there is one channel or server. This model is illustrated in Figure 2.2.

The notation for this is M/M/1, using the Kendall notation, where the first M signifies that the arrival distribution is random and the second M signifies that the service time is also random. The 1 means that there is one channel or server. If *queuing theory* is applied to this model it is possible to derive formulae for the

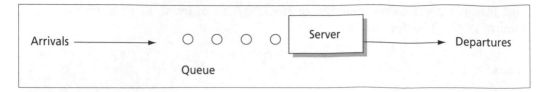

Figure 2.2 ▪ Simple queuing system

calculation of steady state characteristics of the system. For example, the formula for the average time waiting in the queue (W_q) is:

$$W_q = \frac{\lambda}{\mu(\mu - \lambda)}$$

where λ = mean arrival rate and μ = mean service rate.

There are several other more complex queuing models which allow for different arrival and service distributions or for different assumptions. Some of these will be discussed in more detail in Chapter 4.

Simulation models

However, the majority of stochastic models cannot be solved analytically and a numerical technique called **simulation** is often used. Although simulation is a technique or a methodology of solving certain types of stochastic models, we often talk about simulation models. This is because models where simulation can be applied have certain characteristics in common. These models are made up of 'rules', logical expressions and probability distributions as well as mathematical equations. The stochastic nature of the model is handled by *sampling* from the appropriate distribution and this has to be repeated many times to achieve accuracy. Simulation can be carried out on static or dynamic systems, and discrete or continuous systems. When carried out on static systems we often talk about **Monte-Carlo simulation**, while for dynamic systems the choice is between **discrete-event** or **continuous** simulation. All three types of simulation will be discussed in Chapter 5, although only Monte-Carlo and discrete-event simulation will be looked at in subsequent chapters.

▪ **Whiteladies Health Centre** *Scenario 2.4*

This is a dynamic system since we are interested in the flow of patients through the two hours that the surgery is open. It is also discrete since the state of the patient (either waiting or being seen by the doctor) changes at particular times.

Summary

This chapter explored the different types of model and how a model can help us understand and improve a system. A system can be any type of process or collection of items that together achieve a purpose. There are numerous types of systems and we looked at several examples, ranging from a simple stock-control system to a complex airport system made up of many sub-systems. Different systems require different types of models, ranging from physical to symbolic. Even with symbolic models there are many different types, although it is mathematical models that interest us here, particularly stochastic models. Stochastic models have some variability associated with them which makes them very difficult to solve analytically. The technique of simulation is often used to solve stochastic models and we usually refer to these models as simulation models.

Although a system can be extremely complex, we try and make our model as simple as possible. This is achieved by defining the boundaries of the system so that only the important features are included, and by making simplifying assumptions about the system. If the model does not validate, it is necessary to improve the model by redefining the boundaries or relaxing the assumptions. This process, called the modelling cycle, is repeated until we are satisfied that our model represents the system adequately.

▇ Exercises

2.1 Use the categories **static**, **dynamic**, **discrete** and **continuous** to describe the following systems:

    a   Gas flow in a pipe.

    b   Mortgage application and processing.

    c   Queuing at a supermarket checkout.

    d   Monthly accounts for a company.

    e   Steel works where molten steel is poured into a vat before being transported to another part of the process.

2.2 Which type of mathematical model would you use (deterministic or stochastic) to model the following systems?

    a   Accident and emergency department at a hospital.

    b   The transportation costs for a haulage company.

    c   Stock control for a company where the demand is highly variable.

2.3 Why is it necessary to validate a model? What is the difficulty with validating a model of a new system?

2.4 Apply the ideas in this chapter to the queuing mechanism of cars at the Drive Thru Burger restaurant that was described in Chapter 1. In particular, define the system and make a list of the kind of assumptions that might need to be applied to it.

Further reading

Neelamkavil, F. (1987) *Computer Simulation and Modelling* (Chapters 2, 3 and 4), Wiley, Chichester, England.

Watson, J. and Blackstone, J. H. (1989) *Computer Simulation*, Second Edition (Chapter 1), Wiley, Singapore.

3

Statistical aspects of modelling

Les Oakshott

Introduction

A good understanding of probability and statistics is a prerequisite for most forms of model building. Although statistical software packages are generally used for the analysis of data, there is no substitute for having some basic knowledge of the techniques used. Without this knowledge an inappropriate or incorrect technique may be used, or the results misinterpreted. This chapter attempts to explain the basic concepts necessary to follow the ideas and techniques introduced in subsequent chapters, but it is not possible to include every technique and concept in one chapter. A selection of good statistical textbooks is provided at the end of the chapter and readers are encouraged to refer to at least one of these sources.

This chapter is divided into three main sections. The first section is concerned with general descriptive measures of statistics, while the second and third sections are concerned with probability and inferential statistics respectively.

Descriptive statistics

During the modelling process, large quantities of data are frequently collected and/or generated by the model. We use this data either to help build the model or to draw conclusions about the system we are modelling. This data usually forms a *sample* and from this sample we can, hopefully, infer something about the *population* from which the sample came. Later in this chapter we will discuss how to make this inference, but for the time being we will be looking at the data in its own right. That is, we will be describing the data using two main approaches. The first approach is to present the data graphically. Graphical presentation gives us an overview of the data and allows qualitative judgements to be made. The second approach is to calculate numerical measures or statistics, which can help summarise the data. Both approaches are equally important, although graphical presentation is often neglected, particularly now that so much analysis is carried out by computer. This is a pity, since an appropriate graphical display of data will often save vast quantities of number crunching.

Graphical summary of data

There are many methods for displaying data graphically, but not all methods are suitable for all types of data. Data can be **continuous**, **discrete**, **ordinal** or **categorical**. Continuous data is data that is measured on an interval scale and can take on any value, such as time. Discrete data is data that can only take on whole values, such as the number of arrivals to a system. Ordinal data is data that is given a numerical value, but only for comparison purposes. So we might assign a priority value to arrivals to a system. A value of one might have a higher priority than a value of five. Categorical or qualitative data is data that does not have a numerical value and can only be put into a suitable category. Obvious categories are gender or race, but there are many other examples. For example, a company's sales could be placed into a number of categories according to the product.

The simplest form of graphical display is probably the bar chart. This is simply the use of bars to represent the frequency of a category occurring. In the case of sales by department, each bar could represent a department. There are three forms of bar chart. A simple bar chart is where each bar represents one category, while a stacked bar chart allows the total frequency to be split up into its constituent parts, while still allowing the total frequency to be compared. A stacked bar chart can also be in percentage form, in which case information on the totals is lost. A multiple bar chart also allows the components to be compared in a slightly different format. A pie chart is an alternative to a bar chart and has the advantage that the proportion of the total is easily seen. However, a pie chart cannot look at several time periods simultaneously.

■ Whiteladies Health Centre   *Scenario 3.1*

There is a maximum of six doctors available for consultations, although not all the doctors are on duty every day. Table 3.1, opposite, gives the number of patients seen by each doctor for four days during one week. The doctors have been given the names of colours, and the reason for this will become obvious in subsequent chapters.

A simple bar chart is shown in Figure 3.1. This diagram clearly shows the fall in the total number of patients during the week. Figure 3.2 is a stacked bar chart and allows a visual comparison of the numbers of patients seen by each doctor as well as the daily totals. If the sole purpose of the chart is to compare the doctors with each other, Figure 3.3 might be more useful as this is in a percentage format. Another method of comparing the number of patients seen by each doctor is the multiple bar chart shown in Figure 3.4. Finally, Figure 3.5 illustrates the use of a pie chart for the number of patients seen by each doctor on a Monday.

Table 3.1 ■ Number of patients seen by each doctor

Doctor	Monday	Tuesday	Thursday	Friday
Green	17	15	10	6
Pink	12	16	13	15
Yellow	16	0	9	21
Orange	19	14	12	0
Red	19	17	12	0
Blue	17	13	12	20
Total	100	75	68	62

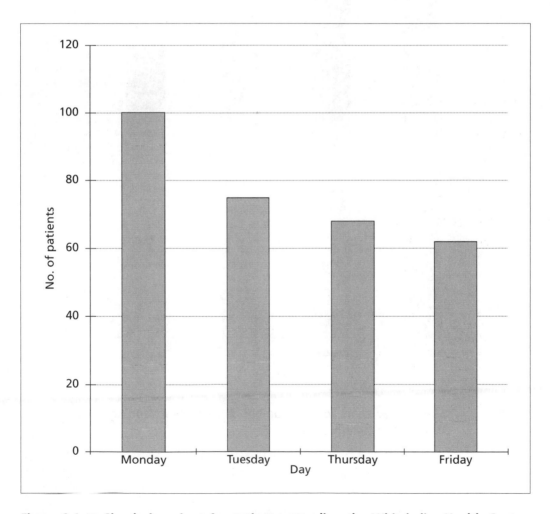

Figure 3.1 ■ Simple bar chart for patients attending the Whiteladies Health Centre

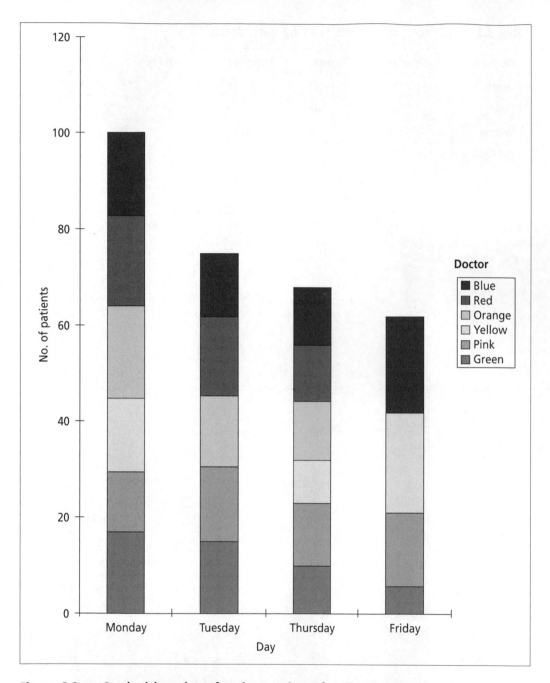

Figure 3.2 ▥ **Stacked bar chart for the number of patients attending the Whiteladies Health Centre**

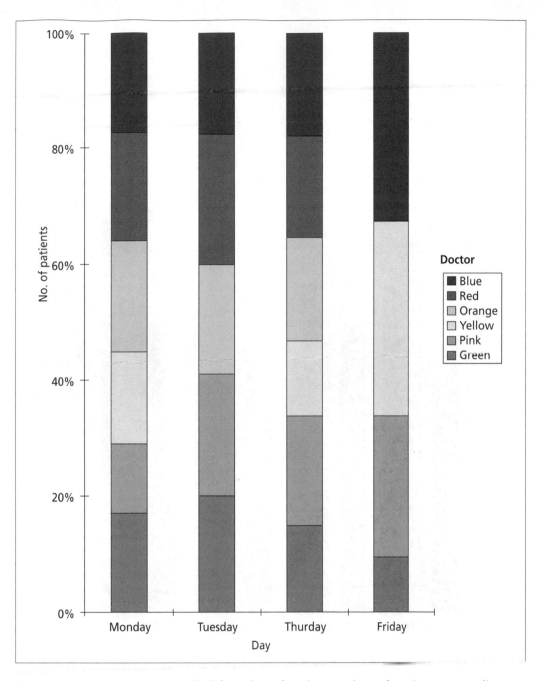

Figure 3.3 ■ **Percentage stacked bar chart for the number of patients attending Whiteladies Health Centre**

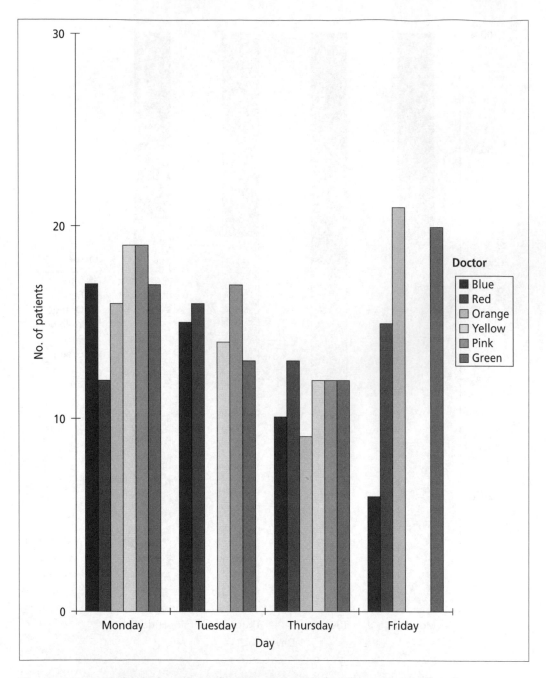

Figure 3.4 ■ **Multiple bar chart for the number of patients attending the Whiteladies Health Centre**

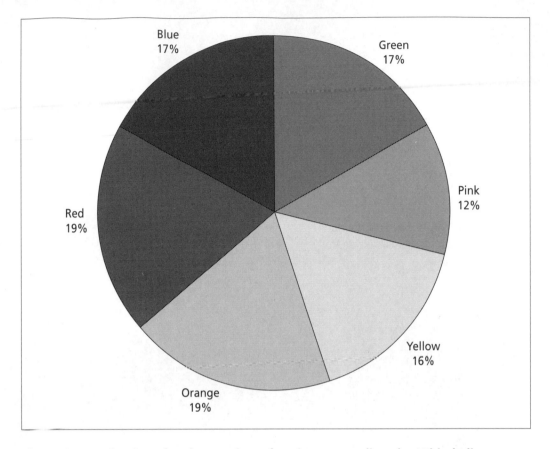

Figure 3.5 ■ Pie chart for the number of patients attending the Whiteladies Health Centre on Monday

Bar charts and pie charts are not normally used for continuous data, although it is possible to group this type of data before displaying on one of these charts. There are, however, better methods of displaying continuous data. The **histogram**, is probably the most useful when information is required on how the data is *distributed* across the range of possible values. Unlike a bar chart, where the comparison is with the height of the bars, it is the area of the histogram that is the important feature. This makes it essential that if the intervals are unequal, the heights of the 'bars' are adjusted accordingly. The shape of the histogram can tell us a great deal about the distribution and for this purpose we categorise the shape into a symmetrical or skewed distribution.

Figure 3.6 illustrates the three different shapes. We shall see later that the shape of the distribution is an important factor in the model-building process.

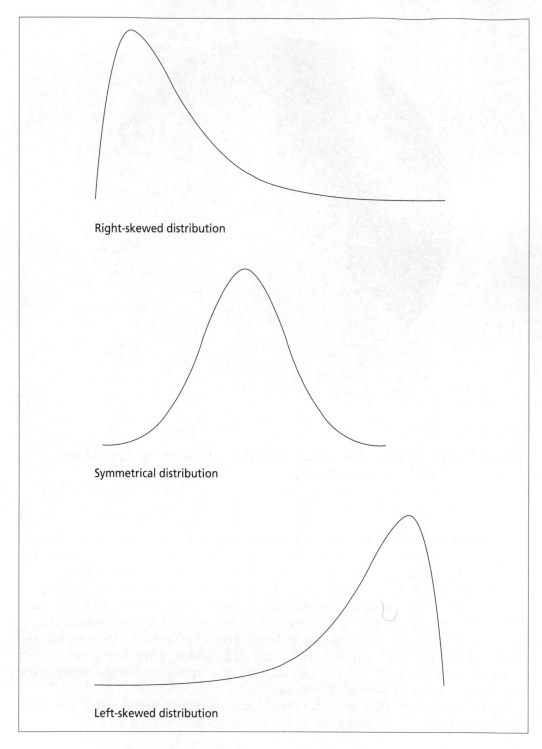

Right-skewed distribution

Symmetrical distribution

Left-skewed distribution

Figure 3.6 ▦ Shapes of distributions

■ Whiteladies Health Centre

The histogram of consultation times for all doctors combined can be seen in Figure 3.7. This distribution has a pronounced right skew with most observations occurring in the five- to ten-minute range.

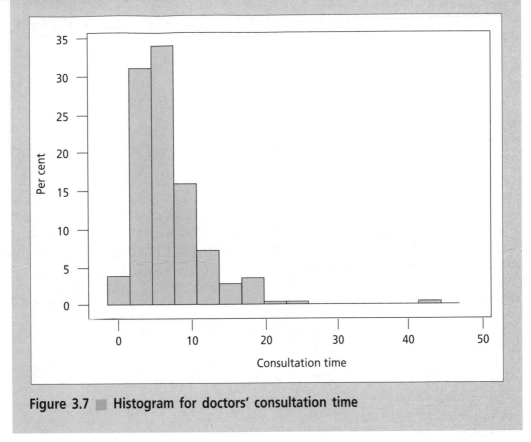

Figure 3.7 ■ Histogram for doctors' consultation time

Two other useful graphs for representing data are the line graph and the X-Y graph. The difference between these graphs is that the *x*-axis for the line graph is always *time*, whereas it is the *independent* variable that is plotted on the *x*-axis for an X-Y graph. An independent variable is a variable that is controlled or has minimal error associated with it. A line graph can be useful if we need to see if a particular variable changes with time. A gradual upward trend may not be obvious until it is plotted on a graph. An X-Y graph, on the other hand, may be useful if we want to see if two variables are related in some way. When used in this way, we do not normally join the points together, and the graph is called a scatter plot.

Numerical summary of data

Although graphical displays of data are very important, we often need to be able to summarise the data using a minimum of numerical descriptors. These descriptors or statistics need to be able to encapsulate the whole set of data in a meaningful way. Two measures are generally required for this purpose: a measure of location to tell us the position of the data and a measure of spread to tell us how the data varies around this central value.

Measures of location

The measure of location is usually taken as some form of average and the most useful are the **mean** and **median**. The mean ($\bar{x}$), is the sum of a set of observations, divided by the number of the observations n, and is defined as

$$\bar{x} = \frac{\sum x}{n}$$

The median is the middle of a set of observations once they have been arranged in order. Both measures have their advantages and disadvantages. The mean is easier to calculate and takes all values into account, while the median is less affected by extreme values (outliers).

■ **Whiteladies Health Centre**   *Scenario 3.3*

The consultation times for Doctor Red on Tuesday are shown in Table 3.2 below.

Table 3.2 ■ Consultation times for Doctor Red on Tuesday

4.33	2.18	2.52	16.35	17.13	17.13	8.27	3.62	6.62
42.37	9.03	3.10	5.88	2.70	2.23	5.82	4.33	

The mean of this set of data is $\bar{x} = \dfrac{153.61}{17}$

$$= 9.04 \text{ minutes}$$

To find the median, the data is ordered as follows:

2.18, 2.23, 2.52, 2.70, 3.10, 3.62, 4.33, 4.33, 5.82, 5.88, 6.62, 8.27, 9.03, 16.35, 17.13, 17.13, 42.37

The middle of this set of data is the ninth value, which is 5.82 minutes. The mean value is larger than the median and this indicates that the data is right skewed. This skewness is partly the result of the outlier of 42.37 minutes. If this outlier was ignored, the mean would be 7.0 minutes.

As indicated in Scenario 3.1, the mean of a set of data can be influenced by an outlier. An outlier is:

an observation (or measurement) that is unusually large or small relative to the other values in a data set. Outliers typically are attributable to one of the following causes:

1. The measurement is observed, recorded, or entered into the computer incorrectly.
2. The measurement comes from a different population.
3. The measurement is correct, but represents a rare (chance) event.

Sincich, 1995

Although we can often recognise an outlier, it is useful to be able to define an outlier in quantitative terms. There are various methods of defining an outlier but a common method is to use the following limits

lower limit $\quad Q_1 - 1.5(Q_3 - Q_1)$

upper limit $\quad Q_3 + 1.5(Q_3 - Q_1)$

where Q_1 is the lower quartile and Q_3 is the upper quartile. A quartile corresponds to a quarter of the data, so that Q_2 will be the 50th percentile. The expression $(Q_3 - Q_1)$ is the *interquartile range* of the data. So, according to this definition, anything below the lower limit or above the upper limit are classified as outliers.

A procedure for detecting outliers, as well as helping to summarise a set of data, is the **box and whisker plot**. The box represents 50 per cent of the data and has limits from Q_1 to Q_3. Within the box, the median is drawn. Outliers are often marked on the diagram as asterisks (*). If a set of data is symmetrical, the length of each whisker would be equal and the median would be at the midway point in the box. When the whiskers are not equal or the median is not at the centre of the box, the data will have a degree of skewness about it. Scenario 3.4 illustrates the use of MINITAB for constructing a box and whisker plot.

▮ Whiteladies Health Centre

Scenario 3.4

MINITAB was used to draw a box and whisker plot for the data in Table 3.2 and this diagram can be seen in Figure 3.8 (overleaf). Notice that the top whisker is longer than the bottom and the median is below the centre of the box. This indicates that the data has a right skew. The outlier of 42.37 minutes is clearly visible in this diagram.

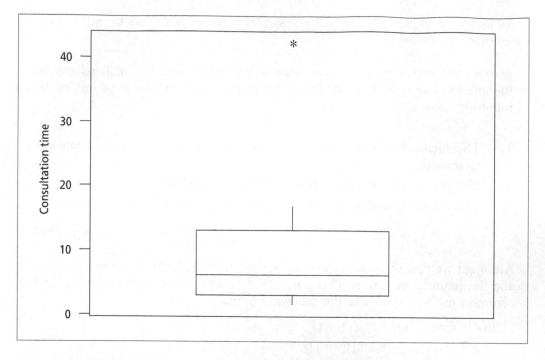

Figure 3.8 ■ Box and whisker plot for the Whiteladies Health Centre

The detection of outliers is an important part of data analysis, but the question of what to do about them then arises. The first stage must be to check the observation for possible error and correct it where necessary. In some cases it may not be possible to verify the accuracy of any particular value, either because the data was collected by someone else, or because the system from where the data was collected has changed in some way. It is tempting to remove outliers in these circumstances, but by doing this we could be ignoring the occurrence of a rare event, which may be important in a modelling context.

Measures of spread

The interquartile range is a measure of the spread or dispersion of the data. The larger this value, the larger the spread of the data. Although this gives some indication of the spread, a better measure that has applications in all areas of statistics is the **standard deviation**. This statistic represents the average deviation of each value from the mean. The formula is:

$$s = \sqrt{\frac{\Sigma(x - \bar{x})^2}{n - 1}}$$

To be precise, this formula is an *estimate* of the standard deviation of the sampled population. This is an explanation for the $n-1$ denominator as it can be shown that this produces an unbiased estimator of the true standard deviation (σ). The square of the standard deviation is called the **variance**, and is denoted s^2 for the sample estimate, and σ^2 for the true variance.

■ **Whiteladies Health Centre**   *Scenario 3.5*

> The standard deviation of the data in Table 3.2 is 10.02 minutes. This is quite a large value as it is larger than the mean. If the outlier is removed, the standard deviation falls to 5.3, which is now less than the new mean of 7.0 minutes.

Probability

Probability plays a central role in modelling systems that have a significant stochastic element. Not only do we need an understanding of probability in the model building phase, but we also need this knowledge during analysis of results obtained from these models.

Probability is measured on a scale of zero to one, where zero represents an impossible event and one a certain event. Probabilities can be obtained in a number of ways. The simplest is the **subjective** method, where an estimate is made of an event occurring. For example, we might say that the probability that it will rain tomorrow is 60 per cent (or 0.6). Another method is the **empirical** or the relative frequency approach. This method uses measurements to estimate the probability. For example, a sample of 100 components may contain ten defective components and we could infer that the probability that a given component is defective is 0.1. A third method is the *a priori* approach. This method allows the probability to be worked out in advance. We can, for instance, calculate the probability of picking an ace from a pack of cards or winning the national lottery.

Probability of compound events

Practical problems of probability involve several events occurring either together or one after the other. We might, for instance, want to know the probability of obtaining two heads in two tosses of a coin or the probability that a selected card from a pack will be both a red card and an ace.

Some events cannot happen together and we call these events *mutually exclusive*. For instance, a card drawn from a pack cannot be an ace and a king. The probability of *either* an ace *or* a king of hearts is:

$$P(\text{ace or king}) = P(\text{ace}) + P(\text{king of hearts})$$

$$= \frac{4}{52} + \frac{1}{52}$$

$$= 0.0962$$

For events that are mutually exclusive, they must also be *mutually exhaustive*. That is, the sum of the probabilities of all the events must equal one. So, the sum of the individual probabilities of *all* cards in a pack must add up to one. This can be a useful fact as it allows us to calculate the probability of an event when we know the sum of the remaining events. We will discover situations later in this chapter where this is important.

When events can occur together, the events are not mutually exclusive. For instance, an ace or a spade can occur at the same time. If we added the probability for two mutually exclusive events, we would be adding the probability of getting an ace of spades twice. To allow for this, the probability is adjusted as follows:

$$P(\text{ace or a spade}) = P(\text{ace}) + P(\text{spade}) - P(\text{ace of spades})$$

$$= \frac{4}{52} + \frac{13}{52} - \frac{1}{52}$$

$$= 0.3077$$

In general, we can state this result as:

$$P(A \text{ or } B) = P(A) + P(B) - P(A \text{ and } B)$$

This is known as the **addition rule**.

If events A and B are mutually exclusive, $P(A \text{ and } B) = 0$ and the rule simplifies to:

$$P(A \text{ or } B) = P(A) + P(B)$$

If two or more events occur one after the other and the occurrence of an event is not affected by the outcome of the preceding event, we say that the events are independent. If a coin is tossed, the probability of a head is 0.5. If it is tossed again, the probability is still 0.5 since the two events are independent of each other. The probability that we would get two heads is:

$$P(2 \text{ heads}) = 0.5 \times 0.5 = 0.25$$

If the probability of event B occurring is dependent on whether event A has occurred, we say that event B is *conditional* on event A and is written $P(B|A)$, which means the probability of B, given A has occurred. For instance, if there are ten defective components in a batch of 100, what is the probability that if we pick two at random, both will be defective? In this case the probability is not independent, since by removing the first defective component, we have changed the probability of a defective component occurring with the second selection. The calculation will be as follows:

$$P(2 \text{ defective components}) = \frac{10}{100} \times \frac{9}{99}$$

$$= 0.00909$$

This rule is known as the **multiplication rule** and is expressed as:

$$P(A \text{ and } B) = P(A) \times P(B|A)$$

If events A and B are independent, the rule simplifies to:

$$P(A \text{ and } B) = P(A) \times P(B)$$

In many situations, the addition and multiplication rules are used together. In these more complex problems, it is often desirable to draw a **tree diagram**. Scenario 3.6 illustrates the technique for a typical problem:

■ **Drive Thru Burger restaurant** *Scenario 3.6*

The restaurant employs a quality control procedure for the purchase of spare parts for its cookers. The procedure is to select two items from a batch and only accept the batch if both items are satisfactory. If both items are defective, they reject the batch, but if only one item is defective they will select a third item. If this third item is satisfactory, the batch is accepted, otherwise it is rejected. From past experience, they know that 5 per cent of the batch will be defective. What is the probability that a batch will be rejected?

Using a batch size of 100 for simplicity, we get the tree diagram shown in Figure 3.9. There are six branches to the tree, three that result in a rejection and three that result in an acceptance of the batch. Each branch consists of a number of events that must happen and the probability of each event is dependent on what happened before. So if the first item was satisfactory, the probability that the next item is defective is $\frac{5}{99}$, since there are still five defective items, but the total has decreased from 100 to 99. The company's quality control procedure is to select a third item and the probability that this will be defective is $\frac{4}{98}$, since the total number of defective items has decreased to 4 and there are 98 items left in total. The probability that these three events would have happened will, by the multiplication rule, be:

$$\frac{95}{100} \times \frac{5}{99} \times \frac{4}{98} = 0.00196$$

This process is repeated to get the remaining probabilities shown on the diagram. Since only one of these branches can occur, the probability that the batch will be rejected is the addition of the three branches that have resulted in a reject decision. That is:

$$P(\text{batch accepted}) = 0.00196 + 0.00196 + 0.00202$$

$$= 0.00594$$

▶

This is a very small probability, so if the restaurant did fail a batch they have either been extremely unlucky or (more likely) the 5 per cent defective rate has increased substantially.

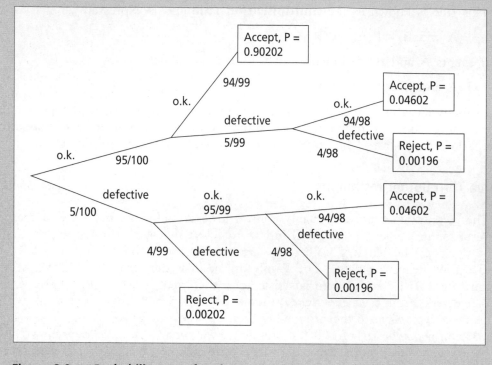

Figure 3.9 ■ Probability tree for the Drive Thru Burger restaurant

Probability distributions

Imagine throwing a die. In probability terminology, we call the set of possible values a random variable (X) and an individual value of X is denoted as x. The probabilities associated with each possible value form a probability distribution. In the case of a die the possible values are discrete, since only the numbers one to six are possible. The probability distribution is uniform, since the probabilities are all the same, that is, $\frac{1}{6}$. In most cases, a large number of values are possible and each may have a different probability of occurring. Sometimes the probability distribution is defined by the data that has been collected. For instance, we may have collected data on the time to carry out a certain task. If we group this data into a frequency table, we get a frequency distribution, and if we now divide each frequency by the total frequency, we get a relative frequency distribution. Because this distribution was obtained from measured data, we call the resulting distribution an **empirical distribution**.

▣ Whiteladies Health Centre
Scenario 3.7

The data for the consultation times at the surgery has been grouped into a frequency table and can be seen in Table 3.3. The column *lcb* refers to the lower class boundary of each group, while column *ucb* refers to the upper class boundary. So, a group of 0 to 2 refers to the 22 observations that were between zero and less than two minutes. In addition to the frequency, the *relative* frequency has been calculated. This has been calculated by dividing each frequency by 305, which is the total number of observations. This is the same data that was plotted in Figure 3.7 and represents the distribution of the consultation times for all doctors.

Table 3.3 ▣ **Empirical distribution of the consultation times at Whiteladies Health Centre**

lcb	ucb	Frequency	Relative frequency
Minutes			
0	2	22	0.0721
2	4	64	0.2098
4	6	91	0.2984
6	8	50	0.1639
8	10	28	0.0918
10	12	21	0.0689
12	14	7	0.0230
14	16	6	0.0197
16	18	11	0.0361
18	20	2	0.0066
20	30	2	0.0066
30	50	1	0.0033
	Total	305	1

Usually, we attempt to assign a probability to a particular value of X using a mathematical function. When the probability distribution assigns integer values to X, we call the distribution a **discrete probability distribution**. We may also have situations where the values are not restricted to whole numbers but can take on any value. The probability distribution in this case is called a **continuous probability distribution**. We shall look at both types of probability distributions in the next two sections.

Discrete probability distributions

A discrete random variable is a variable that can only take on discrete values, such as the rolling of a die or the tossing of a coin. If a coin was tossed three times (or three coins tossed once each), the eight possible outcomes are HHH, HHT, HTH, HTT, THH, THT, TTH and TTT. Each toss of the coin is termed a trial and the tossing of the coins an experiment. The tree diagram for this experiment can be seen in Figure 3.10, where the probabilities of each of the outcomes are shown.

Each of the outcomes has a probability of ⅛ or 0.125, since the probability of a head is equal to the probability of a tail, which is ½.

If the random variable, X, is the number of heads obtained, we can work out the probability of getting $x = 0$, 1, 2 or 3 heads. That is:

$$P(X = 0) = P(0) = 0.125$$
$$P(X = 1) = P(1) = 3 \times 0.125 = 0.375$$
$$P(X = 2) = P(2) = 3 \times 0.125 = 0.375$$
$$P(X = 3) = P(3) = 0.125$$

The sum of these probabilities is equal to 1 since all the possible values of X are included. This list of all possible values of X and the corresponding probabilities form a discrete probability distribution. In some situations it is possible to describe

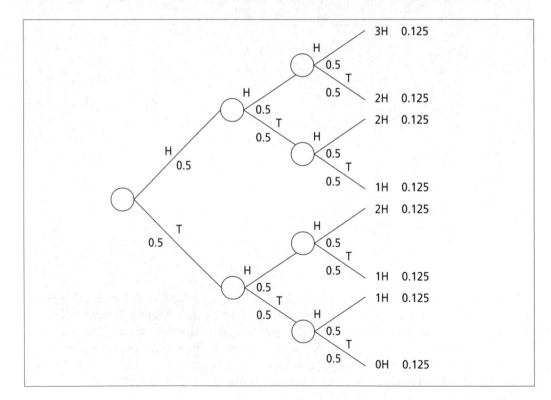

Figure 3.10 ■ Tree diagram for the coin-tossing experiment

the distribution in the form of a mathematical function. When we do this the function is called a **probability mass function** or **pmf**. (Some texts and software use the term probability density function or pdf, but strictly the word density only applies to continuous distributions.) A pmf allows us to calculate the probability for any value x. The requirements for a pmf are:

$P(x)$ is between 0 and 1

and $\sum P(x) = 1$

For the experiment of tossing three coins, it can be shown that the pmf is:

$$P(X = x) = P(x) = {}^3C_x(0.5)^x(0.5)^{3-x} \text{ where } {}^3C_x = \frac{3!}{x!(3-x)!}$$

This is A particular form of the binomial distribution, which we will look at shortly.

We can check to see if this function correctly specifies the probability distribution by substituting the appropriate values of x. That is:

$$P(0) = \frac{3!}{0! \times 3!} \times (0.5)^0 \times (0.5)^3$$

$$= 0.125$$

$$P(1) = \frac{3!}{1! \times 2!} \times (0.5)^1 \times (0.5)^2$$

$$= 3 \times 0.125$$

$$= 0.375$$

$$P(2) = \frac{3!}{2! \times 1!} \times (0.5)^2 \times (0.5)^1$$

$$= 0.375$$

$$P(3) = \frac{3!}{3! \times 0!} \times (0.5)^3 \times (0.5)^0$$

$$= 0.125$$

This correctly specifies the probabilities, and, since the probabilities are all between 0 and 1, and the sum of the probabilities is 1, the requirements for a pmf are met.

As well as the probability mass function, the **cumulative distribution function** (or **cdf**) is important. This is the probability that the value is below a particular value of X and is expressed as $F(x)$

where $F(x) = P(X \leq x) = \sum_{t \leq x} P(t)$ for $-\infty < x < \infty$

So, $F(x)$ is simply the cumulative sum of the probabilities up to the value x. For the coin-tossing experiment, the values of $P(x)$ and $F(x)$ are shown in Table 3.4.

Table 3.4 ■ Values of the pmf and cdf for the coin-tossing experiment

x	$P(x)$	$F(x)$
0	0.125	0.125
1	0.375	0.5
2	0.375	0.875
3	0.125	1.0

We shall see in Chapter 7 that we often require the value of x given $F(x)$. This is defined as $x_p = F^{-1}(p)$, and is the **inverse function** of $F(x)$.

The mean and variance of a discrete probability distribution

We have seen how to calculate the mean and variance of a sample of data consisting of n observations. We now want to be able to specify the mean (μ) and variance (σ^2) of a discrete probability distribution. The expressions for these measures are:

$$\mu = \sum x\,P(x) \text{ for the mean}$$

and

$$\sigma^2 = \sum (x - u)^2\,P(x) \text{ for the variance}$$

An alternative but equivalent expression for the variance is:

$$\sigma^2 = \sum x^2\,P(x) - \mu^2$$

This alternative expression is easier to use, as will be demonstrated for the calculation of the mean and variance of the number of heads obtained in the coin tossing experiment.

For the mean: $\mu = 0 \times 0.125 + 1 \times 0.375 + 2 \times 0.375 + 3 \times 0.125$

$$= 1.5$$

For the variance: $\sigma^2 = (0^2 \times 0.125 + 1^2 \times 0.375 + 2^2 \times 0.375 + 3^2 \times 0.125)$

$$- (1.5)^2$$

$$= 0.75$$

The binomial distribution

In the coin-tossing experiment, there were two possible outcomes that could occur when the coin was tossed: a head or a tail. We can apply this situation to any case where there are exactly two possible outcomes and the probability of a 'success' (p) is constant from trial to trial, and successive trials are independent. If these conditions hold, the probability distribution is called a binomial distribution and the pmf is given by:

$$P(X = x) = P(x) = nC_x\, p^x(1 - p)^{n-x} \quad \text{where} \quad {}^nC_x = \frac{n!}{x!(n - x)!}$$

for $x = 1, 2, 3, \ldots, n$

The mean and variance of the binomial distribution can be shown to be $\mu = np$ and $\sigma = np(1 - p)$.

The pmf for the binomial distribution is quite tedious to calculate manually and it is easier to use tables or a statistical software package. To demonstrate the use of a software package, MINITAB has been used to generate the probabilities for values of p of 0.2, 0.5 and 0.8 respectively and for $n = 10$ in all cases. The results can be seen below, together with bar charts of the resulting distributions.

MTB > PDF c1;
SUB > Binomial 10 .2.

Probability Density Function

Binomial with $n = 10$ and $p = 0.200000$		Binomial with $n = 10$ and $p = 0.500000$		Binomial with $n = 10$ and $p = 0.800000$	
x	$P(X = x)$	x	$P(X = x)$	x	$P(X = x)$
0.00	0.1074	0.00	0.0010	0.00	0.0000
1.00	0.2684	1.00	0.0098	1.00	0.0000
2.00	0.3020	2.00	0.0439	2.00	0.0001
3.00	0.2013	3.00	0.1172	3.00	0.0008
4.00	0.0881	4.00	0.2051	4.00	0.0055
5.00	0.0264	5.00	0.2461	5.00	0.0264
6.00	0.0055	6.00	0.2051	6.00	0.0881
7.00	0.0008	7.00	0.1172	7.00	0.2013
8.00	0.0001	8.00	0.0439	8.00	0.3020
9.00	0.0000	9.00	0.0098	9.00	0.2684
10.00	0.0000	10.00	0.0010	10.00	0.1074

From Figures 3.11 to 3.13, we can see that the distribution will be right skewed for values of p less than 0.5, symmetrical when $p = 0.5$, and left skewed when p is greater than 0.5.

Many binomial problems are concerned with calculating the probabilities of the value of X being greater or less than a certain figure. In these cases the use of the cumulative distribution function is more appropriate. MINITAB can be used to calculate these probabilities as Scenario 3.8 (page 43) shows.

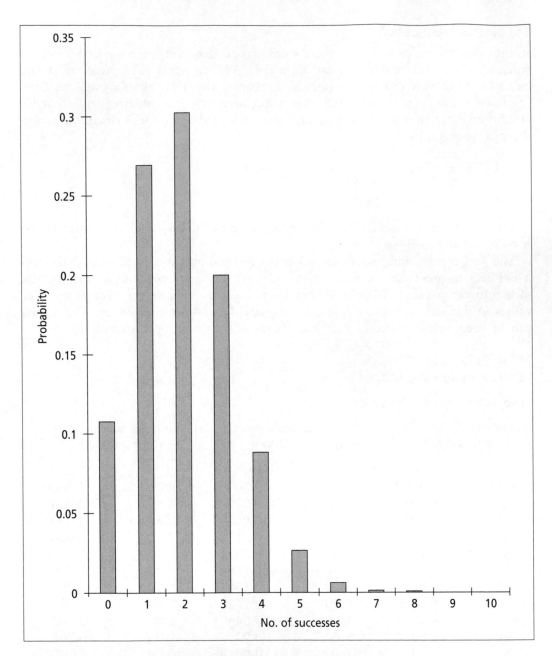

Figure 3.11 ■ Binomial distribution for $p = 0.2$ and $n = 10$

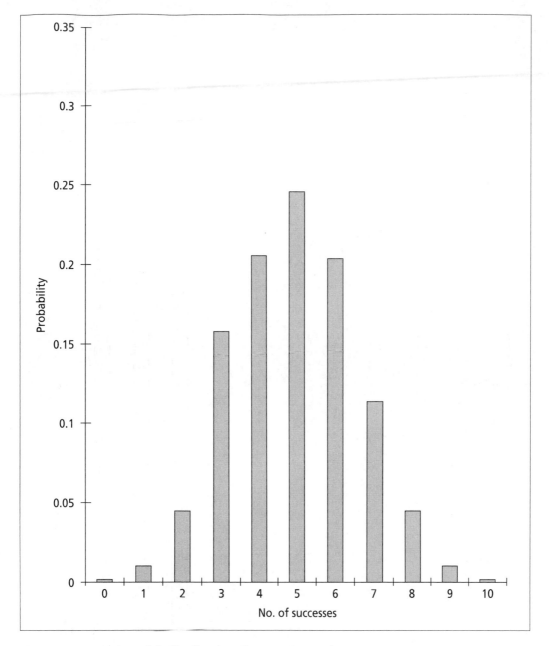

Figure 3.12 ■ Binomial distribution for $p = 0.5$ and $n = 10$

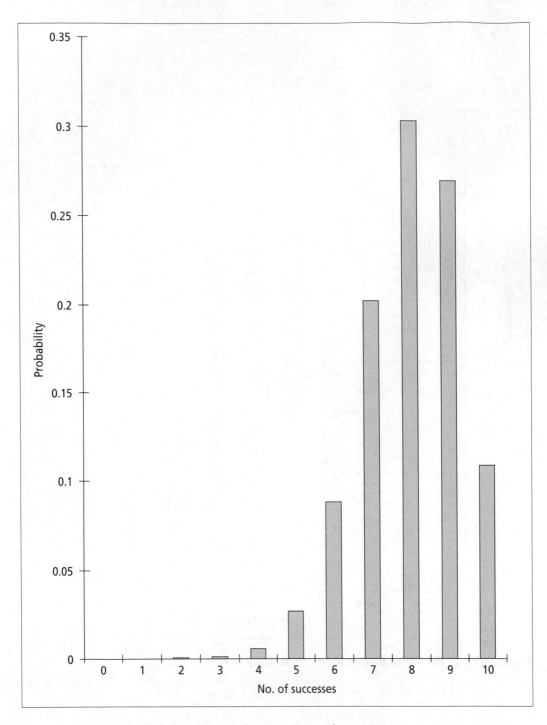

Figure 3.13 ■ Binomial distribution for *p* = 0.8 and *n* = 10

■ **Drive Thru Burger restaurant** *Scenario 3.8*

The selection process for staff at the restaurant involves candidates completing a short numerical test. On past experience, it has been found that the probability that a candidate will pass this test is 0.4. If eight candidates turn up to complete the test, what is the probability that more than three of them will be successful?

This is a binomial problem because there is only success and failure and we can reasonably assume that the candidates are independent of each other. If we assume that the probability of 0.4 is the same for all candidates, then we can use MINITAB to calculate the cumulative probabilities as follows:

```
MTB > CDF C1;
SUBC> Binomial 8 .4.
```

Cumulative Distribution Function
Binomial with $n = 8$ and $p = 0.400000$

x	$P(X < = x)$
0.00	0.0168
1.00	0.1064
2.00	0.3154
3.00	0.5941
4.00	0.8263
5.00	0.9502
6.00	0.9915
7.00	0.9993
8.00	1.0000

These figures tell us that the probability of getting less than or equal to three successes is 0.5941. Therefore, the probability that there will be more than three must be $1 - 0.5941 = 0.4059$, or about 41 per cent. The mean number of successful candidates is $8 \times 0.4 = 3.2$ and the variance is $8 \times 0.4 \times 0.6 = 1.92$.

The Poisson distribution

Another discrete probability distribution is the Poisson distribution and is one of the most useful distributions from a modelling point of view. It is used for counting the number of times an event occurs in a given period of time, and is applicable when events occur at *random*. The most common example is when the event refers to arrivals of people or items, and will apply when successive arrivals are independent of each other. The pmf of this distribution is:

$$P(X = x) = P(x) = \frac{\lambda^x e^{-\lambda}}{x!}$$

where λ is the expected number of occurrences over the time period t and e is the constant 2.7182818...

The mean and variance of the Poisson distribution can be shown to be $\mu = \lambda$ and $\sigma^2 = \lambda$.

■ **Whiteladies Health Centre** *Scenario 3.9*

On average, 43.8 patients per hour arrive at random at the health centre on a Monday. What is the probability that more than three patients turn up during any one minute?

An arrival rate of 43.8 patients an hour implies that on average there will be 0.73 arrivals each minute. Using MINITAB, we can obtain the cumulative probabilities as follows:

MTB > CDF C1;
SUBC> Poisson 0.73.

Cumulative Distribution Function
Poisson with mu = 0.730000

x	$P(X < = x)$
0.00	0.4819
1.00	0.8337
2.00	0.9621
3.00	0.9934
4.00	0.9991
5.00	0.9999
6.00	1.0000
7.00	1.0000
8.00	1.0000

The probability that we will get less than or equal to three patients during one minute is 0.9934 so the probability that we will get more than three is 0.0066.

Continuous probability distributions

A continuous random variable is a variable that can take on any value over some specified range. Unlike a discrete probability distribution, we cannot define a continuous probability distribution that will determine the probability of a particular value. This is because it is impossible to list all possible values of the random variable. What we can do is define a function that gives the probability for a continuous random variable within a range. To do this, the distribution is represented by a curve and the probability found by evaluating the *area* of the appropriate part of the distribution. The function that allows us to calculate this area is called a **probability density function** or **pdf** and should not be confused with the pmf for discrete distributions. To distinguish the pdf from the pmf the notation $f(x)$ is used. In some cases it is quite difficult to obtain the pdf, but fortunately tables are often available, or computer software packages used to obtain the relevant areas. The requirements for a pdf are:

1. $f(x) \geqslant 0$ for all x

2. $\int_{-\infty}^{\infty} f(x)\,dx = 1$

3. $P(a < X < b) = \int_{a}^{b} f(x)\,dx$

Requirement 1. simply says that the function must give positive values and therefore the curve must be above the x-axis. Requirement 2. says that the area under the curve must equal 1 and requirement 3. says that the probability of the random variable being between two limits a and b must be equal to the area under the curve between these limits.

In addition to the probability density function, we can also define the cumulative distribution function $F(x)$ as:

$$F(x) = P(X \leqslant x) = \int_{-\infty}^{\infty} f(t)\,dt$$

We will now look at three continuous probability distributions. The first, the uniform distribution, is an easy one to evaluate, while the normal distribution would be very difficult if it were not for the fact that tables have been produced. The final distribution is the exponential distribution and this is a very important distribution in a modelling context.

The uniform distribution

The uniform or rectangular distribution is where the probability is the same for all values of x. We met this distribution when discussing the throwing of a die, but in that case the distribution was discrete, since only discrete values of x were possible. Figure 3.14 illustrates the case where any value between a and b is possible. The pdf for this distribution is:

$$f(x) = \frac{1}{b - a} \quad \text{for} \ a \leqslant x \leqslant b$$

$$= 0 \quad \text{elsewhere}$$

The mean and standard deviations of this distribution are as follows:

$$\mu = \frac{a + b}{2}$$

$$\sigma = \frac{b - a}{\sqrt{12}}$$

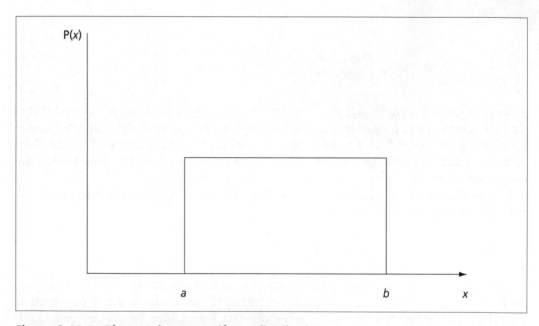

Figure 3.14 ■ The continuous uniform distribution

■ Whiteladies Health Centre

If the time taken by the receptionist to register a patient is uniformly distributed between 10 seconds and 30 seconds, what is the probability that the time taken to register a particular patient will be:

1. less than 8 seconds?
2. between 18 to 25 seconds?

What are the mean and standard deviations of the time taken by the receptionist?

1. Since 8 seconds is less than the minimum value of 10 seconds, the probability is zero.
2. The pdf is $1/(30 - 10) = 0.05$ for all values of x within the range. The area between $x = 18$ to 25 is therefore $(25 - 18) \times 0.05 = 0.35$.

This tells us that the probability that the time will be between 18 and 25 seconds is 0.35 or 35 per cent.

The mean and standard deviation are:

$$\mu = \frac{10 + 30}{2} = 15 \text{ seconds}$$

and

$$\sigma = \frac{30 - 10}{\sqrt{12}} = 5.77 \text{ seconds}$$

These answers are summarised in Figure 3.15.

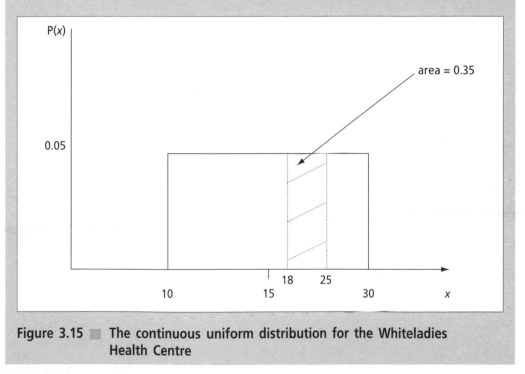

Figure 3.15 ■ The continuous uniform distribution for the Whiteladies Health Centre

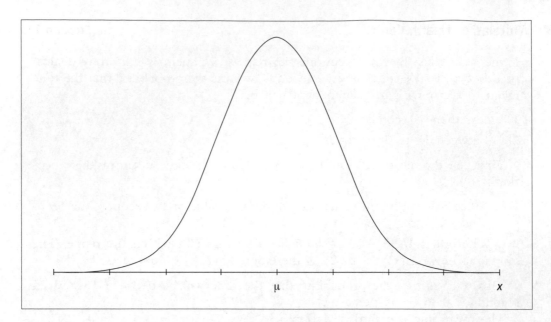

Figure 3.16 ▓ The normal distribution

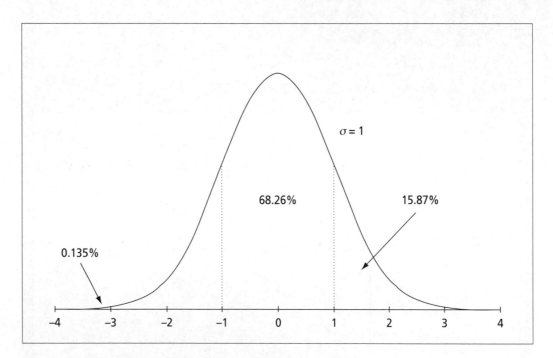

Figure 3.17 ▓ The standard normal distribution

The normal distribution

The normal distribution is an important distribution in statistical inference, which we will meet shortly. The distribution is perfectly symmetrical and the general shape can be seen in Figure 3.16.

The distribution is defined by two parameters, its mean μ and its standard deviation σ. As the standard deviation increases, the curve gets flatter, but it will still maintain its general bell shape. Unlike the uniform distribution, there are no limits either side of the curve, although for practical purposes we can define limits that will cover almost 100 per cent of the area. The pdf of the normal distribution cannot be integrated exactly so tables are normally used to find the required area. These tables refer to the **standard normal distribution**, which is a normal distribution that has a mean of 0 and a standard deviation of 1. The standard normal distribution is illustrated in Figure 3.17.

To transform the observations of any normal random variable X to the standard normal random variable Z, we use the formula:

$$Z = \frac{x - \mu}{\sigma}$$

A value of the random variable Z is often called the **Z-score**. The normal tables in Appendix 2 give the area in the *right*-hand tail of the distribution. For example, for a Z-score of 1.0, the area is 0.1587. As the Z-score gets larger, the area becomes progressively smaller, so that for a Z-score of 3.0, the area is 0.00135. Since the distribution is symmetrical, the area less than −1.0 is 0.1587 and the area less than −3.0 is 0.00135. These Z-scores are effectively the number of standard deviations away from the mean, so that a Z-score of 1.0 infers that the area covered by ± 1 standard deviations is 0.6826 or 68.26 per cent. Similarly, 99.73 per cent of a normal distribution is covered by ± 3 standard deviations.

■ **Drive Thru Burger restaurant**   *Scenario 3.11*

The weight of a burger is known to be normally distributed with a mean of 56.8 grams and a standard deviation of 5.4 grams.

1. What is the probability that if a burger was selected at random it would weigh more than 60 grams?

2. What proportion of burgers should weigh between 60 grams and 65 grams?

3. What is the probability that a burger will weigh more than 50 grams?

4. What is the weight that no more than 5 per cent of burgers will fall below?

1. To answer the first question, we need to find the Z-score corresponding to a value of x of 60. That is:

▶

$$Z = \frac{60 - 56.8}{5.4}$$

$$= 0.5926$$

From tables $P(Z \geqslant 0.5926) = 0.2776$

So there would be a 27.76 per cent chance that the burger would weigh more than 60 grams. This solution is illustrated in Figure 3.18.

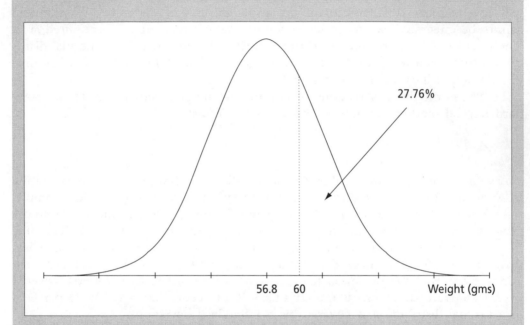

27.76%

56.8   60   Weight (gms)

Figure 3.18 ■ Drive Thru Burger restaurant problem (1)

2. For this question we need to find the area between $x = 60$ and $x = 65$. Since tables only give the area in the tail of the distribution, we have to find the area for both $x > 60$ and $x > 65$ and subtract one from the other. In symbols, this is:

$$P(60 \leqslant x \leqslant 65) = P(x \geqslant 60) - P(x \leqslant 65)$$

We have already calculated the 60 grams case, so we now need to calculate the area corresponding to $x > 65$. We first calculate the Z-score as before:

$$Z = \frac{65 - 56.8}{5.4}$$

$$= 1.519$$

From tables $P(Z \geqslant 1.519) = 0.0643$
Therefore $P(60 \leqslant x \leqslant 65) = 0.2776 - 0.0643$
$= 0.2133$

So there will be a 21.13 per cent chance that a burger will weigh between 60 and 65 grams and this solution can be seen in Figure 3.19.

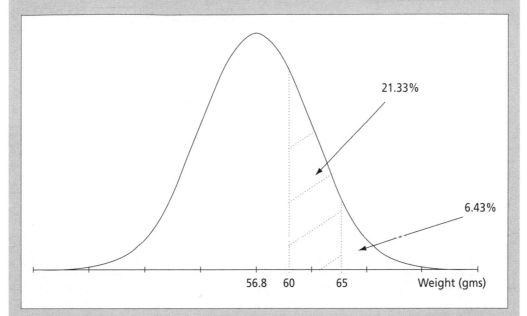

Figure 3.19 ■ **Drive Thru Burger restaurant problem (2)**

3. The difference with this question is that the value of x is below the mean. Since the distribution is symmetrical, we simply ignore the negative sign, but remember that the area lies in the left-hand tail. This area will give us the probability of a value of x less than 50 grams and to find the probability greater than 50 grams, we subtract the value from 1. That is:

$$P(x \geqslant 50) = 1 - P(x \leqslant 50)$$

The Z-score is:

$$Z = \frac{50 - 56.8}{5.4}$$

$$= -1.259$$

Ignoring the negative sign, we find the area to be 0.1038 and the required probability is therefore:

$$P(x \geqslant 50) = 1 - 0.1038 = 0.8962$$

The probability that a burger will weigh at least 50 grams is 0.8962 or 89.62 per cent. The solution can be seen in Figure 3.20.

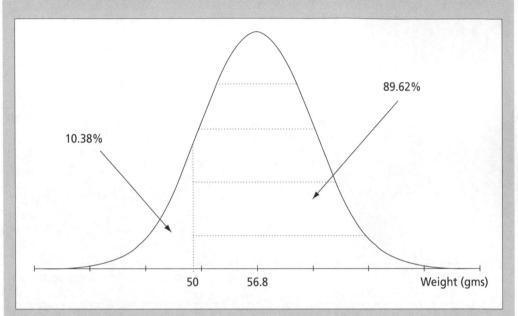

Figure 3.20 ■ Drive Thru Burger restaurant problem (3)

4. Since we are given the probability, we need to use the tables in reverse to find the Z-score. We can then substitute this value into the formula in order to obtain the value of x. For an area of 0.05, the Z-score is approximately 1.645, but this is negative as 50 grams is below the mean. The value of x can then be found from:

$$-1.645 = \frac{x - 56.8}{5.4}$$

that is:

$$x = 56.8 - 1.645 \times 5.4$$

$$= 47.9$$

Therefore, 5 per cent of burgers will be below 47.9 grams in weight. This is shown in Figure 3.21.

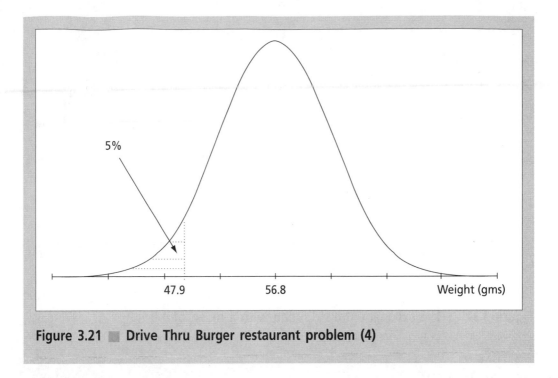

Figure 3.21 ■ Drive Thru Burger restaurant problem (4)

The exponential distribution

The exponential distribution is a very important distribution in stochastic model-ling. The distribution of process times is often approximated by the exponential distribution, and the life times of machines or components can often be modelled using this distribution. It can also be shown that if the number of arrivals follows a Poisson distribution, the *time between arrivals* is exponential. The exponential distribution can therefore be thought of as the continuous equivalent of the Poisson distribution. The mean and standard deviation of an exponential distribution are the same.

The shape of the exponential distribution is a curve that steadily decreases as the random variable decreases. Figure 3.22 (overleaf) illustrates this curve for a mean of 1.

The calculation of the areas for the exponential distribution is somewhat simpler than for the normal distribution, as a calculator can be used (provided it has an exponential function). If X is a random variable from an exponential distri-bution with mean μ and standard deviation μ, the probability density function is given by:

$$f(x) = \frac{1}{\mu} e^{-x/\mu}$$

and the cumulative distribution function is:

$$F(x) = P(X \leqslant x) = 1 - e^{-x/\mu}$$

From this it follows that $P(X \geqslant x) = e^{-x/\mu}$

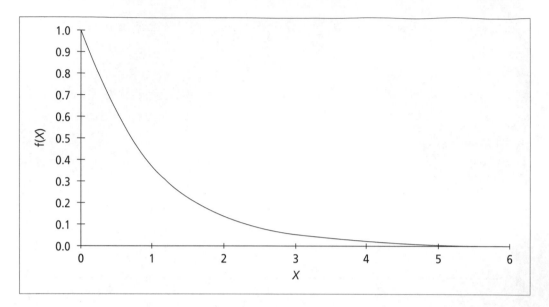

Figure 3.22 ■ The exponential distribution with a mean of 1.0

■ Whiteladies Health Centre

Scenario 3.12

The time between arrivals to the health centre on a Monday is exponentially distributed with a mean of 1.37 minutes. What is the probability that:

1. the time between two arrivals exceeds two minutes?
2. the time between two arrivals is between one and two minutes?

1. For the first case, we simply substitute the values into the formula. That is:

$$P(x \geqslant 2) \quad = e^{-2/1.37}$$

$$= 0.2322$$

2. In the second case we have to calculate both probabilities and subtract the smaller from the larger. That is:

$$P(x \geqslant 1) \quad = e^{-1/1.37}$$

$$= 0.4819$$

So $P(1 \leqslant x \leqslant 2) \quad = \quad 0.4819 - 0.2322$

$$= 0.2497$$

This problem is illustrated in Figure 3.23.

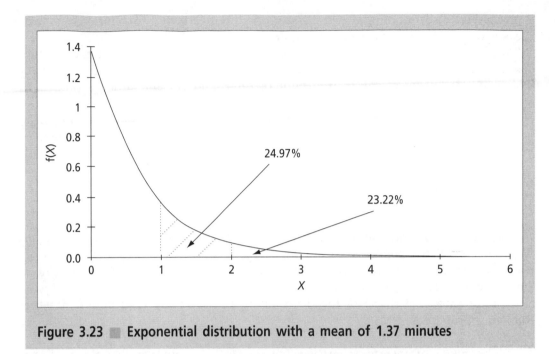

Figure 3.23 ■ **Exponential distribution with a mean of 1.37 minutes**

Inferential statistics

We have already mentioned that the purpose of obtaining samples of data is so that we can infer something about the population. Usually, we wish to obtain estimates of the population parameters, such as the mean and standard deviation. Although the sample parameters will give us *point* estimates of the sampled population, they will not on their own tell us how accurate these estimates are. We might assume that a sample of 100 would be more accurate than a sample of ten, but we really need some quantifiable measure of accuracy. From a modelling point of view, we may want to discover whether our model produces results that are consistent with what we have observed in the real system. In a real system we would expect some variability, so we would not expect our model results to produce identical figures. In addition, we may want to discover whether a change in our model has produced results that are *significantly* different to the results from the original model.

It should therefore be clear that sample results do not in themselves give us the information that we need to draw valid conclusions about the population. Before we can proceed with this quest we need to consider the idea of a **sampling distribution**.

Sampling distributions

If we take many samples and evaluate a statistic such as the mean for each of the samples, it is very unlikely that the values will be identical. The statistic will have a probability distribution and if the statistic is the mean, the distribution is called the **sampling distribution of the mean**.

This sampling distribution will be a continuous distribution and if the sample size is large enough, the shape of the distribution will be approximately normal. This result is known as the **central limit theorem** and is defined as:

> if the sample size is sufficiently large, then the mean $\bar{x}$ of a random sample from a population has a sampling distribution that is approximately normal, *regardless of the shape of the relative frequency distribution of the target population*. As the sample size increases, the better will be the normal approximation to the sampling distribution.
>
> *Sincich, 1995*

The term 'sufficiently large' is usually meant to mean any sample greater than 30. However, if the population from where the sample originated is known to be normally distributed, then the sampling distribution will be normal no matter how small the sample.

In addition to the shape of the distribution, the sampling distribution has the following properties:

1. The mean of the sampling distribution ($\mu_{\bar{x}}$), is equal to the mean of the population (μ), that is:

    $$\mu_{\bar{x}} = \mu$$

2. the standard deviation of the sampling distribution ($\sigma_{\bar{x}}$), is called the **standard error of the mean**, and is given by:

    $$\sigma_{\bar{x}} = \sigma/\sqrt{n}$$

Using the above results, we can apply the ideas already developed with the normal distribution to calculate the probability that a sample will have a mean within a specified range. To do this the Z formula is modified as follows:

$$Z = \frac{\bar{x} - \mu}{\sigma_{\bar{x}}}$$

Not only does the central limit theorem apply to a single sample, but it also applies to two samples taken from two different populations with different means and standard deviations. It can be shown that the difference between the means of the two sampling distributions is normally distributed with a mean equal to the difference of the population means. The variance of the distribution is given by:

$$\sigma^2_{(\bar{x}_1 - \bar{x}_2)} = \frac{\sigma^2_1}{n_1} + \frac{\sigma^2_2}{n_2}$$

The standard error will be the square root of the variance.

■ Drive Thru Burger restaurant

The weight of a burger is known to be normally distributed with a mean of 56.8 grams and a standard deviation of 5.4 grams. What is the probability that a random sample of sixteen burgers will have a mean weight of at least 58 grams?

To answer this question, we need to work out the standard error of the mean and this will be:

$$\sigma_{\bar{x}} = \frac{5.4}{\sqrt{16}}$$

$$= 1.35$$

The *Z*-score will therefore be:

$$Z = \frac{58 - 56.8}{1.35}$$

$$= 0.889$$

From tables, $P(Z \geqslant 0.889) = 0.1867$

So there is an 18.67 per cent chance of the sample mean being greater than 58 grams. This solution is shown in Figure 3.24.

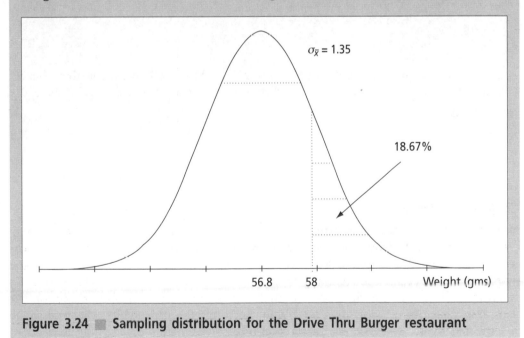

Figure 3.24 ■ Sampling distribution for the Drive Thru Burger restaurant

■ Drive Thru Burger restaurant

Scenario 3.14

Batches of frozen chips are obtained from two different suppliers. Supplier one delivers chips in packets with a mean weight of 5 kilograms and a standard deviation of 0.35 kilograms, while supplier two delivers chips in packets with a mean weight of 3 kilograms and a standard deviation of 0.25 kilograms. If supplier one delivers a batch of 40 packets and supplier two delivers a batch of 50 packets, what is the probability that the difference in the mean weights of the two samples will be less than 1.9 kilograms?

We know that the sampling distribution of the difference of the weights is normally distributed with a mean of $5 - 3 = 2$ kilograms and a variance of:

$$\sigma^2_{(\bar{x}_1 - \bar{x}_2)} = \frac{0.35^2}{40} + \frac{0.25^2}{50}$$

$$= 0.004313$$

and

$$\sigma_{(\bar{x}_1 - \bar{x}_2)} = 0.0657$$

We can now calculate the Z-score as follows:

$$Z = \frac{1.9 - 2}{0.0657}$$

$$= -1.522$$

From tables we find that $P(Z \leqslant -1.522) = 0.0643$, which means that there is a 6.43 per cent chance that the difference in weight will be less than 1.9 kilograms.

Confidence intervals

We normally only take one sample so our best estimate of the population mean must be the mean from this sample. However, we know that there is an error associated with this estimate and this error depends on the sample size. As the sample size increases, the standard error decreases, and so the error decreases. To quantify this error, we first assume that the sample mean is the mean of the sampling distribution, and then we obtain an interval within which the true mean is expected to lie. The size of this interval not only depends on the standard error, but also on the probability that the interval contains the true mean. The convention is to use either a 95 per cent or 99 per cent (sometimes even 99.9 per cent) probability, but as this probability increases, the interval increases. The simplest way to understand this idea is to refer to Figure 3.25, which shows the 95 per cent interval for the standard normal distribution.

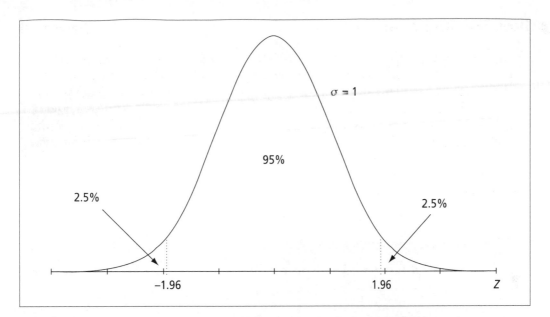

Figure 3.25 ■ Boundaries enclosing 95 per cent of the standard normal distribution

The Z-scores of ± 1.96 correspond to an area of 2.5 per cent or 0.025 in each tail. The sum of these tail probabilities is usually referred to as α, so that the confidence interval will be $1 - \alpha$.

For any interval, the Z formula can be rearranged to make the mean, μ, the subject of the formula. That is:

$$\pm Z = \frac{\bar{x} - \mu}{\sigma_{\bar{x}}}$$

therefore

$$\mu = \bar{x} \pm Z\sigma_{\bar{x}}$$

This formula is called the confidence interval of the true mean μ and it involves adding and subtracting a quantity, $Z\sigma_{\bar{x}}$ which is called the **half-width** of the confidence interval. We interpret this formula by saying that we are $1 - \alpha$ confident that the true mean will be within this interval. This formula is only strictly applicable when the standard deviation of the population is known. However, provided the sample size is large, we can estimate the standard deviation from the sample standard deviation and use this value in the formula. We will discuss the problem of an unknown standard deviation and a small sample size shortly.

■ **Drive Thru Burger restaurant**   *Scenario 3.15*

The restaurant purchases burgers in bulk and randomly weighs eighteen of them. On one occasion the mean weight of the sample was found to be 55.5 grams. If the standard deviation of a burger is known to be 5.4 grams, what is the 95 per cent confidence interval of the true mean weight of a burger?

Although the sample is small, we do know the standard deviation of the population, so the formula using Z is appropriate. The standard error of the sample is:

$$\frac{5.4}{\sqrt{18}} = 1.27$$

The 95 per cent confidence interval for the true mean weight is:

$$55.5 \pm 1.96 \times 1.27 = 55.5 \pm 2.49$$

$$= 53.01 \text{ to } 57.99 \text{ grams}$$

That is, we can be 95 per cent confident that the true mean weight will be between 53.0 to 58.0 grams.

Confidence interval for small samples

It is unlikely that we will know the standard deviation of the population, and we will have to estimate it from the sample. The formula quoted earlier in this chapter provided an unbiased estimate of the true standard deviation. This formula is:

$$s = \sqrt{\frac{\Sigma(x - \bar{x})^2}{n-1}}$$

When we estimate the standard deviation in this way, we cannot strictly use the Z formula, although we can get away with it for large samples. For small samples, it can be shown that provided the population is approximately normally distributed, the sampling distribution follows a *t*-**distribution**. A *t*-distribution is symmetrical like the normal distribution, but it is flatter, which increases the area in the tails. This means that for the same value of α, the half-width is larger, which compensates for the uncertainty in the value of the standard deviation σ. The degree of 'flatness' decreases with increase in the sample size. When the sample size is around 50, there is virtually no difference between the t and the normal distributions. The formula for the confidence interval involving the *t*-distribution is

$$\mu = \bar{x} \pm t\sigma_{\bar{x}}$$

where $\sigma_{\bar{x}} = s/\sqrt{n}$

The value of t depends on the **degrees of freedom** of the sample. Degrees of freedom relate to the freedom lost as a result of estimating the unknown parameters. In this case we have to estimate the standard deviation, so we subtract one from our sample size n. The t-tables provided in Appendix 3 give the area for various degrees of freedom and specific values of α. The bottom row of the table gives the value of t for an infinitely large sample. These values correspond to the Z-scores for the normal distribution.

■ Drive Thru Burger restaurant   *Scenario 3.16*

In Scenario 3.15 we assumed that the standard deviation of 5.4 grams was precise, but suppose this value had been calculated from the sample of eighteen. The sample size is too small to be able to use the Z formula, but provided the distribution of the population is normal, we can use the t-distribution. For a 95 per cent confidence interval (an α of 0.025) and 17 degrees of freedom, the appropriate t-value is 2.110. The confidence interval is therefore:

$$55.5 \pm 2.110 \times 1.27 = 55.5 \pm 2.68$$

The half-width has increased from 2.49 to 2.68 grams and the confidence interval for the true mean weight will be between 52.8 and 58.2 grams.

Hypothesis tests

The calculation of confidence intervals can be very useful when we want to provide some degree of precision around an estimate of a population mean. This can be important when we have some output from a model and wish to compare it with observations from the real system. Model output and the real system will never agree exactly, but the difference may be within the error expected from a sample.

We may also wish to approach the problem in a slightly different way and ask if the sample result could have come from a population with a known mean. When we approach the problem in this way we are conducting an **hypothesis test**. An hypothesis test makes an assumption or hypothesis and then tries to disprove it. This hypothesis is called a **null hypothesis** (H_0). Acceptance of the null hypothesis does not 'prove' that the null hypothesis is true; it merely implies that we do not have sufficient evidence to reject it. However, the rejection of the null hypothesis implies that the sample data is not consistent with the hypothesis, and we accept an **alternative hypothesis** (H_1). The null hypothesis is tested using a **test statistic** at a particular significance level, α. The test statistic is based on an appropriate sampling distribution. The significance level relates to the area or probability in the tail of the distribution being used for the test. This area is called the **critical region** and if the test statistic lies in the critical region, we would infer that the result is unlikely to have occurred by chance. We would then reject the null hypothesis. For example, if the 5 per cent level of significance was being used and the null hypothesis was rejected, we would say that H_0 had been rejected at the

5 per cent (or 0.05) significance level and the result was *significant*. There are many forms of hypothesis tests – some test a statistic of a single sample against the same statistic of the population from where the sample is assumed to have come from, while others test two or more samples simultaneously.

The most important group of hypothesis tests are parametric tests. These tests compare sample statistics with the population parameters and make assumptions about the population. If these assumptions do not apply, it may be necessary to use a non-parametric test. Non-parametric tests make fewer assumptions about the data but are not as powerful as parametric tests; that is, they have less power to reject the null hypothesis when the null hypothesis is false. Non-parametric tests will be discussed later in this chapter.

The steps for carrying out an hypothesis test are as follows:

1. Decide on the appropriate test and sampling distribution to use.

2. Set up the null and alternative hypotheses and determine (usually from tables) the boundaries of the critical region. These boundaries are called the **critical values**.

3. Calculate the test statistic.

4. Decide whether to accept or reject H_0.

The critical values depend on whether the test is two-tailed or one-tailed. A two-tailed test is used when we have *no* reason to believe that a rejection of the null hypothesis implies that the true statistic is either greater than or less than some assumed value. A one-tailed test is when we *have* evidence to suggest that a rejection of the null hypothesis implies that the true statistic is either greater than or less than this value.

Of course, the decision to reject or not to reject the null hypothesis is based on probabilities. To reject H_0, we are making the assumption that if the test statistic falls in the critical region, this result is unlikely. However, if we are using the 5 per cent significance level, then there must be a 5 per cent chance of making an error; that is, we have rejected H_0 when in fact H_0 was true. This is called a type I error. We could reduce the chance of making a type I error by reducing the significance level. Unfortunately, we now increase the chance of making a type II error. A type II error is caused by accepting the null hypothesis when in fact it is false. Table 3.5 summarises the four possible situations that could occur when carrying out an hypothesis test.

Table 3.5 ■ Possible situations that could occur in hypothesis testing

Decision	True situation	
	H_0 is true	H_0 is false
Accept H_0	Correct decision	Type II error
Reject H_0	Type I error	Correct decision

Control of type I errors is usually considered more important, and this has resulted in an α of 0.05 or sometimes 0.01 to be the accepted standard. This rather rigid approach can cause problems when the test statistic is close to the critical value being used for the test. An alternative approach adopted by most computer software packages is to calculate the **P-value**. 'A P-value is the lowest level (of significance) at which the observed value of the test statistic is significant' (Walpole and Myers, 1990). Thus a P-value of 0.001 would indicate that a type I error would only occur once in every 1000 times, while a P-value of 0.049 would indicate that this would occur 49 times in a 1000. In both cases the P-values are less than 0.05, resulting in a rejection of the null hypothesis, but we would be far more confident of our decision in the former case.

It is now time to look at some actual tests so that the ideas discussed above can be put into practice.

Tests involving a single sample

As in the case of confidence intervals, the sampling distribution used depends on whether we know the standard deviation of the population. If we know the standard deviation we can use the normal distribution; otherwise we should use the t-distribution.

The test statistic when the normal distribution is assumed is the Z-score and is expressed in the form:

$$Z = \frac{\bar{x} - \mu}{\sigma_{\bar{x}}}$$

The critical values are the Z-scores for the area covered by $1-\alpha$ of the standard normal distribution. Figure 3.26 shows the case for the two-tailed test when $\alpha = 0.05$ or 5 per cent.

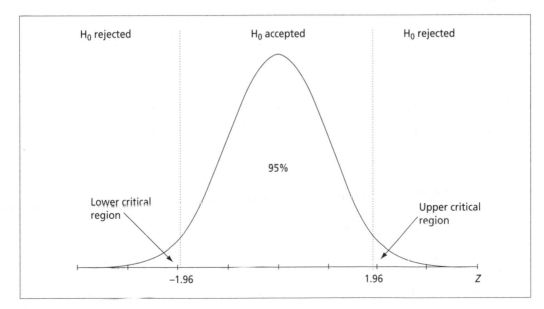

Figure 3.26 ▥ **Two-tailed test at the 5 per cent significance level**

Since the one-tailed test could involve either the lower or upper tail, there are two possible diagrams for this test. These are shown in Figure 3.27.

The difference between the one- and two-tailed tests is that the critical values will be different in the two cases. This is because the area in the tail for the one-tailed case is double that in either of the tails of the two-tailed case. The effect of this is that a one-tailed test is more likely than the two-tailed test to reject the null hypothesis. A one-tailed test should therefore only be conducted if it can be justified. Scenario 3.17 illustrates the case where the one-tailed test is appropriate.

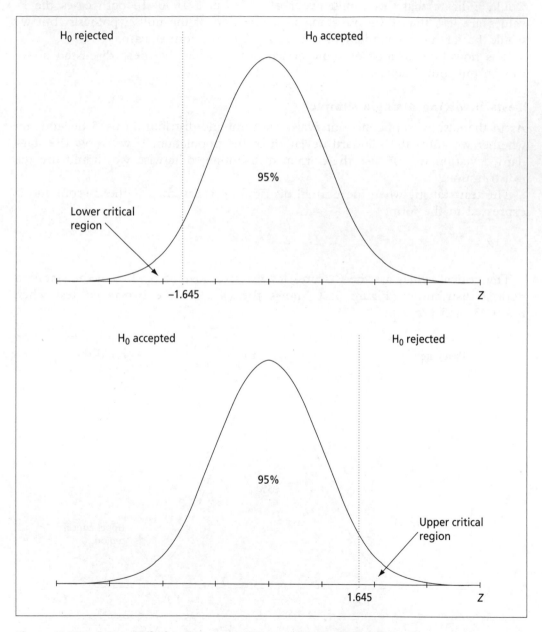

Figure 3.27 ∎ One-tailed tests at the 5 per cent significance level

■ **Drive Thru Burger restaurant**   *Scenario 3.17*

The mean weight of a burger supplied to the restaurant is supposed to be 56.8 grams with a standard deviation of 5.4 grams. A sample of eighteen burgers gave a mean weight of 55.5 grams. Is there any evidence that the true mean weight of a burger is not 56.8 grams?

This example is a one-tailed test since it is unlikely that the restaurant would complain if the mean weight was greater than 56.8 grams. The null and alternative hypotheses are:

$$H_0: \mu = 56.8 \qquad H_1: \mu < 56.8$$

If we reject H_0 we would be able to say that the mean weight of the burgers is less than 56.8 grams. The first stage is to calculate the standard error.

$$\sigma_{\bar{x}} = \frac{54}{\sqrt{18}} = 1.273$$

and

$$Z = \frac{55.5 - 56.8}{1.273} = -1.021$$

The critical value at 5 per cent significance level is -1.645, and since the test statistic is greater than this value, we are unable to reject the H_0. Looking at Figure 3.28, we can see that the test statistic lies in the acceptance region.

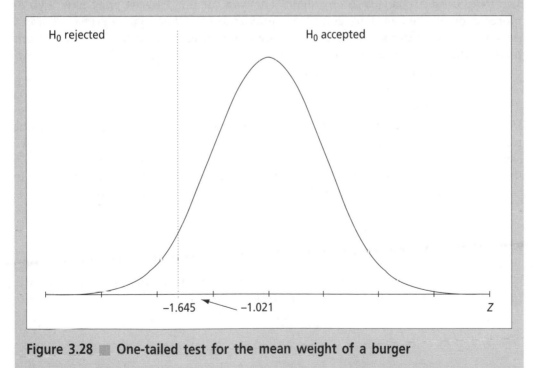

Figure 3.28 ■ One-tailed test for the mean weight of a burger

If the standard deviation has to be estimated from the sample, the t-distribution should be used instead of the normal distribution. The assumption here is that the distribution of the population is approximately normal. The test statistic in this case is

$$t = \frac{\bar{x} - \mu}{\sigma_{\bar{x}}}$$

where $\sigma_{\bar{x}} = s/\sqrt{n}$

The critical values are the values of t on $n-1$ degrees of freedom.

■ Drive Thru Burger restaurant

Scenario 3.18

In Scenario 3.17, we assumed that the standard deviation of 5.4 grams was known exactly. If this value had been estimated from the sample, we would have had to use the t-distribution (assuming the distribution of weights is normal). The value of the test statistic is the same as the previous case but the critical t-value must be found from tables on 17 degrees of freedom and 5 per cent significance level (one-tailed). Since this value is -1.703, we can conclude that there is insufficient evidence to reject the null hypothesis.

Tests involving two or more samples

The process of modelling often requires that changes are made to the model to see if the output changes in any significant way. In this case we may have two or more samples we want to compare simultaneously. The type of test to apply depends on the number of samples we are comparing, as well as the assumptions made of the data. Since we will be looking at tests involving more than two samples in Chapter 12, only the basic details will be presented here.

Tests on two means

For two samples, we are testing to see if both samples have come from the same population. We have already briefly looked at the question of combining two samples that have come from two different populations. The difference between the means of the two sampling distributions is normally distributed with a mean equal to the difference of the population means and a standard error of:

$$\sigma_{(\bar{x}_1 - \bar{x}_2)} = \sqrt{\left(\frac{\sigma_1^2}{n_1} + \frac{\sigma_2^2}{n_2}\right)}$$

If we are testing to see if both samples have come from the same distribution, then $\sigma_1 = \sigma_2 = \sigma$ and the standard error simplifies to:

$$\sigma_{(\bar{x}_1 - \bar{x}_2)} = \sigma \sqrt{\left(\frac{1}{n_1} + \frac{1}{n_2}\right)}$$

The test statistic in this case will be:

$$Z = \frac{(\bar{x}_1 - \bar{x}_2) - (\mu_1 - \mu_2)}{\sigma_{(\bar{x}_1 - \bar{x}_2)}}$$

The null hypothesis will normally be $\mu_1 = \mu_2$ and the alternative hypothesis can be either one- or two-tailed. For a two-tailed test we would have the two means unequal while for a one-tailed test we could have $\mu_1 > \mu_2$ or $\mu_1 < \mu_2$.

On most occasions we do not know the standard deviations, and in these cases we would have to use the t-distribution. The standard error in this case is a little more complicated and is as follows:

$$\sigma_{(\bar{x}_1 - \bar{x}_2)} = \hat{\sigma}\sqrt{\left(\frac{1}{n_1} + \frac{1}{n_2}\right)}$$

where $\hat{\sigma}$ is the estimate of the *pooled* standard deviation of the populations and is given by:

$$\hat{\sigma} = \sqrt{\frac{(n_1 - 1)s_1^2 + (n_2 - 1)s_2^2}{n_1 + n_2 - 2}}$$

The critical value at α significance level and $(n_1 + n_2 - 2)$ degrees of freedom can be found from tables (*see* Appendix 2).

In some cases the data is *paired*; that is, each observation of one sample is paired with an observation in the other sample. This can occur if identical conditions apply to pairs of observations. The null hypothesis is that the difference of the population means μ_d is zero and the alternative hypothesis can be either one- or two-tailed, depending on whether we believe the difference could be positive, negative or not equal to zero. The test statistic for this test is:

$$t = \frac{\bar{x}_d - \mu_d}{\sigma_{\bar{d}}}$$

where $\bar{x}_d$ is the sample mean of the n differences and μ_d is the population mean difference if the null hypothesis is correct. σ_d is the standard error of the mean difference and is given by:

$$\sigma_{\bar{d}} = \frac{s_d}{\sqrt{n}}$$

where s_d is the standard deviation of the differences.

Tests on more than two means

When we have several samples of data, we may wish to see if any of the means differ. The technique to use in these circumstances is the analysis of variance or ANOVA and the null and alternative hypotheses are:

H_0: $\mu_1 = \mu_2 = \ldots = \mu_k$

H_1: At least two of the means differ

The principle behind the analysis of variance is that there will be a spread or variation between the sample means and also between the observations of each sample. The greater the difference in these variations, the more likely that the populations differ. The approach then is to separate out the two sources of variations so that they can be compared. It can be shown that the ratio of the two variations has an F distribution and can be used to test the null hypothesis of no difference between the population means.

There are three different *designs* for the analysis of variance. The first is the **completely randomised design** and corresponds to the two sample t-test.

The second design is the **randomised block design**, which corresponds to the paired samples. The third case is where we want to compare two or more variables or factors, where each factor operates at two or more levels. This is called a **factorial experiment**. ANOVA calculations are normally carried out by computer, and we will be looking at the output from the different designs in Chapter 12.

Goodness-of-fit tests

Another very important test is when we want to see if a population has a specified distribution. There are three main tests that can be applied to a sample of data. The most common and easiest to apply is the Chi-square test (*see below*).

Chi-square test

To illustrate this test, imagine a die was thrown 60 times and the number of times that each face appeared was noted. Let us assume that we got the results shown in Table 3.6.

Table 3.6 ■ Observed and expected frequencies for 60 throws of a die

	Face					
	1	2	3	4	5	6
Observed	7	15	10	16	6	6
Expected	10	10	10	10	10	10

If our hypothesis is that the die is fair, we would expect every face to come up ten times in the long run. We now need to test to see if the differences between the observed and expected frequencies are significant or due to chance.

The test statistic is calculated according to the formula:

$$\chi^2 = \sum_{i=1}^{k} \frac{(O_i - E_i)^2}{E_i}$$

where O_i is the observed value and E_i is the expected value for the ith category. The random variable χ^2, has a sampling distribution that is approximated very closely by the Chi-square distribution. The distribution is right skewed, the level of skewness depending upon the degrees of freedom, ν. Figure 3.29 shows the shape for four degrees of freedom.

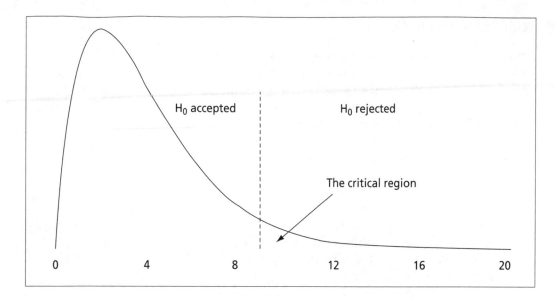

Figure 3.29 ▨ The Chi-square distribution on 4 degrees of freedom

The degrees of freedom can be calculated from:

$$\nu = k - 1 - c$$

where k is the number of categories and c is the number of parameters estimated from the data.

For the case of a uniform distribution, $c = 0$ and the degrees of freedom will therefore be $k - 1$.

To calculate the value of χ^2 for the die, we need to calculate the square difference between the observed and expected frequencies, and divide each by the expected frequency as shown in Table 3.7

The sum of the bottom row of the table is 10.2 and this is the test statistic. The critical value at 5 per cent significance level and 5 degrees of freedom can be found in the Chi-square tables in Appendix 2, and is 11.07. Since the test statistic is less than this value, the null hypothesis is accepted; that is, the die is fair.

Table 3.7 ▨ Calculations for the Chi-square test

	Face					
	1	2	3	4	5	6
Observed	7	15	10	16	6	6
Expected	10	10	10	10	10	10
$O - E$	−3	5	0	6	−4	−4
$(O - E)^2$	9	25	0	36	16	16
$(O - E)^2/E$	0.9	2.5	0	3.6	1.6	1.6

■ Whiteladies Health Centre
Scenario 3.19

Imagine that we made the hypothesis that the distribution of doctor consultation time is normal. The data for 305 consultation times has already been grouped into a frequency table and was shown in Table 3.3, page 35. The histogram has also been plotted in Figure 3.7 and it is evident that the normal distribution would be a rather poor fit, particularly as a result of the outlier at 42 minutes. However, would the normal distribution be a reasonable fit if this outlier was removed?

We can carry out a Chi-square test by calculating the expected frequency within each interval for a normal distribution, with the same mean and standard deviation as our sample. If the outlier of 42 minutes is removed the mean is 6.43 minutes, with a standard deviation of 4.053 minutes. We now need to calculate the area within each interval and multiply these values by 304, the total frequency. For example, the probability within the interval zero to two minutes can be found as follows:

$$Z_0 = \frac{0 - 6.43}{4.053} = -1.586 \qquad\qquad Z_2 = \frac{2 - 6.43}{4.053} = -1.093$$

$$P(Z_0 < -1.586) = 0.0559 \qquad\qquad P(Z_1 < -1.093) = 0.1379$$

$$P(0 < x < 2) = 0.1379 - 0.0559 = 0.082$$

The expected frequency will therefore be $0.082 \times 304 = 24.9$.

This process is rather tedious to do by hand but much easier if a computer is used. Most statistical packages can do Chi-square calculations, although in this case, Excel was used. The worksheet can be found in the attached computer disk (*see* Appendix 4) and the table of results is shown below. (The values will differ slightly compared to those calculated manually due to rounding errors.) You may notice that an additional row has been added to the frequency table; this is because the normal distribution with this mean and standard deviation would have values below a time of zero. If we ignored this, the sum of the probabilities would not sum to one and we would underestimate the value of the test statistic. Therefore, a probability of 0.0564 has been added to the table, giving an expected frequency of 17.15 for consultation times less than zero.

A problem with the results in Table 3.8 is that three of the intervals contain expected values of less than five. The use of the Chi-square distribution is only an approximation and is invalidated for low expected values. To rectify the problem, the four highest groups should be combined. This will give the amended table shown in Table 3.9.

Table 3.8 ■ Chi-square calculations for the doctor consultation times

lcb	ucb	Ob. freq.	P1	P2	P2 – P1	Exp. freq.	Chi
	0	0			0.0564	17.15	17.15
0	2	22	0.0564	0.1374	0.0810	24.62	0.28
2	4	64	0.1374	0.2748	0.1373	41.75	11.86
4	6	91	0.2748	0.4582	0.1834	55.76	22.28
6	8	50	0.4582	0.6511	0.1930	58.66	1.28
8	10	28	0.6511	0.8111	0.1599	48.62	8.74
10	12	21	0.8111	0.9155	0.1044	31.74	3.63
12	14	7	0.9155	0.9692	0.0537	16.32	5.32
14	16	6	0.9692	0.9909	0.0217	6.61	0.06
16	18	11	0.9909	0.9979	0.0069	2.11	37.49
18	20	2	0.9979	0.9996	0.0017	0.53	4.08
20	30	2	0.9996	1.0000	0.0004	0.12	28.57
Total		304			1.00	303.99	140.74

Table 3.9 ■ Amended Chi-square table after grouping cells

lcb	ucb	Ob. freq.	P1	P2	P2 – P1	Exp. freq.	Chi
	0	0			0.0564	17.15	17.15
0	2	22	0.0564	0.1374	0.0810	24.62	0.28
2	4	64	0.1374	0.2748	0.1373	41.75	11.86
4	6	91	0.2748	0.4582	0.1834	55.76	22.28
6	8	50	0.4582	0.6511	0.1930	58.66	1.28
8	10	28	0.6511	0.8111	0.1599	48.62	8.74
10	12	21	0.8111	0.9155	0.1044	31.74	3.63
12	14	7	0.9155	0.9692	0.0537	16.32	5.32
14	30	21	0.9692	1.0000	0.0308	9.37	14.44
Total		304			1.00	303.99	84.98

►

Before we can compare the test statistic of 84.98 with the appropriate Chi-square distribution, we need to determine the degrees of freedom. Since both the mean and standard deviation have had to be estimated from the data, the degrees of freedom will be $9 - 1 - 2 = 6$. The critical value at 5 per cent significance for 6 degrees of freedom is 12.59, and since this is much less than the test statistic, we can reject the hypothesis that the consultation time data are normally distributed.

Although the Chi-square test is fairly easy to understand, care must be taken in its application. One problem that has already been encountered in Scenario 3.19 is that the expected values can sometimes be less than five. Another problem with the Chi-square test is that the result is sensitive to the intervals used to group the data. Changing the number of intervals used to group the data could change the decision reached. Another test that can be used is the **Kolmogorov-Smirnov** test.

Kolmogorov-Smirnov test

The Kolmogorov-Smirnov test compares the difference between the empirical and fitted cdfs. The Kolmogorov-Smirnov test overcomes the problem of the intervals used but it cannot be used for discrete data. It is also only strictly valid when all the parameters of the hypothesised distribution are known. In other words, care should be taken when the parameters have to be fitted from the sample data. (It is possible to use a modified version of the test when the parameters have to be estimated, but this is beyond the scope of this text.)

To apply this test, the relative cumulative frequency for both the observed and theoretical distributions are calculated, and the absolute difference between each pair of cumulative frequencies is found for each class. The null hypothesis is rejected if the largest difference is greater than the critical value found from tables. The largest of these absolute differences is the test statistic and this is compared with the critical value found from tables. If the sample size (n) is large (over 30), the critical value at 5 per cent significance level is approximately:

$$\frac{1.36}{\sqrt{n}}$$

■ Whiteladies Health Centre   *Scenario 3.20*

The Kolmogorov-Smirnov test has been applied to the data from Table 3.9, to see whether the distribution of consultation times is normal. Again, a spreadsheet was used to carry out the calculations, and we can see from Table 3.10 that the largest difference (marked with an *) is 0.1241. Since the sample size is large, the critical value is calculated by:

$$\frac{1.36}{\sqrt{304}} = 0.0780$$

The value of 0.1241 is greater than 0.0780, so the null hypothesis is rejected. That is, the distribution is not normal. This confirms the result obtained from the Chi-square test.

Table 3.10 ▧ **Applying the Kolmogorov-Smirnov test to the consultation time data**

Ob. freq.	Ob. relative freq.	Ob. cumulative freq.	Theoretical freq.	Theoretical relative freq.	Theoretical cumulative freq.	Absolute difference
0	0.0000	0.0000	17.1456	0.0564	0.0564	0.0564
22	0.0724	0.0724	24.6212	0.0810	0.1374	0.0650
64	0.2105	0.2829	41.7466	0.1373	0.2747	0.0082
91	0.2993	0.5822	55.7572	0.1834	0.4581	0.1241 *
50	0.1645	0.7467	58.6624	0.1930	0.6511	0.0956
28	0.0921	0.8388	48.6186	0.1599	0.8110	0.0278
21	0.0691	0.9079	31.7408	0.1044	0.9154	0.0075
7	0.0230	0.9309	16.3225	0.0537	0.9691	0.0382
6	0.0197	0.9507	6.6110	0.0217	0.9909	0.0402
11	0.0362	0.9868	2.1088	0.0069	0.9978	0.0110
2	0.0066	0.9934	0.5297	0.0017	0.9996	0.0061
2	0.0066	1.0000	0.1233	0.0004	1.0000	0.0000

Tests of normality

The easiest method for checking normality is by the use of a **normal probability plot**. In a normal probability plot, the data is plotted against the values that would be expected if the assumption of normality was true. If the points on the graph appear linear, the data is approximately normal, whereas a non-linear set of points suggest that the data is not normal. Special graph paper can be used although the simplest method is to use a statistical software package.

▮ Whiteladies Health Centre

Scenario 3.21

MINITAB was used to obtain a normality plot of the doctor consultation time data, and this can be seen in Figure 3.30. If the data followed a normal distribution, the points would all lie on a straight line. The normal distribution with the same mean and standard deviation as the sample data is superimposed on the diagram, and we can see clearly that the data deviates from this line quite considerably. MINITAB has also carried out the Kolmogorov-

▶

Smirnov test and the largest difference of 0.125 corresponds closely to the value of 0.1241 calculated in Table 3.10. The p-value of < 0.01, indicates that the probability that the null hypothesis is true is less than 1 per cent.

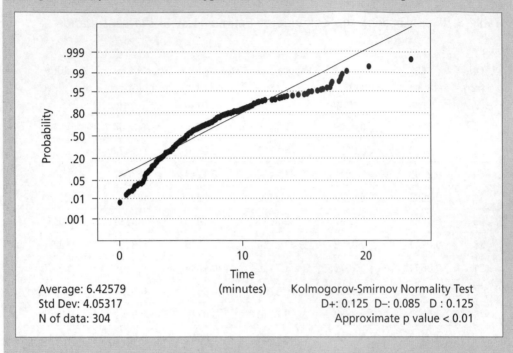

Figure 3.30 ◼ **Probability plot for the consultation time data**

Non-parametric tests

Apart from the Chi-square test, all the tests discussed so far in this chapter are parametric tests. These tests require that the data is measured on an interval scale and that certain assumptions regarding the sampled population are valid. In some cases data can be ordinal (that is, the data can be ranked), while in other cases the assumptions of normality may not be valid. Most of the data obtained during the modelling process will be continuous, so that the problem of data type is unlikely to arise. However, assumptions of normality may be violated, so that alternative methods of hypothesis testing may be required.

Non-parametric tests are distribution-free (that is, very few assumptions are made about the probability distribution of the population). They are not as powerful as parametric tests, though, which means that they have less power to reject the null hypothesis when the null hypothesis is false. Non-parametric tests should therefore only be used when necessary, rather than as a permanent substitute for parametric tests.

There are non-parametric versions of all the tests mentioned so far in this chapter. The **sign test** is used to test the median of any continuous distribution. An equivalent test to the two-sample *t*-test is the **Mann–Whitney test**, while the

Wilcoxon signed ranks test can be used in place of the paired t-test. There are two tests that can be used in place of analysis of variance. For the completely randomised design, the **Kruskal–Wallis test** can be used, while the **Friedman test** can be used for the randomised block design. The Mann-Whitney and the Wilcoxon signed ranks tests are the most important tests from a modelling context and will be looked at in detail in Chapter 12.

Summary

This chapter has introduced some of the more important statistical concepts necessary for an understanding of the remaining chapters in this text. A knowledge of descriptive statistics is necessary in many situations, either when data is collected during the model-building process, or in the analysis of output from some models. Probability is the key to an understanding of the stochastic nature of many systems and as an introduction to the important topic of inferential statistics. The data collected or obtained from a model is usually sample data, and from this sample we attempt to make inferences about the sampled population. There are many tests available to test hypotheses about the population from where the sample originated. Not all tests can be used in all situations and care must be exercised in the choice of test. In some cases it is necessary to use a non-parametric test as these tests do not require so many assumptions about the population.

■ Exercises

3.1 Table 3.11 shows the sales of a company broken down into its four sales regions from 1992 to 1996.

   a   Draw a simple bar chart to show the total sales for the four-year period.

   b   Draw a stacked bar chart to show the sales for the years and how they were broken down between the four sales regions.

   c   Draw a multiple bar chart to compare the sales for each region.

   d   Draw a pie chart to show the breakdown of total sales in 1996.

   e   What can you conclude about the company's sales?

Table 3.11 ■

Sales region	Year (Sales £m)				
	1992	1993	1994	1995	1996
South-west	4.0	2.0	2.2	3.6	3.7
South	6.0	4.9	2.5	3.2	3.7
South-east	7.6	9.1	5.2	4.3	4.2
Wales	1.5	1.4	1.4	1.5	1.6
Totals	19.1	17.4	11.3	12.6	13.2

3.2 The consultation time data for Doctor Blue can be found in Appendix 1 and on the disk that accompanies this text.

    a   Plot a histogram of this data and comment on its shape.

    b   Calculate the mean, median and standard deviation of the data.

    c   Draw a box and whisker plot and identify any outliers.

3.3 A box contains 50 components of which four are known to be defective. What is the probability that if two were removed, both would be defective?

3.4 Customers at the Drive Thru Burger restaurant were asked to state whether they were satisfied or dissatisfied with the service. On previous occasions the probability that a customer was dissatisfied was 0.05. If this probability still holds and is the same for all customers, what is the probability that more than two customers out of fifteen would be dissatisfied?

3.5 On average, 43.8 patients per hour arrive at random at the Whiteladies Health Centre on a Monday. What is the probability that:

    a   no patients arrive in any one-minute interval?

    b   at least three patients turn up in a one-minute interval?

    c   the time between successive arrivals is two minutes?

3.6 Some patients at the Whiteladies Health Centre have to have a hearing test. If the time taken to carry out this test is normally distributed with a mean of five minutes and a standard deviation of 1.5 minutes, calculate:

    a   the probability that the time for a hearing test will be greater than six minutes.

    b   the probability that the time for a hearing test will be between four and six minutes.

    c   the time taken that will not be exceeded by more than 5 per cent of patients.

3.7 The time customers spend ordering their food at the Drive Thru Burger restaurant is normally distributed with a mean of 45 seconds and a standard deviation of thirteen seconds. What is the probability that a random sample of nine customers will spend an average of less than 40 seconds ordering their food?

3.8 The average amount spent by 50 customers at the Drive Thru Burger restaurant is £3.50 with a standard deviation of £1.22. What is the 95 per cent confidence interval of the true mean amount spent by all the restaurant's customers?

3.9 The amount spent by customers at the Drive Thru Burger restaurant is believed to be normally distributed with a mean of £3.65. If a random sample of twelve customers spends £3.50 on average, with a standard deviation of £1.34, does this suggest, at the 5 per cent significance level, that the true mean amount spent has changed?

3.10 The service time data for customers at the Drive Thru Burger restaurant is provided in Appendix 1, and also on the disk that accompanies this text (with name DTB.xls). There is a suggestion that the data is uniformly distributed.

    a   Use the Chi-square test to test this hypothesis.

    b   Use the Kolmogorov-Smirnov test to test this hypothesis.

References and further reading

Black, K. (1994) *Business Statistics* (Chapters 1 to 11 and 16), West Publishing Company, Minneapolis, USA.

Morris, C. (1996) *Quantitative Approaches in Business Studies,* Fourth Edition (Parts 2 and 3), Pitman Publishing, London.

Oakshott, L. (1994) *Essential Elements of Business Statistics*, DP Publications, London.

Sincich, T. (1995) *Business Statistics by Example*, Fifth Edition (Chapters 2 to 11 and 19), Macmillan Publishing Company, Singapore.

Tufte, E.R. (1983) *The Visual Display of Quantitative Information*, Graphics Press, Cheshire, Connecticut, USA.

Walpole, R. and Myers, R. (1990) *Probability and Statistics for Engineers and Scientists*, Fourth Edition (Chapters 1 to 5, 7, 8 and 14), Macmillan Publishing Company, New York.

Wetherill, G. (1981) *Intermediate Statistical Methods* (Chapter 1), Chapman and Hall, New York.

4

Analytical models

Les Oakshott

Introduction

Analytical models are models that can be solved using classical techniques. These techniques can range from simple algebraic manipulation to the use of advanced calculus methods. In this chapter we will be looking at both deterministic and stochastic models, but we shall not be attempting to prove any of the results obtained. The purpose is to demonstrate how a range of problems can be solved analytically and to show that in so doing, we have to make many assumptions. This will pave the way to the use of simulation techniques that we will be discussing in subsequent chapters.

Deterministic models

Deterministic models are models where it is assumed that there is no appreciable uncertainty in the variables or parameters being measured. It represents a kind of utopia where everything is known precisely. Obviously this state will never be found in practice, but the variability may be sufficiently small for this to be a reasonable approximation, at least in the first instance. The advantage of deterministic models is that they are usually much simpler to solve than their stochastic counterparts.

Since we assume that there is no variability, we can guarantee that for the same input we will get the same output. These inputs could, for example, be price, demand and interest rates, while the output could be expected sales volume. No matter how complex the relationship between these variables, the expected sales volume would always be the same for the same values of these input variables. We can think of the model linking the inputs to the outputs as a black box and represent it using the diagram in Figure 4.1.

There are many deterministic models but only two will be mentioned in this chapter. These are **linear programming** and **inventory control models**. The interested reader can look in the 'Further Reading' section at the end of this chapter for references to other models.

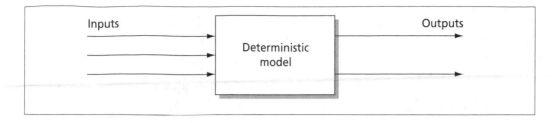

Figure 4.1 ■ **The deterministic model**

Linear programming models

Linear programming (or LP) is a technique used to solve problems where there is an objective and a set of linear constraints. The idea is to obtain values of certain **decision variables**, which will enable the objective to be optimised. This objective could be to maximise the contribution to profits or maximise the throughput of an industrial process. Equally, it could be a minimising objective such as minimising production cost or the risk that an investment will fail. Linear programming can be used in many different areas, but the most common is probably when applied to production situations. When linear programming is used in this context, we say that the technique is concerned with the management of scarce resources. These resources could be materials, labour, money or any resource where there is a finite quantity available. In a typical production system where there are two or more items being produced, these items are competing for the limited resources. If each item provides a certain known contribution towards the company's profits, we would want to determine the quantities of each item to produce so as to maximise the total contribution. Even when we have only two items the solution is not always obvious, and when there are many items to consider it is almost impossible to guess the answer using trial and error methods.

Linear programming assumes that the variables can take on any positive value. In many cases only integer values are sensible, and if this is important we may need to use **integer linear programming**. For simple problems we may be able to adjust the solution, although we must take care that the solution satisfies all constraints.

■ **Drive Thru Burger restaurant**   *Scenario 4.1*

This fast-food restaurant makes and sells a variety of products, ranging from burgers to pizzas. For simplicity, let us assume that only two products are made; these being a beefburger and a cheeseburger. Let us also assume that at the start of the day the company receives the raw materials from a local distributor and that it sells all that it makes. Although the company does not have much control over which product its customers purchase (except through price), it would be interesting to see what quantities of each product they should sell in order to maximise the contribution to profits. Using this

▶

information, the company could decide if they need to change the quantities of raw materials ordered, or whether they should influence demand by a price change.

Each beefburger requires one bun and two 2 oz burgers, and gives a profit of 25p. Each cheeseburger also requires one bun, but only uses one 2 oz burger. It does, however, require one slice of cheese. The profit on this item is 20p.

At the start of the day, 1000 buns, 1000 burgers and 500 slices of cheese are delivered. It is not possible to obtain more of these ingredients until the next day.

The first stage of the linear programming procedure is to formulate the model. To do this we need to express the problem in mathematical terms and the use of algebra becomes indispensable here. If we let the number of beefburgers to make each day be b and the number of cheeseburgers be c, the profit obtained if all were sold is

$$0.25b + 0.20c$$

which is to be maximised. This expression is usually called the **objective function**.

We now need to express the constraints to the problem in the same terminology. The constraints are the quantities of raw materials delivered at the start of the day. In the case of the buns we have 1000, so this means that we cannot make more than this number of items in total. This can be expressed in the form of an inequation. That is:

$$b + c \leqslant 1000$$

A similar procedure is used for the burger resource. In this case there are again 1000 burgers available, but the beefburger requires two of them and the cheeseburger only one. The constraint is therefore:

$$2b + c \leqslant 1000$$

Finally, there is the cheese resource. There are only 500 slices available and the constraint is:

$$c \leqslant 500$$

Notice that in this constraint the variable b does not appear since cheese is not used in the beefburger. We should also specify that the variables must not take on negative values. These are called the **non-negativity constraints** and appear as $b, c \geqslant 0$. This might appear obvious but we must remember that we have reduced our problem into a set of mathematical expressions, and a negative value would be quite legitimate from a mathematical point of view. We would also hope that the values of b and c are integer, but there is no guarantee that this will be the case. If they are not, we will have to adjust the solution accordingly.

To summarise, the objective function and constraints are

$$\text{Max } 0.25b + 0.20c$$
subject to

$$b + c \leqslant 1000$$
$$2b + c \leqslant 1000$$
$$c \leqslant 500$$
$$b, c \geqslant 0$$

Graphical solutions to LP models

Once an LP problem has been formulated, we need to solve it. The method of solution depends on the number of variables there are in the model. In the case of two variables, we can use a graphical method. The inequations can be represented on a graph by a region and to find the boundaries of these regions it is necessary to plot the *equations*. Once the equations have been drawn, the corresponding regions can be identified and the area found that satisfies all constraints noted. Any point within this **feasible region** will obviously be feasible but not necessarily optimal. So how is this optimal point found? Fortunately, the optimum point of an LP model always lies at a corner point of the feasible region, and the problem becomes one of searching for that point. In the graphical method, the simplest method is to evaluate each point.

■ **Drive Thru Burger restaurant**   *Scenario 4.2*

Since the model developed in Scenario 4.1 contained two variables, it can be solved graphically. The equations are:

$$b + c = 1000 \qquad \text{(buns)}$$
$$2b + c = 1000 \qquad \text{(burgers)}$$
$$c = 500 \qquad \text{(cheese slices)}$$

The easiest method of plotting these lines is to find where they cross the axes. The 'bun' equation will cross both axes at 1000, while the 'burger' equation will cross the c-axis at 1000 and the b-axis at 500. The third equation will be a vertical line from the c-axis at 500. This is shown in Figure 4.2. Once the equations have been plotted, it is necessary to identify the regions that are bounded by each equation. Since each region will be either one side or the other of the boundary line, it is simply a matter of investigating one point on the graph. Usually the simplest point to choose is the origin. If $b = 0$, $c = 0$ is substituted into the inequation $b + c \leqslant 1000$, it will be obvious that the required region is that containing the origin (since $0 < 1000$). It is normal practice to shade the unwanted region and this has been done in Figure 4.2. Once the regions have been shaded the feasible region can be identified. This has been marked on the diagram.

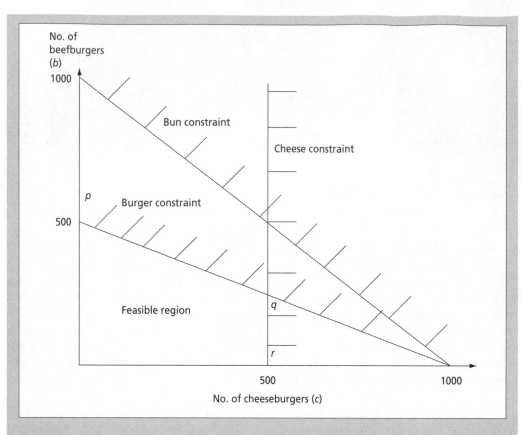

Figure 4.2 ■ Graphical solution for the burger restaurant

Once the feasible region has been identified it is necessary to find the optimum point. As the optimum must occur at a corner point this must be either p, q or r in Figure 4.2. Each of these points will give a feasible combination of b and c and it is a simple matter of comparing the profits in order to select the best combination. In this example the values of b and c can be read from the graph, but in some cases it may be sensible to use simultaneous equations in order to obtain accurate values. The values of b and c and the corresponding profit are shown in Table 4.1, where it will be seen that the optimum combination is to make 250 beefburgers and 500 cheeseburgers, giving a profit of £162.50.

Table 4.1 ■ Corner points of the feasible region

	No. of beefburgers (b)	No. of cheeseburgers (c)	Profit ($0.25b + 0.2c$)
p	500	0	£125
q	250	500	£162.50
r	0	500	£100

More than two variables

Most real-life problems contain many hundreds of variables and an equally large number of constraints. These kinds of problems occur in many industries, particularly the chemical and petroleum industries where a chemical or oil is to be produced from many different ingredients. Although the general principles are the same, the method of solution is completely different. The graphical solution can only be applied to two-variable problems because a normal graph has only two dimensions. In theory we could attempt to solve a three-variable problem graphically as it is possible to visualise a three-dimensional shape, but this is rarely done. The general method of solving linear programming models is by the use of the **Simplex algorithm**. This is rather tedious to do by hand, and a computer package is normally employed. For relatively small problems (say, up to 100 variables) it is possible to use a spreadsheet 'add-on' such as Solver in Microsoft Excel. The Solver routine does not use the Simplex algorithm, and there is no guarantee that it will find a global optimum, although in the majority of cases it will do so. The routine is invoked through the 'Tools' menu and the cells containing the variables are specified together with the objective and the constraints. The advantage with using a spreadsheet-based routine is that it is very easy to try out some 'What-if?' questions, such as, 'What if we have another unit of this material?' or 'What if the profit on this item changed?' All that is needed is for the particular cell to be changed and the problem resolved. We will be looking at sensitivity analysis in the next section.

■ **Drive Thru Burger restaurant**   *Scenario 4.3*

Suppose that in addition to the beefburger and cheeseburger, the company decides to make an eggburger. An eggburger requires one bun, two 2oz burgers and one egg. The profit on this item is 35p. If the company takes delivery of 200 eggs each day, how many of each product should they hope to make in order to maximise profits?

We now have a three-variable problem and the objective and constraints need to be modified accordingly. These become

Max $0.25b + 0.20c + 0.35e$

$b + c + e \leqslant 1000$

$2b + c + 2e \leqslant 1000$

$c \leqslant 500$

$e \leqslant 200$

$b, c, e \geqslant 0$

where e is the number of egg burgers to make each day.

▶

Table 4.2 ▪ Output from Excel for the Drive Thru Burger restaurant model

Microsoft Excel 5.0 Answer Report

Target Cell (Max)

Cell	Name	Original value	Final value
$J$9	Profit=	0	182.5000048

Adjustable Cells

Cell	Name	Original value	Final value
$J$5	b	0	50.00001913
$J$6	c	0	500
$J$7	e	0	200

Constraints

Cell	Name	Cell value	Formula	Status	Slack
$E$5	buns	1000	$E$5>=$B$5*$J$5+$C$5*$J$6+$D$5*$J$7	Not Binding	249.9999809
$E$6	burgers	1000	$E$6>=$B$6*$J$5+$C$6*$J$6+$D$6*$J$7	Binding	0
$E$7	cheese	500	$E$7>=$C$7*$J$6	Binding	0
$E$8	eggs	200	$E$8>=$D$8*$J$7	Binding	0

The Solver routine within Excel was used to solve the model and the output can be seen in Table 4.2 above.

As a result of the additional product, the product mix has changed. The best combination of products is 50 beefburgers (down from 250), 500 cheeseburgers and 200 eggburgers. The daily profit has risen from £162.50 to £182.50.

Sensitivity analysis

An important part of any type of model building is the 'What if?' or sensitivity analysis that should take place after the model has been built and solved. In many cases the sole purpose of building a model is to see what happens if there is a change in one of the model's parameters. In deterministic models we have a particular interest in this type of analysis, since we would have made numerous assumptions regarding the model parameters.

In linear programming, there are a number of procedures that are adopted when sensitivity analysis is applied to a particular model. We are usually interested to see what happens if there are changes to the right-hand side of a constraint and what happens if the objective function coefficients change.

Changes to the right-hand side of a constraint

There are two types of constraints. These are **tight constraints**, which are constraints that are at the limit at the optimal solution, and there are **slack constraints**, which are constraints that have not reached their limits. The tight constraints are the most important since it is these that are limiting any improvement in the objective function. Where these tight constraints represent resources, the resource is said to be *scarce*.

■ **Drive Thru Burger restaurant**   *Scenario 4.4*

To discover the tight constraints for the problem introduced in Scenario 4.1, the optimum value of the decision variables can be substituted into the constraints. If we do this, we should get the following:

$$250 + 500 = 750 \qquad (1000 \text{ buns available})$$
$$2 \times 250 + 500 = 1000 \qquad (1000 \text{ burgers available})$$
$$c = 500 \qquad (500 \text{ cheese slices available})$$

This tells us that all the burgers and all the cheese slices have been used but that there are 250 buns left. The burger and the cheese constraints are therefore tight, whereas the bun constraint is slack. By looking at Figure 4.2 it can be seen that the tight constraints are the constraints that intersect at the corner of the feasible region that gives the optimal solution. This is generally true.

In general, if the right-hand side of a tight constraint is changed, a change will occur to the value of the objective function. In order to compare the effect of changes to different constraints in a problem, we normally evaluate the change to the objective function when the right-hand side of a tight constraint changes by one unit. The change in the objective function is called the **shadow** or **dual** price. When a constraint represents a resource, the shadow price represents the marginal worth of that resource. In order to calculate the shadow prices for two variable problems, one of the tight constraints is increased by one unit and the new values of the decision variables found. The difference between the original value of the objective function and the new value is the shadow price. Since the changes made are so small, it is necessary to solve for the decision variables using simultaneous equations. Reading the values from the graph is not usually accurate enough.

■ **Drive Thru Burger restaurant**   *Scenario 4.5*

Since both the burger and cheese constraints are tight, the shadow prices can be evaluated for these resources. If we increase the number of burgers from 1000 to 1001 our two equations become:

$$2b + c = 1001$$
$$c = 500$$

Substituting $c = 500$ into the first equation gives:

$2b + 500 = 1001$

and $b = 250.5$

The profit is now $0.25 \times 250.5 + 0.2 \times 500 = £162.625$. This represents an increase of 12.5p. The same approach can be adopted for the cheese constraint. In this case, the value of c becomes 501 and this is substituted into the burger constraint to give:

$2b + 501 = 1000$

and $b = 249.5$

The profit is now $0.25 \times 249.5 + 0.2 \times 501 = £162.575$, giving an increase in profit of 7.5p. This suggests that it would be more profitable to increase the number of burgers purchased.

The calculation of shadow prices is an important part of linear programming and in some cases is more useful than the optimal solution. When a resource has a high shadow price there is obvious scope for improving the value of the objective function by increasing the availability of the particular resource. However, there is an assumption that additional units of the resource are not more costly than the original quantity. If they are, the additional cost needs to be subtracted from the shadow price.

Once a scarce resource has been identified, it may be worthwhile to increase the quantity available. But what is the maximum quantity that can be used? There must come a point where additional units of the resource cannot be used and the constraint representing the scarce resource becomes slack. Again this problem is easily demonstrated in the case of two variable models.

■ Drive Thru Burger restaurant   *Scenario 4.6*

If we look at the cheese constraint in Figure 4.2, we see that as additional slices of cheese are obtained, the line moves away from the origin. However, the maximum number of slices that can be used must be 1000 since this is the limit of the other two constraints. At this point the optimal values of b and c become $b = 0$ and $c = 1000$, giving a profit of £200, an increase of £37.50. This is the same answer that would be obtained by multiplying the increase in the quantity of cheese slices by the shadow price. That is, $500 \times 0.075 = £37.50$. The new situation can be seen in Figure 4.3.

For the burger constraint, an increase in the quantity of burgers will move the burger constraint away from the origin, but parallel to its original position. Since at least part of this line must be within the feasible region (controlled by the bun constraint), the furthest it can move is shown in Figure 4.4. The optimum point will now be when $c = 0$ and $b = 1000$, giving a profit of £250, an increase of £87.50. It is not possible to check this figure easily using the shadow price method because the shadow price is not constant; the value of 12.5p is only valid up to point s in Figure 4.4. This is because point q in Figure 4.2 moves up the cheese constraint line until point s and then along the bun constraint line.

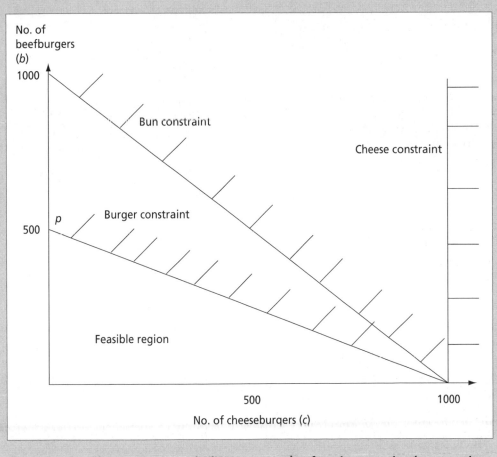

Figure 4.3 ■ **Change in the solution as a result of an increase in the quantity of cheese slices purchased**

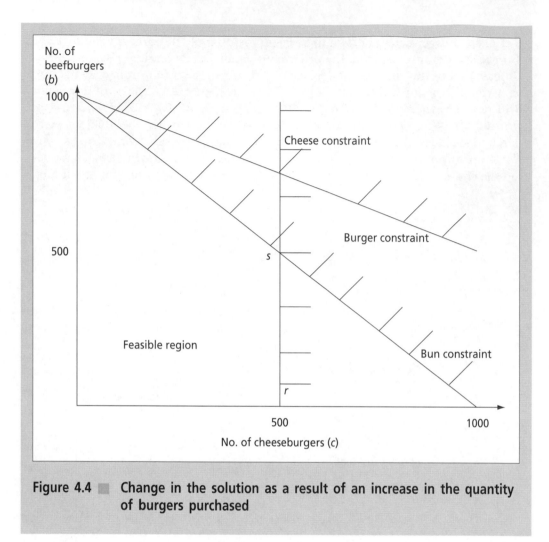

Figure 4.4 ■ Change in the solution as a result of an increase in the quantity of burgers purchased

For three or more variable problems the same principles apply, and most linear programming packages will automatically give details of shadow prices and upper and lower bounds to the right-hand side of the constraints. Although Solver will give some sensitivity information, it is probably easier to make changes to the model and then observe the changes to the objective function.

■ **Drive Thru Burger restaurant**   *Scenario 4.7*

If we want to determine the shadow price of the three-variable model developed and solved in Scenario 4.3, all we need to do is to increase one of the tight constraints by one unit. If we increase the number of burgers from 1000 to 1001 and resolve the model, we get the new report shown in Table 4.3.

Table 4.3 ■ **Solver output when the quantity of burgers is increased by 1**

Microsoft Excel 5.0 Answer Report					
Target Cell (Max)					

Cell	Name	Original value	Final value		
$J$9	Profit=	182.5	182.625		

Adjustable Cells

Cell	Name	Original Value	Final value		
$J$5	b	50	50.5		
$J$6	c	500	500		
$J$7	e	200	200		

Constraints

Cell	Name	Cell value	Formula	Status	Slack
$E$5	buns	1000	$E$5>=$B$5^$J$5+$C$5*$J$6+$D$5*$J$7	Not Binding	249.5
$E$6	burgers	1001	$E$6>=$B$6*$J$5+$C$6*$J$6+$D$6*$J$7	Binding	0
$E$7	cheese	500	$E$7>=$C$7*$J$6	Binding	0
$E$8	eggs	200	$E$8>=$D$8*$J$7	Binding	0

The shadow price is the difference between the original and the new profit, which is 12.5p. This is the same value that was obtained with the two-variable problem (Scenario 4.5). The limit for the burger constraint can be found by increasing the constraint until there is no further increase in profit. A macro could be designed to do this task, or a trial-and-error procedure could be used. (This is left as an exercise for the reader – see Exercise 4.3.)

Changes to the objective function coefficients

One of the problems with deterministic models is that we assume that all the parameters are known with certainty. This, of course, is unlikely to be true and the coefficients of the objective function will only be estimates. What would happen to the values of the decision variables if the profit or cost of an item changed? This question could be investigated by trying different values and observing the effect on the solution. However, a more systematic method of approaching the problem is to find the range of the objective function coefficients within which the solution remains the same. If this range is large, our solution is likely to be robust; that is, the solution will only change for large changes in the coefficients. This could be an important finding, particularly if our coefficients are only guesses or we know that they are likely to change from time to time.

■ Drive Thru Burger restaurant

Scenario 4.8

The feasible region in our original graph (Figure 4.2) contained three corner points (p, q and r). The optimum point is at point q, but what change in the profit per item will cause this to change to either p or r? To answer this question we need to do a little algebra.

If we hold the profit on the cheeseburger constant at 20p and let the profit on the beefburger be y, the objective function becomes $yb + 0.2c$. At point q the total profit will be $250y + 0.2 \times 500 = 250y + 100$.

At point p the total profit will be $500y$. When these profits are the same, there is nothing to choose between p or q, so:

$$250y + 100 = 500y$$

that is: $y = 0.4$

This means that once the profit on a beefburger exceeds 40p it will be worthwhile only selling this item. If we now look at point r the value of the objective function is $500 \times 0.2 = 100$

and $250y + 100 = 100$

that is: $y = 0$

This means that there is no lower limit on the profit of the beefburger. This makes sense as the profit associated with point q will always be greater than the profit associated with point r. The range of profit on a beefburger before the optimal solution changes is therefore 0p to 40p. This is quite a large range so the model is fairly robust for this parameter.

Inventory control models

Inventory control models are in many respects easier than LP models. This is because there are standard models for many situations and therefore the task of building the model is eliminated. In addition, inventory control models are easier to solve, since the equation normally contains one unknown or output variable. Provided the input variables are known, it is simply a matter of substituting these values into the formula and solving for the output variable.

The purpose of most inventory control models is to find the order policy that will minimise the cost of holding stock. It is very expensive to hold products or materials in stock for a number of reasons:

- money tied up or interest charges
- warehouse costs
- damage, deterioration or theft while in storage
- items becoming obsolete

The alternative to holding stock is that items or materials must be ordered more frequently, so incurring ordering and delivery costs. This policy may also prevent the company from taking advantage of discounts for large orders.

All inventory models should answer the following questions:

▓ How much to order?

▓ When to order?

Some models are what are called **periodic review models,** and these models assume that the stock level is reviewed at pre-specified intervals. After each review a quantity of stock is ordered to bring the stock up to some fixed level. There are also **continuous review models.** These models assume that the stock level is continuously monitored and a fixed quantity of stock ordered when the stock level reaches some pre-specified level.

The economic order quantity (EOQ) model

The EOQ model is the simplest of all the inventory control models. This model is applicable when the following assumptions hold:

▓ demand is known and constant

▓ lead (delivery) time is constant

▓ stock is monitored on a continuous basis

▓ when an order arrives, the stock level is replenished instantaneously

▓ stock-outs do not occur

In the EOQ model, an order arrives just as the stock level reaches zero. At this point, an order of quantity Q arrives. This is shown in Figure 4.5.

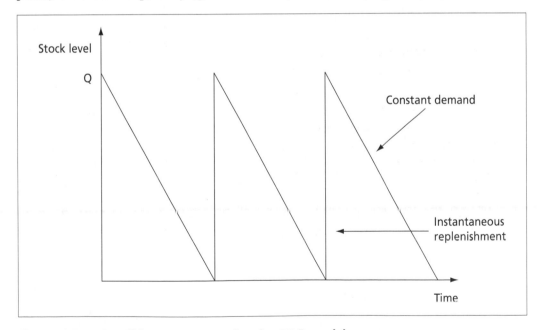

Figure 4.5 ▓ **Conditions necessary for the EOQ model**

The formula for the EOQ model is:

$$Q = \sqrt{\frac{2CD}{h}}$$

where C is the cost of placing an order, D is the demand during a specified period, and h is the cost of holding one unit in stock for the same period of time.

The cost of this policy is made up of two components: the cost of storage and the order cost.

Storage cost: $\dfrac{hQ}{2}$

Order cost: $\dfrac{CD}{Q}$

■ Drive Thru Burger restaurant
Scenario 4.9

The company purchases its food products through a local supplier. One such item is pre-packed sachets of sauce. The demand for this item is reasonably constant at 405 sachets a day. Once an order is placed, delivery takes two days. The cost of placing an order, which includes time spent on the phone and the necessary paperwork, is reckoned to be £5 per order. The cost of holding one sachet in stock for one day has been calculated by the company's accountant to be 0.5p.

From this information we can see that $C = 5$, $D = 405$ and $h = 0.005$. The value of Q is therefore:

$$Q = \sqrt{\frac{2 \times 5 \times 405}{0.005}} = 900$$

So on average an order needs to be placed every two days or so.

The cost of this policy is:

Storage cost: $\dfrac{0.005 \times 900}{2} = £2.25$

Order cost: $\dfrac{5 \times 405}{900} = £2.25$

Total cost = £4.50 per day

Notice that the storage and order cost are the same.

Economic batch quantity (EBQ) model

This model is applicable when the stock level is not replenished instantaneously but over a period of time. This frequently occurs in a batch process in a manufacturing company where items from one process are used in a subsequent process. Since it takes a finite time to make the required items, delivery is made on a gradual basis rather than altogether. The problem is one of deciding the size of each batch that should be made in the first process so that the second process is kept supplied of parts. Figure 4.6 illustrates this situation.

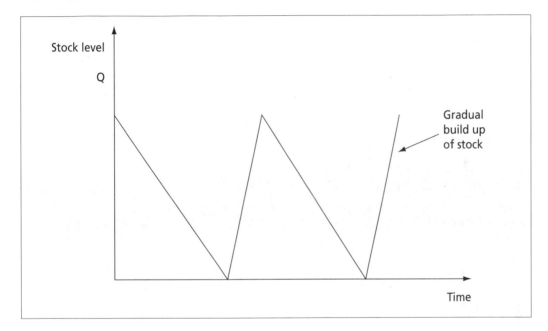

Figure 4.6 ■ The EBQ model

The formula for this model is slightly more complicated than the EOQ formula. It is:

$$Q = \sqrt{\frac{2CD}{h(1 - D/r)}}$$

where r is the rate of production of the first stage. The meaning of C and D are slightly different in this model as D is the *rate* of production of the second stage and C is the *set-up* cost associated with making a batch of items in the first stage. The inventory cost associated with this model is made up of the storage and set-up costs.

Storage cost: $\dfrac{hQ(1 - D/r)}{2}$

Set-up cost: $\dfrac{CD}{Q}$

■ Drive Thru Burger restaurant

The manufacture of the plastic boxes used to hold the food is a two-stage process. The first process involves making rectangular plastic sheets and the second process folds these sheets into boxes. The sheet process can produce sheets at a rate of 2000 an hour while 500 boxes can be produced in an hour by the second process. The set-up cost of the first process is £100 and the cost of holding one sheet in stock is 2p per day. The factory making these boxes works a 24-hour day.

The time period is an hour, and the value of h will therefore be:

$$\frac{0.02}{24}$$

Substituting these values into the formula gives:

$$Q = \sqrt{\left(\frac{2 \times 100 \times 500}{(0.02)/24\,(1 - 500/2000)}\right)} = 12{,}649$$

This tells us to produce sheets in batches of 12,649; enough to supply the main process for just over a day. The cost of this policy is:

Storage cost: $\dfrac{(0.02/24) \times 12{,}649 \times (1 - 500/2000)}{2} = £3.95$

Set-up cost: $\dfrac{100 \times 500}{12649} = £3.95$

Total cost: £7.90 per hour or about £189.60 per day

This model is not restricted to manufacturing problems and can be used in any inventory situation where an order arrives at a gradual rate.

The model for planned shortages

Both the EOQ and EBQ models assumed that stock-outs were not allowed. That is, shortage of stock did not occur. In cases where the cost of the goods are high, it might not be economically viable to maintain sufficient stock to avoid stock-outs. This is often the case with the sale of new cars. It is unlikely that a showroom will keep every model and colour of a particular make of car. In these cases it is assumed that customers are prepared to wait for an order to arrive from the manufacturer. This is known as a backorder. There is a cost associated with a backorder, which is usually some form of goodwill cost. The goodwill cost depends on how long a customer has to wait for delivery. It is a similar cost to the cost of holding a unit in stock for a particular time period, and is expressed in the same form.

When stock is unavailable, it is possible that the customer will go elsewhere and the sale will be lost. However, in the planned shortage model we assume that the customer is prepared to wait for delivery.

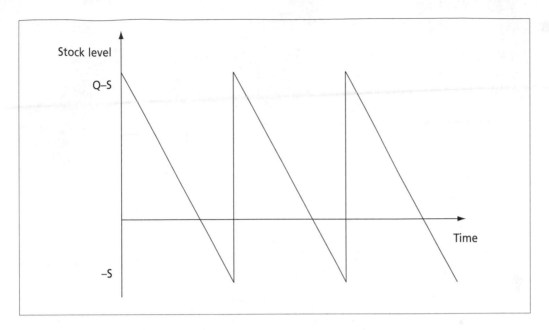

Figure 4.7 ■ Planned shortage model

The diagram for the planned shortage model is similar to the EOQ model except that the demand line now drops below the horizontal axis. A negative stock level in this case means that a number of orders have not been satisfied. As soon as stock arrives these orders are met immediately. As well as an order quantity Q, we now have a number of backorders S. This diagram can be seen in Figure 4.7.

The order quantity for this model is:

$$Q = \sqrt{\left(\frac{2DC}{h}\right)\left(\frac{h + b}{b}\right)}$$

where b is the backorder cost per item per time period. The planned backorders (S) is given by:

$$S = Q\left(\frac{h}{h + b}\right)$$

and the total cost associated with this policy is the sum of the storage cost, order cost and backorder cost.

Storage cost: $\dfrac{(Q - S)^2}{2Q} h$

Order cost: $\dfrac{D}{Q} C$

Backorder cost: $\dfrac{S^2}{2Q} b$

▪ Drive Thru Burger restaurant

The company purchases its kitchen equipment from Kitchen Equipment plc and this company has a policy of maintaining minimum stock levels. If the item required is not in stock, it will ship them to the customer as soon as the next batch has been manufactured.

The demand for its deep-fat fryer is 3000 per year and the cost of this item is £500. The set-up cost to make a batch of fryers is £200 and the company estimates that the backorder cost is around £60 per fryer per year. Holding costs are reckoned to be linked to the cost of capital, which for this company is currently 8 per cent.

Before we can substitute these values into the formulae we need to work out the value of h. Since we know the value of the fryer, we can assume that this cost will incur capital charges. Therefore $h = 0.08 \times 500 = £40$ p.a. The size of the batch should be

$$Q = \sqrt{\frac{2 \times 3000 \times 200}{40} \left(\frac{40 + 60}{60}\right)} = 223.6 \text{ (say 224)}$$

and the planned backorders are:

$$S = 224 \times \left(\frac{40}{40 + 60}\right) = 89.6 \text{ (say 90)}$$

This tells us that the company should make the fryers in batches of 224, which infers that on average they will need to have 13.4 batches a year, or about one every four weeks. They should also expect to have a maximum of 90 unfilled orders at any one time.

The cost of this policy will be:

$$\text{Storage cost: } \frac{(224 - 90)^2}{2 \times 224} \times 40 = £1603$$

$$\text{Order cost: } \frac{3000}{224} \times 200 = £2679$$

$$\text{Backorder cost: } \frac{90^2}{2 \times 224} \times 60 = £1085$$

The total cost is therefore £5367 p.a. If the EOQ model had been used, the order quantity would have been:

$$Q = \sqrt{\frac{2 \times 200 \times 3000}{40}} = 173.2 \text{ (say 173)}$$

The cost associated with the EOQ model would be:

Holding cost: $\dfrac{173}{2} \times 40 = £3460$

Order cost: $\dfrac{3000}{173} \times 200 = £3468$

Giving a total cost of £6928 p.a. The planned shortage model therefore represents a saving of $6928 - 5367 = £1561$. This is equivalent to a reduction in costs of over 20 per cent.

Stochastic models

Unlike deterministic models, stochastic models do not necessarily give the same output for the same input. Within a stochastic model there will be at least one variable that is not known with certainty. The value these variables can take can often be expressed by a probability distribution. A probability distribution is simply a way of defining the range of possible values that a variable can take. The simplest probability distribution is a uniform distribution. This distribution allows the variable to take on any value within a range, with equal probability. If the demand for a product varied from ten to 100 units a week we might decide to assume an average value of 55 units. This value could, for instance, be used in the EOQ inventory control model. Alternatively, we might assume that any value between ten and 100 is equally likely and wish to incorporate this information into our model. The reason for doing this is to reflect more closely what happens in reality. We might, for instance, find that for a few weeks we get a demand for our product near the top end of the range followed by a few weeks when the demand is considerably less. Over the long term, the demand may average out to 55 units, but the fact that demand could fluctuate might be important.

Even where the probability distribution is a simple one, there can be considerable mathematical difficulties in building an adequate model, as well as finding analytical methods of solving the model. Stochastic modelling is an important branch of mathematics and this chapter only touches the surface of this area. In later chapters we will be looking at alternative methods of building and solving models where there is a significant element of variability present. Although these methods may not be as elegant from a mathematical point of view, they have the advantage that they are simpler to understand and are applicable to a wide variety of situations.

However, there are some models of stochastic systems that are worth looking at. These models require many simplifying assumptions to be made about the system but they can be useful, at least as a preliminary investigation, before more suitable models are tried. We will restrict our look at stochastic models to two areas. These are inventory control models and queuing models.

Inventory models with probabilistic demand

Although there could be several sources of variability in inventory control systems, such as the delivery time and the various costs, the major source of variability will be demand. In the discussions so far we have ignored this variability by taking an average value. In practice, the demand could be highly variable and models are needed that take this variability into account. There are many inventory models that have been developed to handle this variability, but only two will be looked at in this chapter. These are the buffer stock model and the single period model.

Buffer stock model

This is an extension of the EOQ model. In the EOQ model, an order was placed when the stock reached a pre-determined level. This means that the variability of demand was not too important up to the point when this order was placed, since all that will happen is that an order may be placed sooner or later than expected. However, once this order has been placed any increase in demand will cause the stock level to fall faster than expected, resulting in a potential stock-out. To attempt to prevent this happening many companies hold a buffer or emergency stock. Figure 4.8 illustrates the idea of a buffer stock in diagrammatic form.

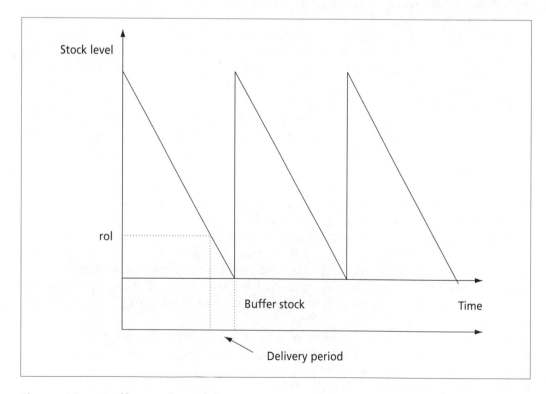

Figure 4.8 ■ Buffer stock model

The buffer stock can be used if demand increases during the delivery period. The question is, how large should this buffer stock be? If too small, a stock-out could still occur, while if too large the company is losing money by having capital tied up in stock unnecessarily. Another problem with a large buffer stock is that the goods might deteriorate. This is an important consideration in the food industry.

To be able to answer this question, it is necessary to have some knowledge of the underlying distribution of demand.

Demand follows the uniform distribution

This is the simplest case, where every value of demand is equally likely. This distribution is illustrated in Figure 4.9, where the demand during the delivery period varies between some minimum value a and a maximum value b. The average demand over the delivery period is μ and this is the average of a and b. A company faced with this distribution of demand may decide that it must always have enough stock to satisfy the highest level of demand. This policy would mean that a buffer stock of $b - \mu$ units should be maintained. Alternatively, it could decide that it would go for a little less and risk the occasional stock-out. It might, for instance, be prepared to be out of stock on 5 per cent of occasions. Since every level of demand is equally likely, the buffer stock is quite easy to calculate. If the area represented by the shaded area in Figure 4.9 is 5 per cent of the total area of the rectangle, the buffer level will be $c-\mu$.

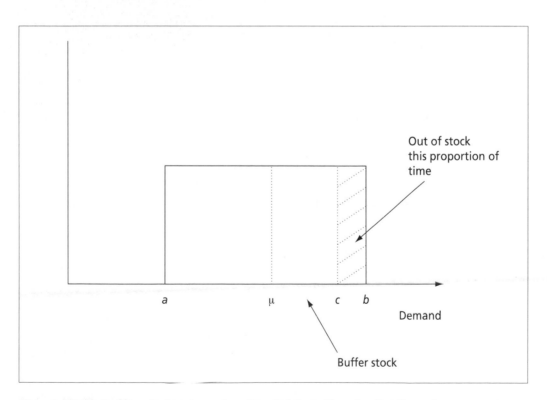

Figure 4.9 ■ Buffer stock when the demand is uniformly distributed

Once the buffer stock has been calculated, it is necessary to decide how to maintain it. On some occasions the demand over the delivery time might be below average, which would mean that the buffer stock might increase. To avoid this problem the buffer stock is taken into account in the calculation of the re-order level (rol). The re-order level is the demand that is likely to occur during the delivery period. The re-order level is shown in Figure 4.8. Scenario 4.12 should enable this idea to be better understood.

Demand follows the normal distribution

It is unlikely that the demand will follow the uniform distribution. It is more likely that the probability of a particular demand occurring will vary, with high probabilities around the mean and rapidly falling off at high and low demand levels. The normal distribution is a useful distribution from this aspect, as it has these attributes and the probabilities are easily obtained from tables.

The normal distribution was discussed in Chapter 3, but essentially it is a symmetrical distribution that requires two parameters: the mean and standard deviation. The standard normal distribution was shown in Figure 3.17, page 48.

The standard normal distribution has a mean of 0 and a standard deviation of 1 and it is in this form of the distribution that the normal tables apply (*see* Appendix 2). Any other normal distribution needs to be transformed into a standard normal distribution using the formula

$$Z = \frac{x - \mu}{\sigma}$$

where x is the value of the random variable (for example, demand), μ is the mean demand and σ is the standard deviation of demand.

▇ Drive Thru Burger restaurant   *Scenario 4.12*

The demand for sachets of sauce varies uniformly with the minimum being 110 a day and the maximum 700. The delivery time is two days. The cost of holding one sachet in stock for one day is 0.5p. What buffer stock of sachets should the company hold in order to only incur a stock-out on no more than 5 per cent of occasions, and what should the re-order level be?

The minimum demand over the two days will be 220 and the maximum demand will be 1400 sachets. If the distribution of demand is assumed uniform, the mean demand will be the average of these two values, which is 810 sachets. The top 5 per cent of the distribution represents $220 + 0.95 \times (1400 - 220) = 1341$ sachets. If the company want the chance of suffering a stock-out to be no more than 5 per cent they will need to re-order when the stock reaches this level and this will maintain a buffer stock of $1341 - 810 = 531$ sachets. The cost of maintaining this buffer stock is $531 \times 0.005 = £2.655$ per day.

Using this formula, it is possible to calculate the probability that the value of x will be in a particular range. Alternatively, if we know the area in one of the tails of the distribution, we can work out the corresponding value of x. For example, if the area in the upper tail was 0.05 or 5 per cent, the corresponding value of Z is 1.65. The formula can now be rearranged as follows.

$$x = 1.65 \times \sigma + \mu$$

Using this formula we can calculate the demand that will occur on no more than 5 per cent of occasions.

■ **Drive Thru Burger restaurant**   *Scenario 4.13*

Instead of the demand for sachets of sauce following a uniform distribution, let us suppose that this distribution is approximately normal. Let us also assume that the mean daily demand is 405 sachets with a standard deviation of 170 sachets. The demand over the two-day delivery period will be 810 sachets as before, but what is the standard deviation over this period? To find this we have to add the variances and square root the answer. That is:

$$\text{Standard deviation over the two days} = \sqrt{(170^2 + 170^2)}$$

$$= 240.4 \text{ sachets}$$

To find the level of demand (x) that is not exceeded on more than 5 per cent of the time, we substitute our values into the formula:

$$x = 1.65 \times \sigma + \mu$$
$$\text{to get: } x = 1.65 \times 240.4 + 810$$
$$= 1206.7 \text{ or about } 1207 \text{ sachets}$$

This will be the re-order level and the buffer level will be $1207 - 810 = 397$ sachets. This represents a cost of $397 \times 0.005 = £1.985$ per day.

Notice that the normal distribution has reduced the buffer level required from 531 to 397 sachets, with a corresponding reduction in cost.

Single period probabilistic model

There are situations where one order is placed for a product and after a certain period any surplus stock is either disposed of or sold at a reduced price. This applies to newspapers, perishable foodstuffs and fashion items. The problem faced by the retailer is that if he/she purchases too much, he/she will lose money on the goods not sold at the end of the period, or if he/she purchases too little, sales will be lost. Obviously, if the retailer knew the demand exactly there would be no problem, but in reality the demand is uncertain. As in the case of the buffer stock model, we can assume that the distribution of demand is known and use the ideas of probability to determine the best strategy for the retailer.

The approach to this problem is to use **incremental analysis** to compute the optimum order level given a particular probability distribution. It can be shown that in general the probability that the demand will be less than the order quantity Q is:

$$P(\text{demand} \leqslant Q) = \frac{C_u}{C_u + C_o}$$

where C_u is the cost of understating demand and C_o is the cost of overstating demand.

If we know the distribution of demand, we can use the probability calculated in the formula to find the value of Q.

Demand follows the uniform distribution

As in the buffer stock model, the simplest case is when all demand values within a range are equally likely. Referring back to Figure 4.9, we can see that the probability of demand being above the average (μ), is equal to the demand being below the average and this probability must equal 0.5. If the cost of overstating demand is equal to the cost of understating demand, then the best decision would be to order the average demand. However, once the values of C_u and C_o differ the optimum demand will move either towards a or b.

■ **Drive Thru Burger restaurant**   *Scenario 4.14*

The company purchases 2 oz burgers on a daily basis and reckons to make a profit of 40p on each burger sold. Any burgers left at the end of the day are sold to its staff at a loss of 10p per burger. The expected daily demand for its burgers is assumed to be uniformly distributed with a minimum of 600 and a maximum of 1400.

The probability that demand will be less than the order quantity Q is:

$$\frac{40}{40 + 10} = 0.8$$

To find the value of Q, we need to move 0.8 of the way from 600 to 1400. This is a range of 800 and so Q is:

$$600 + 0.8 \times 800 = 1240$$

So the company should order 1240 burgers daily.

Demand follows a normal distribution

As in the case of the buffer stock model, the normal distribution is likely to be a more realistic distribution. Again, as in the buffer stock model, we know the probability and we wish to determine the value of the random variable. In this case, however, the probability refers to the area from the *left-hand tail*. The diagram in Figure 4.10 illustrates this situation.

Since the tables in Appendix 2 apply to the area in the right-hand tail, we need to subtract this probability (P) from 1 and use a similar formula as before. That is:

$$Q = Z\sigma + \mu$$

where Z is the value obtained from tables corresponding to the probability $1 - P$

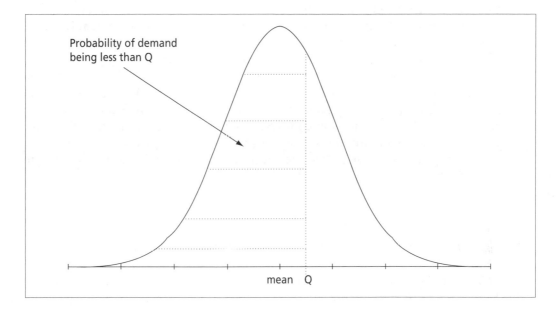

Figure 4.10 ■ **The single period probabilistic model when the normal distribution applies**

■ Drive Thru Burger restaurant

Scenario 4.15

Let us now assume that the daily demand for burgers follows a normal distribution with a mean of 1000 and a standard deviation of 133. The area in the right-hand tail of the normal distribution will be $1 - 0.8 = 0.2$. The Z value corresponding to this probability is about 0.85 so the value of Q will be

$$0.85 \times 133 + 1000 = 1113$$

So under this scenario, we need to order 1113 burgers each day. This is about 10 per cent less than when the demand followed a uniform distribution (Scenario 4.14).

Queuing models

Another class of stochastic models are the models associated with the queuing that result when the demands on a process exceed the current capacity of that process. The most common examples of this type of system are banks, supermarkets, airports and hospitals, but queuing can occur wherever a resource is limited in its capacity to provide a service. For example, queuing occurs in the form of a hospital waiting list since there are a limited number of consultants and beds available.

Queues will form from time to time even when there is apparently sufficient capacity to handle the expected number of arrivals. For example, the rate of customers to a bank cash dispenser may be 30 an hour, while it takes one minute to complete the transaction. If the system was deterministic it would certainly be the case that queues would not form. However, in most queuing systems there is variability in either or both the arrival and service processes and this could mean that a large number of arrivals would occur during one particular period. For example, in the case of the bank, five customers might turn up together.

Queuing systems involve a number of distinct components. The first is the arrivals (*entities*) to the system, the second is queuing that may have to take place, and the third is the process or service concerned. This sequence of components may be repeated several times for complex queuing systems. For example, after service, the entities may join another process as in the case of a doctor's surgery, where a patient joins a queue to see the receptionist before joining another queue to see the doctor.

The structure of queuing systems

Although there are numerous examples of queuing systems, it is fortunately possible to categorise them into one of four main types. The first type is the **single-channel, single-phase** system where an entity arrives, joins a single queue, is served, and finally departs. Supermarket checkouts are usually of this type. The second type is the **multi-channel, single-phase** system, where an entity joins a single queue and is served by the first available server. Many post offices are of this type. Another type is the **single-channel, multi-phase** system, where an entity joins another queue following service from the first. Some petrol stations are of this type, since the driver will queue for a pump and then queue at the payment booth. Finally, there is the **multi-channel, multi-phase system**, such as many production systems. These four types are illustrated in Figures 4.11 to 4.14.

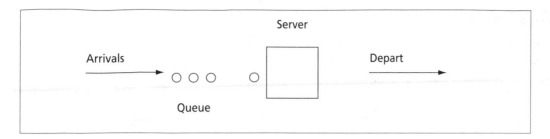

Figure 4.11 ▨ **Single-channel, single-phase system**

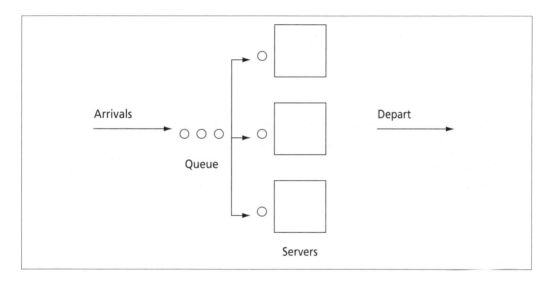

Figure 4.12 ▨ **Multi-channel, single-phase system**

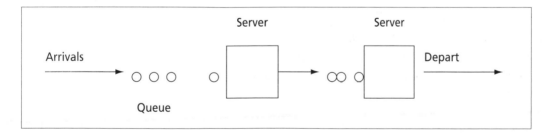

Figure 4.13 ▨ **Single-channel, multi-phase system**

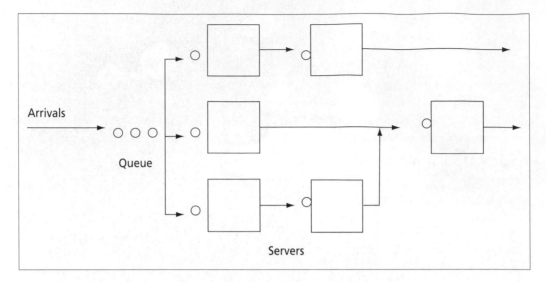

Figure 4.14 ▨ Multi-channel, multi-phase system

In addition to categorising a queuing system, we need to define the mechanism of the:

▨ arrival process
▨ queuing process
▨ service process

For the arrival process we need to know the:

▨ rate of arrivals
▨ distribution of arrivals
▨ size of the population from where the arrivals originated

For the queuing process we need to know:

▨ the queuing discipline (for example, first-in, first-out)
▨ whether *balking* (leaving before being served) from the queue occurs
▨ whether there is any limit on queue length

For the service process we need to know the:

▨ rate of service
▨ distribution of service time
▨ number of servers

Models of queuing systems tend to involve many simplifying assumptions. In particular, the form of the arrival and service distributions are quite restrictive. All models make certain assumptions regarding the queuing mechanism, all assume a first-in, first-out (FIFO) process and all assume that balking does not happen or has a negligible effect. Most models assume that the population from where the entities originate is infinite. This will be approximately true in most systems, but not in the case where machines break down and are repaired by a mechanic. In this situation the machines, of which there will be a finite number, are the entities and the mechanic is the server.

Another restriction with queuing models is that they only apply to the *steady state*. All systems enter a transient phase at the beginning of their operation cycle. For example, when a supermarket opens there will be no one in the checkout queue, but eventually queues start to form. Although the number in the queue will vary, the number will not vary quite as much as at the start, so we say that the system has settled down or reached a steady state. Some systems never reach this state, either because the arrival rate exceeds the service rate or because these parameters are constantly changing.

The derivation of queuing models require a thorough understanding of probability and of advanced calculus, so only the results of the models will be discussed here. These results mainly take the form of average values of the performance measures of a queuing system, such as the average number in the queue and average time waiting to be served. Even taking this limited look at the models requires extensive calculation and a spreadsheet will be used for many of the calculations.

The notation generally adopted for queuing models is that by D. G. Kendal. He used a three-symbol notation usually written as A/B/k, where A represents the probability distribution of the number of arrivals, B represents the probability distribution of the service time and k represents the number of channels. The probability distributions that are commonly used are:

■ M for a Poisson arrival distribution or exponential service time

■ D for constant arrivals or a constant service time

■ G for a general distribution with known mean and variance

The simplest case is where the arrival distribution is Poisson, the distribution for the service time is exponential, and there is one channel or server. The notation for this is therefore M/M/1.

M/M/1 model

A Poisson distribution is a discrete probability distribution and is applicable when entities arrive at random. That is, the arriving entities are independent of each other. This distribution is relevant to a wide range of queuing systems. If the number of arrivals follows a Poisson distribution, it can be shown that the *time between arrivals* is exponential. The service time in the M/M/1 model is also exponential, so using the same argument, the number of services in a given time also follows the Poisson distribution.

In addition to the assumptions regarding the arrival and service distributions, this model assumes that:

■ the population from where the arrivals originate is infinite

■ there is no limit on queue length

■ there is no balking from the queue

■ the queuing mechanism is FIFO

These are very restrictive assumptions, but this model can be useful for simple queuing systems or as a preliminary analysis before more appropriate models are used.

From this model, we are able to derive the following equations:

Probability that there are no units in the system: $P_0 = 1 - \dfrac{\lambda}{\mu}$

Probability that there are 'n' units in the system: $P_n = \left(\dfrac{\lambda}{\mu}\right)^n P_0$

Probability that an arrival has to wait for service: $P_w = \dfrac{\lambda}{\mu}$

Average number in the queue: $L_q = \dfrac{\lambda^2}{\mu(\mu - \lambda)}$

Average number in the system: $L = L_q + \dfrac{\lambda}{\mu}$

Average time in the queue: $W_q = \dfrac{L_q}{\lambda}$

Average time in the system: $W = W_q + \dfrac{1}{\mu}$

Where λ = mean arrival rate, μ = mean service rate and $\lambda < \mu$

To use the M/M/1 model we need the values of λ and μ. We must remember though that both these parameters are *rates*. So if we are told that the average service time was twelve minutes, we would have to convert the twelve minutes into a rate; that is, five an hour.

The probability that an arrival has to wait for service (P_w) will vary between zero and one. A value of zero indicates that the server is always free, while a value of one indicates that the server is always busy. For this reason P_w is sometimes called the *utilisation* of the server and is a very important measure of a queuing system. To illustrate this, the value of P_w and the average time in the queue (W_q) for a value of μ of twelve and values of λ from one to eleven have been calculated and shown in Table 4.4 opposite.

Notice that as the value of P_w exceeds about 0.8, or 80 per cent, the queuing time starts to increase considerably. This can be better illustrated using a graph and this has been drawn in Figure 4.15 (see page 113).

The message here is simple: to prevent excessive queuing, a server should not have an utilisation factor of more than 80 per cent.

Table 4.4 ■ Calculation of the average time in the queue for different values of λ

Average arrival rate (λ) per hour	Utilisation of server (P_W)	Average time in the queue (minutes)
1	0.0833	0.5
2	0.1667	1.0
3	0.25	1.7
4	0.3333	2.5
5	0.4167	3.6
6	0.5	5.0
7	0.5833	7.0
8	0.6667	10.0
9	0.75	15.0
10	0.8333	25.0
11	0.9167	55.0

■ Whiteladies Health Centre
Scenario 4.16

On average, 43.8 patients arrive each hour and are first seen by the receptionist, who takes an average of twenty seconds to see each patient. If we assume that the M/M/1 model is valid, we can calculate average measures of performance of this system.

We first need to calculate the service rate, μ. This is

$$\frac{60 \times 60}{20} = 180$$

an hour. The average number in the queue (L_q) is:

$$\frac{43.8^2}{180 \times (180 - 43.8)} = 0.078$$

The average time a patient spends waiting in the queue (W_q) is:

$$\frac{0.078}{43.8} \times 60 \times 60 = 6.4 \text{ seconds}$$

These are very small values and accurately reflect the situation at the surgery.

M/M/k model

The next stage up in complexity is to have a multi-channel queuing model, with k channels. The formulae for this model are:

Probability that there are no units in the system

$$P_0 = \frac{1}{\sum_{n=0}^{k-1}\left[\left(\frac{(\lambda/\mu)^n}{n!}\right) + \left(\frac{(\lambda/\mu)^k}{k!}\right)\right]\left(\frac{k\mu}{k\mu - \lambda}\right)}$$

Probability that there are 'n' units in the system:

$$P_n = \frac{(\lambda/\mu)^n}{n!} P_0 \quad \text{for } n \leqslant k$$

$$P_n = \frac{(\lambda/\mu)^n}{k!\, k^{(n-k)}} P_0 \quad \text{for } n > k$$

Probability that an arrival has to wait for service:

$$P_w = \frac{1}{k!}\left(\frac{\lambda}{\mu}\right)^k \left(\frac{k\mu}{k\mu - \lambda}\right) P_0$$

Average number in the queue:

$$L_q = \frac{(\lambda/\mu)^k \lambda\mu}{(k-1)!\,(k\mu - \lambda)^2} P_0$$

Average number in the system:

$$L = L_q + \frac{\lambda}{\mu}$$

Average time in the queue:

$$W_q = \frac{L_q}{\lambda}$$

Average time in the system

$$W = W_q + \frac{1}{\mu}$$

These formulae are far more complicated to use than for the M/M/1 model and it is easier if a spreadsheet or tables are used.

■ **Whiteladies Health Centre** *Scenario 4.17*

There are six doctors at the surgery on a Monday and each doctor takes an average of 6.54 minutes to treat each patient. This gives an average service rate of 9.17 treatments an hour. If we assume that the M/M/6 model is valid for this system then the equations shown above can be used to find the average output measures of the surgery, such as the average time spent in the surgery.

Microsoft Excel has been used to do the calculations and the output can be seen in Table 4.5 (see page 112). (As with all the spreadsheet examples, this one can be found on the disk that accompanies this text; *see* Appendix 4 for details.) The output measures for different values of the interarrival time have been calculated to enable a graph of waiting time in the surgery to be plotted against interarrival time. This graph is shown in Figure 4.16 (see page 113).

The time in the surgery for an interarrival time of 1.37 minutes is 9.25 minutes. This is an underestimate of the time that occurs in practice, but at least it is the right order of magnitude. We shall see in subsequent chapters that while the number of arrivals closely follows a Poisson distribution, the service time does not follow an exponential distribution. We have also ignored many other factors, such as the presence of the receptionist in the system.

The graph in Figure 4.16 could be quite useful to the management of the surgery since it will tell them at what point another doctor will be required. We can see that as soon as the interarrival time reaches about 1.15 minutes the queuing time rises dramatically. An interarrival time of 1.15 minutes is equivalent to 52 patients an hour, a 19 per cent rise on the current numbers.

M/G/1 model

Very few service distributions will be exponential, and in some cases it is better to use the *general* distribution which can be represented by the mean and standard deviation. The formulae for this model are a little more complex than the M/M/1 model, but considerably simpler than the M/M/k model. The formulae are:

Probability that there are no units in the system:

$$P_0 = 1 - \frac{\lambda}{\mu}$$

Average number in the queue:

$$L_q = \frac{\lambda^2 \sigma^2 + (\lambda/\mu)^2}{2(1 - \lambda/\mu)}$$

Average number in the system:

$$L = L_q + \frac{\lambda}{\mu}$$

Table 4.5 ■ Excel spreadsheet showing the calculations required for the M/M/6 model

Whiteladies Health Centre

M/M/K MODEL K = 6

Av. service time = 6.54   mu = 9.1743

IAT	lambda	lambda/mu	1	2	3	4	5	sum	P_0	Lq	Wq	W
1.37	43.7956	4.7737	4.7737	11.3942	18.1309	21.6380	20.6588	77.5957	0.006328	1.98	2.71	9.25
1.35	44.4444	4.8444	4.8444	11.7343	18.9488	22.9490	22.2351	81.7116	0.005717	2.23	3.02	9.56
1.33	45.1128	4.9173	4.9173	12.0899	19.8165	24.3609	23.9579	86.1425	0.005129	2.53	3.37	9.91
1.31	45.8015	4.9924	4.9924	12.4619	20.7381	25.8830	25.8435	90.9188	0.004567	2.90	3.80	10.34
1.29	46.5116	5.0698	5.0698	12.8513	21.7177	27.5259	27.9099	96.0745	0.004029	3.34	4.31	10.85
1.27	47.2441	5.1496	5.1496	13.2592	22.7599	29.3012	30.1779	101.6478	0.003516	3.89	4.94	11.48
1.25	48.0000	5.2320	5.2320	13.6869	23.8700	31.2219	32.6706	107.6814	0.003028	4.59	5.74	12.28
1.23	48.7805	5.3171	5.3171	14.1356	25.0534	33.3027	35.4146	114.2234	0.002564	5.51	6.77	13.31
1.21	49.5868	5.4050	5.4050	14.6068	26.3164	35.5597	38.4398	121.3276	0.002125	6.74	8.16	14.70
1.19	50.4202	5.4958	5.4958	15.1019	27.6657	38.0112	41.7804	129.0550	0.001711	8.49	10.11	16.65
1.17	51.2821	5.5897	5.5897	15.6226	29.1088	40.6777	45.4756	137.4744	0.001321	11.15	13.05	19.59
1.15	52.1739	5.6870	5.6870	16.1707	30.6541	43.5821	49.5699	146.6638	0.000955	15.62	17.97	24.51
1.13	53.0973	5.7876	5.7876	16.7482	32.3107	46.7505	54.1147	156.7117	0.000613	24.63	27.83	34.37
1.12	53.5714	5.8393	5.8393	17.0486	33.1839	48.4426	56.5741	162.0885	0.000451	33.68	37.72	44.26
1.11	54.0541	5.8919	5.8919	17.3572	34.0889	50.2120	59.1688	167.7188	0.000295	51.81	57.50	64.04

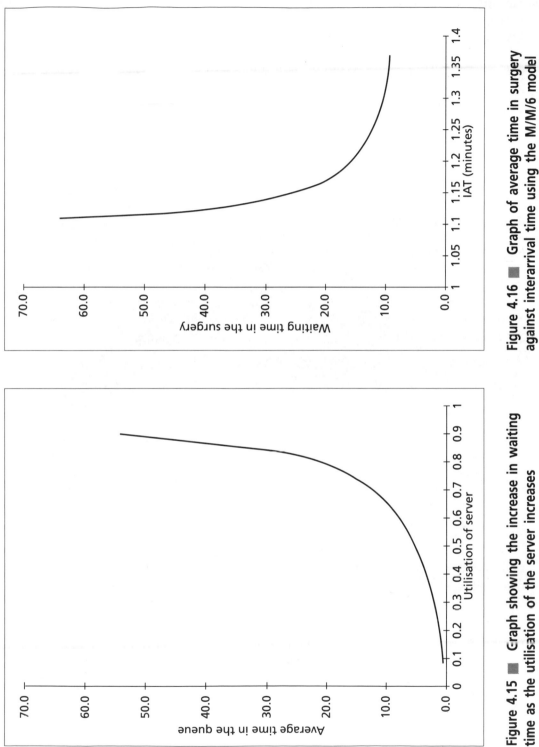

Figure 4.15 ▪ Graph showing the increase in waiting time as the utilisation of the server increases

Figure 4.16 ▪ Graph of average time in surgery against interarrival time using the M/M/6 model

Average time in the queue:

$$W_q = \frac{L_q}{\lambda}$$

Average time in the system:

$$W = W_q + \frac{1}{\mu}$$

where μ is the mean rate and σ is the standard deviation of the service time. It is important to ensure that μ and σ are in the same units; that is, if σ is in minutes then μ should be in services per minute.

■ Whiteladies Health Centre   *Scenario 4.18*

We are now going to re-solve the problem in Scenario 4.16 by using the M/G/1 model. The mean service time is twenty seconds, and the standard deviation is 10.4 seconds.

The service rate is still 180 an hour, or 0.05 per second, while the arrival rate is 43.8 an hour, or 0.01217 per second. The average number of patients in the reception queue is:

$$L_q = \frac{0.01217^2 \times 10.4^2 + (0.01217/0.05)^2}{2(1 - 0.01217/0.05)}$$

$$= \frac{0.07526}{1.5132}$$

$$= 0.050$$

The average time a patient spends waiting in the queue is:

$$W_q = \frac{0.050}{0.01217} \text{ seconds} = 4.1 \text{ seconds}$$

These figures are slightly less than in Scenario 4.16, reflecting the fact that the variability in the service time has been reduced.

M/D/1 model

In some situations, the service time is constant; that is, the system is partly deterministic. This can occur in some manufacturing processes where a machine is set at a fixed rate. The M/G/1 model can be adapted to allow for this deterministic behaviour by setting the standard deviation to zero. The formula for the average number in the queue then becomes:

$$L_q = \frac{(\lambda/\mu)^2}{2(1 - \lambda/\mu)}$$

■ **Whiteladies Health Centre**   *Scenario 4.19*

If the service time is fixed at twenty seconds, the time in the queue and the waiting time become:

$$L_q = \frac{(0.01217/0.05)^2}{2(1 - 0.01217/0.05)} = 0.03915$$

$$W_q = \frac{0.03915}{0.01217} = 3.2 \text{ seconds}$$

These figures are even smaller than with the M/G/1 model, which is sensible, since all variability has now been removed from the service process.

The other formulae remain the same.

M/M/1 model with a finite population

All the models that we have looked at so far have assumed that the population from where the arrivals originate is infinite. This is approximately true for most systems, simply because we do not know the size of the population. However, there are some systems where the arrivals come from a known finite population. The obvious example of this type of system is where machines break down and have to be repaired by one or more mechanics. The machines are the entities, and when they break down they form a 'queue' that is treated on a FIFO basis. The reason why the existing models cannot handle this type of system is that the probability of an arrival will depend on the number of units already in the queue for service. If we have, say, a population of ten machines, the probability of an arrival will be higher when there are no machines in the system than when five of these machines are waiting to be serviced. This is different to the other models, where the probability of an arrival (and hence the arrival rate) is the same no matter how many are currently in the system.

The formulae for the case where there is one channel (that is, one server or mechanic) are:

Probability that there are no units in the system:

$$P_0 = \frac{1}{\sum_{n=0}^{N}\left(\frac{N!}{(N-n)!}\right)\left(\frac{\lambda}{\mu}\right)^n}$$

Average number in the queue:

$$L_q = N - \frac{\lambda + \mu}{\lambda}(1 - P_0)$$

Average number in the system:

$$L = L_q + (1 - P_0)$$

Average time in the queue:

$$W_q = \frac{L_q}{(N - L)\lambda}$$

Average time in the system:

$$W = W_q + \frac{1}{\mu}$$

where N is the size of the population.

The value of P_0 can be tedious to calculate when N is greater than about three, and a spreadsheet or tables are recommended in these cases.

■ Drive Thru Burger restaurant   *Scenario 4.20*

The restaurant has three ovens that occasionally break down, which are then repaired by the resident engineer. The average time between breakdowns of an individual oven is 30 hours, and the repair time is exponentially distributed with a mean of 2.5 hours.

From this information we can deduce that $\lambda = 1/30 = 0.0333$ ovens per hour. The service rate is $\frac{1}{2.5} = 0.4$ ovens per hour. The value of P_0 is found from the following calculation:

$$P_0 = \frac{1}{\displaystyle\sum_{n=0}^{3} \frac{3!}{(3-n)!} \left(\frac{0.0333}{0.4} \right)^n}$$

This expression can be evaluated by noting that $3! = 6$, and $0.0333/0.4 = 0.08325$.

Substituting these values into the denominator, gives:

$$6 \times \left[\frac{(0.08325)^0}{(3-0)!} + \frac{(0.08325)^1}{(3-1)!} + \frac{(0.08325)^2}{(3-2)!} + \frac{(0.08325)^3}{(3-3)!} \right] = 1.29486$$

so, $P_0 = \dfrac{1}{1.29486} = 0.7723$

The average number of ovens that are waiting to be repaired is:

$$L_q = 3 - \frac{0.0333 + 0.4}{0.0333} (1 - 0.7723) = 0.037$$

The average number of ovens out of use is:

$L = 0.037 + (1 - 0.7723) = 0.265$

The average time an oven has to wait before the repair starts is:

$$W_q = \frac{0.037}{(3 - 0.265) \times 0.0333}$$

$= 0.41$ hours or about 24 minutes

The average time an oven is out of use is therefore:

$W = 0.41 + 2.5$

$= 2.91$ hours

Summary

This chapter has demonstrated some models that can be solved by analytical means. The models illustrated are a tiny proportion of those that are available but the purpose of the chapter was to illustrate some of the techniques and problems associated with model building, rather than provide a *Which? Guide to Models*. One of the main problems is that all models require assumptions to be made about the real system. We can improve our model by making less assumptions but this usually makes the model more complex and more difficult to solve.

The simplest models are generally deterministic in nature, since these do not contain any probabilistic elements. However, in some situations these can be quite powerful as in the case of linear programming. The use of sensitivity analysis in deterministic modelling can go some way towards mitigating against the simplistic assumptions necessary in this form of modelling.

Stochastic models are more realistic than deterministic models, although some of the simple queuing models can involve many assumptions. All stochastic models involve probabilistic considerations and this requires some knowledge of probability before these models can be built. Fortunately many stochastic models can be taken 'off the shelf', which minimises the knowledge required.

■ Exercises

4.1 A small company assembles two types of cooker – the Ambassador and the Baron. Each Ambassador that is produced earns £40 contribution, while each Baron earns £50. The company's management need to decide the number of cookers of each type that should be assembled next week in order to maximise contribution.

An Ambassador cooker takes four hours to assemble and a Baron takes six hours. Both cookers need to be assembled by a skilled worker, but currently the company only employs two of these workers, both of whom work a 48-hour week.

The Ambassador cooker has two built-in clocks, while the Baron has only one. As a result of a strike at the suppliers, only twenty of these clocks can be obtained next week.

For marketing reasons, the company has decided that at least six Baron cookers should be produced per week.

a How many cookers of each type should be produced?

b Which are the tight constraints?

c Find the shadow prices of the tight constraints.

d What additional quantity of clocks would it be worth purchasing and what would be the new profit?

4.2 Each Monday, 120 patients on average attend the morning surgery at the Whiteladies Health Centre. During the surgery period, a doctor can see 25 patients, while a nurse can see 30 patients. A nurse is able to treat up to 40 per cent of the patients, but there must be at least three doctors to every nurse. If a doctor is paid £50 for attending the surgery and a nurse is paid £10, how many doctors and nurses would be required to treat all the patients, and at what cost?

4.3 The Bristol Wine Company has developed a range of genetically engineered grape that will grow well in the British climate. They have an accurate forecast of the year's harvest, shown below, and wish to plan production of Vin Speciale and Vin Ordinaire.

Grape	Harvest (kilograms)
Avon Black	120,000
Somerset Pink	37,500
Wiltshire White	80,000

A batch of Vin Speciale requires 30 kilograms of Avon Black, 15 kilograms of Somerset Pink, and 40 kilograms of Wiltshire White. The requirements for a batch of Vin Ordinaire are 60 kilograms of Avon Black, 15 kilograms of Somerset Pink and 20 kilograms of Wiltshire White. The Bristol Wine Company would like to produce at least 800 batches of Vin Speciale. They only have the capacity to produce 2000 batches of Vin Ordinaire. The profit per batch is £60 for Vin Speciale and £40 for Vin Ordinaire. The company wishes to maximise profit.

a How many batches of each type of wine should be produced so as to maximise profits?

b What are the tight constraints in this problem? If it was possible to grow more Wiltshire White grapes, what additional quantity would be worthwhile (if any) and what would the new total profit become?

4.4 This question refers to Scenario 4.7 and uses the spreadsheet file SCEN4_7.XLS to determine the maximum quantity of burgers that the Drive Thru Burger restaurant should purchase. What additional profit would result from this increase in the burger constraint?

4.5 Using SCEN4_7.XLS again, find the range within which the profit on a burger could change without changing the optimal solution.

4.6 An additional product is to be produced, called the baconburger. This product uses one bun, one 2 oz burger, one slice of cheese and one slice of bacon. The profit on this item is 30p, and there are 200 slices of bacon available each day. Extend the linear programming model developed in Scenario 4.7, and solve it by amending the file SCEN4_7.XLS.

4.7 The demand for chips at the Drive Thru Burger restaurant is reasonably constant at 100 bags per week, and every time an order is placed a fixed charge of £20 is incurred. The cost of holding a bag in store for one week is thought to be in the region of 5p.

a Calculate the economic order quantity. What would be the weekly cost of this policy (ignore the purchase cost) and what would be the average time between orders?

b If the standard deviation of weekly demand is 20.4 bags and the lead (delivery) time is two weeks, calculate the level of buffer stock that would prevent the company from running out of stock on no more than 5 per cent of occasions. What is the additional cost of having this buffer stock?

4.8 A company produces a product in a two-stage process. The first stage produces the part-finished article, and operates at a speed of 2000 per hour. The cost of setting up this first stage is £300 and items held in the work-in-progress area incur a holding charge of 2.6p per hour. If an output of 1200 completed items per hour is required, calculate the batch size of items produced in the first stage. What is the cost of this policy?

4.9 A car dealer stocks a particular make, but for economic reasons it only stocks a limited number of cars in the showroom. When a customer buys a car, an order is faxed to the manufacturer and a car is dispatched to the showroom with the next order. The demand for a particular model is 50 a year and the cost of holding a car in stock for one year is £1000. If the cost of ordering (which includes delivery) is £250, and the backorder cost is £300, calculate the quantity to order that will minimise the total inventory cost. What is this cost and what is the number of planned backorders? What would the cost have been if the EOQ policy had been adopted?

4.10 Arrivals to a rail ticket office is Poisson with a mean of 47 an hour. The service time by the single clerk is exponential with a mean of 45 seconds. Assuming that the M/M/1 model applies, calculate the average number of passengers waiting to be served and the average time in the queue.

4.11 Amend the spreadsheet SCEN4_16.XLS that can be found on the disk that accompanies this text, to find the waiting time in the queue when there are five channels.

4.12 The number of patients at the Whiteladies Health Centre has increased to 136 per surgery and another doctor has been employed to handle the additional workload. Amend the spreadsheet SCEN4_16.XLS to obtain the average time a patient spends in the surgery.

4.13 The arrival of lorries is random with a mean of one every twenty minutes. The time taken to unload a lorry is fifteen minutes on average, with a standard deviation of 3.6 minutes. What is the average number of lorries in the queue and the time lorries spend in the system?

4.14 Repeat Question 4.13, for the case where the unloading time is a constant fifteen minutes.

4.15 An amusement arcade has ten simulators that frequently break down and are repaired by the resident engineer. If the time between breakdowns is random, with a mean of twenty hours, and the repair time is exponential with a mean of four hours, calculate the average number of machines that are out of action at any one time. The spreadsheet CHAP4Q15.XLS can be used to help in this calculation.

Further reading

Anderson, D., Sweeney D. and Williams, T. (1994) *An Introduction to Management Science* (Chapters 2, 11 and 12), West Publishing Company, Minneapolis, USA.

Bridge, J. (1989) *Managerial Decisions with the Microcomputer* (Chapter 7), Philip Allan, Great Britain.

Dennis, T. L. and Dennis, L. B. (1993) *Microcomputer Models for Management Decision Making*, Third Edition, West Publishing Company, Minneapolis, USA.

Morris, C. (1996) *Quantitative Approaches in Business Studies*, Fourth Edition (Part 4), Pitman Publishing, London.

Oakshott, L. A. (1994) *Essential Elements of Quantitative Methods* (Chapter 4), DP Publications, London.

Taha, A. T. (1982) *Operations Research*, Third Edition (Chapters 2, 4, 13 and 15), Macmillan Publishers, New York.

5

Simulation modelling

Les Oakshott

Introduction

Simulation is often called a technique of last resort. This modelling approach is used when the system to be modelled is too complex for analytical models to give adequate results. Simulation will be discussed in detail in subsequent chapters, but the intention in this chapter is to give an overview of the technique. This will provide a basic knowledge of the subject for those readers who do not need to take the subject further. However, it should also help to set the scene for those readers who will be studying the subject in depth.

Types of simulation

Before we can distinguish between the different types of simulation, we need some general definition of simulation. Schriber (1987) defines simulation as 'the modelling of a process or system in such a way that the model mimics the response of the actual system to events that take place over time'. The crucial part of this definition is the word 'time', as simulation is generally used for systems that are dynamic in nature (*see* Chapter 2 for the difference between static and dynamic systems). However, we shall meet the use of simulation where time does not play a substantive part, so this definition is not quite accurate as far as this text is concerned. Pegden *et al.* (1995) define simulation as 'the process of designing a model of a real system and conducting experiments with this model for the purpose of understanding the behaviour of the system and/or evaluating various strategies for the operation of the system'. This is a more general definition and better suited to the use of simulation in business-type applications. Although we normally associate simulation as a technique for modelling queuing-type systems, simulation can be used whenever all or part of the system is stochastic in nature. Inventory control, investment appraisal and forecasting problems are all areas where there is some uncertainty present in the system, which can be modelled by sampling from appropriate probability distributions. For these types of problems, a spreadsheet is the most appropriate method for building and running the simulation. The term **Monte-Carlo simulation** is often used for this type of simulation, although strictly the Monte-Carlo technique is for deterministic-type systems. We also talk about **continuous simulation** where the system is varying smoothly over time and we want to model this continuous behaviour. We shall now look at these three types of simulation.

Discrete-event simulation

If the system to be modelled can be represented by a series of discrete events, the method known as discrete-event simulation can be used. An event is where the state of the system changes instantaneously, so an event could be an arrival to the system, the start of a service, or the breakdown of a machine. This method assumes that nothing of interest occurs between these events so the simulation progresses from event to event. Systems that can be modelled using the discrete-event approach are generally systems where queuing mechanisms operate. We have looked at analytical queuing models in Chapter 4, but the systems discussed there were simple systems, where very restrictive assumptions applied. In practice, queuing systems can be quite complex and can contain a number of sub-systems. However, the general principles are the same, no matter how complex the system. The difficulty is more to do with keeping track of all the different events and updating the statistics that a simulation will generate. For this reason, simulation is always carried out by computer, but to demonstrate the general principles, a manual method is usually employed.

Imagine a bank with one cashier. Customers arrive at a rate of two per minute and, if the cashier is busy, wait to be served. Service takes an average of 25 seconds, after which the customer will leave the system. If customers arrived at regular intervals of time and the service time was the same for all customers, a queue would never form and we would have a deterministic system. Unfortunately, customers do not arrive at regular intervals and normally there is some variation around the average service time. In order to model the variability that occurs in real life, we need to sample from an interarrival time distribution and a service time distribution. We will look at sampling from distributions in detail in Chapter 7, but for now we shall demonstrate the process using an empirical probability distribution. These distributions would have been derived from measurements taken of the system. So we might have got the following relative frequency tables:

Table 5.1 ▓ Relative frequency table for the arrivals to a bank

Interarrival time (seconds)	Mid point	Frequency	Relative frequency (%)
0 to under 30	15	66	55
30 to under 60	45	36	30
60 to under 90	75	12	10
90 to under 120	105	6	5

Table 5.2 ■ Relative frequency table for the service time at a bank

Service time (seconds)	Mid point	Frequency	Relative frequency (%)
20 to under 30	25	17	17
30 to under 40	35	28	28
40 to under 50	45	25	25
50 to under 60	55	20	20
60 to under 90	75	10	10

The tables would have been derived from observing times between customers for the interarrival time distribution (Table 5.1) and individual service times for the service time distribution (Table 5.2). These times would have been accumulated into suitable intervals as shown in the tables.

In order to generate arrival and service times, we employ **random numbers**. Random numbers are numbers that are uniformly distributed between any two limits a and b. Computers normally generate random numbers between zero and one, but for our purpose we will use the limits zero to 100, as these correspond to our relative frequency columns in the above tables. Each random number must be allocated to one and only one interval in each table, and we must ensure that in the long term, the correct proportions of times in each interval are sampled. So, in Table 5.1, we want 55 per cent of our random numbers to represent the interval zero to under 30 seconds and 30 per cent to represent the interval 30 to under 60 seconds. The easiest method is simply to let the random numbers 00 to 54 (or 01 to 55) represent the first interval and the random numbers 55 to 84 (or 56 to 85) represent the second interval, and so on. It is helpful if the cumulative frequency values are calculated, as can be seen in Tables 5.3 and 5.4.

We now have a mapping of random numbers to both the interarrival time and service time distributions. Given a random number, a computer would give a precise value by interpolating between the interval limits, but for a manual simulation it is easier to use the mid point value. So a random number of fourteen

Table 5.3 ■ Allocation of random numbers to the arrival distribution

Interarrival time (seconds)	Mid point	Frequency	Relative frequency (%)	Cumulative frequency (%)	Random numbers
0 to under 30	15	66	55	55	00 – 54
30 to under 60	45	36	30	85	55 – 84
60 to under 90	75	12	10	95	85 – 94
90 to under 120	105	6	5	100	95 – 99

Table 5.4 ■ **Allocation of random numbers to the service time distribution**

Service time (seconds)	Mid point	Frequency	Relative frequency (%)	Cumulative frequency (%)	Random numbers
20 to under 30	25	17	17	17	00 – 16
30 to under 40	35	28	28	45	17 – 44
40 to under 50	45	25	25	70	45 – 69
50 to under 60	55	20	20	90	70 – 89
60 to under 90	75	10	10	100	90 – 99

would give an interarrival time of fifteen seconds and a service time of 25 seconds. A computer would generate a stream of random numbers, so imagine that the first eighteen numbers were 08, 72, 87, 46, 15, 96, 04, 00, 52, 27, 46, 73, 95, 76, 10, 25, 02 and 11. Assuming that the clock started at time 0, the first customer would arrive at time 15. Since there is no one being served at the start of the simulation, this customer could be served straight away. The service time corresponding to a random number of 72 is 55 seconds. The service would start at time 15 (the time of arrival of the first customer), and finish at time 70 (15 + 55). The interarrival time (iat) of the second customer is 75 seconds so this customer would arrive at time 90 (15 + 75). By this time the first customer had departed so the second customer could be served straight away. This process is continued for the duration of the simulation, after which various statistics on the performance of the system can be printed out. This method of demonstrating the technique of simulation is often called the **tabular method** of simulation. In Table 5.5, the simulation has been continued until 440 seconds, and data on waiting time in the queue recorded. The average waiting time is the mean of the values in the last column. This is 72.2 seconds, with a standard deviation of 50.4 seconds. The number in the queue has also been recorded and this shows that the maximum number of customers in the queue is three. However, the mean number in the queue is not the simple average of the values in the fourth column. This is because these values need to be weighted by the time a customer spends in the queue. For the first 105 seconds there is no one in the queue, and for the next fifteen seconds there is one person in the queue and so on. The weighted average is therefore:

$$\frac{(0 \times 105) + (1 \times 15) + (2 \times 30) + (3 \times 105) + (2 \times 30)}{285} = 1.58$$

It is also possible to calculate the utilisation of the cashier. Utilisation is the proportion of time that the cashier is busy, and will be the total time spent serving divided by the total time that the system was operational for. The total time spent serving is the sum of the sixth column, which is 405 seconds, and the total time of the simulation was 440 seconds, so the utilisation is 92 per cent.

Table 5.5 ■ Tabular simulation for the bank example

Random no.	Iat	Clock time	No. in queue	Random no.	Service time	Service starts	Service ends	Waiting time
08	15	15	0	72	55	15	70	0
87	75	90	0	46	45	90	135	0
15	15	105	1	96	75	135	210	30
04	15	120	2	00	25	210	235	90
52	15	135	2	27	35	235	270	100
46	15	150	3	73	55	270	325	120
95	105	255	2	76	55	325	380	70
10	15	270	2	25	35	380	415	110
02	15	285	3	11	25	415	440	130

■ **Whiteladies Health Centre**   *Scenario 5.1*

Patients arrive at the health centre and stop briefly at the receptionists' desk before waiting their turn to see a doctor. If we ignore the time spent at the receptionists' desk, this is a simple queuing system. The complication is that there are six doctors, and patients can arrive up to 30 minutes before the doctors start work. We might also want to model the situation where patients are either allocated or choose a doctor on arrival. This could be achieved by allocating a patient to the doctor who has the shortest queue at the time, or randomly making the allocation. Either method would be perfectly feasible, although it would be quite tedious to do manually. A slightly simplified version of this system is provided as an exercise later in this chapter.

Continuous simulation

For some systems, the assumption that there is a set of discrete events is not valid. Examples are mainly in the engineering field and include the flow of a fluid into a tank or the cooling of an ingot after it has been removed from a furnace. In both these examples, the discrete-event approach could be used by making the time between events very short. However, this would be an approximation, and a better approach is to model the continuous change using differential equations. In some cases it may be possible to solve these equations using an analytical model, but in general they have to be solved numerically. It is also possible to have combined discrete-event and continuous simulation in one system. There are simulation packages that specialise in continuous simulation, and packages such as SIMAN that can handle discrete-event, continuous and combined models.

Monte-Carlo simulation

Law and Kelton (1991) define Monte-Carlo simulation to be 'a scheme employing random numbers, that is, $U(0,1)$ random variates, which is used for solving certain stochastic or deterministic problems where the passage of time plays no substantive role'. This technique was developed during World War II where it was applied to problems relating to the atomic bomb. An example of the technique as applied to deterministic problems is to find the area under a curve for functions that cannot be integrated. However, our interest is in the application of the technique to stochastic problems which are essentially static in nature, such as inventory control or risk analysis.

Since Monte-Carlo simulation can be carried out with a spreadsheet, the term **spreadsheet simulation** will be used in future references to the technique. This will help differentiate Monte-Carlo simulation from discrete-event simulation. Spreadsheets cannot easily be used for discrete-event simulations because they do not have the facility to handle time in a meaningful way. We have seen that with discrete-event simulation, the state of the system is not static but changes as the entities interact with the other components of the system. To keep track of the position and state of every entity in a model, an **event calendar** or table is employed. This table provides a means of updating the state of the system after each event. This would be very difficult to achieve with current spreadsheet technology. However, spreadsheets are very good at manipulating expressions and in basic 'number crunching'.

There are many areas where spreadsheet simulation could be used. One of the most common is in inventory control. Although time is part of an inventory system, it is not generally modelled explicitly. If the rows or columns of a spreadsheet represent different time periods, the simulation will simply allow the stock level to be seen to be fluctuating on a period-by-period basis. Decisions on stock ordering can then be made on the basis of some decision rule, such as 'Is the stock level below some re-order level?' The method of inventory simulation is similar to discrete-event simulation in that a stochastic variable is represented by a probability distribution. Instead of generating arrivals to the system, the sampling process randomly generates the demand or other variable in the model. If cells within the spreadsheet are linked by formulae or functions, the effect of varying demand can be transmitted to the output variables. These output variables could include costs or the number of 'stock-outs' that occur in a particular period. Just as in discrete-event simulation, it is possible to demonstrate the method manually. And as in discrete-event simulation, it is easier to use an empirical distribution for the manual simulation.

There are many other areas where this type of simulation can prove useful. These include investment appraisal, some forms of forecasting, and any situation where the level of risk in a particular business venture needs to be evaluated. We will be looking at some of these applications in Chapter 8.

■ **Drive Thru Burger restaurant**   *Scenario 5.2*

The company purchases its food products through a local supplier. One such item is coffee, which it purchases in large catering-size tins. The number of tins used per day varies and the relative frequency table for different levels of usage is shown in Table 5.6.

Table 5.6 ■ **Relative frequency table for the number of tins of coffee used per day**

Number of tins used per day	Mid point	Frequency	Relative frequency (%)
10 to under 30	20	12	17
30 to under 40	35	20	28
40 to under 50	45	25	35
50 to under 60	55	9	13
60 to under 70	65	5	7

Once an order is placed, delivery takes exactly two days. The cost of placing an order, which includes time spent on the phone and the necessary paper-work, is reckoned to be £20 per order. The cost of holding one tin in stock for one day has been calculated by the company's accountant to be 4p.

Before we can simulate the system, we need to allocate random numbers to the distribution shown in Table 5.6. This has been done in Table 5.7. If we approximate the distribution by using the mid point values, we can see what usage figure would be associated with any random number. For example, a random number of 20 would generate a usage of 35 tins, while a random number of 91 would generate a usage of 55 tins.

Table 5.7 ■ **Allocation of random numbers for the demand distribution**

Number of tins used per day	Mid point	Frequency	Relative frequency (%)	Cumulative frequency (%)	Random numbers
10 to under 30	20	12	17	17	00 to 16
30 to under 40	35	20	28	45	17 to 44
40 to under 50	45	25	35	80	45 to 79
50 to under 60	55	9	13	93	80 to 92
60 to under 70	65	5	7	100	93 to 99

▶

To start the simulation, we need to decide the order quantity. The average number of tins, based on the relative frequency table, is about 40 tins a day, and if the usage were constant, we could use the EOQ formula (see Chapter 4) to calculate the optimum order quantity, Q. The EOQ formula is

$$Q = \sqrt{\frac{2CD}{h}}$$

where C is the order cost, D is the demand and h is the cost of holding one item in stock for one unit of time.

Using the figures supplied, we would get:

$$Q = \sqrt{\frac{2 \times 20 \times 40}{0.04}} = 200 \text{ tins}$$

The storage and order costs would be

Storage cost: $\dfrac{hQ}{2} = \dfrac{0.04 \times 200}{2} = £4$

Order cost: $\dfrac{CD}{Q} = \dfrac{20 \times 40}{200} = £4$

giving a total cost of £8 per day or about £240 per month.

Using the EOQ model, we would have placed an order of 200 tins when the stock level reached two days' supply, which is 80 tins. The simulation would generate usage of coffee for each day and if the stock level fell below 80 tins, an order would be placed. The column headings and first few entries for this simulation is shown in Table 5.8.

Table 5.8 ■ Simulation of an inventory system

Day	Stock b/f	Order	Stock available	Rno	Qty	Stock c/f	Order made	Stock out	Order cost	Storage cost	Total cost
1	0	200	200	9	20	180	no	0		£7.6	£7.6
2	180		180	45	45	135	no	0		£6.3	£6.30
3	135		135	67	45	90	no	0		£4.50	£4.50
4	90		90	25	35	55	yes	0	£20	£2.90	£22.90
5	55		55	97	65	0	no	10		£1.10	£1.10
6	0	200	200	83	55	145	no	0		£6.90	£6.90
7	145		145	52	45	100	no	0		£4.90	£4.90
8	100		100	76	45	55	yes	0	£20	£3.10	£23.10
9	55		55	49	45	10	no	0		£1.30	£1.30
10	10	200	210	40	35	175	no	0		£7.70	£7.70

An explanation of the columns in the spreadsheet is as follows

Day	Day number
Stock b/f	Stock brought forward from the previous day
Order	If an order has been made two days previously, this will arrive and be shown in this column
Stock available	Stock brought forward plus the new order (if applicable)
Rno	Random number
Qty	The number of tins generated by the random number
Stock c/f	Stock carried forward is stock available less number of tins used
Order made	If stock carried forward is 80 tins or less, an order is made, for delivery in two days' time
Stock-out	If No. of tins is more than stock available, the difference represents the quantity that cannot be supplied
Order cost	Each time an order is made, a cost of £20 is incurred
Storage cost	This is the average of the stock brought forward and the stock carried forward multiplied by the storage charge of 4p
Total cost	This is the sum of the order and storage costs for each day

This simulation could be repeated for several days, and the total cost and other useful information – such as the number of times there was a stock-out – could be recorded. Over the ten days simulated in Table 5.8, there was one occasion when there was a stock-out. This occurred on Day 5 when a large usage occurred the day after an order had been made. The total costs over the ten days amounted to £40 ordering costs and £46.30 storage costs. Since the EOQ model gave daily costs of £4 for both ordering and storage, the simulation is producing very similar results. Of course, the simulation has shown that stock-outs might occur, which cannot happen with the EOQ model. We could also inject some uncertainty into the delivery process by replacing the fixed two-day delivery period by another probability distribution. This is likely to increase the risk of a stock-out.

Stages of a simulation project

Simulation is a multi-stage process, and each stage must be carried out in a satisfactory manner before the next stage is started. Unlike some types of processes, there is not an agreed set of documented procedures for undertaking a simulation project. This is partly due to the fact that no two projects are the same, but also to the way that the simulation technique has evolved. The following quote, taken from a recent study into the use of simulation in the manufacturing industry, illustrates the problem of the credibility of simulation within industry. 'Unlike computer aided design (CAD), simulation does not mimic an existing technique, and it has not been absorbed culturally into operational decision making' (Simulation Study Group, 1991). With the development of more 'user-friendly' software, at an affordable price, this situation should hopefully improve within the next few years.

The stages in a simulation project generally follow the modelling cycle discussed in Chapter 2, but a simulation model is likely to be far more complex, will involve the use of computers, and will require statistical design and analysis. The following stages relate specifically to the discrete-event type of simulation, although the general ideas are applicable to all types of simulation.

1. Formulate the problem and plan the study

This is the most important stage of a simulation project. The objectives of the study need to be defined in terms of the problems to be addressed and the purpose for which the results will eventually be used. Unfortunately, at the start of many simulation projects there are often a number of conflicting objectives for the project. For example, in the simulation of an airport, one objective might be that the downtime of planes must be kept to a minimum, while another objective might be to minimise maintenance cost. Most simulation projects require the setting up of a project team, and the members of the team should ideally be drawn from many parts of an organisation, each member having different skills and knowledge about the system. This diversity of knowledge can help produce a coherent set of objectives and so increase the chance that the project's recommendations will be implemented.

The boundaries of the system need to be carefully defined at this stage. The boundaries include those aspects of the system that are deemed important and will include the assumptions that can be made about the system. As in any form of modelling, the motto 'simple models are best' applies to simulation. It is far easier to improve a model later than to struggle with a model that is too complex from the start.

Each stage of the project needs to be carefully planned so that the time and the cost of the project can be estimated. The overall cost of the simulation project will be directly proportional to the man-hours of time that the project is estimated to take, but it may also include the cost of any software or hardware that has to be purchased. The benefits of the project should also be estimated at this stage. In many cases there will be a direct financial benefit if the simulation project is able to show that savings can be effected through a change in working practices. In other cases, the benefits may be less quantifiable, but important just the same.

These benefits could include improved customer satisfaction, or a system that is better able to handle unexpected events. If the objectives of the study include the benefits that will accrue, it will be far easier to judge if the project has been a success.

2. Collect and analyse the data

Stages two and three are often worked on in parallel as the data requirements for a model are not always known precisely until the model has been defined. Both stages, however, require a thorough understanding of the current system, which should have been achieved during stage one of the project. The logical relationships within the system must be identified and data collected on these relationships and on all the important parameters. It is at this stage that assumptions are made, either through the need to keep the model simple or because data is not available. There are two basic types of data that are needed by a model; these are the deterministic-type data and the data that is stochastic in nature. Deterministic data is the easiest data to collect and often consists of countable parameters, such as the number of servers or restrictions on queue lengths, scheduled breaks in a process and any other data that is known with a reasonable degree of certainty. Stochastic data, on the other hand, is any data which is known to vary in a random fashion. This could include the number of arrivals to a system, the time taken to process an arrival, or the time between failures of a machine. Collection of data is a very important part of a simulation project, and the time taken for this stage is often underestimated. Some events may only occur rarely and the system may need to be observed for a considerable time in order for some meaningful observations to be made. These rare events can have a significant effect on the long-run behaviour of the system and to ignore them may result in the development of an inadequate model.

Once the data has been collected, it needs to be analysed. This analysis is mainly concerned with fitting appropriate probability distributions to the stochastic variables. We may decide to use the collected data in our model and sample from this. This is called sampling from *empirical* data. Alternatively, we may attempt to fit a theoretical distribution to the data. This is quite difficult to do by hand but much easier if a computer software package, such as BestFit, is used. There are advantages and disadvantages with both approaches. The use of the empirical distribution ensures that the simulation is using only the data that has been observed, while using a theoretical distribution allows the generation of values that are in the tails of the distribution, and therefore only occur rarely. Since we normally hope that our simulation model will allow rare events to occur from time to time, the use of theoretical distributions seems to be the better approach. However, simulation experts disagree on this matter. Whatever the approach, the first stage should be an initial exploration of the data. A histogram will be helpful in observing how the data is distributed across the range of values and to identify any outliers that may need to be investigated. In some cases the fitting of distributions can be difficult. This may be because insufficient data was collected or maybe the model is of a new system, where data is currently unavailable. There is no ideal solution to this problem, although in some cases the form of the distribution can be guessed at, and parameters estimated from a knowledge of similar systems. A panel of experts can often prove useful in estimating these unknown parameters, although numerous research studies have shown that people tend to underestimate extreme values.

3. Build the conceptual model

Concurrently with the collection of the data, a first attempt at the model can be made. A conceptual model is essentially a model where mathematical and logical relationships are defined. A diagram showing the inter-relationships between the main parts of the model will help make the model development easier. An **activity cycle diagram** is a useful diagram for discrete-event simulation, and will be discussed in more detail in Chapter 9.

4. Check the validity of the conceptual model

Although the main validation tests will be carried out once a working computer model has been developed, some checks should be made at all stages of a simulation project. Once the data has been collected and the relationships defined, the users and the rest of the project team should have an opportunity to comment on the model. The terminology used for this form of validation is a 'structured walk-through' of the model. The main idea is that the assumptions made and the relationships defined are scrutinised by key personnel and any basic logic errors or incorrect assumptions identified. It is very easy for an analyst to make an incorrect assumption, perhaps as a result of an inadequate understanding of the system. Time spent identifying these errors at this stage will save much time later on.

5. Develop the computer model

The method of transferring the conceptual model into a computer model depends on the software package or language used. At one time there were simulation **packages** and simulation **languages**. Simulation packages were software that were written for a specific purpose. They were easy to use but not very flexible; that is, they were not very good for using with different situations. Simulation languages, such as GPSS, were essentially high-level programming languages that had an *executive* for carrying out the necessary 'housekeeping' tasks. These tasks consisted mainly of maintaining an *event list* of the time that various events would take place. Simulation languages were very flexible but required a fair knowledge of computer programming. Nowadays, there is less distinction between the two types of software. Most recent software has a graphical user interface (GUI), which allows certain functions to be specified by a click of a mouse. A model can often be completely specified by a few icons placed on the screen, and if further functionality is required, it·is usually possible to use lower-level modules. Some simulation software often allows experienced users to incorporate their own code, so making the software completely flexible. The result of this development is that simulation models can be developed in days, rather than weeks or sometimes months, using simulation languages.

6. Verify (or debug) the computer model

It is very unlikely that a model will work first time. The more complex a model, the more time it will take to identify and fix the problems. The obvious errors, such as syntax errors or basic logic errors, can be easily found, and most software will automatically identify these. There will, however, be some logic errors that cannot easily be identified by the software. If you tell the software to generate an arrival using an exponential distribution of mean ten seconds, it will do this for you, and not realise that you had the time units specified incorrectly. Debugging a simulation model that is developed using a simulation language can be tedious and time consuming. It involves executing (or running) the model under very specific conditions and analysing the output. If the output did not look as expected, an error would be suspected and perhaps a *trace* added to the code. A trace simply prints the contents of specified variables at regular intervals so that it is possible to follow the simulation event by event. Debugging a 'state-of-the-art' simulation package is much easier as these packages are fully animated. An animated simulation shows arrivals (**entities**) passing through the model, which makes it easy to identify mistakes in the specification of the computer model. An incorrect arrival distribution would show up, either by too few or too many entities flowing through the model.

7. Validate the model

Verifying the model simply checks that the computer program is doing what it should do. Validation, on the other hand, checks that the model is reproducing the results expected from the actual or proposed system. There are various types of validation that should be carried out. The easiest and often the most important is the **face validation**. A face validation simply asks whether, on the surface, the model appears to be replicating the real system. This may involve making one run of the model and inspecting the output. Again, the animation can be helpful here, as can plots of important variables. Another form of validation is to check the assumptions made in stage 1. If changing these assumptions changes the output in a detectable way, this may indicate that these assumptions need to be reviewed. Finally, the output needs to be checked statistically. This will require several runs to be made of the model and the average of some key output variables compared with data collected from the real system. Since the model is a simplified representation of the system, it is unlikely that the model and real system will agree exactly, and it is the knowledge and expertise of the project team that will determine whether the results agree sufficiently well. For this reason, it is often preferable to use confidence intervals as a form of comparison rather than hypothesis tests.

Problems arise with validation when the model is of a new system. In this case, actual data will not exist, so statistical validation is impossible. In some cases a similar system is available, which will allow some comparison to be made. In other cases it is necessary for 'experts' to comment on the output and make some qualitative judgements about the credibility of the model.

If serious errors are detected it is necessary to go back to one of the earlier stages before continuing. This may have to be repeated a number of times before a satisfactory valid model is achieved. In some cases it may be necessary either to accept a less than adequate model, to make the model far more complex than was originally intended, or to abandon the project completely. This decision will depend on the time allowed for the project as well as the accuracy required of the model.

8. Design experiments

A simulation model is essentially an elaborate sampling device, but one where the experimenter has full control of the sampling conditions. This means that the output obtained from the simulation must be treated as a sample that has been obtained from an unknown population. In any sampling procedure, we want to be able to estimate parameters of the population that are statistically precise and free of bias. To achieve this in simulation, we need to consider the following factors:

(a) type of system
(b) length of each simulation run
(c) number of independent simulation runs
(d) initial conditions for a simulation run
(e) length of any 'warm-up' period
(f) whether 'variance reduction techniques' need to be considered
(g) number of experiments that are to be carried out on the model

It is frequently the case in simulation modelling that little thought is given to the question of experimentation until after a valid working model is achieved. And even then, experiments are carried out on a piecemeal basis without any real plan as to what is required from the model. To some extent this is understandable, as ideas do not always develop until a simulation model is working. However, it is more efficient and statistically more reliable if some experimental design is decided at the outset of the project. This design need not preclude carrying out other experiments, which will inevitably arise following initial analysis of the results.

9. Make production runs

Once the experimental design has been agreed and a valid model produced, the necessary runs are made. This process can take longer than expected as some designs require a large number of runs, and the model will often need to be amended before each run. Generally, models of non-terminating systems take longer for results to be obtained, as these models have problems with initial conditions, which need to be removed before results are collected.

10. Analyse output data

A well-defined experimental design will have completely specified the analysis that needs to be carried out on the simulation output. Some simulation software packages have an output processor that will perform the necessary calculations. Alternatively, there are several good statistical packages on the market, such as MINITAB, SPSS and SAS. The latest version of these packages are all Windows based and easy to use. However, they will not tell you what technique to use, and neither will they interpret the results of the analyses. Users of these packages are

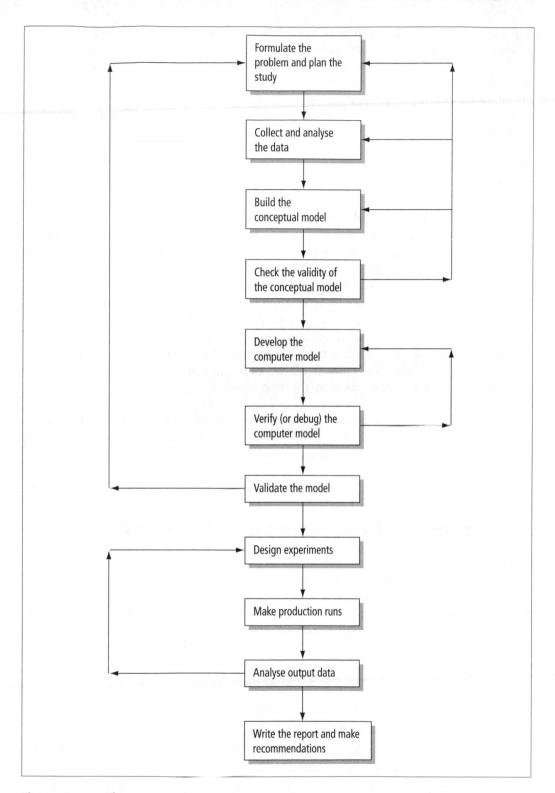

Figure 5.1 ▓ **The stages of a simulation project**

expected to have some statistical knowledge, but one of the dangers of making statistical software more accessible is that inappropriate or incorrect tests will be performed on the data by users without this knowledge. The recent development in simulation software is for the production and analysis of results to be more automated, but we are still some way off from this becoming a reality.

The aims of a statistical analysis of the simulation output will either be a comparison between two or more alternative designs of the system, or to measure the effects of changes to the input to the model. For example, we might want to see the effects of an increase in the arrival rate to the average time entities spend in the system.

11. Write the report and make recommendations

If this step is omitted the whole exercise is worthless! As with most management reports, the report should aim to satisfy three types of reader – the non-technical and/or busy manager who wants the main results and recommendations from the study, a reasonably numerate person who wants to see justification for the conclusions reached, and the person who wants a detailed description of the model and results. The latter may be satisfied by placing the relevant material in an appendix or a separate technical report may be necessary. Often, the most important consequence of a simulation project is that the system is better understood by the client. This sometimes makes the results from the study appear obvious, but this wouldn't have been so without the study in the first place.

There will be several feedback loops between these stages, and like the modelling cycle discussed in Chapter 2, it may take several iterations before a satisfactory model is developed. The eleven stages and the feedback loops are summarised in Figure 5.1.

Advantages and disadvantages of simulation

Simulation has a number of advantages over other modelling techniques but it is not the panacea that some people make out. Listed below are some of the advantages and disadvantages of simulation over analytical models. This is not meant to be an exhaustive list, but it should give some guidelines to situations where simulation can be useful and situations where an alternative method would be more useful.

Advantages

1. Simulation can be used to study complex systems.
2. Simulation can be used to answer What if? type questions.
3. Simulation can be used in the design of new systems or in the modification of existing systems, without disturbing the system.
4. Simulation often gives people a better understanding of a system.
5. Simulation can often help develop team work within an organisation.

6. Bottlenecks in a process can often be identified when simulation is used.

7. It is possible to study the transient nature of a process using simulation.

8. Simulation can help quantify the risk inherent in a system or in an investment decision.

9. Simulation can sometimes be used as a 'real time' scheduling model for certain systems.

Disadvantages

1. Simulation does not guarantee optimal solutions.

2. Simulation cannot solve problems.

3. Simulation is a sampling device so 'exact' solutions are not possible.

4. Statistical knowledge is required to analyse the output from a simulation model.

5. A simulation model can take longer to develop than an analytical model.

6. A simulation model can ignore important variables or relationships that exist in the real system.

7. A simulation project can be expensive to undertake as a major project may require a number of staff for several weeks or months to be assigned to the study.

8. Discrete-event simulation software packages are expensive (typically in the region of several thousands of pounds).

9. Collection of data for a simulation model can be difficult and time consuming.

10. Use of simulation when an analytical solution could have been obtained.

Pitfalls in simulation modelling

Law and McComas (1989) identified eleven pitfalls in simulation modelling. These pitfalls are broken into four categories: the model development process, the selection and use of simulation software, the modelling of system randomness, and the design and analysis of simulation experiments.

In the model development process, the major pitfalls are the failure to set a well-defined set of objectives and the failure to involve the client in all stages of the project. Also mentioned is the lack of simulation and statistical training by the analysts of the project.

The selection and use of simulation software is cited as another potential pitfall. Not all software is suited for all applications, and using an inappropriate package can either cause unnecessary effort or the model has to be changed to accommodate the way that the particular package works. For example, it is possible to use a discrete-event simulation package for a system that is continuous, but the accuracy of the results would suffer.

Possibly one of the main pitfalls in modelling is using an incorrect probability distribution to model the system randomness. This can be caused by lack of data, or a misunderstanding of the part played by a probability distribution in a simulation model. Where data is not available, the form of the probability distribution has to be guessed and an inappropriate choice can cause a large error in the output. Popular distributions for use where little or no data exists are the uniform and triangular distributions. Pegden *et al.* (1995) calls the uniform distribution, the 'distribution of maximum ignorance' as it means that we have no idea what the shape should be. The triangular distribution is a little better, although Law *et al.* (1994) have demonstrated the errors that can arise when this distribution is used inappropriately. The worst situation is where a distribution is replaced by its mean. This completely eliminates all variability associated with a particular variable, and can cause major errors. The only time it can be justified is where the variable is of little importance in the model. This can occur when a process within a model takes a very short time compared to the other processes.

Finally, the last group of pitfalls occurs during the experimental design and analysis phase of a simulation project. The major mistake in this group is to assume that one run of the simulation will be sufficient to enable conclusions to be drawn about the model output. This is equivalent to assuming that a sample of one will allow predictions to be made about the population from where this sample originated. In order for statistically valid conclusions to be made about the simulation output, several independent runs of a simulation model are required and the mean must be obtained for each run. For non-terminating systems, it is necessary to allow the model to reach steady state before data is collected from the model. Failure to carry out this procedure can introduce serious errors into the results.

The management of simulation projects

We have already touched upon the importance of setting objectives for a simulation project and for maintaining close links with the clients of the project. Ideally, the project team should contain members of the client's staff, who will have an intimate knowledge of the existing system or who will know what they want from a new system. Musselman (1993) believes that project success is all about communication. He believes that poor communication is the single biggest reason for the failure of projects. Discussions should be held with the client at all stages of the project, particularly at the beginning. It is at this stage that objectives are agreed and the benefits emphasised. Many people are too eager to start, and do not spend sufficient time planning each stage of the project. It often helps to get the team and client to sit around a table and discuss all the potential problems that could occur. If these potential problems are discussed at this early stage, the problems may not be avoided but at least they will not be a total surprise. More importantly, perhaps, is that solutions to these problems might have been decided in advance, which will help keep delays to a minimum. Once the project has started, the client should be provided with progress reports and meetings should be held at regular intervals. It is important that these reports are honest as it is essential that the analysts and client have a good working relationship. This will not be achieved if the giving of bad news is withheld or delayed.

For really large simulation projects, it will probably be necessary to have a management team to direct the project. In these cases, the project will probably have to be divided into several self-contained modules and some form of **critical path analysis** will be applied to all the activities. Critical path analysis is a technique that allows the total project duration to be estimated, while at the same time identifying those activities that are *critical*. A critical activity is an activity that, if delayed, will delay the entire project. The advantage of applying critical path analysis to a project is that the team is forced to think very carefully about each activity and how long it will take. Data collection is an activity that is often found to be on the critical path, as it can consume a large proportion of the man-hours allocated to the project. It is usually necessary to break this activity down into several sub-activities as this will improve the estimation of time required.

As the project proceeds, it will frequently be found that requests are made to widen the scope of the project or to include more detail. Agreeing to these requests can lead to over-runs in time and money, and should be avoided. It is much better to keep to the original plan, and leave changes until after the original project has been completed. It is for this reason that projects are often designed in phases. The first phase may have been designed to give some basic results before extending the project in other directions. This is sensible when difficulty is found setting the objectives for the project. The initial phase of the project can help consolidate ideas for the second and subsequent phases.

The end of one simulation project can often be the beginning of another! Success breeds success and if the project achieves its objectives, there could well be other parts of the organisation that need the services of the consultant or analyst. However, for a project to be successful, it needs to be seen to be successful. The end of a project is as important as the beginning, and time should be made available for presentations and implementation. Presentations take the form of written as well as verbal reports, and are a key feature of a successful project. Implementation may require that personnel are trained in the recommended procedures, which requires tact and understanding. Many people are reluctant to change as they see it as a threat to their jobs, but this problem can be minimised if all staff have been kept fully informed of the project from the start. In a few cases, the outcome of a simulation project is that recommendations are made regarding staff reductions. These situations are usually handled sensitively by the personnel section of a company, but having to make these kinds of recommendations is not the most pleasant part of a simulation project.

■ Case study 1
1998 SUPPLY BUSINESS SIMULATION AT SWEB

The first case study in this text is an example of the use of discrete-event simulation for a system that does not currently exist. It is always difficult modelling a new system since availability of data is often a problem. However, in this case study, the aim of the simulation was not to make recommendations on design issues, but to explore the repercussions on the clerical workload of the opening up of the electricity supply industry to competition. Senior management were fully committed to this project and one member of staff was seconded to work full-time building the model. Several presentations were made to SWEB management as the project proceeded, and the outcome was that the company were better aware of the resource implications of the changes that will occur in 1998. Although this study could have been completed without simulation, the use of this technique had significant benefits in terms of helping management understand the issues involved, and being able to see the 'big' picture.

Background

On 1 April 1998 the electricity industry will allow competition in the supply of electricity to all customers. This will allow domestic consumers to choose their supplier, rather than having to receive their electricity from their local monopoly REC (Regional Electricity Company). Electricity companies are likely to respond to this new competitive environment in a number of different ways. Some may rely on customer loyalty and hope that their business will not be affected. However, as the telephone industry has shown, the public are prepared to change supplier to gain relatively modest savings. Consumer choice is likely to be an important consideration in the late 90s, and those electricity suppliers that do not respond to this challenge could find their market share collapsing.

SWEB, a subsidiary of Southern Electricity in the United States, currently supplies electricity to 1.2 million domestic customers in an area that stretches from Bristol to the most southern part of Cornwall. In terms of its customer base it is a relatively small supplier. However, it is a very forward-looking company and is expected to be a major player in the electricity industry of the future. They see 1998 as a challenge, and in common with many other suppliers are developing strategies to cope with the increased competition that deregulation will bring.

The system envisaged for 1998

From 1998, a domestic contract customer who wants to receive electricity from SWEB will need to be registered. This involves the customer being sent and returning a contract before he or she can be connected to the supply. Prior to 1998, the customer base was relatively static, with alterations being mainly due to connection of new premises and changes in tenancy. However, from 1998 the situation will be totally different. All SWEB's domestic customers will need to be 'signed up' and re-registered. In addition, SWEB will be attempting to increase its market share. An intense marketing activity will therefore be required, both to keep existing customers and to attract customers from other areas.

This marketing activity will create huge demands on the system since many thousands of customers will need to be registered over a relatively short period of time. In addition, marketing is not seen as simply an advertisement in a newspaper, but as a series of follow-up letters and phone calls. The administrative workload is likely to be immense and the purpose of this simulation study was to measure this workload and help formulate policy on the systems and resources required.

Assumptions

The difficulty experienced with this simulation project was that the processes to be adopted in 1998 are not yet fully understood. This meant that many assumptions had to be made. Some of these assumptions are:

■ There is a peak marketing activity, either one or six months prior to the 1998 cliff edge (depending on the scenario), to communicate with an estimated 50 per cent of the domestic market.

■ Each year a proportion of customers will change supplier, either because they are dissatisfied with their current supplier or because another supplier is offering a more competitive tariff. A 'churn' factor is defined that indicates the proportion of customers who change supplier during the year.

■ The marketing, contracting and registration processes will run on a shift basis, twelve hours per day, six days per week.

■ Many other assumptions had to be made concerning probabilities of particular events occurring, such as the customers responding to 'mailshots' and the number of customers lost at different points in the process. In addition, the times to do various tasks had to be estimated from the existing system. In many cases only the minimum, maximum and most likely values could be estimated, and the triangular distribution was used to give some variability about these values.

The model

A model was developed using ARENA. This package has an excellent graphical user interface which makes modelling by non-experts relatively easy. Its animation facilities are also very good and this was particularly important with regard to presentations to senior management.

ARENA, like many simulation packages, adopts a process approach to modelling. This means that an 'entity' needs to be identified that can be followed through the system. The entity in this case was a consumer that exists in the marketplace. Since there are many millions of potential consumers, it was necessary to group them, first in 10,000s and finally in 100s. The reason that the group sizes could be reduced in this way is that the final number of customers that SWEB is likely to secure will be a small fraction of all consumers. The model contains four sub-modules: a marketing module, a contracting module, a registration module and a billing module.

The marketing module first identifies consumers as either internal or external. An internal consumer is an existing SWEB customer and these customers would receive advertising and promotional material. The model assumes that a proportion of customers will not respond to any supplier's marketing and will remain with their current supplier (SWEB) through default. External consumers are treated in a similar way except that those who respond (either by phone or letter) will be contacted (either by phone or letter).

The contracting module takes the output from the marketing module and sends contracts to all customers who have requested a supply from SWEB. Some of these customers will respond immediately while others will need to be sent reminders. Customers who return their signed contracts progress to the registration module.

In the registration module, the customer is registered on some kind of registration system (various scenarios) as being supplied by SWEB. This is then validated and SWEB makes some alterations to its database to ensure that it has full internal audit control over the amount of electricity it purchases for supply to the customer.

Finally, information is passed to the billing module for subsequent billing of the customer at the relevant time.

These processes can be better illustrated using Figure 5.2.

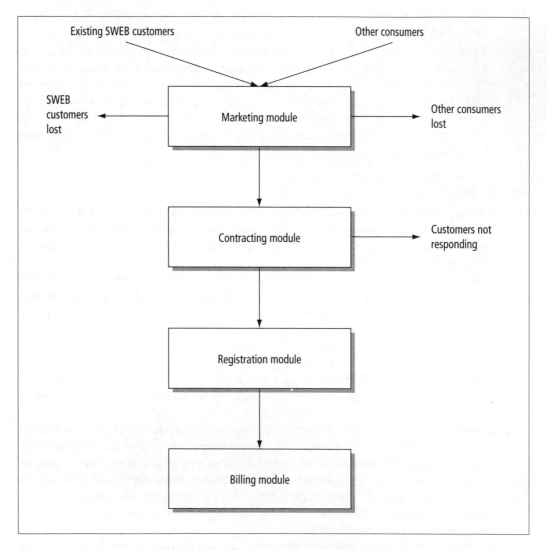

Figure 5.2 ▪ Outline of the simulation model for SWEB

The output from the model consists of numbers of customers gained at the various stages, the workload waiting to be processed at different points in the process and the utilisation of the clerical personnel. These statistics were represented in the form of animated plots as the simulation proceeded.

Validation

Statistical validation was difficult because the model was of a new system and it would be difficult to find data that could be used for any comparison. However, since many of the processes were currently in place, it was possible to make sound judgements on the realism of the model output. This was achieved by personnel at SWEB observing the animated model and commenting on the performance of the simulated system under different conditions. The animated graphical output was of great value in this respect as key variables could be monitored and compared. As a result of comments made it was possible to improve the accuracy of the model.

Conclusions

The main purpose of this model was to observe the effect of 1998 on the clerical processes at SWEB. Clearly, the peak in workload prior to the April of that year is going to cause a strain on the resources, and the simulation was able to provide some idea of the size of the problem. By applying What if? analyses it was possible to determine the possible strategies for dealing with this event. Although the results from the simulation are not likely to be completely accurate, they will at least give the company some idea of what to expect. This is infinitely better than reacting to events after they have occurred.

Another, possibly more important, use of the model was to influence national debate relating to the principles associated with the opening up of competition of electricity supply in 1998. It was possible for SWEB to show that they were approaching this market development in an intellectually rigorous, considered and unemotional fashion. In this respect SWEB were able to demonstrate that they will play a major role within the electricity supply industry of the future.

(The author is indebted to Mike Pool, a former employee of SWEB, for his assistance in writing this case study.)

Summary

This brief account of simulation modelling should give some insight into the different forms of simulation, and how a simulation project should be conducted. From a business context, Monte-Carlo and discrete-event simulation are of most interest, and these will be discussed in more detail in subsequent chapters. Whatever type of simulation is used, a good knowledge of simulation and statistical techniques are essential to avoid drawing incorrect conclusions from a model.

■ Exercises

5.1 Describe the essential differences between discrete-event and continuous simulation.

5.2 Why would it be difficult to use a spreadsheet to carry out a discrete-event simulation?

5.3 Repeat the bank simulation on page 124 by replacing the service time distribution with the mean of the distribution.

5.4 The data given below in Tables 5.9 and 5.10 are the interarrival time distribution and the consultation time distribution for the Whiteladies Health Centre. Assuming that there are six doctors on duty and a patient goes to the first available doctor, demonstrate the tabular method of simulation using the following random numbers:

61, 05, 72, 60, 15, 64, 56, 12, 22, 75, 67, 50, 93, 35, 01, 96, 17, 22, 79, 65, 21, 30, 35, 32, 66, 86, 67, 59, 39, 17, 95, 35, 09, 93, 55, 84.

From your simulation, determine the mean waiting time and the mean number of patients in the queue.

5.5 The relative frequency distribution for the weekly sales of a particular brand of washing machine is given in Table 5.11. It costs £100 to place an order and delivery takes three weeks. The cost of holding one washing machine in stock for one week is £1.

a Use the EOQ model to calculate the order quantity and the order and storage costs.

b Manually simulate the system using the random numbers 41, 10, 18, 14, 96, 67, 64, 62, 69, 53, 22, 76, 72, 63, 52, 74, 07, 25, 79, 75, 39, 37, 58, 00.

5.6 Repeat the simulation in Exercise 5.5, but this time the delivery time varies according to the relative frequency given in Table 5.12.

Table 5.9 ■ Interarrival time distribution for the Whiteladies Health Centre

lcb	ucb	Mid point	Frequency	Relative frequency
Minutes				
0	1	0.5	52	0.52
1	2	1.5	26	0.26
2	3	2.5	8	0.08
3	4	3.5	7	0.07
4	5	4.5	4	0.04
5	10	7.5	3	0.03
		Total	99	1.00

Table 5.10 ■ Consultation time distribution for the Whiteladies Health Centre

lcb	ucb	Mid point	Frequency	Relative frequency
Minutes				
0	2	1	22	0.0721
2	4	3	64	0.2098
4	6	5	91	0.2984
6	8	7	50	0.1639
8	10	9	28	0.0918
10	12	11	21	0.0689
12	14	13	7	0.0230
14	16	15	6	0.0197
16	18	17	11	0.0361
18	20	19	2	0.0066
20	30	25	2	0.0066
30	50	40	1	0.0033
		Total	305	1.0000

Table 5.11 ■ Relative frequency table for the sales of washing machines

Sales	Relative frequency (%)
0 to under 5	20
5 to under 10	50
10 to under 15	15
15 to under 20	10
20 to under 30	5

Table 5.12 ■ Relative frequency table for delivery time

Weeks	Relative frequency (%)
1	5
2	20
3	45
4	20
5	5
6	5

References and further reading

Law, A. M. and Kelton, W. D. (1991) *Simulation Modelling and Analysis*, Second Edition (Chapter 1), McGraw-Hill, Inc., USA.

Law, A. M. and McComas, M. G. (1989) 'Pitfalls to avoid in the simulation of manufacturing systems', *Industrial Engineering*, May, pp. 28–69.

Law, A. M., McComas, M. G. and Vincent, S. G. (1994) 'The crucial role of input modelling in successful simulation studies', *Industrial Engineering*, July pp. 55–59.

Musselman, K. J. (1993) 'Guidelines for simulation project success', *Proceedings of the 1993 Winter Simulation Conference*, pp. 58–64.

Pegden, C., Shannon, R. and Sadowski, R. (1995) *Introduction to Simulation Using SIMAN*, Second Edition (Chapters 1 and 2), McGraw-Hill, Singapore.

Schriber, T. J. (1987) 'The nature and role of simulation in the design of manufacturing systems', from Retti, J. And Wichmann, K. E. (Eds), *Simulation in CIM and Artificial Intelligence Techniques*, Society for Computer Simulation, pp. 5–18.

Simulation Study Group (1991) Horrocks, R. (Ed), 'Simulation in UK manufacturing industry', The Management Consulting Group, Barclays Venture Centre, University of Warwick Science Park, Coventry.

6

Applications of simulation

Les Oakshott, Andrew Greasley and David J. Smith

Introduction

At one time simulation was used mainly in the manufacturing, military and transport sectors. Nowadays, the range of applications is vast, with simulation being used in health care, the service sector, the leisure industry, the financial sector, communications and many other areas. This chapter discusses the use of simulation in some of these areas, and provides a detailed case study of how simulation has helped in the operation of a monorail system for a garden festival.

Types of applications

The 1990s have seen a growth in the variety of simulation projects attempted, and at the same time the user-friendliness of simulation packages has improved. Which occurred first is debatable, but the net result is that simulation is now seen as a technique that can be used by anyone in any business. At one time simulation was essentially a manufacturing technique, although there were significant uses in the military and transport fields. Simulation is still used in these areas and many companies, such as the Rover Group, use simulation as a matter of routine. The military use simulation in a war-gaming mode, as well as in the area of logistics. There are a number of defence-orientated companies and organisations, such as the Defence Research Agency, that have been actively engaged in simulation for a number of years, and will continue to be. Simulation has been frequently used to assist in the planning of port operations and British Airways have carried out numerous simulations into the study and design of airport operations.

The health service has undergone a complete overhaul in the past few years, and there have been a number of simulation projects aimed at improving the effectiveness of hospital departments and health care in general. Although most discrete-event simulation software can be used for health care problems, there have been products developed specifically for this sector. MicroSaint is a product popular with modellers of health care systems.

The service sector is not an area where simulation would be expected to flourish, but there has been a flood of interest from various companies in the service sector, such as the utilities, recruitment agencies, banks, building societies and retail outlets. Machin (1994) describes how simulation was used by the Royal Mail to help in the training of its staff.

Simulation in the financial sector is generally through a form of risk analysis. This can be carried out using a spreadsheet, preferably using a spreadsheet 'add-on' such as @RISK. Risk analysis could be used to evaluate the risk associated with different investment strategies or to determine the best strategy in a commodity market.

Simulation has been used in the leisure and entertainment industries to model the flow of people through an event or to determine the number of exits required in case of emergencies. Simulation can be used to determine whether a restaurant has sufficient resources in the form of staff and tables to handle the expected demand.

The rescue services use simulation for specific needs or to fine-tune their response to a major disaster, such as an aircraft crashing in central London.

A form of simulation is used by British Telecom to route calls over its network. Simulation could also be used to determine the number of phone lines required by a business.

We will now look at a few of these applications in a little more detail.

Manufacturing applications

Since the manufacturing sector is one of the original users of simulation, it is appropriate that this chapter starts by looking at applications that have a manufacturing orientation. The reason that manufacturing industry was one of the first sectors to realise the benefits of simulation is partly the type of problems found in this sector, and partly the fact that manufacturing companies are generally large organisations containing well-qualified staff. Manufacturing processes are complex processes, often involving material-handling devices, such as conveyors and transporters. They also tend to be expensive to operate so that any inefficiencies in the process can result in the waste of large sums of money. Simulation projects often look at ways of improving the throughput of a product by making small changes to the process. However, other *performance measures* might be equally important, such as a reduced amount of work in progress, increased utilisation of machines or staff, and improved quality of the finished product. Simulation can also give management and staff a better understanding of the manufacturing process by highlighting areas that have a major impact on performance.

Within a manufacturing process there are a number of areas of variability that can result in bottlenecks in a process or prevent the process from operating at its full capacity. For example, machines fail from time to time, and the time between breakdowns and the repair time is unlikely to be known precisely, but will vary randomly. The speed of the process may also fluctuate, and the number of rejects may vary. In addition, the resources used in the process, such as machines, people and material-handling devices, will be limited in number, and queues in the form of buffer levels or work in progress will become excessive. In some cases a bottleneck in one process will have serious repercussions in processes 'downstream' of the bottleneck. One of the first industries to benefit from simulation was the car industry. The Rover Group has been using simulation since the late 1970s and has found it has streamlined their business (Grigson, 1993). The technique is used both at factory level to solve local problems and at corporate level to study strategic issues. Other manufacturing industries that have regularly used simulation include the steel industry, the coal industry, the electronics industry and the clothing industry.

Use of material-handling devices, such as conveyors and transporters, are commonplace within the manufacturing sector, and can be the 'weak link' within a manufacturing process. There are many examples in the literature on the subject that demonstrate the improvements in productivity as a result of using simulation to model these devices (*see* Auguston, 1993 for the use of simulation in Alcoa). Problems involving material-handling devices were difficult to model using general-purpose programming languages, and this helped generate a new breed of simulation packages or simulators. These packages, such as SIMFACTORY and WITNESS, contained modules aimed specifically at the kind of problems involving material handling. Material-handling devices are also a common feature in warehouse operation, and the use of simulation in the design of a warehouse can play an important part in its efficient operation.

Simulation in health care

Health care in the United Kingdom was overhauled in the early 1990s, and many hospital managers were faced with the task of improving the effectiveness of their hospital. A hospital is a large organisation, with limited resources and a variable demand for their 'services'. They are now seen as providers of a service and their patients as the customers, who have a right to receive a pre-defined standard of service. Hospitals that are unable to provide an adequate service or overspend their budget can be penalised.

A hospital is a large and complex system, with many interacting parts, and many processes are subject to random variability. Only simulation can attempt to model this type of system, and even then it is usually necessary to break the system down into manageable parts. These sub-systems include the accident and emergency department, operating theatres, day clinics, transport, and all the various departments within a large hospital. The type of problems that need answers include the questions regarding the number of staff needed to provide a given level of service, the number of beds in intensive care, the scheduling of operations, and the amount of stock that should be held. Many of these issues have been tackled at individual hospitals and there is a growing volume of case studies quoted in the literature on the subject. One example is by Huang and Taylor (1995) which describes the simulation model developed for the Accident and Emergency Department at Plymouth Hospitals NHS Trust. This was a successful project in that the recommendations by the project team were accepted. One of the reasons for the successful outcome of the project was that management and clinicians were involved with the project from the very beginning, and the model was properly validated.

All health care problems contain some queuing mechanism. Patients who turn up at a clinic and then wait to be seen by a doctor or consultant is an obvious example, but there are many other queuing situations, such as waiting lists for operations or blood samples waiting to be analysed. The reason that queuing occurs is that the current demand for a service exceeds the capacity to supply the service. It would be possible to eliminate queuing by employing more consultants or more technicians, but these resources are expensive. If queuing did not occur, these expensive resources would be under-utilised, which is a waste of valuable resources. Of course, the Patients' Charter has prevented the queues or waiting lists from becoming too large, and this has increased the pressure on hospitals to cut down on unnecessary delays.

A typical simulation project for a hospital is described in Case Study 4 in Chapter 12.

Simulation in the service sector

The service sector is another area where the use of simulation has increased over the past few years. Part of the reason for this is that the sector has grown, but also because companies are realising that substantial savings can be made by streamlining clerical procedures. 'Business process re-engineering' were the 'buzz words' of the early 1990s, and this involved companies completely redesigning the way they conducted their business. Clerical processes can be as complex as any manufacturing process, and unless procedures are continually monitored and improved, inefficiencies can soon result in rising costs and a declining level of service. To improve a clerical system, it is possible to make changes to the real system and then observe the effect on the system performance. There is, of course, a danger that these changes will not improve the system, and could even make the system performance worse. It is therefore preferable to try out the changes on a model of the system. Simulation can be used to model the system because there are the necessary components to make the technique a viable approach: clerical systems are complex, there are several sources of variability within a typical system, and the resources availability in the form of people and equipment are limited. As an example, imagine an office where enquiries are received by letter and phone. Phone calls arrive at random and must be given priority over the letter enquiries. Both the letters in the in-tray and the phone calls represent arrivals to the system, which have to queue before being served. The workload resulting from an enquiry may vary, so creating further variability within the system. The clerical assistants represent the resources, which are limited in number, and these staff may be off sick or unavailable at certain times of the day. The clerical procedure just described may be only one part of a process, and following an enquiry, further clerical procedures may need to be activated. This is a simplified example of the case study described in Chapter 5, where simulation was used to measure the future resource requirements for a regional electricity supplier.

Transport applications

Transport is a diverse industry and includes all the conventional forms of transport such as land, sea and air. However, we could also include problems that are related to the transport sector, such as port facilities, movement of freight, postal services, rail layout, scheduling of transport services, logistics problems, and many others. Transport applications are different from many systems in that the system contains moving objects (such as trains) that interact with each other. They interact with each other in the sense that the status of one object can affect the status of another similar object. Simulation is a powerful means of studying these transport systems, as it is one of the few techniques that can model this interaction. Modern simulation software contains facilities for the movement of objects (such as guided transporters), which makes the modelling of transport systems relatively easy to handle.

There are a number of examples of the simulation of transport systems in the literature. For example, Danielsen *et al.* (1991) describe the simulation of shipping operations at the Stanlow and Tranmere Waterfronts. An interesting use of simulation in logistics planning is given by Smith (1995). He describes a problem at a Royal Ordnance site, where it was necessary to determine the resources needed to transfer a quantity of explosives from European locations to the RO site where they could be destroyed. The model was written in SIMAN and required the use of material-handling functions, which are well supported in this package.

The modelling of rail transport is a common application and there have been many projects in this area. One of the problems with any form of guided vehicle system is that for safety reasons two vehicles cannot be on the same section of track. This means that if a vehicle stops, those behind must stop too, unless the layout of the track permits overtaking. The second case study is the simulation of a monorail system, and illustrates the problem of 'one stop, all stop'.

■ Case study 2
THE MONORAIL SYSTEM

This case study shows how simulation can be used when a major new facility is being planned. The case highlights the analysis of capacity of an operational system. The authors are Andrew Greasley and David J. Smith.

The context

Increased levels of disposable income, combined with reduced working hours and greater personal mobility, have resulted in dramatic changes in leisure activities. Both the variety and total quantity of leisure facilities available to most sections of the community have increased. Among the new forms of leisure facility that have arisen, one that proved popular in the UK in the early 1990s was the garden festival.

When a garden festival was planned for the north of England, the organisers were required to give considerable thought to managing the flow of visitors through the facility. Although the site covered several acres, the experience of earlier garden festivals caused the organisers to be apprehensive about the large number of visitors, anticipating that this would make visitor movements problematic. In getting round this difficulty, the organisers planned to install a monorail system to move visitors from one side of the complex to another.

The monorail system

The monorail planned for the garden festival comprised a 2.045 kilometre loop, with two stations where trains would stop and one set of passengers would get off, while another set got on. Being a monorail, the track did not need to be located at ground level. Raising the track several metres above the ground left more space for exhibits and provided an excellent observation point from which visitors could view the various gardens. In this way, the monorail was not only of practical value in moving people around the site, but it also provided a 'feature' that, in itself, attracted visitors.

The trains that operated on the monorail track were driverless and continuously circuited the track in an anti-clockwise direction, on a 'merry-go-round' basis. Since the trains were driverless, each was provided with an automatic braking system activated whenever a train reached a specified minimum safety distance between itself and the train in front. Given that they operated automatically, each train always stopped at each station for a specified time interval, termed the 'waiting time', regardless of whether or not there were passengers wanting to leave or join it.

Unfortunately, the decision to use simulation was not taken until construction work on the infrastructure of the garden festival, including the monorail system, was under way. As a result, a number of features of the monorail system were fixed before work on the simulation model began. These included the length and path of the track, the number of stations and the capacity of each of the trains. Hence, there was no scope for using simulation to determine the feasibility of the overall system design. However, the organisers were anxious to ascertain the capacity of the monorail system, especially the maximum number of passengers per hour that it would carry.

The simulation model

A simulation model was developed using the SIMAN-CINEMA simulation package. The basis of the model was that there were resources, in the form of sections of track, that were seized by entities, in the form of trains. The track was divided into twenty sections, ten in front of each of the two stations. The number of sections was determined by the number of trains. Initially, the model was specified with ten trains, hence there were ten sections of track before each station. Each section was denoted on the screen by a signal (in the form of a circle), denoting the section that the train was entering. The logic of the model was that actual movement took place by trains seizing a section of track. This they had to do before releasing the previous section, in order to ensure that two trains were not on the same section of track. The time taken to cover a section of track – in logical terms, the time between seizing one section of track and the next – was

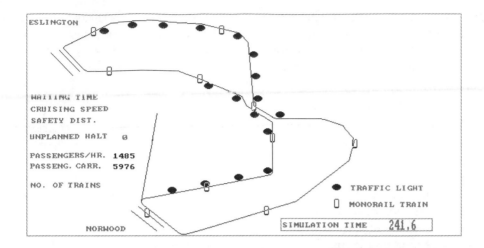

Figure 6.1 ■ Screen display of monorail simulation model

determined by the length of the section of track divided by its speed. Given that the cruising speed of the train was low, acceleration and deceleration were modelled by causing trains to pause as they left and entered stations. Stations, for their part, were no more than storage points, modelled by delaying the trains by a waiting time.

The model was developed in order to study the impact of three variables – cruising speed, the number of trains and the waiting time – on the capacity of the system. Each of these variables was displayed on-screen so that one could see the system configuration with ease.

The screen display above (Figure 6.1) reproduces the key features of the monorail system on the garden festival site.

In Figure 6.1, ten trains can be seen. Although SIMAN-CINEMA provides excellent facilities for accurately reproducing entities such as trains, it was decided that, in view of the limited space available, it was best to model each train in the simplest possible way. This provided more space for on-screen information about the state of the system.

The simulation results are displayed on-screen in the form of tallies of:

■ Passengers carried per hour

■ Total passengers carried

Each tally is continuously updated as the simulation progresses and represents the passenger-carrying capacity of the system.

Thus, in Figure 6.1, after 241.6 minutes, 5976 potential passengers have been carried on the monorail at an average rate of 1485 per hour. Clearly, this is potential capacity, created by this particular system configuration, rather than the actual number of passengers carried.

The number of passengers carried per hour measures the monorail system's ability to move people, and therefore provides a clear indication of the efficiency of the system. The display also shows the number of unplanned halts made by the trains. This measures the number of times trains were forced to make unscheduled stops between stations. Since passengers wanted to be transported from one part of the site to another, an unplanned stop between stations represents a deterioration in the quality of service.

Analysis of the service operations

The system was designed to operate so that the trains were always at least 50 metres apart. At this distance, the trains would always be sufficiently far apart to stop without hitting each other.

The three input variables – cruising speed, waiting time and number of trains – could all be altered. It was therefore decided to undertake a sensitivity analysis to explore the impact of each of the three variables on the passenger-carrying capacity of the system. By carrying out this analysis, it was hoped to identify values for each variable that would ensure a system configuration that maximised capacity, thus ensuring efficient and productive operation.

The first of the three input variables to be considered was the cruising speed of the trains. Initially, the system was operated with the trains running at 1.5 metres per second. As Figure 6.2 shows, increasing the cruising speed resulted in an increase in the passenger-carrying capacity of the system. However, as Figure 6.2 also clearly shows, there were limits to the extent to which capacity could be increased simply by increasing speed. As cruising speed was increased from 2.25 to 2.5 metres per second, capacity actually decreased. Closer investigation of the screen display showed that this was caused by the action of the automatic braking system. As the trains moved faster, so the risk of them getting too close and triggering the automatic braking system also increased. This arose because, at higher speeds, a greater distance was required to enable the trains to stop at the stations. What had not been anticipated was that the automatic braking system had only to stop one train and all the others were very soon forced to stop as well. The impact of this on the passenger-carrying capacity of the system is shown by the reduction in the number of passengers carried per hour as the speed of the trains was increased from 2.25 to 2.5 metres per second. Hence, by a process of experimentation, the limit of the trade-off between higher speed and increased capacity was identified. At the same time, it also led to an increase in unplanned halts. What was surprising was that the limit marked a fairly sudden change. The 'one stop, all stop' behaviour of the system meant that unplanned halts did not occur gradually. It was an 'all or nothing' situation, with important consequences for the quality of service provided, since the service would be subject not to an interruption where a single train made a short, unscheduled stop, but to what was almost a system shutdown, even if it was of a temporary nature. The phenomenon was the direct result of the complexity of the system, where several entities (i.e. trains) interacted.

The next input variable to be considered was the number of trains. Since each train consisted of a two-car set capable of carrying a total of 24 passengers, putting more trains on the track increased the capacity of the system. However, given the need to operate with a minimum distance between trains, there was a point where the system would become congested, stemming the flow of passengers. Figure 6.3

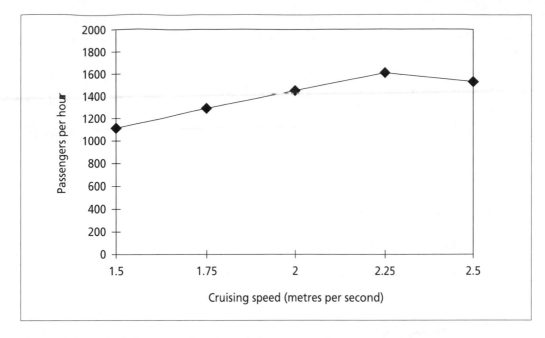

Figure 6.2 ■ **Cruising speed and capacity**

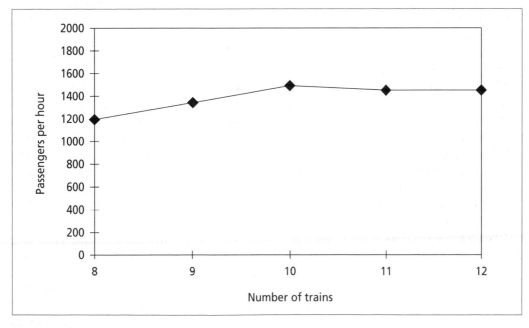

Figure 6.3 ■ **Number of trains and capacity**

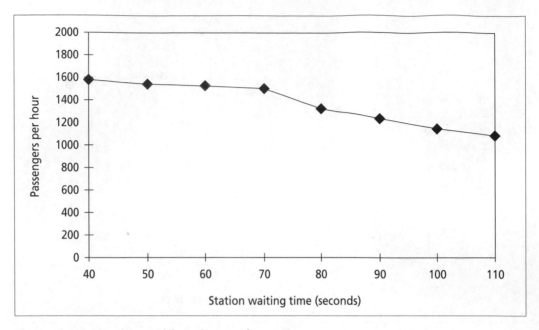

Figure 6.4 ■ Station waiting time and capacity

shows that as the number of trains increased from eight to nine, and then to ten, so the number of passengers carried per hour also rose. Increasing the number of trains beyond ten resulted in a reduction in capacity as the system became congested and the 'one stop, all stop' pattern of unplanned halts occurred again. Hence, a configuration of ten trains, each made up of two cars carrying twelve passengers each, as in Figure 6.1, was identified as the one that provided the highest level of efficiency without compromising quality of service.

Finally, attention turned to the 'waiting' time that trains spent at each station, loading and unloading passengers. Experiments began with the waiting time set to 40 seconds, and this was gradually increased up to 120 seconds. This resulted in a reduction in capacity of 30 per cent. Closer examination of the results revealed that the reduction in capacity did not take place evenly. Increasing the waiting time from 60 to 70 seconds, as shown in Figure 6.4, resulted in a capacity reduction of 2 per cent, or 28 passengers per hour. This was a comparatively small loss of capacity for a 17 per cent increase in loading/unloading time. A further increase in the waiting time by 14 per cent, to 80 seconds, resulted in a much bigger loss of capacity, amounting to a reduction of 11.5 per cent, or 159 passengers per hour. Detailed scrutiny of the screen display showing the monorail at work revealed that this break of trend, resulting in a sharp decline in capacity, was again caused by the 'one stop, all stop' behaviour of the trains. In view of this, a waiting time of 70 seconds was selected as the best compromise between reduced efficiency, in the form of lost capacity, and improved quality of service, in the form of extra time for passengers to get on or off trains.

The value of animation

The SIMAN-CINEMA simulation package was specifically used because it provided the benefit of animation for analysing the operation of the two stations, Eslington and Norwood, particularly the arrangements for loading and unloading passengers. These arrangements were governed by the 'waiting time', and it was the animated nature of the model, showing the movement of trains in and out of both stations, that brought home to the company's engineers that the waiting time had a human dimension. Whatever the efficiency gains of a short waiting time, there was a potential cost in terms of service quality, if entering and exiting the trains was an unpleasant experience for passengers. More significantly, if entry and exit arrangements were not carefully planned, there was a risk of safety problems that could jeopardise service quality even more seriously. Fortunately, seeing the system at work highlighted this dimension and as a consequence, much effort was directed at planning entry and exit arrangements.

Conclusion

The 'one stop, all stop' behaviour of the trains was not anticipated. The company's staff were used to working with comparatively simple systems involving only a small number of trains. They were unaware of the problems that could be encountered when operating several trains making short journeys and frequent stops. It was the model that highlighted the 'one stop, all stop' behaviour, thus enabling the company's engineers to configure the system so as to avoid this phenomenon and the rapid deterioration in service quality that passengers would have suffered if the trains were forced to stop between stations.

The case study also demonstrates the value of simulation as a planning tool where various aspects of a proposed system can be thoroughly evaluated prior to construction. In one respect, the case study is disappointing because the decision to use simulation was taken after the overall design had been finalised and construction work had already started. This meant that there was no point in using simulation to evaluate key design features of the planned system, such as track length and the location of stations. Despite this, the case study does show how simulation can aid planning by helping to 'fine-tune' a design. The identification of appropriate values for key system variables, such as cruising speed and waiting time, helped ensure the most productive use of resources, while minimising the risk of system failures (i.e. unplanned stops between stations) that would have jeopardised the quality of service.

The case study also shows how unanticipated behaviour can be identified through simulation.

Finally, the work undertaken in simulating the monorail highlighted the value of simulation in identifying, anticipating and rectifying 'bugs' in a system prior to it becoming operational, so as to ensure customers get a better quality of service. This was certainly the case with the arrangements for loading and unloading passengers at the two stations. At the design stage, little thought had been given to these arrangements. It was not until the animated nature of the simulation model enabled the company's staff to see the system at work that the significance of loading and unloading passengers within a specified time interval was appreciated. A delay in loading and unloading could, potentially, bring the entire system to a halt. When this was acknowledged, much effort went into designing the layout of each of the stations, and when the system was commissioned, it did not encounter operating problems of this type.

This case study is adapted from D.J. Smith (1994), 'Computer simulation applications in service operations: A case study from the leisure industry', *The Service Industries Journal*, Vol. 14, No.3, pp. 395–408.

Summary

Simulation is no longer seen as a technique to be used solely by the manufacturing sector. It is now used to help solve problems in most industries and sectors, and the areas of application are growing. Some areas have seen more activity than others. Health care and the service sector are two areas where there has been a significant growth in the past few years. Transport is an area where simulation has always had a presence, and modern simulation software allows transportation problems to be modelled using material-handling devices.

References and further reading

Auguston, K. A. (1993) 'How simulation helped Alcoa save $12 million/year', *Modern Material Handling*, Vol. 48, Issue 3, March.

Danielsen, P., Eldridge, D. and Brown, S. (1991) 'On the waterfront', *OR Insight*, Vol. 4, No. 1, January–March.

Grigson, A. (1993) 'Driving change – Rover's experience of simulation', *Manufacturing Engineer*, Vol. 72, No. 4, August.

Huang, X. and Taylor, C. (1995) 'Potential applications of simulation in hospital logistics management', *OR Insight*, Vol. 8, No. 2, pp. 15–23.

Machin, S. (1994) 'What-ifs for the Royal Mail', *OR Insight*, Vol. 7, No. 2, April–June.

Smith, V. (1995) 'Ship to magazine in four days?', *OR Insight*, Vol. 8, Issue 4, October–December.

7

Sampling from probability distributions

Les Oakshott

Introduction

In order to reproduce the randomness that occurs in a stochastic system, it is necessary to generate random variates by sampling from a probability distribution. A simplified demonstration was given of the technique in Chapter 5, using an empirical distribution. That demonstration used the tabular method of simulation, but in practice, simulations are carried out using a simulation software package and the distributions used are usually one of the standard theoretical distributions. Although users of simulation packages do not need to know exactly how the distributions are sampled, it is useful to have some knowledge as this gives a better understanding of the strengths and limitations of the technique. Since all sampling involves random numbers, this chapter starts with a look at the generation of random numbers.

Random numbers

Random numbers are numbers that are uniformly distributed between 0 and 1, and variates that have this property are said to be distributed according to the $U(0,1)$ distribution. The probability density function (pdf) for the $U(0,1)$ distribution is:

$$f(x) = \begin{cases} 1, & 0 < x < 1 \\ 0, & \text{otherwise} \end{cases}$$

The mean (μ) of a $U(0,1)$ distribution is 0.5 and the variance (σ^2) is $\frac{1}{12}$.
The pdf is shown in Figure 7.1 (overleaf).
Random numbers can be generated by physical devices, such as a roulette wheel, and these are true random numbers as they cannot be predicted in advance. Tables

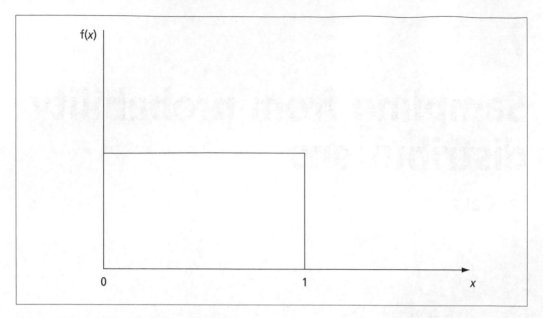

Figure 7.1 ■ The *U*(0,1) distribution

of random numbers can be generated from physical devices, but random numbers in this form are not particularly convenient for computer simulation. The normal method of random number generation is through an arithmetic procedure, and random numbers generated in this way are often called **pseudo random numbers**. Pseudo random numbers are numbers that behave like true random numbers in that they should pass all the tests for randomness. The advantage with pseudo random numbers is that since they are calculated they can be reproduced. Being able to reproduce a stream of random numbers is very important in simulation, as we will find out in subsequent chapters.

Generating random numbers

The requirement for a good random number generator is that it should:

1. have a long cycle length
2. generate random numbers that can be reproduced
3. not degenerate
4. be fast and not require much computer memory
5. produce random numbers that pass all the tests for randomness

All random numbers generated by an arithmetic procedure will eventually recycle the same numbers, and clearly it is important that this cycle length should be very long, relative to the number of random numbers used in a simulation. Since simulations can use in excess of one million digits, the cycle length is an important factor. The random number generator in the SIMAN simulation package is claimed to have a cycle length of about two billion digits (Pegden *et al.*, 1995).

Being able to reproduce random numbers is important in the analysis of simulation experiments as it enables the analyst to control the experimental conditions. By using the same random numbers in two or more versions of the model, we are able to reduce the variability in the results and hence more easily detect any real differences between versions.

Under certain conditions, some random number generators cause the sequence to degenerate. That is, the same number or pattern is repeated continuously. The repetition of the value zero does happen with some generators.

The most popular method of random number generation is the **multiplicative congruential method**. This method uses a recursive procedure, which will generate numbers between 0 and m, and these numbers can then converted to the $U(0,1)$ form; that is, lie in the range 0 to 1. The procedure is in the form of three steps:

Step 1   Select a starting value (x_0)

Step 2 $x_{i+1} = ax_i \pmod{m}$

$r_{i+1} = x_{i+1}/m$

Step 3   Repeat Step 2

The starting value, x_0 is called the *seed* and will give a unique stream of random numbers. The 'mod m' stands for modulo m and means dividing the product ax_i by m and keeping only the remainder. For example, suppose $a = 10$, $m = 7$ and the seed is chosen as 25. The first random number would be calculated as follows:

$ax_1 = 10 \times 25 = 250$

dividing 250 by 7 gives 35 remainder 5

the normalised random number will be 5/7 = 0.7143

The second random number will be found in a similar manner, except that x_0 is replaced by x_1. That is:

$ax_2 = 10 \times 5 = 50$

Dividing 50 by 7 gives 7 remainder 1 and the normalised random number will be 0.1429.

This process has been continued and the results can be seen in Table 7.1. Notice that the same numbers start repeating after the sixth iteration. The *cycle length* in this case is 6, and all random number streams produced by the multiplicative congruential method will eventually recycle the same numbers. The cycle length depends on the value of a and m; in the simulation package SIMAN, the value of a is 16,807 and m is $2^{31} - 1$.

Table 7.1 ■ Random numbers generated by the multiplicative congruential method

i	x_i	$10 \times x_i$	$10 \times x_i/7$	$U(0,1)$
0	25	250	35 r 5	0.7143
1	5	50	7 r 1	0.1429
2	1	10	1 r 3	0.4286
3	3	30	4 r 2	0.2857
4	2	20	2 r 6	0.8571
5	6	60	8 r 4	0.5714
6	4	40	5 r 5	0.7143
7	5	50	7 r 1	0.1429

Testing random numbers for randomness

Most simulation packages generate a good stream of random numbers, in that they pass all the tests for randomness. The most important tests include: goodness-of-fit test, runs test and autocorrelation test.

Goodness-of-fit test

The goodness-of-fit test is a test to see if the numbers are uniformly distributed. The main tests are the Chi-square test and the Kolmogorov-Smirnov test, both

Table 7.2 ■ Results obtained using the Chi-square goodness-of-fit test

lcb	ucb	Observed frequency	Expected frequency	Chi-square
0	0.1	100	100	0
0.1	0.2	101	100	0.01
0.2	0.3	101	100	0.01
0.3	0.4	90	100	1
0.4	0.5	106	100	0.36
0.5	0.6	99	100	0.01
0.6	0.7	90	100	1
0.7	0.8	99	100	0.01
0.8	0.9	112	100	1.44
0.9	1	102	100	0.04
	Total	1000	1000	3.88

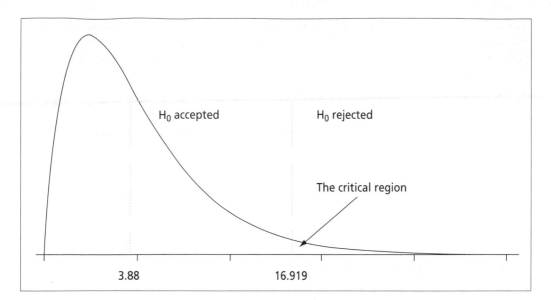

Figure 7.2 ■ The Chi-square distribution on 9 degrees of freedom

described in Chapter 3. To demonstrate the Chi-square test, 1000 random numbers were generated in Excel and the results obtained are shown in Table 7.2.

The Chi-square value at the 5 per cent significance level on 9 degrees of freedom is 16.919 and this distribution is shown in Figure 7.2. Since the test statistic of 3.88 is not in the critical region, the null hypothesis that the distribution is uniform cannot be rejected. The generated numbers therefore passed this test.

The Kolmogorov-Smirnov test was applied to the same 1000 numbers using SPSS, and the results are shown below.

> SPSS for MS WINDOWS Release 6.0
> - - - - - Kolmogorov-Smirnov Goodness-of-Fit Test
> RNO   Random numbers
>
> Test distribution - Uniform Range: .0052 to .9987
>
> Cases: 1000
>
> Most extreme differences
> Absolute Positive Negative K-S Z 2-Tailed P
> .01689   .01081   –.01689   .5341   .9379

The probability that the null hypothesis is true is 0.9379, or 93.79 per cent, so this is strong evidence that the numbers are uniformly distributed.

The runs test

The goodness-of-fit test simply tests whether the data taken as a whole is uniform. The data could pass this test yet not be random. For example, we could find that the data follows a sequence such as 0.0, 0.1, 0.2, 0.3, 0.4, 0.5, 0.6, 0.7, 0.8, 0.9, 0.8, 0.7, 0.6, 0.5, 0.4, 0.3, 0.2, 0.1 . . . This is clearly not a random sequence.

There is a pattern in this case, which is a long upward cycle or run of numbers, followed by a long downward run of numbers. We would normally expect that a random sequence of numbers would give us runs of varying length and the number of runs over the sequence would be neither too large nor too small. It can be shown that the mean number of runs in a sequence of N random numbers is:

$$\mu = \frac{2N - 1}{3}$$

and a standard deviation of

$$\sigma = \frac{16N - 29}{90}$$

Table 7.3 ■ Demonstration of the runs test

0.0052
0.3562
0.4550+
0.4485–
0.8613+
0.1534
0.0547–
0.4119
0.4747+
0.4292–
0.9981+
0.9113
0.0598–
0.2067
0.7168+
0.6505
0.0098–
0.2939
0.3262+
0.1646–

For a large sample of numbers (at least twenty), the distribution of the number of runs is approximately normal. We can therefore use the normal distribution to test to see if the observed number of runs is significantly different to the expected number of runs. To illustrate the *runs test*, we shall take twenty of the 1000 random numbers already generated. These numbers are shown in Table 7.3 where it can be seen that the first three numbers are increasing; that is, they are showing an upward run, so a + is placed alongside the third number. The next number, 0.4485, is a decrease or a downward run and a − is put alongside it. The number 0.8613 is an upward run, while 0.1534 and 0.0547 are both downward, and so on.

The number of runs in Table 7.3 is twelve, but the expected number of runs should be

$$\mu = \frac{2 \times 20 - 1}{3} = 13$$

with a standard deviation of:

$$\sigma = \sqrt{\frac{16 \times 20 - 29}{90}} = 1.798$$

The null and alternative hypotheses are:

H_0: $\mu = 13$ H1: $\mu \neq 13$

The Z-score is:

$$Z = \frac{12 - 13}{1.798} = -0.556$$

Figure 7.3 shows that the value of −0.556 is not in the critical region of the standard normal distribution, so the null hypothesis cannot be rejected. The sequence of the twenty numbers therefore passes the runs test.

The runs can also be tested against the mean. That is, each number is compared with the mean of the data. A sequence of numbers above the mean is an upward run, while a sequence of numbers below the mean is a downward run. This test has been carried out using SPSS on all 1000 numbers, and the results are:

SPSS for MS WINDOWS Release 6.0

- - - - - Runs Test

RNO   Random numbers

Runs: 308   Test value = .503835 (Mean)

    Cases: 503 LT Mean
    497   GE Mean Z = .4441

    ─────
    1000   Total 2-Tailed P = .6570

Since the P-value is above 5 per cent, we are unable to reject the null hypothesis. Therefore the sequence of 1000 numbers passes this test.

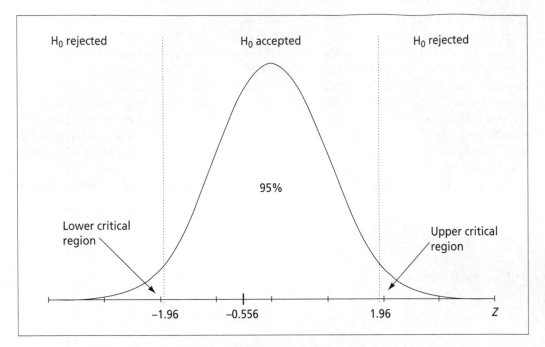

Figure 7.3 ■ The standard normal distribution at the 5 per cent significance level

Autocorrelation test

In a sequence of random numbers, we may find that every mth number is correlated in some way. For example, every tenth value may be high or the value may alternate between low and high. The value of m is called the *lag* and if we find a significant correlation for lag m, we say that there is *autocorrelation* present. This is not a particularly reliable test as the chance of finding some correlation between all possible values of m will be quite high, even for data that is known to be random.

MINITAB was used to test for autocorrelation for the 1000 generated random numbers. The output, in the form of a graph and individual calculated correlations, can be seen in Figure 7.4. The y-axis is the value of the autocorrelation function (between 1 and –1) and the x-axis is the lag number. MINITAB has calculated the value of the autocorrelation function for lags from 1 to 73, and has plotted these, together with an upper and lower limit (shown dotted). These limits specify the range of the correlations that would be expected if the data was random. The limits in this case are very narrow due to the large number of values, but all the calculated values are contained within the limits. The sequence of 1000 random numbers therefore passes this test.

The tests described above and others, such as the gap test and the poker test, are fully explained by Banks *et al.* (1996).

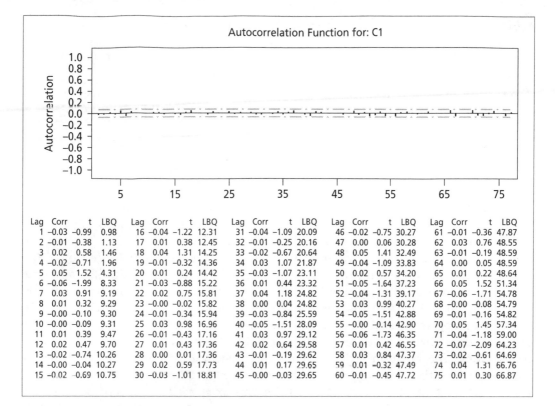

Lag	Corr	t	LBQ	Lag	Corr	t	LBQ	Lag	Corr	t	LBQ	Lag	Corr	t	LBQ	Lag	Corr	t	LBQ
1	-0.03	-0.99	0.98	16	-0.04	-1.22	12.31	31	-0.04	-1.09	20.09	46	-0.02	-0.75	30.27	61	-0.01	-0.36	47.87
2	-0.01	-0.38	1.13	17	0.01	0.38	12.45	32	-0.01	-0.25	20.16	47	0.00	0.06	30.28	62	0.03	0.76	48.55
3	0.02	0.58	1.46	18	0.04	1.31	14.25	33	-0.02	-0.67	20.64	48	0.05	1.41	32.49	63	-0.01	-0.19	48.59
4	-0.02	-0.71	1.96	19	-0.01	-0.32	14.36	34	0.03	1.07	21.87	49	-0.04	-1.09	33.83	64	0.00	0.05	48.59
5	0.05	1.52	4.31	20	0.01	0.24	14.42	35	-0.03	-1.07	23.11	50	0.02	0.57	34.20	65	0.01	0.22	48.64
6	-0.06	-1.99	8.33	21	-0.03	-0.88	15.22	36	0.01	0.44	23.32	51	-0.05	-1.64	37.23	66	0.05	1.52	51.34
7	0.03	0.91	9.19	22	0.02	0.75	15.81	37	0.04	1.18	24.82	52	-0.04	-1.31	39.17	67	-0.06	-1.71	54.78
8	0.01	0.32	9.29	23	-0.00	-0.02	15.82	38	0.00	0.04	24.82	53	0.03	0.99	40.27	68	-0.00	-0.08	54.79
9	-0.00	-0.10	9.30	24	-0.01	-0.34	15.94	39	-0.03	-0.84	25.59	54	-0.05	-1.51	42.88	69	-0.01	-0.16	54.82
10	-0.00	-0.09	9.31	25	0.03	0.98	16.96	40	-0.05	-1.51	28.09	55	-0.00	-0.14	42.90	70	0.05	1.45	57.34
11	0.01	0.39	9.47	26	-0.01	-0.43	17.16	41	0.03	0.97	29.12	56	-0.06	-1.73	46.35	71	-0.04	-1.18	59.00
12	0.02	0.47	9.70	27	0.01	0.43	17.36	42	0.02	0.64	29.58	57	0.01	0.42	46.55	72	-0.07	-2.09	64.23
13	-0.02	-0.74	10.26	28	0.00	0.01	17.36	43	-0.01	-0.19	29.62	58	0.03	0.84	47.37	73	-0.02	-0.61	64.69
14	-0.00	-0.04	10.27	29	0.02	0.59	17.73	44	0.01	0.17	29.65	59	0.01	-0.32	47.49	74	0.04	1.31	66.76
15	-0.02	-0.69	10.75	30	-0.03	-1.01	18.81	45	-0.00	-0.03	29.65	60	-0.01	-0.45	47.72	75	0.01	0.30	66.87

Figure 7.4 ■ Autocorrelation test for random numbers

Generation of random variates

Random numbers are numbers that are uniformly distributed between 0 and 1. These values can easily be transformed into any other uniform distribution by a simple transformation. For example, if it is desired to obtain uniform random variates between 5 and 15, we would simply multiply the random number by 10, the range of the distribution, and then add 5. So for a random number of 0.3562, the uniform random variate would be $5 + 10 \times 0.3562 = 8.562$. The uniform distribution is a simple distribution to generate, but some other distributions can be more difficult. Modern simulation software packages use a number of efficient algorithms for generating random variates from a distribution and all we shall do here is look at some of the general principles. We shall start with an empirical distribution as this should help in understanding the process.

Empirical distribution

An empirical distribution is a distribution that has been obtained from measurement. In Chapter 5, we used an empirical distribution in order to demonstrate

Table 7.4 ■ Relative frequency table for the arrivals to a bank

Interarrival time (seconds)	Mid point	Frequency	Relative frequency	Cumulative frequency	Random numbers
0 to under 30	15	66	0.55	0.55	0.00 to under 0.55
30 to under 60	45	36	0.30	0.85	0.55 to under 0.85
60 to under 90	75	12	0.10	0.95	0.85 to under 0.95
90 to under 120	105	6	0.05	1.00	0.95 to 1.00

the tabular method of simulation for a queuing problem at a bank. The table for the interarrival time distribution used in that example is reproduced above. The random numbers used in this case were two-digit integers between 00 and 99, but in order to standardise the process, these values have been divided by 100.

In Chapter 5, we simplified matters by using the mid point value for any time within the range of random numbers. So, for any random number between 0.00 and less than 0.55, we would have used an interarrival time of fifteen seconds. This is an approximation as, say, a random number of 0.20 should generate a different time than a random number of 0.40. What we have to do is to *interpolate* within the range in order to get a more accurate value. This can be easily explained by estimating the *cumulative distribution function*, or cdf (*see* Chapter 3 for an explanation of the cdf). The cdf for this example can be represented by a graph; the *upper-class boundaries* of each interval are plotted against the upper values

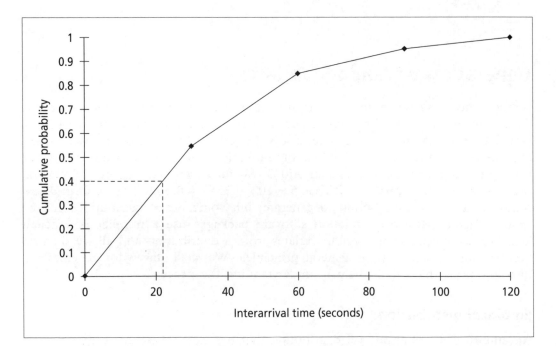

Figure 7.5 ■ The cumulative distribution plot for the interarrival time at the bank

of the random numbers, and straight lines drawn between the points. These random numbers are equivalent to the probability that the time will be less than the specified upper-class boundary. To find the interarrival time for a given random number, we can simply draw a horizontal line from the given random number until it intersects the plotted line, and then drop a vertical line until it meets the x-axis. We can then read off the value for the interarrival time. To illustrate this, imagine that we generated a random number of 0.4. Figure 7.5 shows that the interarrival time will be approximately 22 seconds.

Of course, a computer would not use a graphical method, but would have to calculate the random variate using an algebraic procedure. Since the segments are all straight lines, a linear interpolation method can be used. It can be shown that for a continuous empirical distribution the value of a random variable, X, is given by:

$$X = \frac{(R - r_i)}{a_i} + x_i$$

where R is the random number, x_i is the value of X at the ith segment, and r_i is the corresponding cumulative probability. a_i is the gradient of the relevant segment and is given by:

$$a_i = \frac{r_{i+1} - r_i}{x_{i+1} - x_i}$$

So, when the random number $R = 0.4$, the segment $i = 1$ and the calculation will be as follows:

$$a_1 = \frac{.55 - 0}{30 - 0} = 0.01833$$

and

$$X = \frac{(0.4 - 0)}{0.01833} + 0 = 21.82$$

This agrees with the graphically estimated value of 22 seconds. This process has been repeated for a few more random numbers and the results can be seen in Table 7.5.

We will look at the practical methods of implementing this procedure using a spreadsheet in Chapter 7.

Table 7.5 ▥ Calculation of randomly generated interarrival times for arrivals to the bank

R	Segment (i)	a	X
0.9981	4	0.001667	118.85
0.8613	3	0.003333	63.39
0.7168	2	0.010	46.68

The uniform distribution

We have already mentioned how easy it is to generate a uniform variate from a $U(0,1)$ distribution. To formalise the situation, we define a uniform distribution as having a pdf of:

$$f(x) = \begin{cases} 1/(b-a), & a \leqslant x \leqslant b \\ 0, & \text{otherwise} \end{cases}$$

The cdf is:

$$F(x) = \begin{cases} 0, & x < a \\ (x-a)/(b-a), & a \leqslant x \leqslant b \\ 1, & x > b \end{cases}$$

Using the same procedure as in the empirical distribution, we substitute R for $F(x)$. That is

$$R = \frac{X-a}{b-a}$$

and by rearranging, $X = a + (b-a)R$, which is the same result obtained from an intuitive approach.

The pdf and cdf for a uniform distribution with limits of 5 and 15 are shown in Figures 7.6 and 7.7.

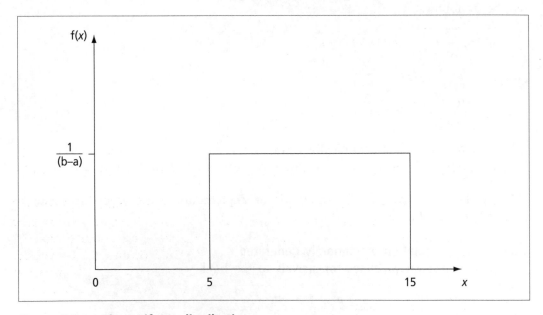

Figure 7.6 ■ The uniform distribution

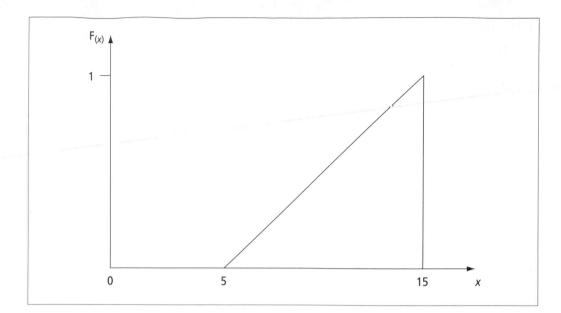

Figure 7.7 ▪ The cumulative distribution function for the uniform distribution

The exponential distribution

The exponential distribution was discussed in Chapter 3 and the probability density function is given by:

$$f(x) = \begin{cases} (1/\mu) \ e^{-x/\mu}, & x \geqslant 0 \\ 0, & x < 0 \end{cases}$$

The cumulative distribution function is:

$$F(x) = P(X \leqslant x) = 1 - e^{-x/\mu}, \quad x \geqslant 0$$

where μ is the mean of the distribution.

The cumulative distribution function for the exponential distribution for a mean of 34.5 is plotted in Figure 7.8.

For both the empirical distribution and the uniform distribution, we obtained the value of the random variable, given information about the cdf. In the case of the empirical distribution we can demonstrate the process using a graphical procedure, but in general we need a method that can be carried out by a computer. For both these distributions, we used an algebraic expression and this expression is called the *inverse function* of $F(x)$ and is defined as $F^{-1}(x)$. The inverse function for the exponential distribution is quite easy to obtain and is

$$X = -\mu \ ln \ (1 - R)$$

where *ln* is the logarithm to base e. (The *ln* function should be found on most good calculators.)

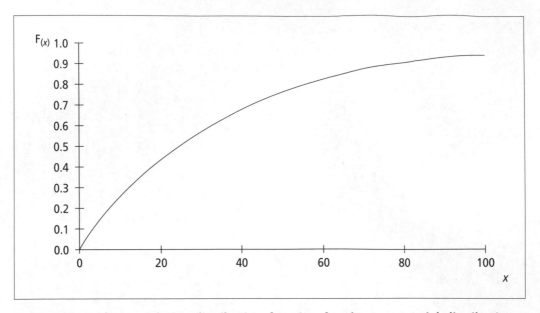

Figure 7.8 ■ The cumulative distribution function for the exponential distribution with a mean of 34.5

We can simplify the equation somewhat by noting that if R is a $U(1,0)$ variable, then so is $(1 - R)$. We could therefore replace $(1 - R)$ by R, and the equation becomes:

$$X = -\mu \ln R$$

To use this inverse function, we simply generate a random number, R, and substitute it into the equation. If the mean (μ) of the distribution was 34.5 and a random number of 0.4 was generated, the value of x would be:

$$
\begin{aligned}
x &= -34.5 \ln 0.4 \\
&= -34.5 \times (-0.9163) \\
&= 31.6
\end{aligned}
$$

A few more values have been calculated in Table 7.6.

Table 7.6 ■ Calculation of random variates from the exponential distribution with mean of 34.5

R	x
0.9981	0.07
0.8613	5.15
0.7168	11.49

The normal distribution

It may be recalled that tables are used to evaluate the areas for the normal distribution. This is because the pdf cannot be integrated exactly and therefore the cdf is not of a *closed* form. Since it is not possible to obtain the cdf, the inverse function is also unobtainable, which means that the method used for the exponential distribution is not applicable. There are, however, a number of approximate methods that can be used.

The Box-Muller method

The Box-Muller method uses two random numbers to generate a standardised normal variate. The expression is:

$$Z = (-2 \ln r_1)^{1/2} \cos (2\pi r_2)$$

To obtain a normal variate with the required mean and standard deviation, the following transformation is applied:

$$x = \mu + Z\sigma$$

Imagine we wanted to sample from a normal distribution with a mean of 34.5 and a standard deviation of 12.2. If the two generated random numbers were 0.1534 and 0.3562, the calculation would proceed as follows:

$$Z = (-2 \ln 0.1534)^{1/2} \cos (2\pi \times 0.3562)$$
$$= 1.9363 \times 0.9992$$
$$= 1.9348$$

and

$$x = 34.5 + 1.9348 \times 12.2$$
$$= 58.10$$

The central limit theorem method

Another method is to use the central limit theorem. This theorem was discussed in Chapter 3 but essentially it states that as the sample size increases, the sampling distribution is approximately normal no matter what the shape of the sampled population. If uniform random variates $U(0,1)$ are generated, then the sum of the variates will be normally distributed. The mean of the $U(0,1)$ distribution is 0.5 with a variance of $\frac{1}{12}$, so if twelve random numbers are generated the mean of the *sum* will be $0.5 \times 12 = 6$, and the variance will be $12 \times \frac{1}{12} = 1$. The standard deviation is therefore 1 also. If 6 is subtracted from the sum, we will have generated a random variate from a standard normal distribution. These standard normal variates can then be transformed into any normal distribution with a mean, μ, and a standard deviation, σ, using the transformation given in the previous method.

To illustrate this, suppose that we generated the first twelve random numbers in Table 7.3.

$$\sum_{i=1}^{12} x - 6 = 5.5595 - 6$$

$$= -0.4405$$

If we require to sample from a normal distribution with a mean of 34.5 and a standard deviation of 12.2, the required variate will be:

$$x = 34.5 + (-0.4405) \times 12.2$$

$$= 29.13$$

The rejection method

The third method is the *rejection* method. This method can be used with any continuous distribution and the principle behind this method is that a randomly chosen point in an area surrounding the curve of the pdf will either be inside or outside the area bounded by the curve. If the point is inside the curve, the point will be accepted, otherwise it will be rejected. To illustrate this procedure for the normal distribution, Figure 7.9 has been drawn. Although the normal distribution continues to infinity in both directions, the area in the tails diminishes quite rapidly outside the range of ±3 standard deviations and is virtually zero outside ±5 standard deviations. The pdf of a standard normal distribution is:

$$f(x) = \frac{e^{-Z^2/2}}{\sqrt{2\pi}}$$

The maximum height of the standard normal curve is when $Z = 0$, and this height is given by:

$$f(x) = \frac{1}{\sqrt{2\pi}} = 0.3989$$

So, a rectangle can be drawn round the standard normal distribution with a width of 10 and height of 0.4.

Two random numbers are now generated. The first one, (r_1), is transformed into a $U(-5, 5)$ by the transformation $-5 + 10r_1$. This effectively generates the Z value. The height of the curve at this point can then be calculated using the pdf. The second random number (r_2) is transformed into a $U(0, 0.4)$ by the transformation $h = 0.4r_2$. If h is less than or equal to the height of the curve, the Z value is accepted, otherwise it is rejected and a new pair of random numbers are generated. This ensures that the probability of accepting a calculated Z value diminishes as the absolute value increases.

To illustrate this procedure, we shall assume that two random numbers have been generated. These are 0.3562 and 0.1534.

Step 1 $Z = -5 + 10 \times 0.3562 = -1.438$.

The height of the curve at this point will be:

$$f(x) = \frac{e^{-1.438^2/2}}{\sqrt{2\pi}} = 0.1419$$

Step 2 $h = 0.4 \times 0.1534 = 0.06136$

Step 3   Compare this value of h with the value from Step 1. As 0.06136 is less than 0.1419, the Z value is accepted. This can be confirmed by noting that 0.06136 is under the curve shown in Figure 7.9.

Step 4   Transform the Z value into the required normal distribution. If, as before, we wanted to generate normal variates with a mean of 34.5 and a standard deviation of 12.2, the value of x would be:

$$x = 34.5 + (-1.438) \times 12.2$$

$$= 16.96$$

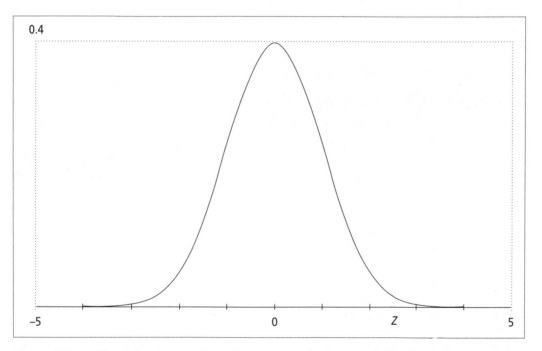

Figure 7.9 ▧ **The rejection method for the standard normal distribution**

The Poisson distribution

The Poisson distribution is an example of a discrete probability distribution. This distribution is closely related to the exponential distribution, and in many modelling applications it is usual to use the exponential distribution instead of the Poisson, except where actual counts are required. This might occur where entities arrive in groups and we wish to randomly vary the number in a group.

The probability mass function for the Poisson distribution is:

$$P(n) = \frac{\lambda^n e^{-\lambda}}{n!}$$

where λ is the expected number of occurrences over the time period t.

To sample from the Poisson distribution, the usual procedure is to use the exponential distribution to obtain the time between successive occurrences and then to count the number of occurrences, (n), that take place in the specified interval. To illustrate the method, imagine a system where arrivals to a system follow a Poisson distribution with a mean of four per hour. If we wanted to sample from this distribution and obtain the number of arrivals in intervals of 30 minutes, we would proceed as follows:

Step 1 If the mean number of arrivals is four per hour, the mean time between arrivals will be 15 minutes. Using the random number 0.4550, the value from the exponential distribution will be

$$x = -15 \times \ln 0.4550$$
$$= 11.81$$

So, the first arrival will turn up 11.81 minutes into the interval.

Step 2 Repeat Step 1 for the next random number. That is:
$$x = -15 \times \ln 0.4485$$
$$= 12.03$$

Step 3 There have now been two arrivals in a time of $11.81 + 12.03 = 23.84$

Step 4 Continue this process until the time is *greater* than the required interval of 30 minutes. The sampled Poisson value will be equal to the number of times the exponential distribution has been sampled, *less one*. This process is shown in Table 7.7.

Table 7.7 ■ Sampling method for the Poisson process

n	R	x	Σx
1	0.4550	11.81	11.81
2	0.4485	12.03	23.84
3	0.8613	2.24	26.08
4	0.1534	28.12	54.2

From this table we can see that the Poisson value will be 3, as on the fourth repetition of the procedure, the time exceeds 30 minutes.

This is not a particularly efficient method for generating Poisson variates, as several random numbers are required to generate one Poisson value. Other, more efficient methods are available, and the texts by Dagpunar (1988) and Devroye (1986) give details of these methods.

Summary

Random variate generation is the 'engine' that drives a simulation model. By obtaining values from an appropriate distribution, the variability that occurs in a real system is replicated in the model. All simulation software contain algorithms that sample from a variety of common distributions, and these algorithms are efficient in that they are fast and accurate. All these algorithms require a good random number generator, and by this we mean that the random numbers have a long cycle length and pass all the tests for randomness. All random number generators allow the same sequence of numbers to be reproduced by specifying a unique seed. The ability to reproduce random numbers is important in simulation as this allows the analyst to control the experimental conditions.

There are various methods of generating a random variate from a specified distribution. In some cases the inverse of a cumulative distribution function can be found, and this will give exact values. For functions where the inverse cannot be found, such as the normal distribution, other methods must be used. The rejection method is a method that can be used for any continuous distribution, and involves sampling from an area bounding the curve of the probability density function. Discrete distributions do not tend to be used very much in modelling. The only discrete distribution that is sometimes used is the Poisson distribution, and this distribution is closely related to the exponential distribution. The easiest method of sampling from the Poisson distribution (although not the most efficient), is to sample from the exponential and to count the number of occurrences in a specified time period.

■ Exercises

7.1 Use the multiplicative congruential method of random number generation to generate the first three random numbers for the case where $a = 17$, $m = 13$ and the seed is 6.

7.2 Use a spreadsheet to generate 100 random numbers and test for randomness using one or more of the tests suggested earlier in this chapter.

7.3 The data in Table 7.8 represents the empirical distribution for the consultation times at the Whiteladies Health Centre. Using the random numbers 0.6505, 0.3262 and 0.1646, a sample from this distribution is required.

   a Use the graph of the cdf to obtain the required values.

   b Use an algebraic method to obtain the required values.

Table 7.8 ■ Relative frequency table for the consultation time at Whiteladies Health Centre

lcb	ucb	Frequency	Relative frequency
Minutes			
0	2	22	0.0721
2	4	64	0.2098
4	6	91	0.2984
6	8	50	0.1639
8	10	28	0.0918
10	12	21	0.0689
12	14	7	0.0230
14	16	6	0.0197
16	18	11	0.0361
18	20	2	0.0066
20	30	2	0.0066
30	50	1	0.0033
	Total	305	1

7.4 Using the random numbers 0.6505, 0.3262 and 0.1646, sample from a uniform distribution with limits 3.2 and 9.5.

7.5 Using the random numbers 0.6505, 0.3262 and 0.1646, sample from an exponential distribution with a mean of 5.75.

7.6 Using the Box-Muller method and the random numbers 0.6505 and 0.3262, sample from the normal distribution with a mean of 6.1 and a standard deviation of 1.8.

7.7 Use the central limit theorem method and the *last* twelve random numbers in Table 7.3 to sample from the normal distribution with a mean of 6.1 and a standard deviation of 1.8.

7.8 Use the rejection method and the random numbers in Table 7.3 (starting from the top of the table), to generate two values from the normal distribution with a mean of 6.1 and a standard deviation of 1.8.

7.9 Arrivals to a system follow the Poisson distribution with an average of two every five minutes. Obtain the number of arrivals in an interval of 20 minutes, using the random numbers in Table 7.3.

7.10 (For the computer-literate student.) Use a spreadsheet to implement the rejection method for the normal distribution. Generate at least 100 values and plot a histogram of the data. Does the histogram look approximately normal?

References and further reading

Banks, J., Carson, J. S. and Nelson, B. (1996) *Discrete-Event Simulation*, Second Edition (Chapters 8 and 9), Prentice Hall, New Jersey, USA.

Dagpunar, J. (1988) *Principles of Random Variate Generation*, Clarendon Press, Oxford.

Devroye, L. (1986) *Non-Uniform Random Variate Generation*, Springer-Verlag, New York.

Law, A. M. and Kelton, W. D. (1991) *Simulation Modelling and Analysis*, Second Edition (Chapters 7 and 8), McGraw-Hill, Inc., USA.

Pegden, C., Shannon, R. and Sadowski, R. (1995) *Introduction to Simulation Using SIMAN*, Second Edition (Chapter 4), McGraw-Hill, Singapore.

Watson, H. J. and Blackstone, J. H. (1989) *Computer Simulation*, Second Edition (Chapter 6), Wiley, Singapore.

8

Spreadsheet simulation

Les Oakshott

Introduction

As spreadsheets become more powerful, the range of applications increases. At one time, spreadsheets were used for basic accounting purposes, but now they are used for a variety of modelling applications as well. In Chapter 4 we saw how spreadsheets could be used to solve linear programming models, using a spreadsheet 'add-on' called Solver. Linear programming is an example of a deterministic model, but spreadsheets can also be used for a category of stochastic model where time does not need to be modelled explicitly. The main examples in this category are inventory models and models involving risk analysis. Risk analysis is an important and increasingly complex exercise in business, and spreadsheets are seen as an essential tool in this exercise. Although spreadsheets can be made to perform simulations, it is much easier if an add-on, such as @RISK is used. This package allows simulations to be performed on standard spreadsheet models and also handles the analysis of the results. This chapter discusses some of the techniques used in spreadsheet simulation and provides some guidance in using Excel and @RISK software.

General principles

All stochastic systems have an element of variability, which causes the uncertainty in the real world. If we could exactly predict the cash flow resulting from a particular investment or if the delivery of an item of stock always took the same time to arrive, life would be much simpler. Unfortunately, cash flows can vary for no apparent reason, as can delivery times, so creating an element of risk in business. Models of stochastic systems attempt to take this uncertainty into consideration by allowing a variable or variables within the model to be represented by a probability distribution. As in all forms of simulation, it is necessary to sample from this probability distribution in order to mimic the variability that occurs in a particular variable.

In Chapter 5, we explained that the correct term for simulation where time does not play an important part is **Monte-Carlo simulation**. The original purpose of Monte-Carlo simulation was to provide approximate solutions to certain deterministic equations that were difficult to solve analytically. However, we will be using Monte-Carlo simulation for models of stochastic systems that are essentially static in nature. In these cases, the treatment of time is not an important issue, and it is possible to use a spreadsheet to model the process. Where dynamic systems are concerned, as in queuing systems, discrete-event simulation is necessary. This technique will be discussed in subsequent chapters.

Spreadsheet modelling

A spreadsheet has a number of advantages for simulating a system where time is not an important variable. These include:

1. The accessibility of the package; almost every business uses a spreadsheet for deterministic type applications, such as accounts, budgeting and scenario analysis.

2. The entry level, in terms of the cost and experience necessary, is low.

3. Modern spreadsheets have a variety of statistical functions built in.

4. Macros are becoming more powerful and easier to use.

5. The ability to perform 'What-if?' analysis by changing a single parameter.

6. The model can be built in a logical manner without the recourse to complicated mathematics.

7. A number of 'add-ins' have been developed that make simulation a task that almost anyone can master.

We will now look at the use of spreadsheets in the simulation of some typical business problems.

Inventory models

We discussed inventory models in Chapter 4, where both deterministic and stochastic models were developed. For the stochastic models, we looked at relatively simple models where only the demand was allowed to vary and the form of the variability was limited. In practice, both the demand and delivery time can vary, and this variability can be described by a number of different probability distributions. Spreadsheets have a number of functions and statistical distributions that allow simulation to be performed on a model of an inventory system. If we allow a variable to vary according to some probability distribution, we need to be able to sample from the appropriate distribution. The technique of generating random variates was explained in Chapter 7, and all the standard distributions can be generated using most spreadsheets. The spreadsheet used in this text is Excel version 5, but the same ideas should apply to all good spreadsheets. However, the function names may vary from package to package.

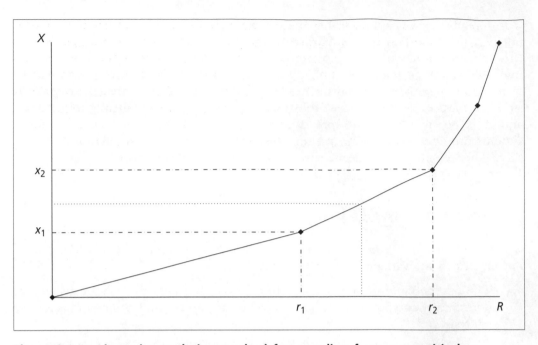

Figure 8.1 ■ Linear interpolation method for sampling from an empirical distribution

The first distribution we shall look at is the empirical distribution. Recall that to sample from this distribution, we used a linear interpolation method to obtain the value of the variable given a generated random number. Rather than use the expression from Chapter 7, we will use an equivalent expression that is more suited for use by a spreadsheet. Since each segment is a straight line, we can express the random variable, X, by

$$X = aR + b$$

where a is the gradient of the straight line segment, b is the value of X when $R = 0$ (the 'intercept'), and R is the generated random number. This expression implies that the vertical axis represents the random variable, and the horizontal axis represents the random number. Since cumulative relative frequency and random number are equivalent, we can use the cumulative relative frequency to calculate the values of a and b for each segment. Figure 8.1 illustrates the situation.

In Figure 8.1 there are four segments and we will use the second segment to illustrate the method. The gradient of this segment is:

$$a = \frac{x_2 - x_1}{r_2 - r_1}$$

and by re-arranging $X = aR + b$ and letting $x = x_1$, $R = r_1$:

$$b = x_1 - ar_1$$

For each segment we can calculate the values of a and b in advance so that the only calculation needed is to multiply the gradient by the random number, R, and then add the value of b. Of course, we need to determine the segment and this can be done using an appropriate look-up table. In Excel, the function for obtaining a particular value in a look-up table is =VLOOKUP. The following explanation of the VLOOKUP function is taken from the on-screen help menu of Excel:

VLOOKUP(lookup_value, table_array, col_index_num, range_lookup)
Lookup_value is the value to be found in the first column of the array. Lookup_value can be a value, a reference, or a text string.

Table_array is the table of information in which data is looked up. Use a reference to a range or a range name, such as Database or List.

Col_index_num is the column number in table_array from which the matching value should be returned. A col_index_num of 1 returns the value in the first column in table_array; a col_index_num of 2 returns the value in the second column in table_array, and so on. If col_index_num is less than 1, VLOOKUP returns the #VALUE! error value; if col_index_num is greater than the number of columns in table_array, VLOOKUP returns the #REF! error value.

Range_lookup is a logical value that specifies whether you want VLOOKUP to find an exact match or an approximate match. If TRUE or omitted, an approximate match is returned; in other words, if an exact match is not found, the next largest value that is less than lookup_value is returned. If FALSE, VLOOKUP will find an exact match. If one is not found, the error value #N/A is returned.

To illustrate the technique, we will develop a relatively simple model where only the demand is known to vary.

■ Drive Thru Burger restaurant
Scenario 8.1

In Scenario 5.2 of Chapter 5, we manually simulated an inventory system for the usage of tins of coffee. Recall that the usage of coffee was given by an empirical probability distribution – this is reproduced in Table 8.1. There is a slight difference from the table given in Chapter 5 – here the relative frequency has been divided by 100 and the mid point of each interval has been removed from the table.

As in Chapter 5, delivery of an order takes exactly two days. The cost of placing an order is £20 per order and the cost of holding one tin in stock for one day is 4p. When we carried out the manual simulation, we first calculated the EOQ. Using the EOQ model, we would have placed an order of 200 tins when the stock level reached two days' supply, which is 80 tins. The order and storage cost for this order quantity both turned out to be £4 per day.

We are now ready to use Excel to simulate the system. However, instead of approximating the process by using the mid point figure, we are going to

▶

Table 8.1 ■ Relative frequency table for the number of tins of coffee used per day

Number of tins used per day				
lcb	ucb	Frequency	Relative frequency	Cumulative relative frequency
0	10	0	0.0000	0.0000
10	30	12	0.1690	0.1690
30	40	20	0.2817	0.4507
40	50	25	0.3521	0.8028
50	60	9	0.1268	0.9296
60	70	5	0.0704	1.0000

use the linear interpolation method to find a precise value. To explain this it will help to draw the graph of the cumulative distribution function, and this graph is shown in Figure 8.2, where usage of coffee is plotted on the vertical axis and cumulative frequency is plotted on the horizontal axis.

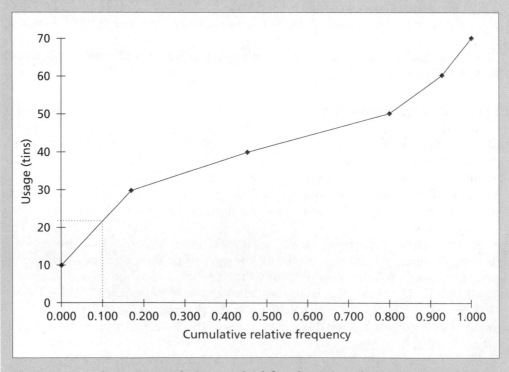

Figure 8.2 ■ Linear interpolation method for the Drive Thru Burger restaurant

From this graph we can see that a random number of 0.1 should yield a usage of about 22 tins. To confirm this using the linear interpolation method, we first calculate the gradient and intercept:

$$a = \frac{30 - 10}{0.1690 - 0.0000} = 118.34$$

and

$$b = 10 - 118.34 \times 0.0000 = 10$$

In this case the intercept of 10 could be read from the graph, but the method used is applicable for any segment. If we now use these values to calculate the usage given a random number of 0.1, we get:

$$\text{No. of tins} = 118.34 \times 0.1 + 10$$

$$= 21.83$$

This agrees with the value read from the graph. We now need to automate the process and the first task is to get the spreadsheet (Excel) to calculate the values of a and b for each segment. This is a simple task and Table 8.2 is a copy of the appropriate cells from Excel.

Table 8.2 ■ Calculated values of a and b using Excel

Cumulative relative frequency	Usage ucb	gradient a	intercept b
0.0000	10	118.34	10.00
0.1690	30	35.50	24.00
0.4507	40	28.40	27.20
0.8028	50	78.86	−13.31
0.9296	60	142.05	−72.05
1.0000	70	70.00	0.00

We now use the VLOOKUP function to find the appropriate segment for a given random number, R. The range of cells in Table 8.2 were given the name 'dist', so that to locate the appropriate value of a, the arguments of the function would be vlookup(R,dist,3), and to locate the appropriate value of b, the arguments would be vlookup(R,dist,4). For a random number of 0.1, the function would search down the first column until it found a value greater than 0.1, which would be 0.1690. The function would return the values of a and b that are in the row one less than the row containing 0.1690. In this case the values of a and b would be 118.34 and 10 respectively.

▶

Table 8.3 ■ Generated number of tins of coffee used

Random number	Usage
0.091	21
0.447	40
0.666	47
0.249	33
0.974	67

In order to generate a random number between zero and one, we would use the function =RAND(). The first few random numbers and corresponding usage of coffee are shown in Table 8.3.

Comparing this table with Figure 8.2, we can see that the values are correct. The next stage is to incorporate a re-order process. As a starting point, we could use the EOQ value, so that we would place an order of 200 tins when the stock level reaches 80 tins (two days' supply). Using the same column headings as for the manual simulation (see page 128), we get the spreadsheet shown in Figure 8.3. This spreadsheet, called SCEN8_1.XLS, can be found on the disk that accompanies this text (*see* Appendix 4 for details).

It is assumed that an order of 200 tins arrives at the start of the month and that there is no stock in hand. (This assumption can cause 'start up' problems, which can be minimised by making a longer run and ignoring the first few days. We shall return to this problem in subsequent chapters.) Once the simulation has started, orders are made when the stock level falls below 80 tins and we have assumed that only one order can be outstanding at any one time. A column for stock-outs has been added and order and storage costs have been calculated for each day. At the end of 30 days, totals have been shown for the appropriate columns. The average quantity generated over the month is 44.3 tins per day, which is close to the expected average of 40 tins. The simulated total cost is also close to that calculated using the EOQ model; the difference being caused by the slightly higher than expected storage costs.

Figure 8.3 also shows that there was a stock-out on day 5, due to the high potential usage of 67 tins that day. There is also a stock-out on day 14 and day 28. Since there were three occasions in the month when there was a stock-out, we could evaluate the risk of a stock-out as three days in 30, or about 10 per cent. The problem with this measure of risk is that no account is taken of the size of the stock-out. We may have a situation where there is stock-out of one tin several times a month. Is this worse than having a large stock-out on fewer occasions? Another method of evaluating the risk might be to compare the size of the stock-out with the total potential usage during the month. Using this method, we would see that over the month there was a total stock-out of

				Drive Thru Burger Restaurant							
	INPUT PARAMETERS			Model	Empirical usage distribution						
	Order quantity:	200			Constant delivery time (2 days)						
	re-order level:	80									
	Order cost:	£20.00			SUMMARY						
	Storage cost:	£0.04		No. stock-outs		3					
				Value of stock-outs		23					
				A. usage		44.3					
				Order cost	£120.00						
				Storage cost	£143.24						
				Stock-out cost	£115.00						
				Total cost	£378.24						

Day	Stock b/f	Order	Stock available	Rno	Quantity	Stock c/f	Order made	Stock out	Order cost	Storage cost	Total cost
1	0	200	200	0.091	21	179			£0.00	£7.58	£7.58
2	179	0	179	0.447	40	139			£0.00	£6.36	£6.36
3	139	0	139	0.666	47	92			£0.00	£4.62	£4.62
4	92	0	92	0.249	33	59	y		£20.00	£3.02	£23.02
5	59	0	59	0.974	67	0		8	£0.00	£1.18	£1.18
6	0	200	200	0.834	53	147			£0.00	£6.94	£6.94
7	147	0	147	0.523	43	104			£0.00	£5.02	£5.02
8	104	0	104	0.758	49	55	y		£20.00	£3.18	£23.18
9	55	0	55	0.494	42	13			£0.00	£1.36	£1.36
10	13	200	213	0.401	39	174			£0.00	£.74	£7.74
11	174	0	174	0.687	47	127			£0.00	£6.02	£6.02
12	127	0	127	0.555	43	84			£0.00	£4.22	£4.22
13	84	0	84	0.641	46	38	y		£20.00	£2.44	£22.44
14	38	0	38	0.425	40	0		2	£0.00	£0.76	£0.76
15	0	200	200	0.735	49	151			£0.00	£7.02	£7.02
16	151	0	151	0.338	36	115			£0.00	£5.32	£5.32
17	115	0	115	0.853	54	61	y		£20.00	£3.52	£23.52
18	61	0	61	0.125	25	36			£0.00	£1.94	£1.94
19	36	200	236	0.899	58	178			£0.00	£8.28	£8.28
20	178	0	178	0.604	45	133			£0.00	£6.22	£6.22
21	133	0	133	0.855	55	78	y		£20.00	£4.22	£24.22
22	78	0	78	0.031	14	64			£0.00	£2.84	£2.84
23	64	200	264	0.755	49	215			£0.00	£9.58	£9.58
24	215	0	215	0.414	39	176			£0.00	£7.82	£7.82
25	176	0	176	0.467	41	135			£0.00	£6.22	£6.22
26	135	0	135	0.552	43	92			£0.00	£4.54	£4.54
27	92	0	92	0.874	56	36	y		£20.00	£2.56	£22.56
28	36	0	36	0.734	49	0		13	£0.00	£0.72	£0.72
29	0	200	200	0.680	47	153			£0.00	£7.06	£7.06
30	153	0	153	0.912	59	94			£0.00	£4.94	£4.94
	TOTAL	1400			1329			23	£120.00	£143.24	£263.24
	AVERAGE				44.3	No. stock-outs		3			

Figure 8.3 ■ Printout from the Excel spreadsheet

▶

23 tins compared to the potential usage of 1329 tins. This represents a 1.7 per cent stock-out risk. If it is possible to give a cost to a stock-out, we could evaluate the effect of an inventory policy in terms of the stock-out cost. For example, if each tin of coffee generated profits of £5, we could estimate the cost of different inventory policies. However, it is not a simple case of calculating the cost of lost sales. We also have to take account of the order and storage costs, as more stock-outs will mean lower storage costs. For the present policy, the stock-out cost would be $23 \times 5 = £115$, and the total cost would therefore be £378.24.

There is one problem that we haven't yet considered. Is the run of 30 days sufficient, and what would happen if we repeated the exercise for another 30 days? The simulation run length is important, but what is more important is the effect of a repeat of the simulation. This can be demonstrated by getting the spreadsheet to re-calculate, using a new set of random numbers. Normally, a spreadsheet will re-calculate automatically but this has been turned off in SCEN8_1.XLS. To get this spreadsheet to re-calculate, the function key *F9* should be pressed. A new set of random numbers will generate a new set of usage figures, which will change all related figures, such as stock-outs and costs. Table 8.4 gives the relevant totals for each of five runs.

Table 8.4 ■ **Summary information from five runs of the spreadsheet model**

	Run				
	1	2	3	4	5
Average usage	44.3	42.07	45.70	41.87	36.80
No. of stock-outs	3	1	2	1	0
Quantity of stock-outs	23	19	36	27	0
Order cost	£120.00	£120.00	£140.00	£120.00	£100.00
Storage cost	£143.24	£146.06	£141.94	£146.26	£163.28
Stock-out cost	£115.00	£95.00	£180.00	£135.00	£0.00
Total cost	£378.24	£361.06	£461.94	£401.26	£263.28

Each run of the simulation is effectively replicating what happens in reality, as not only will there be day-to-day changes, but there will also be month to month changes. If we average the figures for the five runs, we should get a good estimate of the performance of the system. The average total cost is £373.16 with a standard deviation of £72.31.

Often, the purpose of a simulation model is to try out 'What-if?' experiments on the model. That is, we want to see the effect of changing the model in some way. For inventory models there are many changes that we might consider. These include changes to the:

■ order quantity

■ re-order level

■ inventory costs

■ delivery period

There could also be a change in the structure in the model itself. We might, for example, want to see what would happen if the delivery time changed from a fixed value to a variable time period, or the demand distribution changed.

To see the effects of these changes we would simply change the model and repeat the simulation. If we made several runs of the model, we could compare the results with the original model and hopefully draw some conclusions. There is one problem though. The results are sample *values* and if we repeated the runs, we might draw different conclusions. We should therefore compare our results statistically. If we wish to compare two sets of results, we should use the **two-sample *t*-test**. We will not go into details of the test here as we will be returning to the statistical interpretation of simulation experiments in Chapter 12. Scenario 8.2 uses MINITAB to compare the results from two spreadsheet models.

■ **Drive Thru Burger restaurant** *Scenario 8.2*

In Scenario 8.1 we used the EOQ value as the order quantity. What effect would a larger order quantity have on the results? Would the reduction in stock-outs be more than offset by the additional storage charges? Table 8.5 gives the results for a change in the order quantity from 200 tins to 300 tins,

Table 8.5 ■ **Summary information after increasing the order quantity from 200 to 300 tins**

	Run				
	1	2	3	4	5
Average usage	40.00	43.03	39.1	43.27	43.8
No. of stock-outs	1	2	0	0	1
Quantity of stock-outs	18	27	0	0	2
Order cost	£80.00	£80.00	£80.00	£80.00	£80.00
Storage cost	£190.36	£199.00	£199.86	£208.36	£202.64
Stock-out cost	£90.00	£135.00	£0.00	£0.00	£10.00
Total cost	£360.36	£414.00	£279.86	£288.36	£292.64

▶

and from this table we see that the total cost has dropped. The average over the five runs is now £327.04, with a standard deviation of £58.26.

To check to see if this reduction is statistically significant, MINITAB was used and the results are shown below:

Twosample T for C1 vs C2

	N	Mean	StDev	SE Mean
C1	5	373.2	72.3	32
C2	5	327.0	58.3	26

95% C.I. for mu C1 − mu C2: (−52, 144)
T-Test mu C1 = mu C2 (vs not =): T = 1.11 P = 0.30 DF = 7

The probability that the two samples have come from populations with the same mean is 0.30 or 30 per cent, which is high. We would therefore conclude that there does not appear to be any significant difference between the two sets of results. However, a sample of five is very small and for spreadsheets it is normally recommended that at least 100 simulations are performed to achieve stable results.

Rather than compare two different inventory policies, we might want to look at the distribution of one of the output variables. We could do this by running the simulation many times and looking at a chart of the output variable. This could be in the form of a histogram, or we might be interested in the cumulative distribution. A histogram would show us how the data was distributed across the range, while a cumulative distribution curve would give us some idea of the probability that the true value of the output variable is below a certain limit.

In order to be able to obtain a meaningful plot, we would need to run the simulation at least 100 times. This would be rather tedious unless a macro was used. A macro is simply a way of automating a process, and is a set of instructions that tells the spreadsheet what to do. Each spreadsheet has its own macro language and in Excel version 5, it is Visual Basic. Visual Basic is a programming language in its own right and it provides a very powerful and easy-to-use macro language. To make matters even easier, Excel has a macro recorder. A macro recorder records the key strokes, which then provides the basis of the macro.

The advantage of the cumulative distribution plot shown in Scenario 8.3 is that we can estimate the probability that the stock level or cost will be below a certain value. We might, for instance, know that if the cost of holding stock exceeds a known value, the item would cease to be profitable to stock. Using the analysis demonstrated, we could easily estimate the probability that this figure will be exceeded. There is, however, an easier method of obtaining these kinds of results. This is to use an 'add-on', such as @RISK. This package provides additional capabilities to either Excel or LOTUS 1-2-3, and will allow the analysis previously carried out to be done quicker and more easily.

@RISK is designed to allow users to replace fixed values with probability distributions, and to automate the simulation procedure. Analysis of the results, in the

■ Drive Thru Burger restaurant

To plot the distribution of the total cost of the inventory system discussed in Scenario 8.2, we need to repeat the simulation a number of times. This can be done with the following macro:

```
Do  While counter < 100              'Loop.
        counter = counter + 1        'Increment Counter.
        Sheets("model1").Select      'Select model1 sheet
        Calculate
        Range("H13").Select          'Select output cell
        Selection.Copy
        Sheets("Analysis").Select    'Select Analysis sheet
                                     'and paste output results
                                     'starting in cell A1
        Range(Cells(counter, 1), Cells(counter, 1)).Select
        Selection.PasteSpecial Paste:=xlValues, Operation:=xlNone, _
        SkipBlanks:=False, Transpose:=False
    Loop
```

This provides a simple means of repeating the simulation by incrementing a counter 100 times. Each time through the loop, the spreadsheet is recalculated

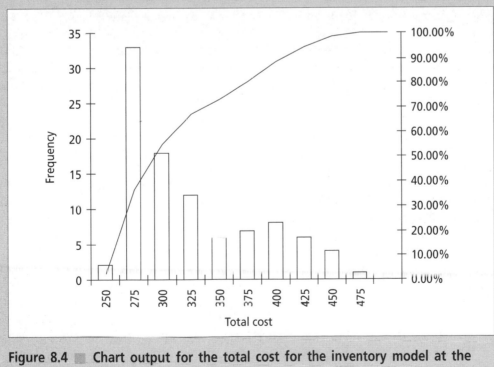

Figure 8.4 ■ Chart output for the total cost for the inventory model at the Drive Thru Burger restaurant

and the cell containing the total cost moved to another sheet. When the simulation is complete, the data in this new sheet (*Analysis*) can be grouped and plotted.

The mean and standard deviation of the total cost for the 100 simulations are £313.77 and £55.27 per month respectively. A histogram and cumulative distribution curve has been plotted in Figure 8.4 where it can be seen that the distribution is positively skewed. The mode of the distribution occurs at a cost in the range £250 to £275, and from the cumulative distribution curve we can see that there is a probability of about 10 per cent that the cost will be in excess of £400 per month.

form of statistics and graphical output, is also done automatically. The procedure is very simple; any fixed value variable can be replaced by a probability distribution by specifying a function name. For example, if a variable was to be replaced by a normal distribution, the expression would be $=RiskNormal(\mu, \sigma)$, where μ is the mean of the distribution and σ is the standard deviation. In addition to specifying the distributions to be used, the output variables also need to be specified. These variables contain the results of the simulation, and could be cost, number of stock-outs, or any other variables where analysis is required.

■ Drive Thru Burger restaurant   *Scenario 8.4*

The inventory policy for the usage of coffee is to be simulated using @RISK. The distribution is an empirical distribution and the @RISK function name for this distribution is $=RiskCumul(minimum, maximum, \{x_1, x_2,...,x_n\}, \{p_1, p_2,...,p_n\})$, where x is the value of the upper class boundary, corresponding to the cumulative probability p. The cell references containing the x and p values can be defined in range terms, so for the spreadsheet SCEN8_4.XLS, the expression is:

=RiskCumul(0,80,N4:N9,M4:M9)

The output variables are those shown in the summary box in Figure 8.3.

The simulation was run 100 times and the results are shown in Table 8.6

We can see from this table that the results generally agree with the figures that we obtained in Scenario 8.2. The statistics given in Table 8.6 should be more accurate as they are the results from 100 runs. The advantage with having a large number of runs is that we are more likely to see an extreme result. From Table 8.6, we see that although the maximum number of stock-outs was only three, the quantity of stock-outs has reached 82 on one occasion. Since the average value of the stock-out is only 13.89, large values must be rare. To demonstrate this, we could get @RISK to plot this output variable. A histogram and a cumulative distribution curve are shown in Figures 8.5 and 8.6.

Table 8.6 ■ Results from the @RISK simulation

Simulation Results for SCEN8_4.XLS
Iterations = 100
Simulations = 1
# Input Variables = 30
# Output Variables = 7
Sampling Type = Monte Carlo
Runtime = 00:00:21
Summary Statistics

Cell	Name	Minimum	Mean	Maximum
I7	No. stock-outs	0	1.09	3
I8	Quantity of stock-outs	0	13.89	82
I9	Av. usage	34.47	41.52	47.4
I10	Order cost	£100	£120.6	£140
I11	Storage cost	£132.48	£145.20	£163.7
I12	Stock-out cost	£0	£69.45	£410
I13	Total cost	£258.88	£335.25	£668.8

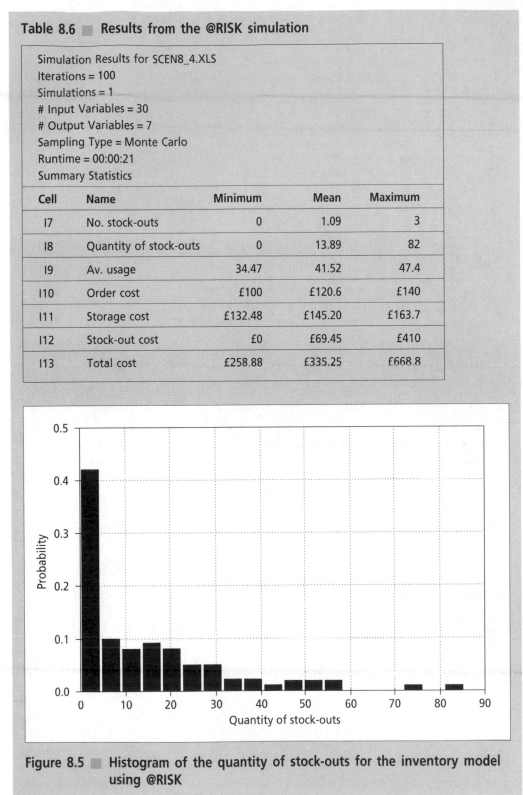

Figure 8.5 ■ Histogram of the quantity of stock-outs for the inventory model using @RISK

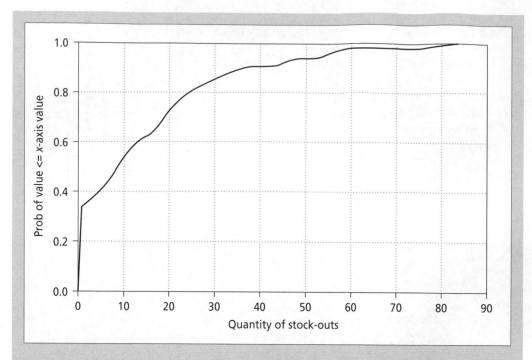

Figure 8.6 ■ Cumulative distribution curve for the inventory model using @RISK

Figure 8.5 illustrates the skewness of the distribution. Most of the time there were none or few stock-outs but occasionally the quantity of stock-outs exceeded 50 per month. This can be put into perspective by looking at Figure 8.6. From this graph we can see that the probability that the quantity of stock-outs is less than 50 is about 0.95, so the probability that a value of 50 is exceeded is around 0.05 or 5 per cent. We can also use Figure 8.6 to deduce that the value of the stock-outs will be less than about 8 on 50 per cent of occasions. This of course is the median of the distribution.

The advantage of using a package like @RISK is that most of the procedures for incorporating probability distributions and for running the simulations are automatic. We could easily replace the fixed delivery time of two days with a probability distribution. Imagine that the delivery time could vary from one to five days according to the discrete probability distribution shown in Table 8.7.

This table shows that there is a 30 per cent chance that the delivery time could be greater than two days. To incorporate this distribution into our simulation, we need to have a column for delivery time and a column that specifies the delivery day. The amended spreadsheet is shown in Figure 8.7.

Although the spreadsheet appears to generate a new order frequently, this order is ignored if the previous order has not yet arrived. So in the example shown, we can see that new orders arrived on days 1, 6, 10, 15, 18, 24 and 30.

				Drive Thru Burger Restaurant						
	INPUT PARAMETERS			Model 2	Empirical usage distribution					
	Order quantity:		200		Variable delivery time					
	re-order level:		80							
	Order cost:		£20.00				SUMMARY			
	Storage cost:		£0.04			No. stock-outs		4		
						Quantity of stock-outs		54		
	Delivery data					Av. usage		42.67		
	Days	Prob.				Order cost		£280.00		
	1	0.3				Storage cost		£131.88		
	2	0.4				Stock-out cost		£270.00		
	3	0.15				Total cost		£681.88		
	4	0.1								
	5	0.05								

Day	Stock b/f	Order	Stock available	Quantity	Stock c/f	Order made	Delivery time	Delivery day	Stock out	
1	0	200	200	47	153		0	1		
2	153	0	153	39	114		0	2		
3	114	0	114	33	81		0	3		
4	81	0	81	45	36	y	2	6		
5	36	0	36	46	0	y	2	6	10	
6	0	200	200	63	137		0	6		
7	137	0	137	68	69	y	3	10		
8	69	0	69	56	13	y	3	10		
9	13	0	13	43	0	y	3	10	30	
10	0	200	200	39	161		0	10		
11	161	0	161	35	126		0	11		
12	126	0	126	41	85		0	12		
13	85	0	85	45	40	y	2	15		
14	40	0	40	48	0	y	1	15	8	
15	0	200	200	49	151		0	15		
16	151	0	151	33	118		0	16		
17	118	0	118	50	68	y	1	18		
18	68	200	268	38	230		0	18		
19	230	0	230	43	187		0	19		
20	187	0	187	45	142		0	20		
21	142	0	142	41	101		0	21		
22	101	0	101	45	56	y	2	24		
23	56	0	56	46	10	y	1	24		
24	10	200	210	31	179		0	24		
25	179	0	179	37	142		0	25		
26	142	0	142	64	78	y	4	30		
27	78	0	78	52	26	y	3	30		
28	26	0	26	19	7	y	2	30		
29	7	0	7	13	0	y	1	30	6	
30	0	200	200	26	174		0	30		
TOTAL	1400			1280			Quantity of stock-outs		54	
AVERAGE				42.67			No. stock-outs		4	

Figure 8.7 ■ The spreadsheet model using @RISK

►

Table 8.7 ■ Distribution of delivery times

Days	Probability
1	0.3
2	0.4
3	0.15
4	0.1
5	0.05

Table 8.8 ■ Results for the inventory model with variable delivery time

Simulation Results for SCEN8_4.XLS
Iterations = 100
Simulations = 1
# Input Variables = 60
# Output Variables = 7
Sampling Type = Monte Carlo
Runtime = 00:00:53
Summary Statistics

Cell	Name	Minimum	Mean	Maximum
I7	No. stock-outs	0	3.1	9
I8	Quantity of stock-outs	0	88.92	262
I9	Av. usage	34.77	41.21	45.2

This corresponded to delivery times from one to four days. A delivery time of two days was most common, which is not surprising since this had the highest probability.

Using this model, the simulation was repeated another 100 times and some of the results obtained can be seen in Table 8.8. Notice that the mean quantity of stock-outs has increased from 13.89 to 88.92. This is a very large change, which has been caused by the variability in the delivery time. Figures 8.8 and 8.9 allow us to see this increase more clearly. Comparing the two histograms, we see that the distribution has become less skewed, with a higher proportion of values in the upper ranges. From Figure 8.9 we can see the probability that the quantity of the stock-outs will exceed 50 during the month has changed from 0.05 to 0.62. The median has also increased from eight to about 80 tins, a ten-fold increase.

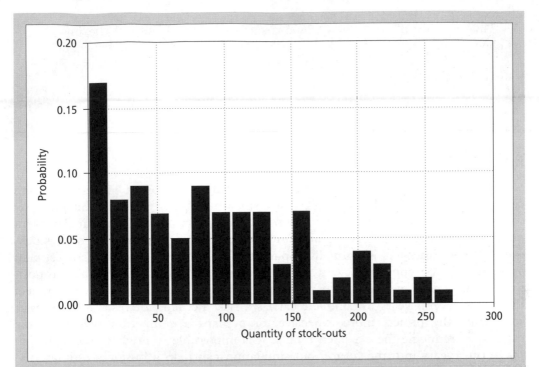

Figure 8.8 ■ **Histogram for the inventory model with variable delivery times**

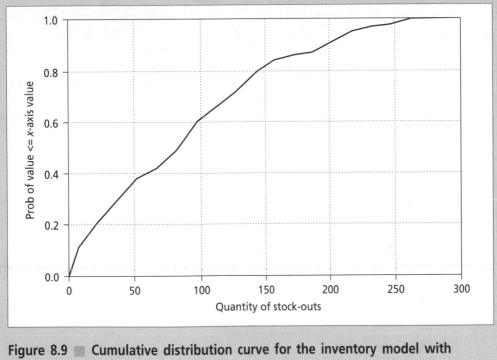

Figure 8.9 ■ Cumulative distribution curve for the inventory model with variable delivery times

▶

This number of stock-outs would probably be too high and the inventory policy would need changing. The simulation could be repeated for changes in the order quantity or for changes in the re-order level. These are left as exercises for the reader.

Risk analysis

As we have seen in the previous section, the simulation of an inventory system can be used to obtain the probability of a stock-out. When used for this purpose, we say that we are using the simulation to evaluate the risk of a particular event occurring. In the inventory example, we were referring to the risk of a stock-out, but **risk analysis** is normally applied to **investment appraisal**. Investment appraisal can be concerned with deciding whether a project is a viable proposition, or it can be used in choosing between two or more projects. Any project that takes several years to complete carries a risk. Perhaps interest rates will rise, so making the project more expensive, or perhaps a competitor will enter the market, so reducing the expected profits. It is impossible to predict outcomes that may occur years into the future, but simulation can help a business estimate the risks of failure.

Spreadsheet simulation can be useful here as it is possible to simulate the life of the project and to determine the **present value** of the income received. Present value is a method of discounting future sums of money. We need to discount these future amounts because money in the future is not worth as much as the same amount of money available now. We might say that £1000 to be paid in a year's time is only worth £950 now, because that is the amount of interest we would have lost by not having the money now. To calculate the present value of a future sum of money we usually apply a *discount* rate to the money. (This discount rate will vary from company to company and it is usually connected to the opportunity cost of the capital being invested.)

The formula for present value (P_0) is

$$P_0 = P_n \frac{1}{\left(1 + \dfrac{r}{100}\right)^n}$$

where P_n is the amount of money in n years time and r is the discount rate (as a percentage). So, if the discount rate was 12 per cent and we wanted to find the present value of £1000 in 5 years' time, the calculation would be:

$$P_0 = 1000 \times \frac{1}{(1 + 0.12)^5}$$

$$= 1000 \times 0.5674$$

$$= £567.43$$

The value 0.5674 is the *discount factor* for this problem and can also be obtained from tables.

Most projects involve some capital expenditure at the start of the project and, hopefully, produce income in future years. A project would only be viable if the **net present value (NPV)** of all cash flows is positive; that is, the income exceeds the expenditure. To determine the net present value we subtract the initial expenditure from the discounted net cash flows. This is quite an easy task, but this assumes that there is no uncertainty about these future sums of money. To try and estimate the risk that a project will generate a negative NPV, we need to repeat the calculations many times with different estimates of the cash flows. The easiest method of doing this is through a spreadsheet.

A spreadsheet has a number of financial functions already built in, and these, together with @RISK, can enable the simulations to be performed easily. In Excel, the function name to calculate the NPV is $= NPV(rate, x_1, x_2, ..., x_n)$, where *rate* is the discount rate and x is the net income for each of n years. @RISK has two methods of sampling, the first is the Monte-Carlo method and the second is the **Latin Hypercube method**. The disadvantage with the Monte-Carlo method is that there is a chance that part of the cumulative density function (cdf) will not be sampled. This chance increases if the number of simulations is small, which may be the case with some spreadsheet simulation models. The Latin Hypercube method ensures that all the distribution is sampled, by dividing the cdf into the same number of intervals as the number of times that the spreadsheet is to be simulated. The order in which intervals are sampled is random, and once an interval has been sampled, it will not be sampled again. Where relatively few values are sampled, this can ensure that the sampled values are a closer match to the actual distribution. This method is recommended by @RISK as it takes less runs of the simulation to achieve stable results. @RISK measures stability of results using three convergence measures. These are the percentiles, the mean and the standard deviation. The results are deemed stable when the percentage change in these measures falls below some threshold figure.

In order to vary the cash flows, we need to replace the fixed value with a probability distribution. The problem is in the choice of distribution. Since investment projects tend to be one-off projects, it is unlikely that we will have any useful data that could be used in the choice of distribution. The normal distribution is often a popular choice although this assumes that the distribution of cash flows is symmetrical about the mean. If there is evidence that large cash flows are more or less likely than small cash flows, a skewed distribution, such as the triangular distribution, may be more appropriate. However, all risk analysis is based on assumptions, and therefore these assumptions need careful consideration. For example, is the spread of the distribution the same for all years, or does the spread increase with time? Another factor that should be considered is whether the income is independent from year to year, or whether there is correlation from year to year. This can easily be arranged in @RISK by making the mean of a distribution the cell reference of the previous year's sampled cash flow.

■ Drive Thru Burger restaurant

The company is considering a deal with a European company to establish a network of fast-food restaurants in Europe. This deal would involve the Drive Thru Burger restaurant in an initial cost of £7m and the income for each of the five following years would be £2m a year on average. If the cost of capital for the company is 10 per cent, should it proceed with the deal?

We could work out a deterministic value by assuming that the £2m income each year is certain. In this case we would calculate the present value for each year and sum the values.

Table 8.9 ■ Calculation of present values for the overseas venture

Year	Discount factor	Cash flow	Present value (£m)
1	0.9091	2	1.818
2	0.8264	2	1.653
3	0.7513	2	1.503
4	0.6830	2	1.366
5	0.6209	2	1.242

The total of the present values is £7.582m, so the net present value is £7.582 − £7 = £0.582m. Since this figure is positive, the project appears worthwhile. However, how certain are the cash flows? Perhaps the income varies according to the normal distribution, with a mean of £2m and a standard deviation of £0.25m. We could use @RISK to simulate the NPV calculations and the spreadsheet model for this problem is quite simple and is shown in Table 8.10.

The default setting on @RISK is for the expected value to be shown, but as soon as the simulation is started these figures will change. To achieve stability of results, the simulation was repeated 1500 times. The mean of the simulations was £0.582 as expected, but the range was from −£0.828m to £1.896. The histogram and cumulative distribution curve has also been produced and can be seen in Figures 8.10 and 8.11.

The shape of the histogram is normal, and this would be expected as the sum of a number of normal distributions is also normal. From the cumulative distribution curve, we can see that the probability that the NPV will be negative is about 0.08 or 8 per cent. We can also obtain exact values without using the graph by specifying a target value or values within @RISK. Three targets were set. The first one asked for the probability that the NPV would be negative, the second that the NPV was less than £1m, and the third for the value that would correspond to a probability of 5 per cent. The values were 8.6 per

Table 8.10 ■ Spreadsheet model for the overseas project

SCEN8_5A.XLS	NPV calculations for the overseas project					
	Year					
	0	1	2	3	4	5
Expenditure	7					
Income		2	2	2	2	2
NPV at 10%	£0.5816					

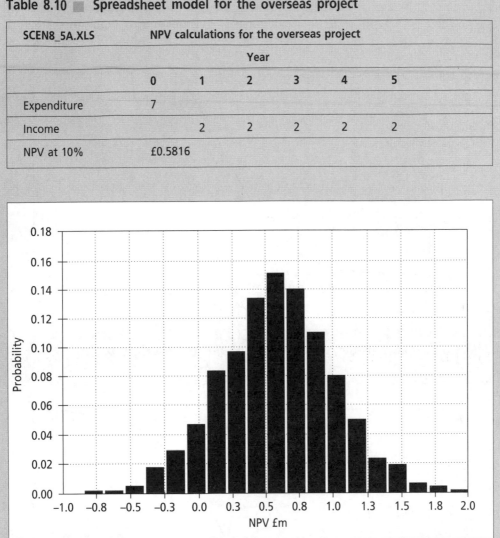

Figure 8.10 ■ NPV for the overseas project

cent, 84.4 per cent, and −£0.119m respectively. If we wish to find the probability that a value is greater than a particular value, we need to subtract the 'less than' value from 100 per cent. Therefore the probability that the NPV is greater than £1m is 100 − 84.4 = 15.6 per cent. All these values can be confirmed from Figure 8.11.

In the above analysis, we had the same standard deviation for each year. Since the standard deviation represents the spread in the distribution, we are effectively assuming that the uncertainty is the same from year to year. This

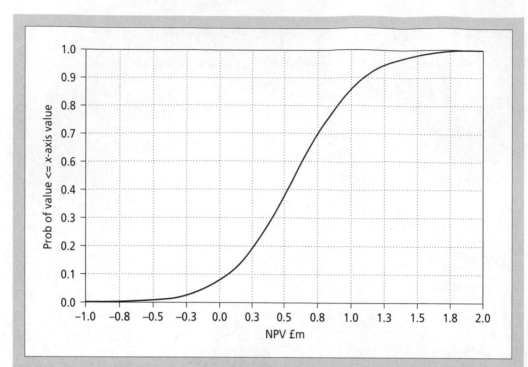

Figure 8.11 ■ Cumulative distribution curve for the overseas project

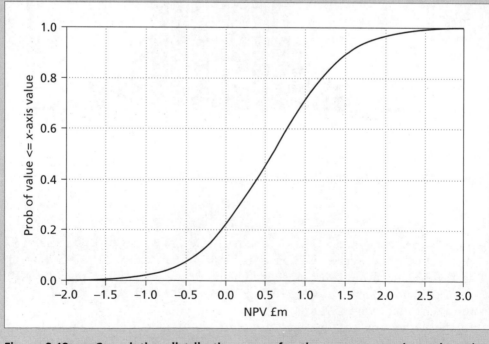

Figure 8.12 ■ Cumulative distribution curve for the overseas project when the uncertainty increases with time

is unlikely to be true, as uncertainty tends to increase with time. To reflect this idea we need to change the standard deviation for each year and repeat the simulation. In this model (SCEN8_5B.XLS) the standard deviations for years one to five were 0.25, 0.35, 0.45, 0.55 and 0.65 respectively. The result was the same mean NPV of £0.582, but the range has increased. The minimum is now −£1.668m and the maximum is £2.831. The values for the targets of £0m, £1m and 5 per cent were now 23.0 per cent, 71.3 per cent and −£0.654m respectively. The cumulative distribution curve is shown in Figure 8.12.

Another limitation of the analysis so far is that we have assumed that the cash flows are independent from year to year. This is unlikely to be true, as a poor year is likely to be followed by another poor year. To improve our model, we need to introduce correlation from year to year. One way of achieving this is to make the mean of the distribution in years two to five the value randomly selected in the previous year. So, if the value sampled in year one was 0.7, this would be used as the mean in year two. To do this, we use the cell reference of the income for the previous year. For example, the cell reference for year one was D8, so the formula for the cash flow in year two is =RiskNormal(D8,0.25). The simulation was repeated for a constant and increasing standard deviation, and all the results are summarised in Table 8.11.

We can see from these results that although the mean NPV is the same for each model, the chance that the NPV will be negative depends on our assumptions. The simplest model would suggest that the chance of a negative NPV is quite small, but the more realistic models suggest that the chance of making a loss on the project is too high to make the project a viable proposition. Of course, the chance of making a large profit has also increased, because the variability in the results has increased.

Table 8.11 ▦ **Summary of results from the different models**

Model	Summary statistics			Target values		
	Mean	Minimum	Maximum	≤ £0m	> £1m	5%
SCEN8_5A (constant std)	£0.582m	−£0.828m	£1.896m	8.6%	15.6%	−£0.119m
SCEN8_5B (increasing std)	£0.582m	−£1.668m	£2.831m	23.0%	28.7%	−£0.654m
SCEN8_5C (correlated – constant std)	£0.582m	−£4.510m	£5.025m	33.4%	37.3%	−£1.582m
SCEN8_5D (correlated – increasing std)	£0.581m	−£5.467m	£6.672m	36.9%	41.3%	−£2.552m

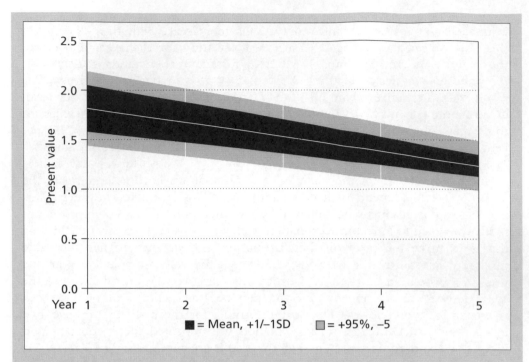

Figure 8.13 ■ Summary graph for constant spread (Model 4)

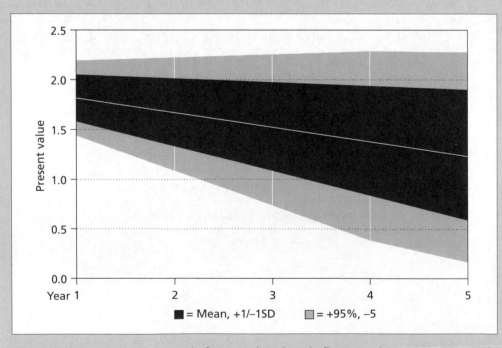

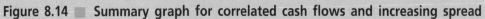

Figure 8.14 ■ Summary graph for correlated cash flows and increasing spread

Another method of comparing the different assumptions is to look at how the risk changes over time. @RISK does this automatically if the summary graph is chosen. In a summary graph, the centre line represents the trend in the mean value across time, while the two outer bands represent ± 1 standard deviation and the 95 percentile. Figure 8.13 represents the case where the spread was constant from year to year, while Figure 8.14 is a summary graph where the spread is increasing and the cash flows are correlated from year to year. Not only does this show that the present value is decreasing rapidly during the life of the project, but that the variability of cash flows is far higher in the second graph.

Summary

Spreadsheets are almost indispensable in business, and each day brings new features and products that can be added to a normal spreadsheet. One use of spreadsheets is in the area of simulation. Spreadsheet simulation can be applied to situations which are essentially static in nature, such as inventory control and risk analysis. In both of these cases, variables within the model are represented by probability distributions and the spreadsheet is made to sample from these distributions. These sampled values are then used to reduce the stock available or to vary the cash flows, for example. By repeating the simulation a sufficient number of times, a distribution of the output variable can be formed. In some cases we may only be interested in the mean of the distribution, but in most cases we are more interested in the percentiles. The percentiles allow us to estimate the probability that the value of the output is below a certain value. If the output variable represents some financial measure, such as net present value, we can use the simulation in the decision-making process.

▮ Exercises

8.1 Which of the following models could be solved by spreadsheet simulation?

   a Queues forming at a supermarket checkout.

   b The inventory model for a supermarket.

   c Forecasting of sales, where each forecast is subject to an error.

   d Movement of transporters in a warehouse.

   e Decision on choice of site for a new warehouse.

8.2 The probability of demand for a product is given by the relative frequency distribution in Table 8.12.

a Calculate the gradient and intercept for all the segments of the cumulative distribution curve.

b What would be the demand for a random number of 0.6514?

Table 8.12 ▨

lcb	ucb	Relative frequency
0	5	0.05
5	10	0.22
10	20	0.30
20	30	0.15
30	50	0.18
50	100	0.15

Questions involving the use of a spreadsheet

8.3 Using the spreadsheet model, SCEN8_1.XLS, try out the following experiments:

a Decrease the re-order level to 50 tins.

b Increase the order quantity to 500 tins.

c Make one order of 1200 once a month.

For each experiment, make twenty runs of the simulation and calculate the average monthly total inventory cost. Analyse the results and decide whether any of the experiments are likely to lead to a reduced cost.

8.4 Change the order quantity to 300 and make 100 simulations of the model SCEN8_1.XLS. Plot the cumulative probability distribution and determine the probability that the total inventory cost will be greater than £400 per month.

8.5 Amend the model SCEN8_1.XLS so that an order can be obtained the next day by payment of a £100 delivery charge. Does this significantly reduce the total inventory cost?

Questions involving the use of @RISK

8.6 Use the model SCEN8_1.XLS to see the effect of increasing the order quantity from 200 to 500. What is the probability that the quantity of stock-outs exceeds 50 per month?

8.7 Change the model SCEN8_3.XLS so that the order quantity is 500. What is the probability that the quantity of stock-outs exceeds 50 per month?

8.8 Change model SCEN8_5A.XLS so that the mean cash flows increase by £1m each year. The cash flows will be 2, 3, 4, 5 and 6 million pounds for each of the five years. Obtain the cumulative distribution of the NPV and determine the probability that the NPV will be negative.

8.9 The sales of a company (in £000s) for the years 1996 to 2001 are 500, 700, 750, 800, and 800 respectively. There is an error in these figures, which can be assumed are normally distributed. Simulate these forecasts by multiplying them by a normal distribution with a mean of 1 and a standard deviation of 0.05. Plot a summary graph and interpret it.

Further reading

Bridge, J. (1989) *Managerial Decisions with the Microcomputer* (Chapters 1 and 3), Philip Allan, England.

Dennis, T. L. and Dennis, L. B. (1993) *Microcomputer Models for Management Decision-Making*, Third Edition, West Publishing Company, Minneapolis, USA.

Goodwin, P. and Wright, G. (1991) *Decision Analysis for Management Judgement* (Chapter 6), Wiley, Chichester, England.

Jackson, M. (1988) *Advanced Spreadsheet Modelling with LOTUS 1-2-3*, Wiley, Chichester, England.

Targett, D. (1996) *Analytical Decision Making* (Chapter 5), Pitman Publishing, London.

Thesen, A. and Travis, A. (1992) *Simulation for Decision Making* (Chapter 3), West Publishing Company, St Paul, USA.

Watson, H. and Blackstone, J. (1989) *Computer Simulation* (Chapters 3 and 4), Wiley, Singapore.

Willis, R. J. (1988) *Computer Models for Business Decisions* (Chapters 5, 7 and 9), Wiley, Chichester, England.

9
Construction of simulation models

Les Oakshott

Introduction

At the heart of all simulation packages is a computer program that contains the basic instructions for controlling the way the package works. The way that this program works depends on the world view (*see* page 211) adopted, and this ultimately determines how easy the package is to use. Although it is possible to use a simulation package without any knowledge of the underlying computer program, a basic understanding of the ideas involved can make simulation a more rewarding task. It can also help to explain why some systems can be easier to simulate than others. This chapter will start at looking at the terminology used in simulation before discussing the different methods that can be adopted in the design of a simulation model. Finally, the use of a diagram in the design stage of a computer model will be demonstrated.

Terminology

Unfortunately, there is not a universal terminology used in simulation. The terminology varies from country to country and from software manufacturer to software manufacturer. This is partly the way that the discipline has evolved, but also due to the fact that there are different ways of designing simulation packages. The terminology used in this text is that adopted by many leading simulation software manufacturers.

A discrete-event model is a model whose **system state variables** change at discrete intervals of time. A system state variable is a variable within the model which we have chosen as being an important element of the system. Discrete-event models are dynamic models with respect to time, which mean that time plays an important part in the modelling process. Time is advanced from one event to the next, and at each event the system state variables are updated. We assume that nothing of interest occurs between events, and events themselves occur in zero time.

A system can contain a number of interdependent components, such as people, objects, machines, conveyors and transporters. These components interact with each other, so causing the system to change state at discrete points in time. Strictly speaking, we should use the term **entity** to refer to any object within a system that can cause the system to change state. However, it is probably less confusing to restrict the term entity to those objects that 'move' through the system. Entities can be created, destroyed, undergo delays or cause other entities to be created, destroyed or undergo delays. An entity can have an attribute (or several attributes), such as size, type of transaction or priority status, and this can influence the length of any delay. In the simulation of a high street bank, the customer is the entity and the attribute could be the type of transaction. A customer who wants to withdraw cash will suffer a smaller delay than someone who wants to change foreign currency.

When the delay can be calculated in advance, we use the term **activity**. An example of an activity is the time taken for an entity to progress through some operation, such as carrying out a transaction. The time taken to complete this activity can be found by sampling from the appropriate probability distribution. So, in the bank example, the time taken to complete a particular transaction can be found by sampling from the service time distribution. Some delays cannot be calculated in advance, and these include the time an entity spends in a queue or in a storage area. In these cases, the delay is dependent on some conditional event, such as entities at the front of the queue being served first. The *time between arrivals* of an entity is an activity, even though the actual arrival is an event and occurs in zero time. So, if an arrival occurs at time t_1, the interarrival time of the next entity can be found from sampling from the interarrival time distribution. If this is time T, the next arrival will then occur at $t_1 + T$.

Most activities are controlled by a **resource**, which is a static object. That is, the resource remains idle unless acted on by an entity. A resource provides a service to an entity and may contain a number of identical units. The number of units of a resource is called its *capacity*. If all units of a resource are *busy*, the entity requiring service will either have to wait and join a queue of other waiting entities, or it might take some other action, such as leaving (*balking*) the system. If at least one unit of a resource is *idle*, the entity will *seize* the resource and will not *release* it, until either the service is complete or unless some other event takes place, such as a scheduled or unscheduled break. A scheduled break occurs when the resource is timed to become *inactive*, due to the end of a shift or other known event. An unscheduled break however, occurs as a result of an unexpected event, such as a machine breakdown or the arrival of an entity that has a higher priority than the current entity, and *pre-empts* the service of the first entity. The sequence of activities is called a **process**, so in a high street bank, the process is the arrival of customers, followed by the service required. Another, slightly more complex system is a port, where ships are unloaded by cranes and then depart. The ships are the entities and they can have an attribute, such as size. The process consists of three activities: the arrival of ships, the docking, and the unloading operation. The resources in this case are the berths and cranes, which are limited in number. The activity of unloading a ship may have to be suspended due to the end of the shift, a change in the weather or a crane breakdown. The ending of the shift is

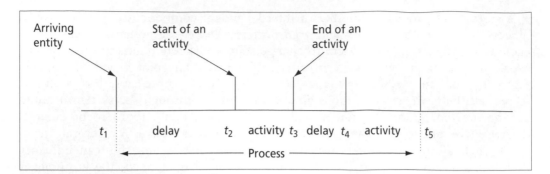

Figure 9.1 ▨ A diagram to illustrate discrete-event terminology

predictable, but the change in the weather or the breakdown is not and is modelled by an appropriate probability distribution. Ships may have to wait for a free berth or crane and this waiting time is conditional on a berth or crane becoming free.

The objects do not have to move physically to be classed as entities. For example, in a production system breakdowns of machinery may occur, which need to be repaired by mechanics. The entities in this case are the machines, even though they are stationary and the process is the activity of repairing them by the mechanic resource.

Figure 9.1 should help explain the ideas discussed above. In this diagram, an entity arrives at time t_1, which is the first event to take place. This entity may have to wait until time t_2 before it can initiate an activity. This delay may have been caused by a resource having a scheduled or unscheduled break; in either case the time of the start of the activity can be calculated in advance. In other cases the resource may be in the idle state so that the entity can be served immediately, which means that $t_2 = t_1$. Of course, all units of the resource may be busy, in which case the entity will have to join a queue. The delay caused by this situation cannot be calculated and the start of the service for this entity will be initiated by the completion of the previous entity's service. The time spent in the queue by the entity will form part of the output statistics generated by the computer.

▪ Whiteladies Health Centre   *Scenario 9.1*

The entities in this case are the patients passing through the system, and they have attributes, such as type of illness or age. The arrival of a patient is obtained by sampling from an interarrival time distribution, and the arriving patient will first register with the receptionist, before obtaining a consultation with a doctor. Both the registration and consultation times can be obtained by sampling from service time distributions. Delays are caused by patients having to wait to register or having to wait for a doctor to become available. Patients who arrive early will also have to wait until the doctors arrive; that is, the doctor resource will have to change from the inactive state to the idle state.

World views

The *executive* of a simulation package or program has to ensure that events occur at the correct time and in the correct sequence. The method of achieving this is dependent on the *world view* adopted. A world view is a way of looking at the system. We could consider a system to be made up of several events that occur at discrete points in time. An event changes the state of the system, and our simulation could model the way these changes occur. If we take this approach, we are using the **event scheduling** method. Alternatively, we could look at the activities that occur in a system, and see which activities are currently active. This approach is called the **activity scanning** method. Finally, we could model the life history of an entity as it passes through the system. This is called the **process interaction** method. All approaches incorporate an internal clock that controls the time in a simulation model. This clock will be reset to zero at the start of each simulation run, and will be advanced at the appropriate points in time. The time units used in a simulation are implicitly set by the data incorporated in the model. So, if interarrival times are in seconds, all the time data must be in seconds, which includes information on the length of the simulation run.

Event scheduling

As its name suggests, this approach is concerned with events and how each event affects system states. An event is an instantaneous occurrence that changes the state of a system. The event can be the end of an activity, which can be calculated in advance, and is often called an unconditional or *primary* event. An event can also be a conditional event that is caused to occur as a result of the current system state. There is also a start event and a stop event. A stop event can either be a primary event if the simulation is run for a specific time or it can be a conditional event (for example, stop if the queue size exceeds ten). An *event calendar* is created that includes the type of event that is to occur and the timing of the event.

The event scheduling approach is implemented as follows:

1. The model is initialised and the simulation clock set at time zero.
2. The simulation clock is advanced to the next event as listed in the event calendar and the actions specified in the calendar executed.
3. Any conditional events are executed at this clock time.
4. The current event is removed from the calendar and the calendar updated.
5. If the stop event has not been reached, Steps 2, 3 and 4 are repeated.

To illustrate the event scheduling approach, we shall use the bank system as an example. We have already manually simulated this system in Chapter 5, and we obtained a table (Table 5.5), giving details of the first 440 seconds of simulated time. The essential parts of this table are reproduced in Table 9.1 overleaf.

Table 9.1 ■ Results of the tabular simulation method from Chapter 5

Iat	Clock time	Service time	Service starts	Service ends
15	15	55	15	70
75	90	45	90	135
15	105	75	135	210
15	120	25	210	235
15	135	35	235	270
15	150	55	270	325
105	255	55	325	380
15	270	35	380	415
15	285	25	415	440

At the start of the simulation, all queues and times are initialised. The simulation clock is set to zero and the event calendar is created giving the time of the next arrival and the time of the end of the first service. In this example, the first entity will arrive at time 15 and the first service will end at time 70. There will therefore be three entries in the event calendar, these are the two times mentioned above and the time of the stop event. Let us imagine that the simulation was intended to be performed for 240 seconds. The entries in the event calendar would be 15, 70 and 240. The simulation clock is now advanced to the next imminent event, which is the arrival at time 15, and this event is removed from the calendar. There are no conditional events to be executed at this time, since there are no entities in the queue. The next arrival event is obtained, which is clock time 90. The entries in the event calendar are now 90, 70 and 240. The next event now occurs at time 70, and this corresponds to an end-of-service event. The entry of 70 is removed from the calendar and the next end of service calculated. This process is continued until time 240, when the simulation will stop. This process is demonstrated in Table 9.2, where A stands for an arrival event, E stands for an end-of-service event and S is the stop event. During the simulation, statistics on the time customers spend in the queue and other output measures are stored and summarised at the end of the simulation.

This is a very simplified description of what happens in practice, but it does illustrate the main principle, which is that the simulation clock moves from event to event. One problem that occurs in this and other methods is when more than one event is timed to happen at the same simulated time. Normal computers are serial machines and can only handle one event at one time. Therefore some rule is needed to decide on the event to execute first. On some occasions, this may be achieved using a priority rule, while on other occasions, the order is taken as they occur in the event calendar.

Table 9.2 ▪ Event scheduling method applied to a simple queuing system

Entity	Clock time	Primary event	Conditional event	Entries in event calendar		
				A	E	S
	0	Initialisation		15	70	240
1	15	A		90	70	240
	70	E		90	135	240
2	90	A		105	135	240
3	105	A		120	135	240
4	120	A		135	135	240
5	135	A				
	135	E	Wait ends for entity 3	150	210	240
6	150	A		255	210	240
	210	E	Wait ends for entity 4	255	235	240
	235	E	Wait ends for entity 5	255	270	240
	240	STOP				

The event scheduling method is the traditional approach to simulation and this is the approach frequently adopted by analysts who still develop simulation models in a general purpose language such as FORTRAN or C. Unfortunately, this approach requires some programming knowledge and takes significantly longer to develop models than other approaches. The advantage with this world view is that it is a very flexible approach and can be applied to almost any system.

Activity scanning

Unlike event scheduling, activity scanning does not maintain an event calendar. The simulation works by scanning activities at set intervals of time and those activities which satisfy the necessary conditions are immediately scheduled and the appropriate segments executed. Activity scanning has an advantage over event scheduling in that event lists do not have to be maintained. However, its disadvantage is that it is slower to operate, as all activities have to be scanned and time intervals do not always correspond to an event. A modification to this approach called the **three phase approach** is a combination of event scheduling and activity scanning, and is supposed to be more efficient as not all activities need to be scanned.

The three phase approach divides activities into two categories. These are the primary activities and the conditional activities. The three phases consist of:

■ phase A – advance the clock to the next event

■ phase B – execute the primary activities

■ phase C – scan the conditions that determine the conditional events

Pidd (1992) describes the three phase approach in detail.

Process interaction

The process interaction approach follows the life cycle of an entity as it flows through the system. This is the intuitive approach to simulation and is ideal for people with little understanding or interest in computer programming. It is for this reason that most commercial simulation packages adopt this approach.

If we think in terms of the bank example, the entity (customer) is generated and then attempts to *seize* the resource (cashier). If all units of the resource are busy, the entity will join a queue. Once the entity has completed its service, it will *release* the resource and depart the system. This simple description can easily by represented by a flow or **block** diagram.

The process interaction approach is easy to understand and is good for queuing-type applications, where an entity is moving between activities. Since most discrete-event applications involve queuing, this is an appropriate method. However, where there is no obvious entity present in the system, such as an inventory control system, this approach is quite difficult to use. In the case of inventory simulation, a spreadsheet simulation is often an easier alternative (*see* Chapter 8).

■ **Whiteladies Health Centre** *Scenario 9.2*

To develop a model of the Whiteladies Health Centre in terms of the process interaction approach, we need to specify the life cycle of a patient. A patient arrives, waits to obtain the service of the receptionist, and then waits to see a doctor. Once the patient has seen the doctor he or she will depart. This life cycle is illustrated in block diagram form in Figure 9.2.

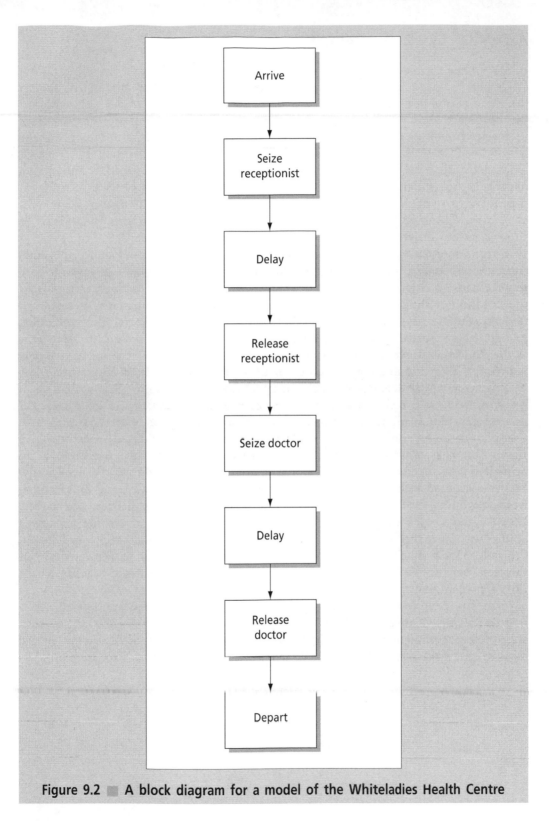

Figure 9.2 ■ A block diagram for a model of the Whiteladies Health Centre

Activity cycle diagrams

In all but the simplest of systems, a conceptual model of a system should be developed before specifying the computer model. The conceptual model will specify the interactions between the different components of the system, as well as define the necessary logic and expressions. A diagram is an important step in this stage in model building. Although a block diagram can be useful in representing the life cycle of an entity, it will not necessarily show how all the components interact. The block diagram approach is also only applicable for the process interaction approach to simulation modelling. A useful diagram to use for all approaches is the **activity cycle diagram**. In an activity cycle diagram, all components in a system are assumed to have a life cycle, and the purpose of this diagram is to show how the different life cycles combine to create the system.

A component in a system is assumed to be in either an *active* state or a *dead* state. Active states are normally represented by rectangles, while dead states are represented by circles. The difference between an active and a dead state is that the duration of the activity of an active state can always be calculated in advance. A dead state, on the other hand, is where the component is waiting for something to happen and usually means that the component is in a queue or storage. This is the conditional event that was referred to in the event scheduling world view approach. The duration that a component spends in the dead state cannot be calculated and will depend on other components in the system. The executive of the simulation will record the times that components spend in the dead state, as this information is often required as a performance measure of the system.

It may be a surprise to hear that the arrival process is considered to be an active state. This is because we can think of the arrival activity as the generation of an arrival, which takes a finite time to carry out. The time referred to here is the time between successive arrivals, which can be calculated in advance by sampling from the interarrival time distribution. The service process is also an active state because the service time can be calculated in advance, and the same argument applies to the failure of a machine or the downtime of a failed machine. Again, the failure of a machine may not immediately be thought of as an activity, but the time between failures can be calculated in advance in the same manner as the time between arrivals.

Each component of a system has its own sequence of active and dead states and the sequence must form a loop. An entity must always pass through a dead state before completing an activity, although in some cases the duration of the time in the dead state will be zero. Scenario 9.3 illustrates the procedure.

■ Whiteladies Health Centre

Using the details provided in Scenarios 9.1 and 9.2, we can easily construct an activity cycle diagram for the Whiteladies Health Centre system. There are three cycles to the system: the patient cycle, the receptionist cycle and the doctor cycle. If we first consider the patient cycle, we see that there are three active states. These are arriving, registering with the receptionist, and consultation with the doctor. The dead states of the patient are the waiting or queuing to see the receptionist, the waiting to see the doctor and the return to the outside world. This last dead state is necessary because the loop must be complete and must alternate between dead and active states. The activity cycle for the patient can now be drawn (*see* Figure 9.3).

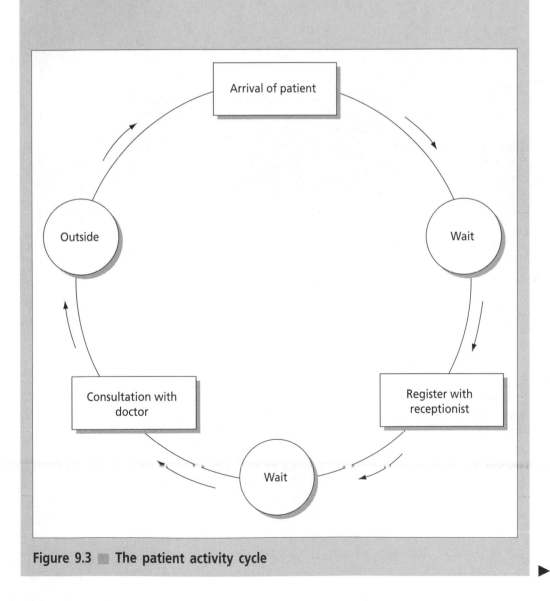

Figure 9.3 ■ The patient activity cycle

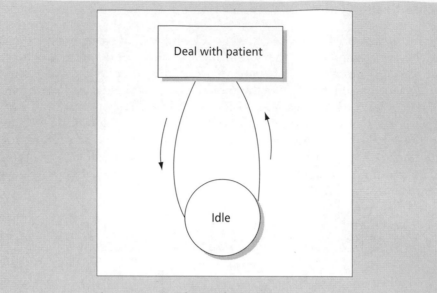

Figure 9.4 ■ The receptionist activity cycle

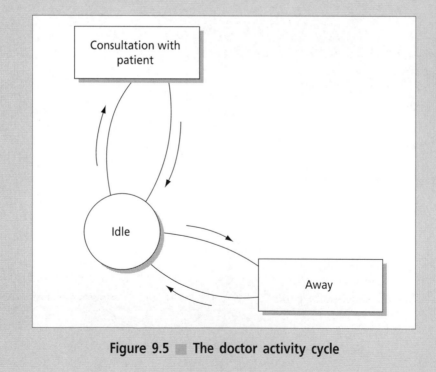

Figure 9.5 ■ The doctor activity cycle

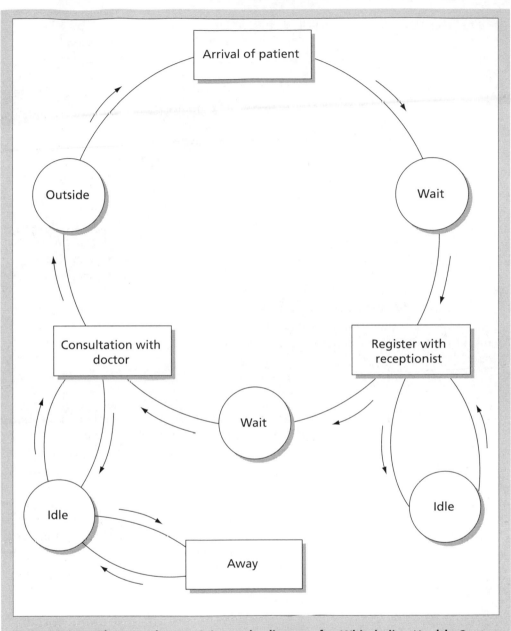

Figure 9.6 ■ **The complete activity cycle diagram for Whiteladies Health Centre**

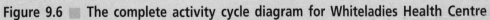

The receptionist activity cycle is much simpler in that he or she is either busy with a customer or not. The time taken to deal with a patient can be calculated, and so is an active state. If we assume that the receptionist is idle when not busy, the idle condition is a dead state, since it cannot be calculated in advance. (In practice, of course, the receptionist will be involved with other tasks when not busy with a patient.) The doctor cycle diagram is slightly different, in that he or she arrives after the surgery has opened and may be called away to deal with urgent enquires. The doctor therefore has two active states: these are 'busy with patient' and 'away'. A doctor must pass through a dead state ('idle') when going from the busy state to the away state, and vice versa. The activity diagrams for the receptionist and doctor are shown in Figures 9.4 and 9.5.

From the three diagrams, we notice that the activities 'deal with patient' and 'register with receptionist' are the same activity, and similarly for the activities 'consultation with patient' and 'consultation with doctor'. We can therefore combine all three diagrams to get the activity cycle diagram for the whole system. This is shown in Figure 9.6.

We could add further information to this diagram to help in the design of the computer model. For example, we could add information on any important attributes or the probability that the doctor might move to the 'away' state.

Activity cycle diagrams can be far more complicated than shown in Scenario 9.3, but the same principles apply. In complicated models, it will probably be necessary to break the system into several parts and draw activity cycle diagrams for each. The advantage with drawing this type of diagram is that it helps to sort out the logic before attempting to produce the computer model. It can also be a useful diagram for validation purposes. If used in discussions with the client or users of the system, any errors in understanding will become apparent. There is a simulation package called Hocus, which uses the activity cycle diagram as a means of building the computer model. With this package, the analyst draws up an activity cycle diagram of the system and then transfers the information directly to the package.

Summary

This chapter has explained some of the fundamentals of construction of simulation models. The terminology used in simulation varies, but essentially a system consists of different components or entities (in this text we have reserved the word 'entity' to represent an object that moves through the system). Entities are delayed in their progress through a system by initiating an activity. An activity can be a resource of some kind that is limited in number. This means that if the resource is busy the entity will have to wait in a queue or storage area. The type of simulation model built depends on the world view adopted. There are three such views: the event scheduling, the activity scanning and the process interaction approach. In the event scheduling approach, the model is described in terms of the events that take place, while in the activity scanning approach each activity is scanned at fixed intervals of time, and any necessary action taken. The event scheduling approach is the more traditional approach but the logic involved in maintaining an event calendar can be quite difficult. The activity scanning approach is simpler in terms of the logic but it is an inefficient method since all activities are scanned whether or not anything has changed. The three phase approach is supposed to be a compromise between the more complex event scheduling approach and the inefficient but simpler activity scheduling method. Most commercial simulation packages use the process interaction approach as it is the easiest for non-programmers to understand. This approach considers the life cycle of an entity as it passes through the system. A block diagram of the system can be drawn when using the process interaction approach and this can help in the model design. Another type of diagram that can be drawn is the activity cycle diagram. This diagram allows the life cycle of all the components in a system to be defined.

■ Exercises

9.1 An item is manufactured on a production line using two machines in sequence. At the end of the line an inspector checks the item for quality. Describe this system in terms of the entities, the activities and the system state variables.

9.2 Draw an activity cycle diagram for the Drive Thru Burger restaurant scenario. The details of this system can be found in Chapter 1.

9.3 Freighters enter a port and wait for an available berth before docking. They then have to wait until a crane and crew are available to unload it. Draw an activity cycle diagram for this system.

Further reading

Banks, J., Carson, J. S. and Nelson, B. (1996) *Discrete-Event Simulation*, Second Edition (Chapter 3), Prentice Hall, New Jersey, USA.

Carson, J. S. (1993) 'Modelling and simulation world views', *Proceedings of the 1993 Winter Simulation Conference*, pp. 18–23.

Pegden, C., Shannon, R. and Sadowski, R. (1995) *Introduction to Simulation Using SIMAN*, Second Edition (Chapters 1 and 2), McGraw-Hill, Singapore.

Pidd, M. (1992) *Computer Simulation in Management Science*, Third Edition (Chapters 3, 4 and 5), Wiley, Chichester, England.

10

Data collection and analysis

Les Oakshott

Introduction

The collection of data for a simulation model is probably the most important part of a simulation project. If insufficient care is taken over this process the whole project can be a failure. This chapter looks at the practical aspects of data collection and how to analyse the data once it has been collected. Reference is made to some statistical ideas first mentioned in Chapter 3, so some readers may prefer to check their understanding of topics such as probability distributions and goodness-of-fit tests before proceeding.

General considerations

There are two types of data required by a simulation model. The first type is deterministic data such as number of processes, restrictions on queue lengths, scheduled breaks in a process and any other data that is known with a reasonable degree of certainty. The second type of data is the **stochastic** variety. This is data that is known to vary in a random fashion and is the reason why a simulation model is needed in the first place. The stochastic data required will vary from project to project but the two main ones are normally the arrivals of entities to a system and process times. Since we are mainly concerned with discrete-event simulation, the arrival data will consist of data on the times that entities arrive. This is normally expressed as the time between successive arrivals or *interarrival time*. This data can be obtained by subtracting the time of arrival of one entity from the time of arrival of the previous entity. The process or service time is the time from the start of a process to its end. It does not include the time waiting in a queue or the time waiting for the server to become active (e.g. a server having a scheduled or unscheduled break). In addition to this data, there is likely to be information required on many other parts of the system such as the frequency of machine breakdowns, the proportion of entities that balk, the proportion of entities that fail an inspection process and the transfer times if an entity is to be moved from one location to another. Some of this data, such as machine breakdowns, may be available in the form of report 'logs', while other data may have to be collected by observing the system.

■ Whiteladies Health Centre   *Scenario 10.1*

The deterministic data collected included the following:

■ the number of doctors on duty

■ the opening and closing time of the surgery

■ the time the doctors started consultations

The stochastic data included:

■ the interarrival time of patients

■ the time taken to 'book in' each patient by the receptionists

■ the consultation time of each patient

■ the number of patients who didn't wait to be seen

Practical problems with data collection

There are many cases where a simulation project has failed because of problems that have occurred during the data collection exercise. These problems can be categorised into four types. First, there is the problem of inaccurate recording of data. Second, insufficient data may have been collected to enable appropriate analysis to be carried out. Third, important elements of the system have been ignored and therefore data has not been collected on these parts of the system. Finally, if the simulation is for a new system then the data required may simply not exist.

Inaccurate recording of data

If data is obtained from existing sources, questions need to be asked as to the accuracy of the data. Are there set procedures for recording the data or does this depend on the operator? Is the information checked on a regular basis or is it simply filed away and forgotten about? Never accept data as correct without having asked these and other questions. If data is found to be unreliable it is better to find out at the start rather than in the middle of the project.

Even when data is collected at source, inaccuracies can still occur. This can result from either inaccurate measuring devices, insufficient resources available to collect the data or an incomplete understanding of the system. The accuracy necessary for recording will depend to a certain extent on the frequency or duration of the activity. When entities are arriving close together or the process times are short, the accuracy should be high, whereas if there are large gaps between arrivals the precision can be less. This can be easily demonstrated for the case where an error of only one second is made. If the average time is twenty seconds, an error of 5 per cent has been made, whereas if the average is 100 seconds the error is only 1 per cent. Although stop watches and other timing devices can record times to a hundredth of a second, it is unlikely that we could achieve an accuracy of better than half a second unless the timing was done automatically.

Unless the data collection is being carried out automatically, a number of people are normally required for the task. Again, the number of people required will depend on how busy the system is. For a very busy system more than one person will be required for each part of the system, whereas for other systems it may be possible to use the same person to collect all the required data. If insufficient people are available then it is very easy for mistakes to be made.

The other source of error is not fully understanding the system. In the simulation of a ferry terminal we may have ignored the impact of the tides on the arrival rate of ferries. If vessels can only enter the terminal at fixed states of the tides then arrivals will only occur at specific times. If we had ignored this, our inter-arrival data would be totally misleading.

Although it is difficult to achieve 100 per cent accuracy in data collection, it is possible to reduce errors by a pilot study before the full data collection starts. A pilot study should highlight any problems that might arise and it should allow the number of observers to be determined. It should also be of help in devising suitable forms or methods to improve the collection of the data.

■ Whiteladies Health Centre
Scenario 10.2

An initial pilot study of the system indicated that the system was quite busy with patients arriving every couple of minutes. In such a busy system with a short turnaround of patients, it was difficult to distinguish patients who were arriving and those who were leaving or waiting to be seen. Since it was not desirable to ask patients their names or to interfere in the overall process, a method was needed to keep track of the patients. The solution was for the receptionist to give each patient a card on arrival. These cards were coloured so it was possible to use this to distinguish which doctor the patient had been assigned to. When the patient had been treated by the doctor, the patient would return the card to the receptionist. Using this method it was possible for one person to record the arrival times, and two further people to record the consultation times. One unexpected benefit of the coloured cards was that to maintain confidentiality, doctors were referred to by colour. So we had Doctors Blue, Green, Orange, Pink, Red and Yellow.

Insufficient data collected

The time required for the data collection exercise is often underestimated and the consequence of this is that the amount of data collected is considerably less than was originally planned. In the simulation of the clerical procedures at a building society, it might have been thought necessary to collect data at different times of the day, week and month. If time is short, one of two things might happen. Either the quantity of data at each time period is reduced or perhaps some of the time periods are ignored. Since the data collected is a sample, the smaller the quantity collected the smaller the sample, which means reduced accuracy. This reduction of accuracy could affect the reliability of the distribution fitted to the data. We will look at this problem later in the chapter.

If data is not collected for some time periods or parts of the system, the result will be a model that is unlikely to validate or will only be applicable for certain conditions. In some cases data is not collected for specific time periods or processes simply because it is impractical to do so. For instance, having to wait several months before all the data is collected may simply not be feasible because results from the model would have been required before then. Where the validation of the model fails because data is missing, the obvious answer would be to collect further data and try again. This is not always possible because the time when the data should have been collected has passed.

▪ Whiteladies Health Centre   *Scenario 10.3*

A doctors' surgery is likely to be busier on a Monday than other days of the week, so arrival times were collected for all open surgery clinics during one week. These were on Monday, Tuesday, Thursday and Friday. It is likely that more people will be ill in the winter months than other seasons but it was only possible to collect data for one week in October. Data on consultation times were collected for all doctors but the quantity of data collected for each doctor was small. Combining the data will give a much larger sample but we will then have to make the assumption that all doctors work at the same rate, which may not be true.

Model too simple

Another source of error occurs when important elements of the system have been ignored either intentionally or unintentionally. Simplifying assumptions are normally made with models since simple models are quicker to build and easier to amend. This is part of the modelling cycle (*see* Chapter 5) and most models will need to be improved before they validate satisfactorily. This is quite legitimate, and hopefully a valid model can be created that contains just sufficient detail for it to be a useful device for answering 'What-if?' questions. The problem really arises when the model will not validate and the reason for this is not immediately apparent.

Validation will be looked at in more detail in Chapter 11, but essentially it is a comparison between the output from the model and some aspect of the real system. Since simulation is really a sampling device it is unlikely that the comparison will be perfect, but statistical techniques can be used to judge whether any differences are significant.

■ **Whiteladies Health Centre**   *Scenario 10.4*

The pilot study indicated that the time spent at the reception desk was minimal and very few people had to wait here (*see* Appendix 1 for the data that was collected at the reception desk during the pilot study). To simplify the model, the reception area could be ignored and patients assumed to go immediately to the waiting room, where they would be seen on a 'first come, first served' basis.

Data not available

In some cases data is not available. This is normally the case when simulation is to be used to help design a new system. This is a very important use of simulation and various methods are used to obtain some realistic data. One method is to use a similar system while another method is for 'experts' to agree some likely values. The former method can be useful, particularly when the similar system bears close resemblance to the new system. For instance, a new warehouse may be required by a company and simulation is required to determine the number of material-handling devices for different levels of activity. If the company already has a similar system, then data on arrival rates of orders and times for retrieving items could be obtained from this system.

If it is not possible to find a similar system then the only solution is to 'guess' possible values. This 'guessing' is done by people who have a good knowledge of the business. An example could be the planning of an event that has not occurred before, such as the deregulation of the domestic electricity market (*see* Case study 1, Chapter 5). If it is required to estimate the resources required to handle possible increases in the electricity business, then some information is required on the number of customers who are likely to change supplier. The data may be obtained by one or two experts in the company, or a **brain-storming session** could be held. A brain-storming session is where a group of people spend a short time concentrating on a specific topic. Whatever the mechanism, it is important that a range of data should be obtained rather than an average value. This is because an average value will not allow for the stochastic nature of the system to be simulated. Although a range for the variable is not perfect, we shall see later that this range can be used in the form of a simple distribution.

Interpreting stochastic data

By its very nature, stochastic data contains a high degree of variability. This variability can be described in a number of ways. Statistical measures such as means and standard deviations can be found to represent the data, while histograms, box plots and other charts and diagrams can be used to show the *distribution* of the data. We will see later in this chapter how important it is to understand how our data is distributed.

Statistical measures

It is always a good idea to summarise the data that has been collected. This will give a 'feel' for the data and may provide evidence that there are some problems with the data collection procedures. The two most important measures are the mean and the spread of the data. The standard deviation is the universally preferred measure of spread and will indicate the amount of variability in the variable being measured. An excessively large standard deviation could indicate either that there are errors in the data or that there are other factors present that have not been taken into account. There is no point in proceeding with the project if there are serious doubts about the validity of the data.

■ **Whiteladies Health Centre**   *Scenario 10.5*

Statistical measures for the interarrival time data for each day are shown in Table 10.1.

Table 10.1 ■ **Statistical summary for the interarrival time data**

	Number of arrivals	Mean (minutes)	Standard deviation (minutes)
Monday	99	1.37	1.53
Tuesday	74	2.0	2.36
Thursday	68	2.04	1.92
Friday	61	2.23	2.48

The mean for Monday is smaller than the other three days, which suggests that Mondays are busier. This is confirmed by the larger number of arrivals for Mondays. Since the means for Tuesday, Thursday and Friday are similar it may be possible to combine the data for these days. The importance of this is that only two simulation models are required; one for Mondays and one for all other days. The combined statistics are shown in Table 10.2.

Table 10.2 ■ **Statistical summary for the interarrival time data when days are combined**

	Number of arrivals	Mean (minutes)	Standard deviation (minutes)
Monday	99	1.37	1.53
Tuesday, Thursday and Friday combined	203	2.08	2.25

▶

A similar analysis has been carried out for consultation times, which is shown in Table 10.3.

Table 10.4 ■ Statistical summary for the consultation time data

Doctor	Number of patients	Mean (minutes)	Standard deviation (minutes)
Blue	62	5.58	3.55
Green	48	5.48	2.83
Orange	45	6.21	4.88
Pink	56	7.36	3.86
Red	48	8.07	7.02
Yellow	46	6.74	3.83

These figures suggest that Doctor Green has the smallest average consultation time while Doctor Red has the largest. However, the standard deviations for all the doctors are quite large, particularly for Doctor Red, so it may be justifiable to combine the data for all doctors. If this is done the model is made considerably simpler since it will not be necessary to distinguish between doctors. If the data is combined then the mean and standard deviation for the consultation times are:

mean = 6.54 minutes

standard deviation = 4.54 minutes

Diagrammatic representation of data

Although it is necessary for statistics to be generated for the data that has been collected, the information that can be obtained from these statistics is limited. For example, you cannot very easily see how the data is *distributed* across the range. As we shall see later, the purpose of collecting stochastic data is to be able to define the distribution of the data. We discussed different types of diagram in Chapter 3, and a histogram was recommended when an idea of the distribution of the data is required.

A histogram will indicate whether the data is symmetrical or skewed and this information can be useful in defining the underlying distribution.

If there are several sets of data to be compared a more effective diagram is the box and whisker plot. This diagram allows the data to be summarised and can be a useful means of detecting outliers.

■ **Whiteladies Health Centre**   *Scenario 10.6*

The box and whisker plot in Figure 10.1 shows very clearly the difference in interarrival time between Mondays and the other days. It supports the earlier suggestion that the data for Tuesdays, Thursdays and Fridays can be combined.

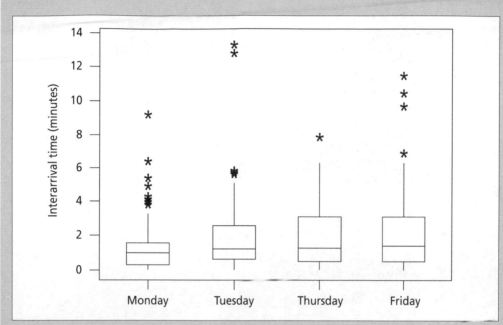

Figure 10.1 ■ **The box and whisker plot for interarrival time**

The diagram also indicates that the data is skewed; that is, there is more data on one side of the mean than the other. This skewness can be seen more clearly in the histograms shown in Figures 10.2 and 10.3.

Figure 10.4 is a box and whisker plot for the consultation times for the different doctors. This diagram confirms that there is little overall difference between the doctors, although there are differences in the spread of data, with Doctors Blue, Green and Yellow having less variability than Doctors Orange, Pink and Red.

On the basis of this chart and the comments already made about the consultation times, the data for each doctor was combined and a histogram drawn. This is shown in Figure 10.5. The distribution is again positively skewed although the skewness is caused partly by one or two outliers. In particular there is one consultation time of 42 minutes that is far in excess of any other observed time. It is tempting to remove this value on the basis that this is a freak result. However, this time did occur and it would therefore be wrong to omit it. It is only one figure in more than 300, so its effect on the model is not likely to be great.

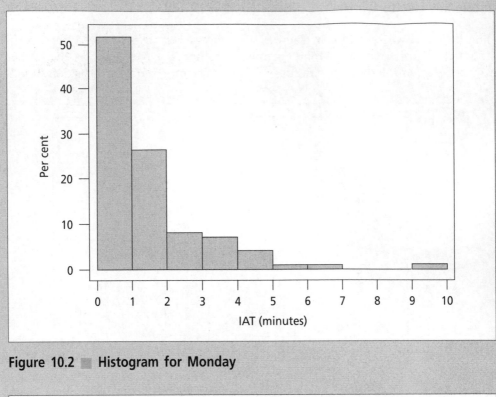

Figure 10.2 ■ Histogram for Monday

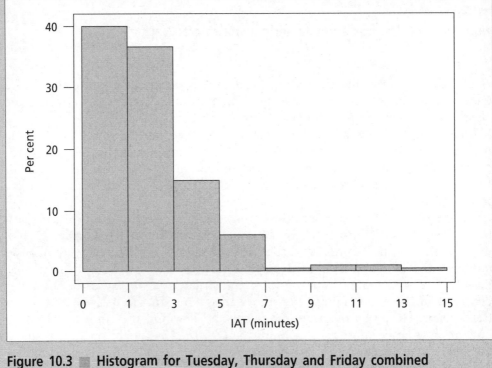

Figure 10.3 ■ Histogram for Tuesday, Thursday and Friday combined

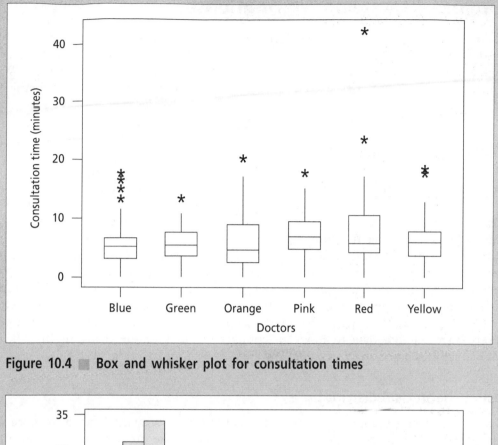

Figure 10.4 ■ Box and whisker plot for consultation times

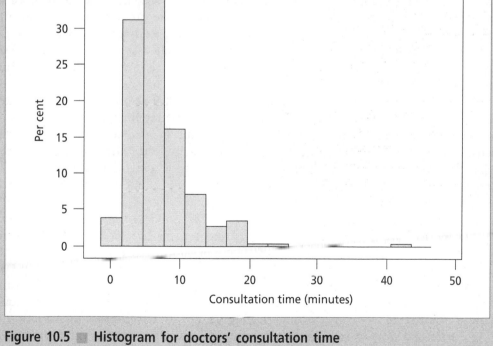

Figure 10.5 ■ Histogram for doctors' consultation time

Choice of sampling distributions

A simulation model works by randomly selecting data that is used to 'drive' the model. This random process ensures that the model behaves like the real system in that we cannot predict precisely what will happen at any particular time. We can either use an empirical distribution to sample from, or a theoretical distribution can be used.

Using empirical distributions

We looked at the interpolation method for sampling from an empirical distribution in Chapter 7. The advantage of using the empirical distribution is that since actual data is being used, validation should be much easier. However, there are disadvantages with this method. In particular, it is only possible to use values that were observed during the time that data was collected. So, if the range of our data was from 0 to 120 seconds, it would not be possible for the simulation to generate values above 120 seconds, even though we might think that this could happen in reality. By ignoring the values in the 'tail' of the distribution, the simulation will only apply to a specific set of circumstances and will not be as useful in looking at new situations. However, against this argument is the point that we rarely have enough data to model accurately the tails of the distribution. These points are discussed in more detail by Fox (1981) and Kelton (1984).

Using theoretical distributions

There are several theoretical probability distributions that can be used in place of an empirical distribution. We have already looked at the uniform distribution, the normal distribution and the exponential distributions (*see* Chapter 3). The simplest is the uniform distribution, which is a distribution that assumes that every value within a range is equally likely. This distribution can apply to both continuous and discrete data.

The triangular distribution (Figure 10.6) is a distribution that only requires information on the range and the modal value. It is better than the uniform distribution and is particularly useful when little data is available. The triangular distribution can be used instead of the normal distribution. The problem with the normal distribution is that the tails of the distribution extend to infinity in both directions, and negative values can occur if the mean is small or the standard deviation is large.

The exponential distribution is a distribution that models time between random events. In the case of arrivals to a system, the arrivals are likely to be independent of each other so that the arrival time of entities are random. The only parameter required for an exponential distribution is its mean, μ (the standard deviation is equal to the mean), so this is an easy distribution to fit. If the time between arrivals is exponentially distributed, then the number of arrivals in a unit of time follows the Poisson distribution (Figure 10.7). The Poisson distribution is an example of a discrete probability distribution and again models random events.

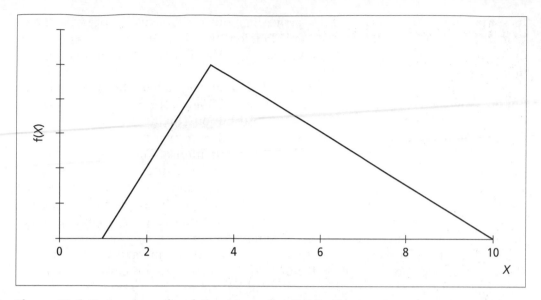

Figure 10.6 ▧ **An example of the triangular distribution**

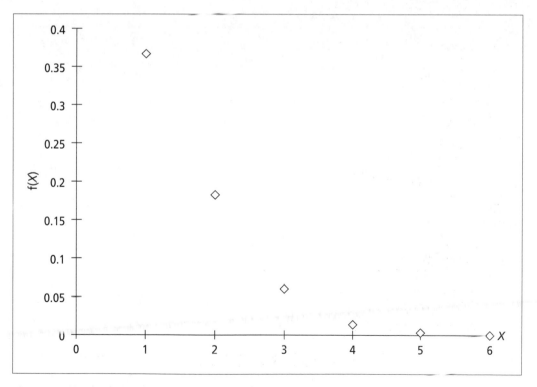

Figure 10.7 ▧ **The Poisson distribution with a mean of 1**

In some simulations where entities arrive in groups, the arrival process is represented by both the exponential and Poisson distributions – the exponential distribution for the time between arrivals and the Poisson distribution for the number of entities in each group.

Other distributions that are used in simulation models include the **gamma** distribution (Figure 10.8), the **Weibull** distribution (Figure 10.9), the **log normal** distribution (Figure 10.10) and the **beta** distribution (Figure 10.11).

The gamma, Weibull and beta distributions all have two parameters, α and β, which determine the shape and scale of the distributions. When α of the gamma distribution is an integer and is equal to the mean, the distribution is called the **Erlang** distribution. And when α has a value of 1 and β is again equal to the mean, the gamma becomes the exponential distribution. The gamma distribution is quite a useful distribution for modelling process times as well as being a better fit than the exponential distribution in some situations.

The Weibull distribution is another distribution that can take on a variety of shapes. It is used for modelling lifetimes of machinery or processes although it can again be used instead of the exponential distribution.

Unlike the normal distribution, the log normal distribution is a skewed distribution. It occurs naturally when several normal distributions are multiplied together. The advantage of the log normal distribution is that it has a long tail, which can be useful for modelling data where there are a few extreme values.

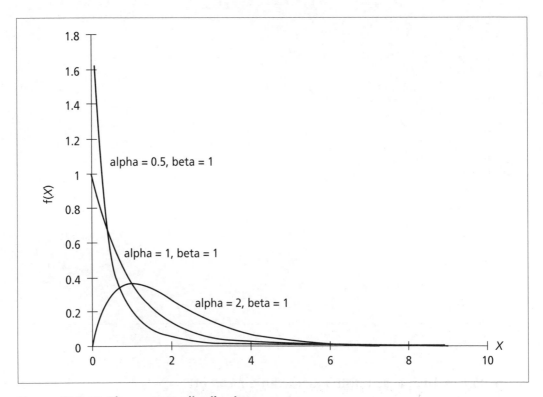

Figure 10.8 ▨ The gamma distribution

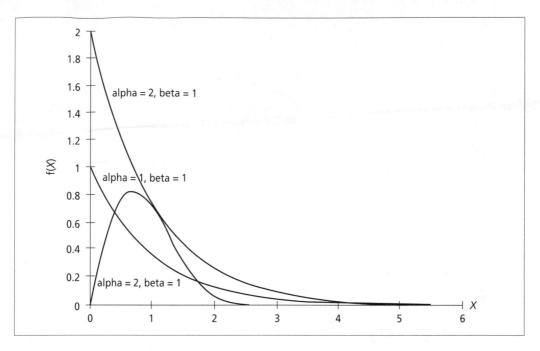

Figure 10.9 ■ **The Weibull distribution**

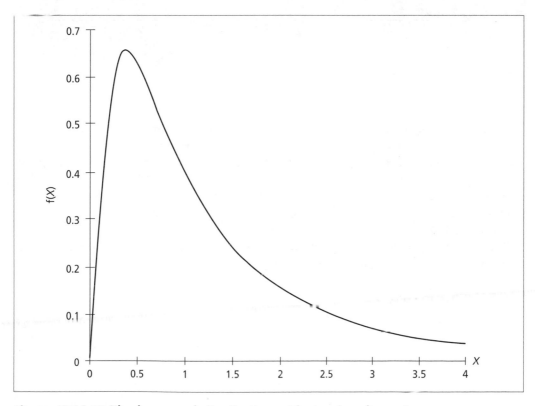

Figure 10.10 ■ **The lognormal distribution with $\mu = 0$ and $\sigma = 1$**

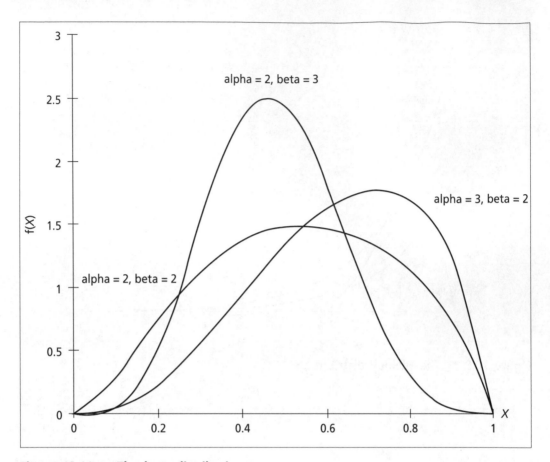

Figure 10.11 ■ The beta distribution

Finally, the beta distribution, like the triangular distribution, can model situations where information is only available on the minimum, maximum and most likely values. However, it is not as convenient to use as the triangular distribution as the parameters should be obtained using *maximum likelihood estimators*. This method of parameter estimation is described by Law and Kelton (1991) and Wetherill (1981). It is possible though to estimate the α and β parameters using an approximate method.

If a and b represent the minimum and maximum values of our data and the most likely value is m, the mean (μ) can be estimated as:

$$\mu = \frac{a + 4m + b}{6}$$

The two parameters can be estimated from:

$$\alpha = \frac{(\mu - a)(2m - a - b)}{(m - \mu)(b - a)} \quad \text{and} \quad \beta = \frac{(b - \mu)}{(\mu - a)}\alpha$$

Choosing a suitable distribution

To fit a distribution to a set of data by hand requires a good level of statistical knowledge. Fortunately, most simulation packages these days have an input processor built in so that a distribution can be fitted to a set of data automatically. Alternatively, there are products on the market such as BestFit which can be used. However, it is essential that the distribution chosen is sensible and fits the data well. If the steps suggested earlier have been adopted, an analysis of the data would already have been done and diagrams drawn. This should have narrowed down the possible distributions that will be suitable.

■ Whiteladies Health Centre   *Scenario 10.7*

Since the arrival of the patients is expected to be random, the interarrival time distribution is likely to be exponential with a mean equal to the mean of the data. This hypothesis is supported by the shape of Figures 10.2 and 10.3 and the fact that the mean and standard deviation of the data are very similar (*see* Table 10.3). Figure 10.12 has been obtained from ARENA and shows the exponential distribution with a mean of 1.37 minutes superimposed on to the histogram of Monday's interarrival time data. Figure 10.13 is a similar diagram for the interarrival time data for the rest of the week. The mean in this case is 2.08 minutes. Both diagrams indicate that the data is a good fit to the exponential distribution.

The consultation time histogram (Figure 10.5) is made up of the sum of the distributions from the six doctors and the fitting of a distribution in this case may not be so easy. The gamma distribution is likely to be a possibility and so is the beta distribution. The log normal might also be worth trying since the data has one or two extreme values. These three distributions have been fitted to the data and are superimposed on to the consultation time histogram. These are shown in Figures 10.14 to 10.16. The parameters for the gamma distribution are $\alpha = 3.52$ and $\beta = 1.86$ and for the beta they are $\alpha = 2.17$ and $\beta = 11.7$. The beta distribution also needs to be scaled by a multiplying factor of 43. The mean and standard deviation for the log normal distribution are 9.62 and 16.3 respectively.

None of these fits looks particularly good although there are other distributions that could be tried. BestFfit has 26 distributions, so there may be a distribution that was not available within ARENA that might be a better fit to the data. The advantage with BestFit is that it is an 'add-in' to Excel or Lotus 1-2-3. BestFit was used on the consultation time data and the PearsonVI distribution was fitted. This distribution is a function of the beta distribution we have already met. This is shown in Figure 10.17, where it will be seen that the fit appears slightly better than the other distributions tried.

►

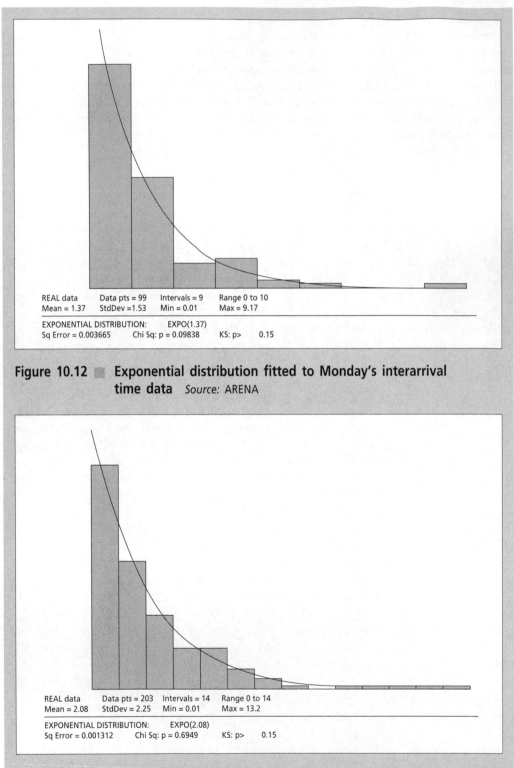

| REAL data | Data pts = 99 | Intervals = 9 | Range 0 to 10 |
| Mean = 1.37 | StdDev =1.53 | Min = 0.01 | Max = 9.17 |

EXPONENTIAL DISTRIBUTION: EXPO(1.37)
Sq Error = 0.003665   Chi Sq: p = 0.09838   KS: p>   0.15

Figure 10.12 ■ **Exponential distribution fitted to Monday's interarrival time data** *Source:* ARENA

| REAL data | Data pts = 203 | Intervals = 14 | Range 0 to 14 |
| Mean = 2.08 | StdDev = 2.25 | Min = 0.01 | Max = 13.2 |

EXPONENTIAL DISTRIBUTION: EXPO(2.08)
Sq Error = 0.001312   Chi Sq: p = 0.6949   KS: p>   0.15

Figure 10.13 ■ **Exponential distribution fitted to the interarrival time data for Tuesday, Thursday and Friday combined** *Source:* ARENA

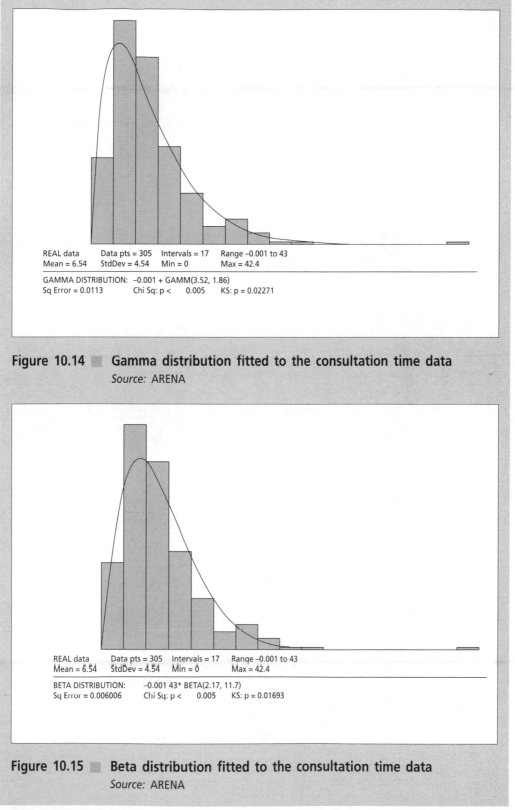

Figure 10.14 ▪ **Gamma distribution fitted to the consultation time data**
Source: ARENA

Figure 10.15 ▪ **Beta distribution fitted to the consultation time data**
Source: ARENA

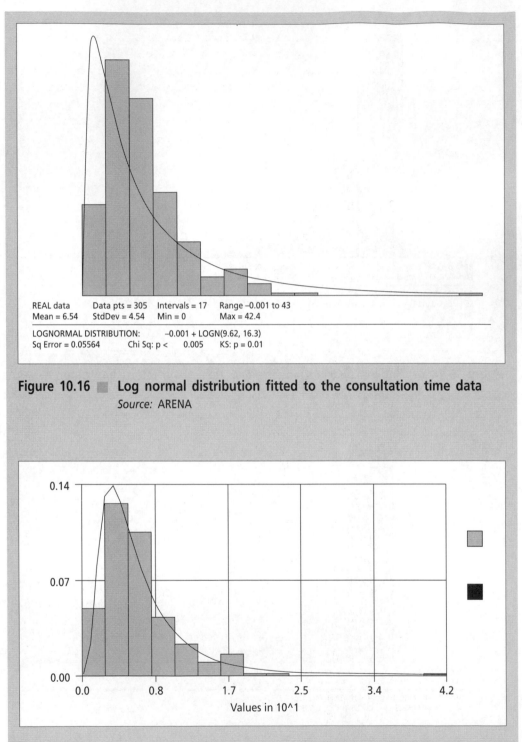

Figure 10.16 ■ **Log normal distribution fitted to the consultation time data**
Source: ARENA

Figure 10.17 ■ **Pearson VI distribution fitted to the consultation time data**
Source: BestFit

Testing for goodness-of-fit

Having chosen a particular distribution to fit some data, the next step is to use a suitable test to see how well the data fits the distribution. Packages that fit the distribution should also give you this information. Many packages will calculate the sum of squared errors; an error being the difference between the observed and expected value. Using this measure, the distribution with the smallest value should be preferred. Although this method will differentiate between different distributions, it will not be able to determine how good the fit is. A statistical test is necessary to decide this question.

A popular statistical test to use is the Chi-square test. The test was described in Chapter 3, but essentially it tests the *hypothesis* that the data and the chosen distribution fit perfectly and any discrepancy is the result of chance. The Chi-square calculations can sometimes be carried out by the software that has fitted the distribution. Both ARENA and BestFit will do this and they give the probability that the null hypothesis is true. If this probability is *less* than some specified value (usually 5 per cent or 0.05), the hypothesis can be rejected, otherwise we would say that the data appears to fit the specified distribution.

■ **Whiteladies Health Centre** *Scenario 10.8*

The Chi-square test results can be seen in Figures 10.12 to 10.16, for each distribution fitted. These results are summarised below:

Monday arrivals	probability = 9.84%	for exponential distribution
Other arrivals	probability = 69.5%	for exponential distribution
Consultation times	probability < 0.5%	for gamma distribution (squared error = 0.0113)
	probability < 0.5%	for beta distribution (squared error = 0.0060)
	probability < 0.5%	for log normal distribution (squared error = 0.0556)

The exponential distribution appears to be a good fit to the arrival process but neither the gamma, beta or log normal appear to fit the consultation time data. Although the beta distribution has the smallest square error, it still fails the Chi-square test. It might therefore be wise to sample from the empirical distribution for the consultation times rather than attempt to use a distribution that is a poor fit.

The disadvantage with the Chi-square test is that it is only applicable for large samples of data. The Kolmogorov-Smirnov is a better test although it cannot be used for discrete data, and strictly the parameters of the theoretical distribution should not have been fitted by the sample data.

■ Whiteladies Health Centre   *Scenario 10.9*

Again referring to Figures 10.12 to 10.16, the Kolmogorov-Smirnov test results are:

Monday arrivals	probability > 15%	for exponential distribution
Other arrivals	probability > 15%	for exponential distribution
Consultation times	probability = 2.3%	for gamma distribution
	probability = 1.7%	for beta distribution
	probability < 1%	for log normal distribution

This confirms the conclusions reached following the Chi-square test.

Estimating a distribution when no data exists

In situations where data does not exist or has not been collected in sufficient quantities, three options are possible.

The first option is to use mean values for variables where the data is missing. Even though data may not exist, it is often possible for an average value to be estimated reasonably accurately. The use of a mean value in place of a distribution was briefly discussed in Chapter 5. Law and McCommas (1989) have shown that this method can produce very misleading results. In order to demonstrate the inaccuracies that can result, imagine that entities arrive at a system with a mean interarrival time of five minutes and the mean service time is 4.9 minutes. If we ignored all randomness (that is, we assume that an entity arrives every five minutes exactly and takes 4.9 minutes to be served) a queue would never form. However, if both the arrival time and service time distributions were exponential, queueing theory (*see* Chapter 4) would indicate that there would be 48 in the queue on average! Using a mean value should therefore be avoided wherever possible. It may, though, be justified in situations where the variable concerned does not vary very much or is unlikely to affect the model to any significant degree. To illustrate this, suppose a simulation is to be carried out on a production system where faulty items are sent to another process for repair. If the number of faulty items is small, the time taken to repair the item may have little influence on the overall performance of the system. In this situation the use of a mean value for the repair time may be justified.

■ Whiteladies Health Centre   *Scenario 10.10*

Data was not collected on the time patients spend with the receptionist, but it was known from the pilot survey that the average time is around twenty seconds. Since this time is so small compared with the time patients spend with the doctor, an average value may be justified here.

The second option is to fit a simple distribution to the data. This requires that more than one estimate is available for the data. If these estimates are in the form of minimum, maximum and most likely values, then it is possible to fit either the triangular or the beta distribution. The most convenient distribution to fit is the triangular since the data can be used directly, while for the beta distribution the parameters must be estimated using either maximum likelihood estimators or the approximate method illustrated on page 236.

■ **Whiteladies Health Centre**   *Scenario 10.11*

Estimates of the minimum, maximum and most likely times were available for the time spent at the reception. These estimates were five seconds, ten seconds and 50 seconds respectively. These figures could be used directly in a triangular distribution; alternatively, the parameters of the beta distribution could be estimated as follows:

$$\mu = \frac{5 + (4 \times 10) + 50}{6} = 15.83$$

and

$$\alpha = \frac{(15.83 - 5)(2 \times 10 - 5 - 50)}{(10 - 15.83)(50 - 5)} = 1.445$$

$$\beta = \frac{(50 - 15.83)}{(15.83 - 5)} \times 1.445 = 4.559$$

A third option is to abandon the simulation. This is a drastic step but it may be necessary if it is important that the model is accurate.

Collecting data for validation purposes

In addition to the data that is collected to 'drive' the model, data for validation is also required. Validation is discussed in detail in Chapter 11, but essentially the purpose of validation is to check to see if the model gives results that are similar to the real system. These results will refer to any of the many outputs from a model, such as the time people spend in a queue, or the utilisation of a machine. It is extremely unlikely that the two sets of results will agree exactly and it is the skill of the simulation analyst that decides whether the two set of results are close enough.

It also requires skill to decide what type of data should be collected for validation and how this data will be collected. In some ways it is more difficult to make these decisions than the decisions regarding the main data collection exercise. This is because the data required for a model is usually obvious as there will be variables and distributions within the model that need to be defined. However, since there will probably be so much output generated by the model, some choice will probably have to be made as to which variables are most important and which data is easiest to collect. In the simulation of a computer network, both the time that documents spend waiting to be printed and the number in the queue may be quite difficult to obtain, while the total time that a document is in the system may be easier to collect. In a manufacturing system, the number of items waiting to be processed could be easily collected, whereas the utilisation of the machine that carries out the process would require more effort to obtain.

Once it has been decided which variables should be monitored, the question of when to collect the data needs to be answered. The data for validation could be collected during the same period that the model data were collected, or they could be collected for another period entirely. If both types of data are collected at the same time, the overall time and effort for data collection will be minimised. Also, validation is likely to be more successful since the simulation will relate to the same conditions. However, the drawback of this approach is that the model will only relate to a specific period and may not be so useful for experimentation purposes. As we shall see in Chapter 12, experiments are conducted on models by changing the model in some way. If we have demonstrated that our model is *robust* (that is, valid for a wide range of conditions) we will have more confidence in the results of the experiments. To illustrate this, imagine the simulation of a plasterboard production line. We may have collected data during the period when a specific type of plasterboard was being manufactured. If the data for validation was also collected at the same time our model should validate satisfactorily, but the model will not be so useful if we want to simulate the manufacture of a different type of plasterboard. If, though, we validate the model using data for several different types of plasterboard, we may find that the model needs to be far more detailed for it to validate satisfactorily. This is unnecessary if all we want is a model to be valid for a specific range of circumstances.

▓ Whiteladies Health Centre   *Scenario 10.12*

A patient attending a surgery normally wants to be seen as quickly as possible so it is the time in the queue that is the main interest here. Unfortunately, time in the queue was not easy to collect because the large number of people in the surgery at any one time makes identification difficult. The use of the card system (*see* Scenario 10.2) enabled the total time in the surgery to be calculated for all patients and it was this, rather than queuing time, that was to be used for validation. Although this was the main validation data collected, observations were also made of the number of patients in the queue from time to time and the throughput of patients during the two and a half hours that the surgery was open.

Once the decision was made on what was to be collected, the decision on when to collect the data had to be made. Since the data was being collected over a relatively short period of a week, there was really no option but to collect the validation data at the same time as the interarrival and consultation time data. As the system is relatively simple, this should not affect any conclusions made. The time spent in the surgery for about every third patient was timed and recorded. In addition to this, the number in the surgery during these times was noted. The data collected can be seen in Table 10.4.

Table 10.4 ■ Validation data for Whiteladies Health Centre

Patient	Arrival time	Departure time	Waiting time (minutes)	Number in surgery
1	8:41	8:59	18	3
2	8:52	9:58	66	5
3	8:59	9:14	15	7
4	9:12	9:42	30	4
5	9:18	9:46	28	12
6	9:21	9:34	13	6
7	9:23	9:44	21	4
8	9:25	9:46	21	2
9	9:30	9:52	22	8
10	9:37	10:15	38	7
11	9:46	10:25	39	7
12	9:49	10.03	14	6
13	9:50	10:17	27	13
14	9:53	10:01	8	5
15	9:54	10:10	16	6
16	10:01	10:40	39	9
17	10:16	10:42	26	2
18	10:18	10:28	10	2
19	10:24	10:57	33	4
20	10:30	10:43	13	7

From this table we can see that the time in the surgery varies from a low of eight minutes to a high of 66 minutes, with a mean of 25 minutes. This is fairly typical of the times that occur in practice. The numbers waiting to see a doctor varied from two to thirteen, which again reflects the normal situation.

Summary

Data collection is one of the most important parts of a simulation project and this chapter has looked at the tasks involved as well as the problems that can occur. Before the data collection phase is started, careful thought needs to be given to the data required, the data currently available, and whether some data will be difficult or impossible to collect. A pilot study should help answer some of these question as well as identify the resources required and procedures for collecting the data.

Once the data has been collected it needs to be analysed. The main purpose of the analysis is to identify what distributions can be used to represent the stochastic variables within the model. The two options are to use the existing data in the form of an empirical distribution or to use a theoretical distribution. There are many theoretical distributions that can be used but care must be taken to ensure that the distribution chosen is a good fit to the data. Distribution fitting can be done automatically these days and statistics generated that allow the goodness-of-fit to be determined.

When very little data is available or when specific parameters are estimated the choice is either to use the mean to represent the variable or to use a simple distribution such as the triangular distribution. Unless the variable concerned has little variation or is of minor importance, the use of the mean is not to be recommended as this will prevent the stochastic nature of the system from being replicated.

As well as collecting and analysing data for the purposes of model fitting, data should also be collected to assist in the validation of the model. This is not necessarily an easy exercise and thought needs to be given as to whether the data for validation should be collected during the same period as the model data or at different times. It is generally easier to collect it at the same time but this could mean that the model is only valid for specific circumstances.

■ Exercises

10.1 The following variables relate to a bank. Which of the variables are deterministic in nature and which are stochastic?

   a Number of counter staff

   b Interarrival time of customers

   c Time spent being served

   d Probability that a customer will balk from the queue

   e Number of counter staff on duty during the lunch period

   f Probability that a member of staff is called away from the counter

10.2 In the simulation of an airport, what time periods might it be necessary to collect data for?

10.3 Name three theoretical probability distributions that are symmetrical.

10.4 Would you expect the arrivals to a cinema to be random? Why/why not?

10.5 Analyse the interarrival time data for the Drive Thru Burger restaurant given in Appendix 1 and on the disk that accompanies this text. What distribution might fit this data? Repeat this exercise for the ordering and service time distributions.

References and further reading

Dagpunar, J. (1988) *Principles of Random Variate Generation*, Oxford University Press, New York, USA.

Fox, B. L. (1981) 'Fitting standard distributions to data is necessarily good: dogma or myth', *Proceedings of the 1981 Winter Simulation Conference* Oren, Delfosse and Shub (eds), IEEE 81CH1709-5, pp. 305–7.

Kelton, W. (1984) 'Input data collection and analysis', *Proceedings of the 1984 Winter Simulation Conference* Sheppard, Pooch and Pegden (eds), IEEE 84CH2098-2, pp. 91–5.

Kleijnen, J. and Groenendaal, W. (1992) *Simulation: A Statistical Perspective*, Wiley, Chichester, England.

Law, A. and McCommas, M. (1989) 'Pitfalls to avoid in the simulation of Manufacturing Systems', *Industrial Engineering*, May, pp. 28–69.

Law, A. and Kelton, W. (1991) *Simulation Modelling and Analysis*, Second Edition (Chapter 6), McGraw-Hill, Inc., USA.

Pegden, C., Shannon, R. and Sadowski, R. (1995) *Introduction to Simulation Using SIMAN*, Second Edition (Chapter 2), McGraw-Hill, Singapore.

Rothschild, V. and Logothetis, N. (1986) *Probability Distributions*, Wiley, USA.

Wetherill, G. (1981) *Intermediate Statistical Methods*, Chapman and Hall, New York.

11

Validation of simulation models

Les Oakshott, Andrew Greasley and David J. Smith

Introduction

Following building of the model and the collection of data, the next stage in the modelling cycle is to check that the model is an adequate representation of the system. This is not a trivial exercise and great care should be taken to ensure that the methods used are appropriate to the system being modelled. Systems can be categorised into one of two basic types and the method of obtaining results from a model depends on the type of system that is being modelled. This chapter starts by explaining the differences between the two types of system before looking at methods of validation. An understanding of the term *confidence interval* is assumed in this chapter, and this idea was explained in Chapter 3.

Types of system

Many systems have specific periods of time when they are operational or active and other periods of time when they are inactive. In the majority of these systems the system is empty at the start of the active period so that all resources are available and arriving entities do not have to queue. These systems are called terminating systems since they terminate after a specific period of time. Shops, banks and many production processes are of this type.

There are some systems that do not terminate or whose cycle is so long that they are effectively non-terminating. These systems are called non-terminating and include hospitals, airports, traffic control systems and some production processes. A system is also non-terminating if at the end of the active period any entities in the system remain there until the next active period. Many administrative systems are of this type since the 'in-tray' contains the waiting entities and will remain in the queue for subsequent processing.

It is important to know the type of system that is being modelled since the method of obtaining and analysing the results is different for the two types of system.

Terminating systems

Although models of terminating systems can be quite complex, obtaining results and analysing them are straightforward. For example, if a system was active for, say, six hours each day, then a 'run' of the simulation model would be for this length of time. At the start of the run, the state of the various queues within the model would be set to zero and all service facilities and processes would be in the idle state. The simulation would proceed on an event-by-event basis and the system status and statistics would be updated following each event.

■ Whiteladies Health Centre   *Scenario 11.1*

> Since the surgery is open for a specific period each day and the system starts in the empty state, it is a terminating system.

In Chapter 5 the simulation of a bank was performed using the tabular method. The table used in Chapter 5 is reproduced in Table 11.1 and from this table the various events can be seen. The first customer arrived fifteen seconds after the bank was opened. The time the customer waited in the queue to be served (in this case zero) is also recorded. A full simulation would continue for six hours at which time the run would end and statistical information would be generated concerning the many performance measures. These measures may refer to numbers in the queue, time in the queue or utilisation of the cashier resource.

Table 11.1 ■ Tabular simulation for the bank example

Random no.	Iat	Clock time	No. in queue	Random no.	Service time	Service starts	Service ends	Waiting time
08	15	15	0	72	55	15	70	0
87	75	90	0	46	45	90	135	0
15	15	105	1	96	75	135	210	30
04	15	120	2	00	25	210	235	90
52	15	135	2	27	35	235	270	100
46	15	150	3	73	55	270	325	120
95	105	255	2	76	55	325	380	70
10	15	270	2	25	35	380	415	110
02	15	285	3	11	25	415	440	130

The common mistake that many people make, particularly those new to simulation, is to assume that one run would be sufficient for conclusions to be drawn about the system. That is, one run would adequately allow the model and the real system to be compared. The argument that is made is that one run consists of many measurements, which would allow statistical analysis to be carried out. The problem is that the data will not be *independent*. For example, if the data refers to the time in the queue, then the time of, say, the tenth person depends on how long the ninth person spent in the queue. The time spent in the queue by the ninth person depends on how long the eighth person had been in the queue for, and so on.

Table 11.1 can be used to demonstrate this lack of independence. The first customer completed his service before the next person arrived so this second person did not have to wait. However, the customer who arrived at clock time 150 joined a queue of two others. The waiting time of this customer was determined by the length of time that the two others spent in the queue.

Another reason the individual data from one run should not be used is that normality assumptions are usually necessary for most statistical analyses. This is unlikely to be true for the variables of interest, such as time in a queue, which is likely to be heavily skewed.

A final reason that one run is not sufficient is that the results will depend on the stream of random numbers used. If a different stream were used, different results would be obtained. This is what should happen as random numbers are used to represent the variability that occurs in real life. So, for example, the bank could be busy one day and less busy the next day.

To overcome these problems, several runs of a simulation are made and the method to achieve this is called the **method of independent replications**.

Method of independent replications

To overcome the problems of independence in terminating systems, several runs of a simulation are made and the *average* value of a particular variable found for each run. The length of each run can be fixed according to time and this is typical of many queuing systems. Alternatively, the length can be based on the number of arrivals or departures. This may be typical of production systems where production ends once a certain number of items have been produced.

Provided different streams of random numbers are used for each run and the simulation is reset between runs, the average values obtained across all the runs will be independent. This set of averages obtained over all the runs constitutes a *sample* and since this sample is made up of averages the central limit theorem applies. This means that normality assumptions can be made and confidence intervals or statistical tests calculated for the true mean in the normal way.

The advantage with samples obtained from simulation is that we have full control of the accuracy of the simulation results by increasing the number of runs when necessary. This is not true with normal sampling where it may be impossible or expensive to obtain additional samples.

Non-terminating systems

Non-terminating systems are systems that do not terminate or whose cycle is so long that they are effectively non-terminating. The problems associated with lack of independence still apply with non-terminating systems but there is now the added problem that a simulation does not have a 'natural' end. We could arbitrarily choose a suitable length of a simulation run and proceed using the method of independent replications. However, there is now a new problem associated with **initial bias**.

Initial bias

When a simulation starts we normally assume that all queues are empty and all service facilities are in the idle state. This may be true for terminating systems but not if the system is non-terminating. If empty queues and idle servers are assumed then a bias is introduced into the simulation, the effects of which will diminish with time. To avoid problems with initial bias we have to ensure that the system has reached **steady state** before results can be collected. A system is in a steady state if its current state is independent of the starting conditions. The length of time necessary for a system to reach steady state can only be found by experimentation. That is, we would plot a graph of, say, the mean time in a queue for different periods. If we do this we should get a graph similar to the one in Figure 11.1. Steady state is reached once the graph has stopped fluctuating and has reached some reasonably constant level. Some packages (for example, ARENA) allow us to display the graph while the simulation is running. For other packages we may have to do several small runs of the simulation and then smooth the data using moving averages.

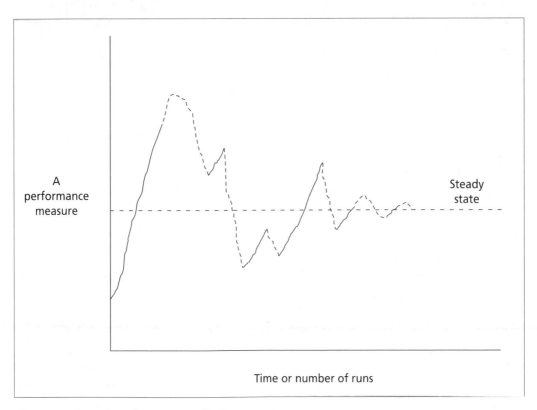

Figure 11.1 ■ **Steady state analysis**

Batch means method

Once the time taken to reach steady state has been found, we have to decide how to obtain the required sample. Provided the simulation run ended *after* steady state was reached, we could still use the method of independent replications. We would have to remove the data before steady state was reached for each run and averages found for the remainder of the data. This is a wasteful method as a large amount of data would have to be discarded. Advances in computer technology have made this less of a problem but there is a better method in which we only need to find steady state once. In this method we would make one very long run of the simulation and halt it at regular intervals. At the end of each interval statistical information would be recorded for that interval or batch. The data before steady state is reached can be discarded and only data from that point need be analysed. This method is called the **batch means** method. This is illustrated in Figure 11.2.

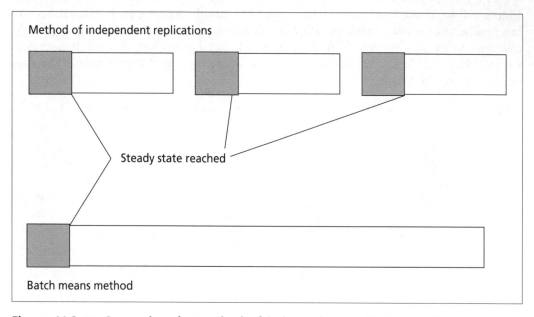

Figure 11.2 ■ Comparing the method of independent replications with the batch means method

However, this method does not tell us how many or how long each batch should be. Intuitively it should seem that the larger the number and length of each batch, the greater the accuracy. But how large is large? Even with fast computers simulations can take a considerable time. If there is a maximum length of the simulation run that is feasible, how should we divide this between number of batches and length of each batch? If the length of each batch is large, then this implies that the number of batches will be small, which increases the half-width of the confidence interval. On the other hand, if the length of each batch is too short, problems of independence can arise. This is because the starting conditions of one batch

Table 11.2 ■ A summary of the problems regarding the number and size of each batch

	Batch size large	Batch size small
Large number of batches	Ideal but probably not feasible	Likely to be problems with independence
Small number of batches	Half-width of the confidence interval likely to be large	Problems with independence and large half-width

are the same as the ending conditions of the previous batch. For example, if during one batch large queues formed, then the effect of these large queues could still be felt during the next period. The larger the batch, the greater the chance that these effects would have worked themselves out before the end of the batch (*see* Table 11.2). This means that successive batches are likely to be correlated (*autocorrelated*) and therefore the average values obtained from each batch will not be independent. Tests for independence can be performed within many simulation packages, or statistical software can be used. According to Pegden *et al.* (1995) at least ten batches are normally required to obtain an adequate half-width, and about 1000 departures per batch should guarantee independence for moderately busy queuing systems. Beyond twenty batches, the gain in the half-width progressively diminishes.

Validation methods

Schlesinger (1974) defined validation as, 'The process of substantiating that the model within its domain of applicability is sufficiently accurate for the intended application.' This definition is just as appropriate today as it was twenty years ago. It doesn't say that the model and system should agree perfectly but that the model should be *adequate* for its intended purpose.

Naylor and Finger (1967) developed the 'three-step approach' to model validation. This has been extended by Law and Kelton (1991). The three phases are:

(a) face validity

(b) testing the assumptions of the model empirically and

(c) statistical comparisons between the real system and the model output

Face validity

Face validity is concerned with deciding whether, *on the surface*, the model seems to be producing reasonable results. One of the advantages of the latest simulation packages is that the model can be animated so that a visual check can be made on the model's behaviour. Assuming that the model has already been verified, a run of the model should indicate whether any unexpected events are happening. For example, is throughput of the system correct? Do excessive queues form from time to time? Are there rather too many rejects occurring at a particular time?

Some statistical output from the model can also be useful. Do the figures look reasonable? Although averages are important, do not ignore minimum and maximum values. A simulation of an enquiry desk might indicate that the maximum number in the queue is much larger than expected. This could have arisen because the problem of balking from a queue had not been included in the model.

Graphical displays can also help in the validation process. Many simulation packages allow plots to be made while the simulation is proceeding and this should indicate whether anything unusual has happened. A histogram can be a useful graph for looking at the *distribution* of the variable. Many output variables will be heavily skewed; that is, a few large or small values will occur but generally the values will cluster around a central figure.

■ Whiteladies Health Centre   *Scenario 11.2*

The simulation of Whiteladies Health Centre for Mondays was repeated ten times and a selection of the results obtained are shown in Table 11.3.

On a normal Monday, at least 100 patients are expected. From Table 11.3 it can be seen that the number of patients varied from 96 to 120, with an average over the ten runs of 109.6 The model therefore seems correct from this aspect. The surgery can become crowded from time to time but this is usually at the start of the period. The model replicated this busy period quite well.

The time in the surgery for the ten runs varied from 3.1 minutes to 47.6 minutes with an average of 20.0 minutes. These figures look rather low as the

Table 11.3 ■ Output statistics for Monday's model

No. of patients	Time in surgery (minutes)			Time waiting to see a doctor (minutes)			Number waiting to see a doctor		
	Av.	Min.	Max.	Av.	Min.	Max.	Av.	Min.	Max.
96	20.3	3.1	47.6	12.8	0.0	29.5	5.9	0	27
113	17.3	3.1	40.0	10.2	0.0	29.5	5.5	0	20
112	18.8	3.1	44.2	11.4	0.0	29.7	6.1	0	26
110	23.9	3.1	45.6	16.5	0.0	31.1	8.6	0	25
111	23.2	3.1	45.4	16.3	0.0	30.9	8.6	0	28
120	24.0	10.6	41.1	16.4	7.4	29.5	9.4	0	20
100	19.7	3.4	38.2	12.6	0.0	29.5	6.0	0	26
111	18.3	3.1	36.1	11.3	0.0	29.5	6.0	0	24
111	19.0	3.1	41.5	11.8	0.0	29.5	6.2	0	21
112	15.3	3.1	46.2	8.2	0.0	29.5	4.4	0	22

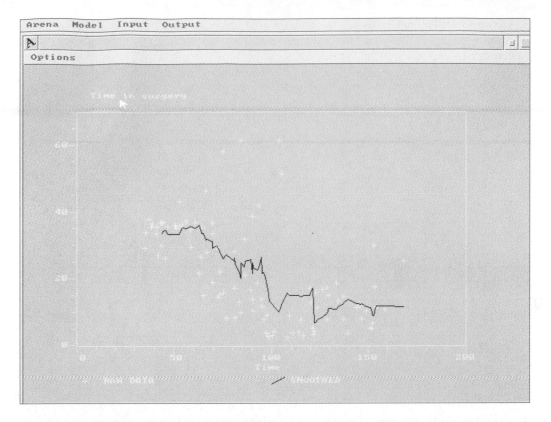

Figure 11.3 ■ Plot of time in the surgery *Source:* ARENA

data collected from the real system indicated that patients can sometimes spend over an hour in the surgery (*see* Scenario 10.12).

Figure 11.3 is a plot of the time in the surgery for the first run. This plot indicates that the time in the surgery starts off quite high but soon starts to fall to around twenty minutes. The reason for this early peak is the result of patients arriving before the start of the session.

A histogram of the number waiting to see a doctor is shown in Figure 11.4. This diagram indicates clearly the long tail of the distribution. That is, there is a peak around 0 to 4 patients but there are several instances where the numbers have been far in excess of this figure.

Another important variable is the time waiting to see a doctor. This varied from zero to 31.1 minutes, which again is low.

Although the results suggest that the model appears to represent many aspects of the system reasonably well, there does seem to be a tendency for the model to underestimate the time spent at the surgery. A possible reason for this is that the model is *more* efficient than the real system. The model has assumed that a patient is allocated on a 'first come, first served' basis to the first doctor

▶

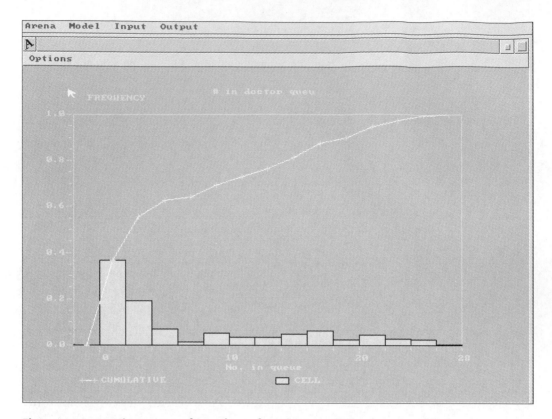

Figure 11.4 ■ Histogram of number of patients waiting to see a doctor
Source: ARENA

that is free. In reality, patients are allocated to a doctor when they first arrive at reception and it is possible that patients who arrive later will be seen sooner. In addition, some patients will want to see a particular doctor and will be prepared to wait longer as a result. Another reason is that we assumed that there are no gaps between consultations; that is, as soon as one consultation finishes another starts. We also assumed that the average arrival rate of patients is constant throughout the 150 minutes. This may not be correct as more patients may arrive at the start of the session than at the end.

In order to achieve more realistic figures, a relatively simple modification was made to the model. This was to have six separate doctors, and patients would be allocated to the doctor that has the shortest queue at the time. This doesn't account for the patients who choose a longer queue intentionally, but it should go some way towards making the model more realistic.

By making this modification it is possible to use a different probability distribution for each doctor, rather than have the same distribution for all six doctors. The results of using this modified model are shown in Table 11.4.

This amended version of the model does seem to give more realistic figures. The maximum time anyone spends in the surgery has increased from nearly

Table 11.4 ■ Output statistics for the amended model

No. of patients	Time in surgery (minutes)			Time waiting to see a doctor (minutes)			Number waiting to see a doctor		
	Av.	Min.	Max.	Av.	Min.	Max.	Av.	Min.	Max.
99	21.2	2.4	61.5	15.6	0.0	51.8	6.6	0	27
109	23.5	2.8	67.5	18.9	0.0	49.9	8.7	0	28
113	18.0	0.7	55.1	13.0	0.0	45.0	6.4	0	24
111	14.0	1.9	44.2	6.8	0.0	31.5	3.7	0	17
109	21.2	2.0	49.8	14.3	0.0	44.0	7.3	0	22
101	14.3	0.7	40.2	9.3	0.0	29.6	4.0	0	21
104	25.9	6.2	93.9	22.6	0.0	83.6	9.2	0	21
107	15.5	1.1	40.5	8.6	0.0	29.5	4.3	0	19
108	19.9	1.4	47.8	13.5	0.0	33.1	6.6	0	22
84	19.8	1.8	41.1	14.3	0.0	33.2	5.0	0	20

48 minutes to over 90 minutes and the maximum time patients have to wait to be seen by a doctor has increased from 31 minutes to 84 minutes. However, what is surprising is that the average time in the surgery over all ten runs has hardly changed at 19.3 minutes. What has increased is the variation from run to run. This reflects what happens in reality (that is, a variation from week to week) so this model does seem to be generally better than the first attempt.

Testing assumptions

All models will involve assumptions to be made about some aspects of the system. For example, the average arrival rate of customers to a bank may have been assumed constant. Or a particular probability distribution may have been assumed to apply to a model parameter. Some validation will probably have been done during the data collection and analysis phase (see Chapter 10) and distributions fitted to the data. However, what effect would a different distribution or a different parameter value have on the output? If the output changed, is this change expected?

When changes are made to a model it is important that all other conditions are kept the same. So the model should be run the same number of times and the same stream of random numbers used. The use of **common random numbers** will be discussed in Chapter 12 but the important point to remember is that the variability from one run to another is caused by the different random numbers used. If totally different random number streams are used in two different sets of runs, the differences in the output will be partly the result of the random numbers

■ Whiteladies Health Centre

Scenario 11.3

A mean value of twenty seconds was assumed for the time a patient spends at the reception so it would be interesting to see what would happen if this mean was changed to a distribution. A triangular distribution was tried with a minimum value of five seconds, a modal value of ten seconds and a maximum value of 50 seconds.

Although results from individual runs changed, the average time in the surgery over the ten runs was exactly the same at 19.3 minutes. The standard deviation increased from 3.92 to 5.11 minutes suggesting that the variation from run to run has increased.

From these results we can conclude that the time a patient spends at the reception has little effect on the overall performance of the system.

used and partly the result of the changes made. By keeping the random number streams the same, the difference in the output should be the result of the changes made only.

Even when the assumptions and parameter values are known to be reasonable, it is interesting to see what happens if a small change is made to one of the parameters in the model. A small change to an input parameter would be expected to make a small change in the output variables. This is known as *sensitivity analysis* and can highlight those variables that are sensitive to change. It is important to ensure that any parameters that are particularly sensitive should be as accurate as possible and it may be necessary to check a parameter by collecting more data. Another use of sensitivity analysis is that it helps create a better understanding of the system. For instance, the discovery that a small reduction in the number of rejects is likely to reduce a bottleneck in another process could have significant benefits to a company.

■ Whiteladies Health Centre

Scenario 11.4

In order to see how sensitive the model is to changes in the arrival rate, the mean interarrival time was reduced from 1.37 minutes to 1.30 minutes, a change of 5 per cent. The model was then run for a further ten times and the new average time in the surgery obtained.

The average time in the surgery changed from 19.3 minutes to 20.9 minutes over the ten runs, which is a change of 8 per cent. An increase was expected since a reduction in the interarrival time means that more patients will arrive. However, since the percentage change in the average time is greater than 5 per cent, this may suggest that this variable is quite sensitive to changes in the arrival rate. This could suggest possible experiments to try out on the model (this will be discussed in Chapter 12).

Statistical comparisons

The final validity step is to see if the differences between the real system and the model are statistically significant. This, of course, can only be done if the real system exists. In models of new systems more emphasis should be directed towards the first two validity steps.

There is some controversy in the value of statistical tests to simulation data. Law and Kelton (1991) state three reservations they have about the use of statistical tests. They are:

(a)   the data is *non-stationary*

(b)   the data is autocorrelated

(c)   the use of a 'null hypothesis' is not appropriate

The reservation concerning non-stationary data refers to the fact that data changes over time. Most statistical tests assume that the distributions from which the data has been obtained is independent of time, but of course both the model data and the data from the real system are time dependent.

Autocorrelation is only a problem for models of non-terminating systems, and these can be minimised if the batch means method was used to collect the output data. However, the data collected from the real system for the purpose of validation is almost certain to be autocorrelated. This is because the measurements taken are influenced by what has gone on before.

The use of the null hypothesis to test the difference between the real system and the model output assumes that the two should, in theory, agree. Since the model is only an approximation of the real system, this is perhaps rather an unfair comparison. What we really want is some idea as to the discrepancy between the system and the model. The most effective method of observing this discrepancy is by the use of **confidence intervals**.

Confidence intervals

The formula for a confidence interval is

$$\mu = \bar{x} \pm \frac{t \times s}{\sqrt{n}}$$

where μ is the 'true' mean, $\bar{x}$ is the mean from the sample (in the case of simulation it is the 'mean of means' from n replications), s is the sample standard deviation and t is the value of the t-statistic on n degrees of freedom with p per cent confidence. The level of confidence (p) is normally taken as 95 per cent.

The confidence interval tells us that we are, say, 95 per cent confident that the true mean of the population lies between the two limits calculated in the formula above. If these limits are felt to be too wide, the number of replications should be increased. This process can be continued until the half-width is considered satisfactory or the number of replications becomes excessive. As the number of replications increases, the improvement in the half width will progressively diminish, so it is rarely worthwhile making more than about 30 replications.

If we have a value of a particular parameter obtained from the real system, we can see whether this value lies within the calculated limits. If it does lie within the two limits, this is a good indication that the model is a valid representation of the real system. If it lies outside the limits, it *may* suggest that there is an error with the model. However, in both cases we should use our judgement and other information to decide if the model is valid or whether it needs modifying. The statistical analysis should be seen as only one part (admittedly, an important part) of the validation process. As more validation checks are made, our views about the model should start to converge.

If differences are found between the real system and the model, we first need to discover possible reasons for this discrepancy. It is more than likely that these differences are a result of the assumptions made at the model-building stage. If these differences are deemed important it is necessary to make adjustments to the model and go through the validation phase again. This process may be necessary several times before a valid model is achieved.

We should not forget the definition quoted at the start of the validation section, which states that the model should be 'accurate for the intended application'. In many simulation models the purpose is to make comparisons between several different alternatives rather than to obtain an absolute value for one chosen scenario. In these cases a simulation model that is less than perfect may still be a useful tool in deciding which option to choose.

■ Whiteladies Health Centre   *Scenario 11.5*

The 'mean of the means' for the time in the surgery is 19.3 minutes with a standard deviation of 3.92 minutes. This mean of means will be the best estimate of the true mean time in the surgery. The 95 per cent confidence interval for the true mean time that a customer would spend in the surgery is

$$19.3 \pm 2.262 \times \frac{3.92}{\sqrt{10}}$$

(t is 2.262 on 9 degrees of freedom)

which is 19.3 ± 2.8, or 16.5 to 22.1 minutes. That is, we would be 95 per cent confident that the true mean time in the surgery is somewhere between 16.5 minutes and 22.1 minutes. This is illustrated in Figure 11.5.

From Scenario 10.12 in Chapter 10, we discovered that the mean waiting time in the system is around 25 minutes. Since this confidence interval does not include the observed mean, we must conclude that the model is not validated using this criterion. To improve the model it would probably be necessary to incorporate the situation where patients *choose* the doctor to see. This would involve assigning a certain proportion of patients to each doctor regardless of queue size. This would be feasible but is it really worth it? The purpose of this model (*see* Chapter 1) is to compare the existing system with possible alternatives. It is therefore not essential that the model is perfect in the absolute sense. For this reason and because the model does replicate the system in other respects, no further improvements will be attempted.

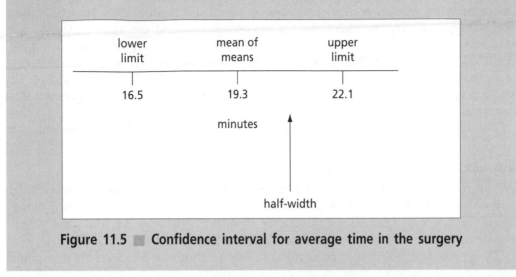

Figure 11.5 ■ **Confidence interval for average time in the surgery**

In addition to normal statistical procedures, the **Turing test** can be used (Turing, 1950). This test involves giving 'experts' two sets of statistical data, one from the real system and one generated by the model. They are not told which is which and if they are unable to differentiate between the two, this is evidence that there is no difference between the model and system.

Validation when an existing system does not exist

When a model is built of a new system, validation becomes difficult, although not impossible. Statistical comparisons will not be possible but face validity and the testing of assumptions will still be possible to some extent. In these situations it is often possible to gather together a number of 'experts' who have a good knowledge of the business. If the software being used allows animation, these experts will be able to see the model running and will be able to comment on its correctness. The statistical output will also need to be looked at and comments made on the reasonableness of the figures.

If the model is to be used for future planning, it is possible to test the model retrospectively. That is, once a simulated event has occurred the model forecasts can be compared with actual data. The model can then be amended if necessary and hopefully further forecasts will be more accurate. The danger with this method of 'calibration' is that the model is made to fit a particular set of conditions rather than be more general and potentially a more useful model.

■ Case study 3
ASHBURTON PRODUCTS

This next case study involves a non-terminating system and demonstrates the importance of validation in a simulation project. The model indicated that there was a major discrepancy between the model output and the actual system, and this was caused by activities being carried out by the workforce that were not included in the model. These activities were unproductive in the sense that they were not part of the production process. One of the recommendations from the project was that these activities could be eliminated through management of a reorganised and revised system.

The authors of this case study are Andrew Greasley and David J. Smith.

Introduction

Ashburton Products manufactures fireplaces. They have a retail showroom in which various models are displayed. Attached to the showroom is a workshop where stone, bricks and other items are cut and polished prior to dispatch and on-site construction.

Two years ago, Ashburton responded to requests for wooden mantels to complement their fireplaces. A small additional workshop close to the showroom was taken on a short-term lease, and various items of second-hand woodworking machinery were acquired. Two joiners were taken on to build the mantels which, for the most part, were custom built to customer requirements. This part of the business has thrived and four people are currently employed.

The process

A mantel consists of three sub-assemblies comprising two legs and a shelf. Sub-assemblies are made from wood which has been cut, sawn, planed and routed. At the sub-assembly stage, the various items are brought together, glued and then clamped. The glue takes time to dry, so clamped sub-assemblies are left overnight. The assembly stage is similar. As with sub-assembly, assembly takes place on a specifically designed workbench.

Ashburton employs four staff. One person operates the cutting and planing machines, together with the saw. Another operates the router. Two men are employed in sub-assembly and final assembly work.

Two main categories of mantel are produced from hardwood and medium density fibreboard (MDF). The ratio of MDF mantels to hardwood is 85 per cent to 15 per cent. With current staffing levels, output normally averages slightly over 25 per week.

Demand for mantels has been rising for some time. Sales which were, in the past, based exclusively on single orders for individual customers have recently been supplemented by multiple orders from two local builders.

In view of this trend, Ashburton's management is concerned about how best to meet the increase in demand. Unable to expand the current site because of planning restrictions, and reluctant to spend large sums on new equipment, the management is uncertain what to do. In order to evaluate the capacity of the current system and explore the options available, it was decided to carry out a simulation of the plant.

Simulation model

The logic of the model was that entities in the form of jobs moved through a production system comprising a number of resources. The resources were of two types: equipment and staff. The equipment resources were grouped together to represent the various stages of production. Jobs queue at each stage of the process (i.e. they form work in progress), waiting until the operator is free. Effectively, jobs move through the system, being either in an 'active' state where they are being processed, or a 'dead' state where they are queuing. Having checked and agreed the logic of the model with the staff concerned, processing times for the various operations were collated by observing and timing each of the processes.

Actual model construction was very straightforward. The ARENA simulation software was used, which generates its own code thus eliminating the need for coding. Instead, the model was built up on-screen, using a number of predefined 'icons' to model each of the equipment resources. Each icon or group of icons was set to engage an entity (representing a queue), seize a resource, delay (to represent processing) and release. The overnight drying of sub-assemblies and assemblies was modelled by delaying jobs for an appropriate length of time. The people involved in the process were also represented as resources. A resource was seized for the duration of the cutting, sawing and planing operation to represent that member of staff. The router was in effect dedicated to another member of staff. In addition, two 'benchers' were allocated to the sub-assembly and main assembly tasks as required. This allowed both staff to work on either sub-assembly or main assembly or a member of staff could be allocated to each operation. The number of staff involved in the process could be changed by adjusting the appropriate resource capacity in the model. The screen display of the model is shown in Figure 11.6. During the execution of the model the MDF and hardwood mantels are represented by different coloured squares which move through the simulation and queue at a process if it is busy. The display also incorporates output variables showing lead time and output achieved and a graph of the total number of products in the system at any one time; i.e. the work in progress (WIP). The graph shows how the WIP increases during the 'warm-up' phase of the simulation and then reaches 'steady state' for the remainder of the simulation run.

Model coding

As noted earlier, no coding is necessary using the ARENA system but the software can generate coding in the SIMAN language. This aids understanding of the model and is a useful tool in the debugging phase of a simulation project. The 'model' element of the SIMAN program, representing the program logic and the 'experimental' file, which contains the parameters for the simulation run, are provided in Appendix 1. As described in the experimentation section of this case study there are two versions of the model which simulate jobbing and batch

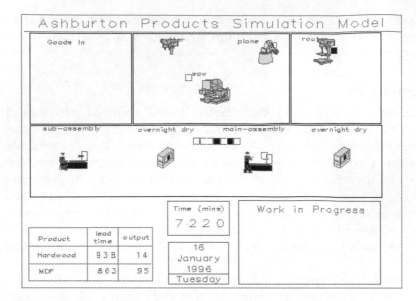

Figure 11.6 ■ Screen display of simulation model

production systems. The coding for both the jobbing and batch versions of the simulation model are identical apart from the initial generation of demand into the model. The jobbing version generates MDF mantels with a 0.85 probability and hardwood mantels with a 0.15 probability. They are then assigned a batch size of one. The batch version generates a batch of eight hardwood mantels on every seventh day and generates a batch of ten MDF mantels on every other day.

The work progresses through the model, seizing people and machine resources as appropriate. The process times are represented by a delay on the relevant machine. The delay formula is:

Delay Time = setup time + (jobtype * extra setup time) + (process time + (jobtype * extra process time)) * batchsize

where jobtype = 0 for MDF and 1 for hardwood mantels

This formula enables the simulation to allocate a set-up time for a machine when changing between batches. An extra set-up period is allocated for the more complex hardwood mantels. The process time (plus an extra process time period for hardwood mantels) is multiplied by the batch size to give a total delay time.

Process times would not normally be fixed on a simulation model but would be represented by a distribution reflecting the variation in process time that would occur for an operation repeated a number of times. However, it was felt that because this was a 'prototype' and demonstration model for the client, it should be kept as simple as possible. If more detailed information were collected on process times, distributions could be incorporated into the model providing scope for further statistical analysis.

When sub-assemblies and assemblies have been glued they require drying time. This is represented by the time remaining in the present day. Finally, the completed mantels are directed to appropriate tallies which calculate the time in the system (i.e. lead time) and count the number processed. The time of entry is marked at the beginning of the simulation code at the CREATE statement using the MARK parameter. This ability of each entity to be associated with certain attributes as they pass through the model is one of the key features of discrete-event simulation.

Experimentation

Jobbing system

The model was run to simulate four weeks (twenty days) of operation. This produced the following results (*see* Table 11.5).

The system generated 105 units of output over a month's operation and appeared to be at steady state, with no build-up of work in progress.

Table 11.5 ■ Jobbing simulation results

Jobs per day	6	
Product	Lead time (mins)	Output
MDF	939	95
Hardwood	1024	10
Total		105

Table 11.6 ■ Resource utilisation: jobbing

Jobs per day	6
Machine utilisation	
Cutter	14%
Saw	39%
Plane	27%
Router	39%
Staff utilisation	
Cut/Saw/Plane (1)	99%
Router (1)	39%
Assembly (2)	60%

Detailed analysis of resource utilisation showed that the system was operating close to capacity. The cutting/sawing/routing area was a bottleneck, with the operator in this area working at 99 per cent capacity (*see* Table 11.6).

This level of utilisation differed markedly from actual practice. The real-life system was running at a considerably lower level of output, producing approximately twelve to fifteen units per week, i.e. three units per day. Furthermore, the level of activity showed that the workforce was fully employed and there was a build-up of work in progress, indicating that the system was, in fact, running at or slightly beyond full capacity. There was clearly a major discrepancy between the model and actual practice. This caused some consternation, and the immediate reaction was that the model was flawed, with major errors either in the data or in terms of model construction.

In order to highlight what appeared to be flaws in the model, the actual system was subjected to close scrutiny. Further observations were conducted and these showed that the operating times that had been used to provide the data for the various resources were accurate. Similarly, the logic of the model was correct. However, there were excessive amounts of work in progress in the plant and, to that extent, the plant was working at capacity. Closer examination revealed that the workforce – particularly those in the sawing and cutting area – was heavily engaged in finding materials, moving materials and sorting materials. When asked to describe the system and the various activities that took place, no member of the workforce had indicated that these types of activity took place, but further observation revealed that they were being carried out and that they were taking substantial amounts of time. These activities had not been mentioned previously because they were not considered to be 'real' and had certainly not been thought about. They were taking place and they were diverting effort away from productive tasks. Effectively, what was happening was that the workforce was engaged in a number of unproductive activities.

The consultant's conclusion was that the model was correct, was working effectively, and did describe the system. But there were operational problems in the running of the plant which were causing the workforce to engage in a variety of unproductive activities. The solution was not to acquire more equipment or more people but to avoid time being wasted on unnecessary activities, through management of a reorganised and revised system to ensure that only appropriate, productive activities were carried out.

The model was then adapted to discover ways of finding additional capacity. An extra resource, i.e. another person, was added to the saw/planing facility and additional demand was fed into the system, at the rate of nine jobs per day. This produced a 50 per cent increase in output. Results showed that the system would work satisfactorily on this basis, achieving a better balance of workload, with the cutting/sawing area working at 78 per cent utilisation and the assemblers working at 91 per cent utilisation.

Batch system

Although the addition of another person in the jobbing system would solve the short-term problem of a lack of capacity, it was felt that there was a fundamental problem in the match between market needs and operational capability within the workshop. In other words, the firm had moved from competing in a market based on a requirement for a 'one-off' customised product to one where a batch of products was required. Thus, there was now a mismatch between market needs and operational capability. If the firm continued to try to supply products on a batch basis using a jobbing operation it is most likely they would not be cost competitive in the market. It was decided to simulate the performance of the facility using a batch method of production in order to quantify any improvement in efficiency. The model was run using a batch size of ten MDF and eight hardwood mantels. For six days out of seven MDF mantels would be produced. On the seventh day the facility would produce hardwood mantels. The model was run to simulate four weeks (twenty days) of operation which produced the results shown in Tables 11.7 and 11.8.

The system generated 164 units of output over a month's operation and appeared to be at steady state, with no build-up of work in progress. This output indicated that a considerable improvement in performance could be gained by moving to a batch system without any additional personnel. A summary of the results is presented in Table 11.9.

Table 11.7 ■ Batch simulation results

Batch size	10 MDF, 8 hardwood	
Product	Lead time (mins)	Output
MDF	1645	140
Hardwood	1920	24
Total		164

Table 11.8 ■ Resource utilisation: batch

Batch Size	10/8
Machine utilisation	
Cutter	13%
Saw	45%
Plane	25%
Router	44%
Staff utilisation	
Cut/Saw/Plane (1)	86%
Router (1)	44%
Assembly (2)	64%

Table 11.9 ■ Summary of simulation experiment results

Model	Output level (mantels)
Jobbing simulation	105
Jobbing simulation with additional person	161
Batch simulation	164

Conclusion

The study illustrates a number of features that commonly occur when simulation is applied to practical problems in the field of operations management. At the same time it indicates the potential value of simulation in helping to solve the problems frequently encountered in the running of even small-scale manufacturing facilities.

In this instance, the work to develop and run a simulation model gave the management of the facility a much better understanding of the production system itself. From this it proved possible to identify major deficiencies in the way in which the facility was being operated.

The simulation was also able to show the potential impact of making changes to the facility. The effect of providing additional resources was highlighted, together with the impact of moving from a jobbing to a batch production system.

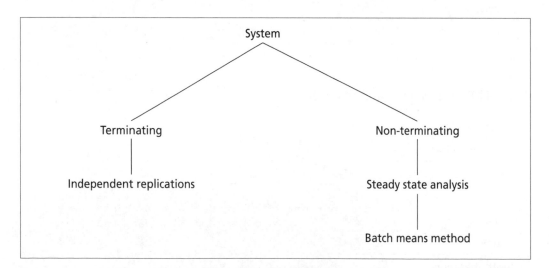

Figure 11.7 ■ Summary of the methods of obtaining data from models of the two types of system

Summary

This chapter has been concerned with the process of validating a simulation model. Validation involves analysing the data obtained from runs of a simulation model and comparing this data with how the real system behaves or is thought to behave. Where the system already exists the process of validation is easier since it is possible to use statistical techniques, such as confidence intervals, to help comparison. However, validation involves more than statistical comparisons and it should be remembered that the model and real system will never show perfect agreement. The main criterion for a valid model is that it is adequate for the intended purpose.

Before data is collected from a simulation model, the type of system must be taken into account. The two types of system are terminating and non-terminating and Figure 11.7 summarises the main differences in the way that data is obtained from models of the two systems.

■ Exercises

11.1 Label the following systems as either terminating or non-terminating:

    a   a restaurant

    b   a 24-hour petrol station

    c   an accident and emergency ward in a hospital

    d   a road junction

    e   a telephone switchboard that is manned for twelve hours a day

    f   mortgage-approval process at a building society

11.2 A simulation of a non-terminating system has been run for 100 hours. Which would be better: analysing the data by five batches of twenty hours or twenty batches of five hours?

11.3 An insurance company has built a model of its claims procedure in order to try out different ideas for reducing the time to process claims. Describe the procedure for obtaining data from this model that could be used for validation purposes. What performance measures would be needed for the validation?

11.4 A company manufactures components for the computer industry and has developed a model of one of its production systems. The measure of interest is the time that a component has to wait in one of the processes. The production process operates for twelve hours a day and the system starts each day in the empty state. The model was run five times and the average times the component had to wait are 12.3, 14.6, 20.9, 9.5 and 17.5 minutes. What is the confidence interval for the true mean time from the model? If measurements from the real system gave a mean figure of 22 minutes, what would you conclude about the validity of the model?

The next exercise is for those students who have access to simulation software.

11.5 Use the activity cycle diagram developed in Exercise 9.2 to develop a model of the Drive Thru Burger restaurant. The data for the model can be found in Appendix 1, or on the disk that accompanies this text. Validate your model using the information supplied in Appendix 1.

References and further reading

Carson, J. S. (1986) 'Convincing users of model's validity is challenging aspect of Modeller's Job', *Industrial Engineering*, June (18) 74–85.

Harrell, C. R., Bateman, R. E., Gogg, T. J. and Matt, J. R. A. (1992) *System Improvement Using Simulation* (Chapter 6), Promodel Corporation, Orem, Utah 84058, USA.

Kleijnen, J. and Groenendaal, W. (1992) *Simulation: A Statistical Perspective* (Chapter 11), Wiley, Chichester, England.

Law, A. M. and Kelton, W. D. (1991) *Simulation Modelling and Analysis*, Second Edition (Chapter 5), McGraw-Hill, Inc., USA.

McHaney, R. (1991) *Computer Simulation: A Practical Perspective* (Chapter 6), Academic Press Limited, London.

Naylor, T. H.and Finger, J. M. (1967) 'Verification of computer simulation models', *Management Science*, (14) 92–101.

Needlamkavil, F. (1987) *Computer Simulation and Modelling* (Chapter 4), Wiley, Chichester, England.

Pegden, C., Shannon, R. and Sadowski, R. (1995) *Introduction to Simulation Using SIMAN*, Second Edition (Chapter 4), McGraw-Hill, Singapore.

Sargent, R. (1988) 'A tutorial on validation and verification of simulation models', *Proceedings of the 1988 Winter Simulation Conference*, San Diego, 12–14 December, pp. 33–9.

Schlesinger, S. (1974) 'Developing standard procedures for simulation, validation and verification', *Proceedings of the 1974 Summer Computer Simulation Conference*, pp. 927–33.

Schmeiser, B. (1982) 'Batch size effects in the analysis of simulation output', *Operations Research*, Vol. 30, pp. 556–68.

Schruben, L. W. (1982) 'Detecting initialisation bias in simulation output', *Operations Research*, Vol. 30, pp. 569–90.

Turing, A. M. (1950) 'Computing machinery and intelligence', *Mind* 59, pp. 433–60.

Van Horn, R. L. (1971) 'Validation of simulation results', *Management Science*, 17, pp. 247–58.

Watson, H. J. and Blackstone, J. H. (1989) *Computer Simulation*, Wiley, USA.

12

Interpretation of simulation experiments

Les Oakshott

Introduction

The main purpose of developing a simulation model is to be able to try out some 'What-if?' experiments on the model. If the model is a good representation of the real system, the results from these experiments should give a good indication of what would happen if these experiments were to be made on the real system. Unfortunately, experimentation usually comes at the end of a simulation project and this aspect of simulation is not always given the time it deserves. This could be because of lack of time or money or because the project team does not have sufficient statistical expertise to make a proper attempt at the analysis. The purpose of this chapter is to explain the ideas behind simulation experimentation and to demonstrate some of the statistical analysis that can be performed on data obtained from a simulation model. Although the statistical analysis will be shown in detail, some underlying knowledge of statistics is required in this chapter. Readers who have doubts regarding their level of statistical knowledge are advised to read Chapter 3 before proceeding.

General considerations

A simulation model is usually developed for a specific purpose. This could be because a manager wants to see the effect of a change or changes to a current system. These changes could be to increase the number of operators for a production system, to change the priority for trains entering a junction, or to see what happens if a hospital had to handle a major emergency. In the design of a new system, the purpose of the model could be to compare alternative designs.

In some situations the number and type of experiments can be defined in advance of building the model. This is the most efficient approach as this will allow appropriate techniques to be used and the amount of time required for this part of the project to be determined more accurately.

Unfortunately, this is rarely the case, as it is only after the model has been developed that ideas start to develop. For example, a simulation model of a port might have been built with the intention of seeing the effect of providing another berth. The results might have indicated that a larger throughput could be achieved with more cranes rather than an additional berth. As experiments are performed on this model, other ideas start to develop, such as changing the priority for use of these cranes. Experimentation therefore proceeds on a piecemeal basis until either no further experiments are needed or the time (or money) for the project has been reached. It is the experience of the author that it is usually for the latter reason that the project is finally deemed to have been completed! Many simulation consultants will give a fixed charge for the model building and validation but will charge for experimentation on a daily basis.

There are two basic types of experiment that can be performed on a model. The first type is where the absolute value of some output measure is required and the second is where a comparison is to be made with either the original model or different alternatives of the same model. The simplest case is where an absolute measure is required. In both cases, however, the methods of obtaining the output data as discussed in Chapter 11 still apply. That is, the method of independent replications should be used for terminating systems and the batch means method used for non-terminating systems.

Absolute measures for a single model

Absolute measures are likely to be used when it is known that a change in the model *will* make a change in an output variable. For example, if the speed of a process is increased, it would be expected that the queues for the process would decrease. The point of the experiment in this case may be to decide if the improvement can be justified on cost grounds.

If changes are made to the model, it will be necessary to obtain a new set of replications for each modification. (To avoid unnecessary repetition the word 'replication' will be used when referring to either independent replications or batches.) The analysis will be similar to that carried out during the validation phase (*see* Chapter 11), where confidence intervals were calculated for the variable of interest. The important difference between validation and experimentation, however, is that during validation the confidence interval is compared with a value obtained from the real system. The purpose of experimentation is to see the effect of changes to a model, assuming that the basic model is valid. If the validation process was not sufficiently thorough, the experimentation stage may indicate errors in the model. If this occurs, further experimentation should be abandoned until the errors have been investigated and, if necessary, corrected.

■ **Whiteladies Health Centre**   *Scenario 12.1*

As the number of patients increases, the time a patient spends waiting to see a doctor will increase, assuming other factors remain constant. Currently about 110 patients visit the surgery on a Monday morning, and according to the model, spend about fourteen minutes on average waiting to see a doctor. What would happen to the queuing time if the number of patients doubled? To simulate this event the mean interarrival time was halved from 1.37 minutes to 0.685 minutes and ten replications of the model were made. The results for the original and amended models are shown in Table 12.1.

Table 12.1 ■ **Mean waiting time when the number of patients is doubled**

Replication	Mean waiting time to see a doctor (minutes)	
	Original model	Amended model
1	15.6	60.1
2	18.9	62.5
3	13.0	62.0
4	6.8	52.2
5	14.3	55.8
6	9.3	60.6
7	22.6	61.2
8	8.6	51.8
9	13.5	63.3
10	14.3	61.5
mean	13.69	59.1
standard deviation	4.762	4.253

The mean queuing time over the ten replications was 59.1 minutes with a standard deviation of 4.253 minutes. This suggests that a doubling of the number of patients will cause the mean waiting time to increase by over 400 per cent.

The confidence interval of the true mean waiting time is:

$$\mu = 59.1 \pm \frac{2.262 \times 4.253}{\sqrt{10}}$$

(where 2.262 is the t-value on 9 degrees of freedom) and

▶

$$\mu = 59.1 \pm 3.04$$

$$= 56.1 \text{ to } 62.1 \text{ minutes}$$

That is, we are 95 per cent confident that the true mean waiting time will lie somewhere between 56.1 and 62.1 minutes.

If the sample variance is high, the half-width of the confidence interval might be higher than desired. If this occurs, it is normal practice in simulation to increase the number of replications until some target value of the half-width is reached. Unfortunately, as the number of replications increases, the gain in the half-width progressively diminishes. For models where the variance is particularly high, the target may not be realistically obtainable. In this case it may be necessary to accept an inferior half-width or to use a **variance reduction technique**, such as **antithetic variates**. The idea behind this technique is to make pairs of replications that are negatively correlated. To achieve this, each random number of the second replication of the pair is the complement of the first replication of the pair; that is, if r is a random number in the first replication, then $1 - r$ will be the random number of the second replication. This should ensure that a large observation in the first replication would be offset by a small observation in the second replication. By taking the average of the two observations, the value obtained is closer to the expected value of the variable. Implementation of the antithetic variate procedure depends on the package used, but it is important that the random numbers between pairs of replications are synchronised; that is, each random number is used for the same purpose in both replications. To understand this, imagine a simple model where entities arrive, queue for service and then depart. If the random number in the first replication generated a large service time, then the complement of this random number should generate a smaller service time in the second replication. Since it is the service time (together with the rate of arrivals) that determines the time waiting for service, the average of the two replications should give a figure that is closer to the expected value. If synchronisation is not achieved, it is quite likely that the complement of the random number that was used to generate a service time in the first replication may be used to generate a small interarrival time in the second replication. A small interarrival time will mean that the next entity arrives sooner and the waiting time for this entity will be greater than if the antithetic variate procedure had not been used.

To improve the chances that the replication pairs are synchronised, each source of variation within the model should have its own unique random number stream. Most simulation packages have the facility for specifying random number streams, although complex models may require more streams than the package permits.

■ **Whiteladies Health Centre**   *Scenario 12.2*

Since each source of variation within the model has its own random number stream, the method of antithetic variates was tried and ten replications made. The results are shown in Table 12.2.

Table 12.2 ■ Replications using antithetic variables

| | Mean waiting time to see a doctor (minutes) | | |
| | Pair | | |
Replication	1	2	Average
1,2	60.1	49.2	54.7
3,4	60.8	53.3	57.1
5,6	59.0	49.8	54.4
7,8	53.6	63.5	58.6
9,10	55.6	60.9	58.3

Although ten replications were made, each replication was paired to give a sample size of five. The mean of the average of the pairs was 56.6 minutes with a standard deviation of 1.974 minutes. The 95 per cent confidence interval is therefore:

$$\mu = 56.6 \pm \frac{2.776 \times 1.974}{\sqrt{5}}$$

(where 2.776 is the *t*-value on 4 degrees of freedom) and

$$\mu = 56.6 \pm 2.45$$

$$= 54.2 \text{ to } 59.1 \text{ minutes}$$

Notice that the half-width of the confidence interval has been reduced from 3.04 to 2.45 minutes. The use of antithetic variates does not give much of an improvement in this case since the variance is quite small.

Comparisons of multiple alternatives of a model

Frequently, simulation experiments are performed in order to *compare* one version or alternative of the model with another. In these cases it may not be obvious that a change will have the desired result and statistical tests can be used to decide if any differences are indeed significant.

When data from two or more alternatives of a simulation model are to be compared statistically, consideration needs to be given to the random numbers used by the model. Each replication of a simulation model should use a different random number stream. This ensures that the model replicates the randomness that occurs in a real system. However, when experiments are carried out on a model, the question arises as to whether to use the same random number streams for the amended model or to use totally different streams. We will see that this is an important decision as it influences the form that the statistical analysis will take.

Even when this decision has been made, the choice of the correct statistical test to use may appear bewildering at first sight. Law and Kelton (1991), as well as many other authors, discuss methods of analysing simulation output obtained from two or more alternatives. There are literally dozens of techniques that can be used but fortunately it is possible to narrow down the choice by a systematic approach to the problem. This approach starts by looking at the number of alternatives that need to be compared.

Comparison of two alternatives

This is the simplest and probably the most common use of a simulation model. It does not necessarily mean that only one experiment is to be conducted, but that one experiment is done at a time. After each experiment a comparison is made with the original version before proceeding with other experiments.

The next decision to be made is whether the output data *between* alternatives of the model are independent and whether the distribution of the output data can be assumed normal. The output data *within* an alternative should be independent if either the method of independent replications (terminating system) or the batch means method (non-terminating system) has been used to obtain the data. The data will be independent *between* alternatives of the model if different random number streams have been used for both alternatives. If, though, both alternatives use the same random number streams, independence cannot be assumed. We will see later that there are certain advantages in using the same random numbers for both alternatives.

Data independent between alternatives

If different random number streams have been used for both alternatives of the model, the output data will be independent and statistical tests that demand independence can be used to determine whether any differences in the data are significant. The most common test to use is the two-sample *t*-test (*see* page 277) but this requires that the data is normally distributed. In most cases this will be true since the average value of the output variable is made up of many (often thousands) measurements and the central limit theorem will apply. (*See* Chapter 3 for an explanation of the central limit theorem.) However, there may be occasions when the simulation model represents a 'quiet' system where very few events occur, or the replication time is too short for many observations to be collected. In these situations it *may* be necessary to use the appropriate non-parametric test, which in the case of two samples is the **Mann–Whitney** test. The advantage with non-parametric tests is that they are 'distribution-free' and require fewer assumptions to be made about the data. However, non-parametric tests are not as *powerful* as their parametric equivalents. This means that they will not have the same power to identify real differences between two sets of data.

It is possible to check whether the assumption of normality is correct. The easiest method is by the use of a **normal probability plot**, which was described in Chapter 3 (*see* page 73).

■ Whiteladies Health Centre   *Scenario 12.3*

The sample of ten average waiting times for the original model (*see* Table 12.1) was tested for normality using MINITAB. The normal probability plot obtained is shown in Figure 12.1, where the line of best fit has been drawn between the points. There is no evidence of non-linearity in this plot so the assumption of normality is reasonable.

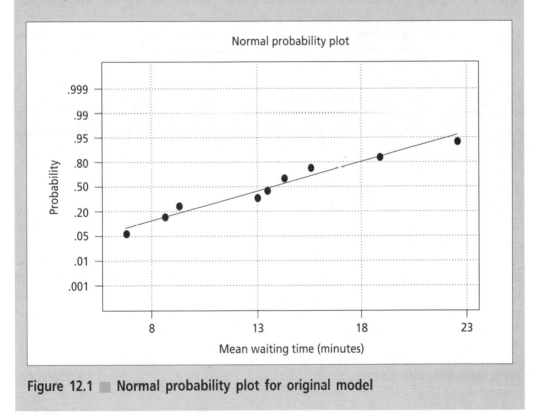

Figure 12.1 ■ Normal probability plot for original model

Two-sample *t*-test

When normality is assumed, the two-sample *t*-test can be used. As with all hypothesis tests, a null and alternative hypothesis must be defined. In the case of the two-sample *t*-test the null hypothesis (H_0) is that the two means are equal. If the test result provides evidence to reject the null hypothesis, the alternative hypothesis (H_1) is accepted. This alternative hypothesis can be one of two types. It can either be two sided, in which case we are only testing to see if the means are different, or it can be one sided. A one-sided test is when we have good reason to believe that the means must be either less than or greater than each other. In statistical terms the hypothesis is stated as follows:

$$H_0 : \mu_1 = \mu_2 \qquad H_1 : \mu_1 \neq \mu_2 \qquad \text{(two sided)}$$

$$H_1 : \mu_1 > \mu_2 \qquad \text{(one sided)}$$

$$H_1 : \mu_1 < \mu_2 \qquad \text{(one sided)}$$

The formula for the test statistic is

$$t = \frac{(\bar{x}_1 - \bar{x}_2) - (\mu_1 - \mu_2)}{\sigma_{(\bar{x}_1 - \bar{x}_2)}}$$

where $\bar{x}_1 - \bar{x}_2$ is the difference between the means from the original and amended models and $\mu_1 - \mu_2$ is the difference in the population means (equal to zero in our case) according to the null hypothesis. The expression $\sigma_{(\bar{x}_1 - \bar{x}_2)}$ is the estimated standard error of the difference between the two means and is calculated by

$$\sigma_{(\bar{x}_1 - \bar{x}_2)} = \hat{\sigma} \sqrt{\left(\frac{1}{n_1} + \frac{1}{n_2} \right)}$$

where $\hat{\sigma}$ is the estimate of the pooled standard deviation of the populations and is given:

$$\hat{\sigma} = \sqrt{\frac{(n_1 - 1)s_1^2 + (n_2 - 1)s_2^2}{n_1 + n_2 - 2}}$$

The critical value at α significance level and $(n_1 + n_2 - 2)$ degrees of freedom can be found from tables (*see* Appendix 2).

This formula assumes that the two sample variances are simply two estimates of the true population variance. If there is evidence that the variances are different, the test is modified. This will not be discussed here but the interested reader can refer to Sincich (1995) or other texts mentioned in the further reading section. Alternatively, most good statistical packages will do both types of tests.

■ Whiteladies Health Centre   *Scenario 12.4*

A possible change to the system was to make the surgery 'appointment only'. Groups of five patients were given appointments at five minute intervals. The model was modified accordingly and ten replications were made of the amended model. The results are shown in Table 12.3.

Since it has already been shown that the data from the simulation is approximately normal, a two-sample *t*-test can be performed. The null hypothesis is that the means are two estimates of the same population mean. That is, there

Table 12.3 ■ Comparison of with and without appointments

Mean waiting time to see a doctor (minutes)		
Replication	Original model (no appointments)	Appointments
1	15.6	10.8
2	18.9	7.8
3	13.0	8.1
4	6.8	8.9
5	14.3	5.2
6	9.3	9.6
7	22.6	9.1
8	8.6	9.6
9	13.5	7.7
10	14.3	7.6
mean	13.69	8.44
standard deviation	4.762	1.534

is no significant difference between the sample means; any difference is the result of chance effects. The alternative hypothesis is that the population means are different. This is a two-sided test since we have no reason to believe that one model should give waiting times that are shorter than the other. That is:

$$H_0: \mu_1 = \mu_2 \qquad H_1: \mu_1 \neq \mu_2$$

If we assume that the variances are equal we can calculate the pooled estimate of the standard deviation, which is:

$$\sqrt{\frac{(10-1) \times 4.762^2 + (10-1) \times 1.534^2}{10 + 10 - 2}} = 3.538$$

and the standard error is $3.538 \times \sqrt{\left(\frac{1}{10} + \frac{1}{10}\right)} = 1.582$

and the value of t is: $\dfrac{(13.69 - 8.44 - 0)}{1.582} = 3.319$

▶

The critical value of t at 5 per cent significance level and 18 degrees of freedom is 2.101 (*see* Appendix 2), so it appears that the appointment system will make a difference to the mean waiting time.

Using MINITAB the results shown below were obtained.

MTB > TwoSample 95.0 'No app.' 'appoint.';
SUBC> Alternative 0;
SUBC> Pooled.

Two Sample T-Test and Confidence Interval

Twosample T for No app. vs appoint.

	N	Mean	StDev	SE Mean
No app.	10	13.69	4.76	1.5
appoint.	10	8.44	1.53	0.49

95% C.I. for mu No app. - mu appoint.: (1.9, 8.57)
T-Test mu No app. = mu appoint. (vs not =): T= 3.32 P=0.0038 DF= 18
Both use Pooled StDev = 3.54

Although the MINITAB calculations are set out differently to that carried out manually, the figures correspond to that already obtained. For instance, the t-statistic is 3.32. The advantage with using a package like MINITAB is that the probability that the null hypothesis is correct is given; this avoids having to use tables to find the critical value. In this instance the probability (P) is 0.0038 or 0.38 per cent. This is well below 0.05 (5 per cent) so the hypothesis that the means are the same is rejected. That is, the appointment system does appear to change the mean waiting time. In fact, the figures suggest that an appointment system would reduce this time. This makes sense as a source of variability has been removed from the system.

The calculations above have assumed that the variances of the two samples are equal. To test this assumption, MINITAB has been used and the output in the form of a diagram is shown in Figure 12.2.

This diagram and the accompanying statistics suggests that the two variances are indeed different. If this is true, the two-sample t-test needs to be modified and this has been done using MINITAB. Notice that the only difference between the commands is that the word 'pooled' is not used for the modified test.

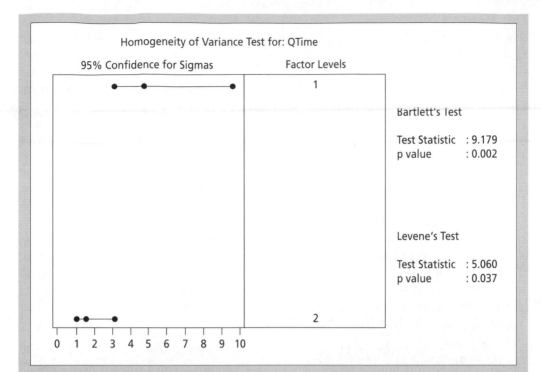

Figure 12.2 ■ **Test for homogeneity of variance**

MTB > TwoSample 95.0 'No app.' 'appoint.';
SUBC> Alternative 0.

Two Sample T-Test and Confidence Interval

Twosample T for No app. vs appoint.

	N	Mean	StDev	SE Mean
No app.	10	13.69	4.76	1.5
appoint.	10	8.44	1.53	0.49

95% C.I. for mu No app. - mu appoint.: (1.7, 8.78)
T-Test mu No app. = mu appoint. (vs not =): T= 3.32 P=0.0078 DF= 10

Although the test statistic for the modified test is the same, the degrees of freedom are different and this results in a different value of *P*. In this case the conclusion that the means are different has not changed since the probability is still well below 5 per cent.

The Mann-Whitney test

When the assumption of normality cannot be made, it is necessary to use a non-parametric test. For two samples, the appropriate test to use is the Mann-Whitney test. The null hypothesis for this test is that the two samples come from the same probability distribution, while the alternative hypothesis is that they come from different distributions.

To perform the Mann-Whitney test, the data from the two models are merged and sorted in ascending order. To avoid losing the identity of the data it is easiest to sort the data in their original columns. Each data item is then given a rank according to its position in the table. Whenever there are two or more ties, the ranks are averaged. So if the tenth and eleventh values are equal, the ranks for these values will both be 10.5 and the next rank will be twelve.

If the data has come from the same distribution there should not be any pattern in the way that the values appear in the table referred to above. However, if one of the models gives lower values on average, values from this model are more likely to appear near the top of the table. To test the hypothesis that there is no difference between the models, the *rank sum* is calculated. This is the sum of the ranks of the values in the first model and is denoted as W_1.

The 'U' value is then calculated. This is

$$U = n_1 \times n_2 + \frac{n_1(n_1 + 1)}{2} - W_1$$

where n_1 and n_2 are the numbers of values in alternatives 1 and 2 respectively.

If n_1 and n_2 are both at least 10, we can assume that U is normally distributed with a mean of:

$$\mu_U = \frac{n_1 \times n_2}{2}$$

and a standard deviation of:

$$\sigma_u = \sqrt{\frac{n_1 \times n_2 \times (n_1 + n_2 + 1)}{12}}$$

The value of Z is calculated in the normal way; that is:

$$Z = \frac{U - \mu_U}{\sigma_U}$$

■ Whiteladies Health Centre   *Scenario 12.5*

Since it has been demonstrated that the sample data comes from a population that is normally distributed, there is no need to use a non-parametric test. However, the use of the Mann-Whitney test in this situation is not wrong and it will be useful for demonstration purposes.

To apply the test, the data given in Table 12.3 is sorted into ascending order. The new table with the ranks is given in Table 12.4.

Table 12.4 ■ **Rankings of the data from Table 12.3**

Mean waiting time to see a doctor (minutes)		
Rank	Original model (no appointments)	Appointments
1		5.2
2	6.8	
3		7.6
4		7.7
5		7.8
6		8.1
7	8.6	
8		8.9
9		9.1
10	9.3	
11.5		9.6
11.5		9.6
13		10.8
14	13.0	
15	13.5	
16.5	14.3	
16.5	14.3	
18	15.6	
19	18.9	
20	22.6	

This table clearly shows that the data from the appointment system is clustered near the top of the table, while the no appointment data is at the bottom.

To apply the Mann-Whitney test to this data, the rank sum for this table is calculated as follows:

$$W_1 = 2 + 7 + 10 + 14 + 15 + 16.5 + 16.5 + 18 + 19 + 20 = 138$$

and

$$U = 10 \times 10 + \frac{10 \times 11}{2} - 138 = 17$$

Since the values of n_1 and n_2 are both 10, we can assume that U is normally distributed with a mean of

$$\frac{10 \times 10}{2} = 50$$

and a standard deviation of:

$$\sqrt{\frac{10 \times 10 \times 21}{12}} = 13.2$$

$$Z = \frac{17 - 50}{13.2} = -2.5 \quad \text{(or 2.5 if the sign is ignored)}$$

The critical value for Z at 5 per cent significance level is 1.96 (*see* Appendix 2) and since the calculated Z value is greater than this figure, there does appear to be a difference between the alternatives.

As with most statistical tests it is easier to use a statistical software package. The output from *SPSS* is shown below.

SPSS for MS WINDOWS Release 6.0

- - - - - Mann-Whitney U - Wilcoxon Rank Sum W Test

QTIME   waiting time
by MODEL   model number

Mean Rank	Cases
13.80	10 MODEL = 1 no appointment
7.20	10 MODEL = 2 appointment
	20 Total

Exact Corrected for ties

U	W	2-Tailed P	Z	2-Tailed P
17.0	138.0	.0115	−2.4964	.0125

These results show that the probability that the null hypothesis is correct is 0.0125 or 1.25 per cent. This is below 5 per cent used in the manual calculations and confirms the conclusion that there is a significant difference between models.

Common random numbers used for both alternatives

In certain situations it is possible and desirable to use the same stream of random numbers for both the original model and the alternative. The reason for this is that if different streams of random numbers are used, the difference between the output data is the result of the difference between the two models *and* the different random numbers used. In some cases, real differences between two alternatives of a model cannot be detected due to the *noise* caused by the model's randomness. This 'noise' *may* be reduced by using the same random number streams for both models. This statement is qualified because it is not always possible to ensure that the exact same stream is used in both cases. To illustrate this, imagine a simulation of a production process where a machine is prone to breakdowns. These breakdowns occur at random and have been included in the model through the use of an appropriate probability distribution. A number of replications are made of this model and results obtained. Two experiments are to be performed on this model. The first is where there is a change in the priority of this machine and the second is where the machine is taken out of service at regular intervals to be serviced. In the first case the model is essentially the same, and it would be expected that the same random numbers are generated at exactly the same time. This means that particular events, such as the machine breakdown, would occur at exactly the same time for both models. The randomness is therefore controlled and any differences in the output variables should be caused by the change in the model and not the random numbers used. However, in the second case there is a structural change in the model and there is no guarantee that similar events will occur at the same time. This problem can be minimised to a certain extent by ensuring that each source of variability within a model has its own random number stream. If this can be achieved, the breakdown of the machine may be triggered at the same time (although this could occur during the period of overhaul). The practical problem with this solution is that a typical model may require more streams than the simulation package allows.

Another problem with this method is that of synchronising the random number streams at the start of each replication. Many hundreds of thousands of random numbers may be used in a single replication and the chance that the alternative model would finish with the same random number as the original model must be very small indeed. This means that after the first replication the random numbers used in both the original and alternative models get out of step. Many simulation packages overcome this problem by discarding a large number of random numbers at the end of a replication. This effectively allows a break or gap to be inserted in the random number stream so that the next replication starts with the same random number for both models. Figure 12.3 illustrates this procedure in diagrammatic form.

The technique of common random numbers is another example of a variance reduction technique. Common random numbers are probably the most popular and potentially the most useful variance reduction technique, but like any technique it should be used with care. If there are any doubts whether the assumptions underlying the method are met, it is better to use a completely different stream of random numbers for the alternative model and analyse the results using one of the methods for independent data.

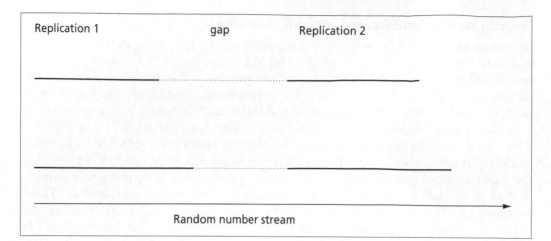

Figure 12.3 ■ Mechanism to ensure that each replication starts with the same random number

When common random numbers are used correctly, the data from the models will be correlated since both models have been tested under identical random conditions. Although the tests already mentioned cannot be used because they assume independence, there are other tests that can be used. If the data is normally distributed the **paired t-test** can be used, while the **Wilcoxon signed ranks test** can be used if normality cannot be assumed.

Paired t-test

To use the paired t-test the *difference* between the outputs for the two alternatives is calculated for each replication. The mean and standard deviation of these differences are found and if the data from both models came from the same distribution, the mean of the differences will be zero. In order to test the null hypothesis that the difference of the population means μ_d is zero, the test statistic shown below is calculated.

$$t = \frac{\bar{x}_d - \mu_d}{\sigma_{\bar{d}}}$$

where $\bar{x}_d$ is the mean of the n differences and μ_d is the population mean difference if the null hypothesis is correct. $\sigma_{\bar{d}}$ is the standard error of the differences and is given by:

$$\sigma_{\bar{d}} = \frac{s_d}{\sqrt{n}}$$

where s_d is the standard deviation of the differences.

The critical t value can be found from tables (*see* Appendix 2) for α significance level (normally 5 per cent) and $n-1$ degrees of freedom.

■ **Whiteladies Health Centre**   *Scenario 12.6*

If the experiment of an appointment system is to be repeated using common random numbers, consideration needs to be given to the suitability of the technique in this situation. Use of an appointment system is a structural change since the arrival pattern of patients will change. This means that services will occur at different times, which could destroy any 'matching' between alternatives. However, each source of variability had been given a unique random number stream and this should ensure that the same pattern of service times occurs for both alternatives. Since it is the service times that cause the main delay in the system, the use of common random numbers should be valid in this case.

The results from ten replications using the amended and original models can be seen in Table 12.5.

Table 12.5 ■ **Comparison of with and without appointments using common random numbers**

	Mean waiting time to see a doctor (minutes)		
Replication	Original model (no appointments)	Appointments	Difference
1	15.6	10.9	−4.7
2	18.9	10.3	−8.6
3	13.0	7.1	−5.9
4	6.8	7.9	1.1
5	14.3	8.8	−5.5
6	9.3	9.2	−0.1
7	22.6	10.3	−12.3
8	8.6	6.2	−2.4
9	13.5	10.9	−2.6
10	14.3	6.3	−8.0
mean	13.69	8.79	−4.90
standard deviation	4.762	1.831	4.083

The mean difference is −4.90 minutes with a standard deviation of 4.083 minutes. The standard error is therefore:

$$\frac{4.083}{\sqrt{10}} = 1.291$$

and

$$t = \frac{-4.90 - 0}{1.291} = -3.80$$

(or 3.80 if the sign is ignored)

Since the critical value is 2.262 on 9 degrees of freedom and 5 per cent significance level, the hypothesis that the mean differences are equal to zero is rejected. An inspection of the data suggests that the appointment method gives lower waiting times on average. This is the same conclusion that was reached with the tests involving independent samples.

The results using MINITAB are shown below. These results confirm the conclusions reached with the manual calculations since the probability that the null hypothesis is correct is 0.0043 or 0.43 per cent. This is well below the 5 per cent level.

MTB > let c4=c3-c1

MTB > ttest c4

T-Test of the Mean

Test of mu = 0.00 vs mu not = 0.00

Variable	N	Mean	StDev	SE Mean	T	P-Value
diff.	10	-4.90	4.08	1.29	-3.80	0.0043

Wilcoxon signed ranks test

This test is used if normality cannot be assumed. It is a non-parametric test and ranks the absolute differences (sign ignored) between the two models and then the sum of the ranks for both the positive and negative differences are found. Zero differences are ignored and the sample size n reduced accordingly. Any ties are given an average rank. The sum of either the positive or negative ranks are compared with the critical value obtained from tables.

For large samples, the sampling distribution for the Wilcoxon signed ranks statistic is normally distributed and the formula is:

$$Z = \frac{T^+ - [n(n + 1)/4]}{\sqrt{[n(n + 1)(2n + 1)/24]}}$$

where T^+ is the sum of the ranks of the positive differences.

■ **Whiteladies Health Centre** *Scenario 12.7*

To use the Wilcoxon signed ranks test the data from Table 12.5 is ranked as shown in Table 12.6.

Table 12.6 ■ **Comparing alternatives using the Wilcoxon signed ranks test**

	Mean waiting time to see a doctor (minutes)			
No appointment	Appointment	Difference	Absolute difference	Rank
15.6	10.9	4.7	4.7	5
18.9	10.3	8.6	8.6	9
13.0	7.1	5.9	5.9	7
6.8	7.9	–1.1	1.1	2
14.3	8.8	5.5	5.5	6
9.3	9.2	0.1	0.1	1
22.6	10.3	12.3	12.3	10
8.6	6.2	2.4	2.4	3
13.5	10.9	2.6	2.6	4
14.3	6.3	8.0	8.0	8

The rank sum $T^+ = 53$. Using the normal approximation we get:

$$Z = \frac{53 - 10 \times 11/4}{\sqrt{10 \times 11 \times 21/24}}$$

$$= -2.60 \ (2.60 \text{ if sign ignored})$$

This value of Z is greater than 1.96 (the critical value at 5 per cent significance level) so it confirms that there is a difference between the two models. The output obtained from SPSS is shown below:

SPSS for MS WINDOWS Release 6.0

- - - - - Wilcoxon Matched-Pairs Signed-Ranks Test

APPOINT appointment
with NOAPP no appointment

▶

Mean Rank Cases

2.00   1 – Ranks (NOAPP LT APPOINT)
5.89   9 + Ranks (NOAPP GT APPOINT)
*   0 Ties (NOAPP EQ APPOINT)*
              —

*   10 Total*

$Z = -2.5992$ *2-Tailed P = .0093*

The probability that the null hypothesis is correct is 0.0093 or 0.93 per cent, which is below the 5 per cent level.

Comparisons of several alternatives

In some situations a comparison is required between several alternatives. This may be the situation when a model of a new system has been built and a comparison is required between several different designs.

In these cases we could compare each alternative with each other, but when we have several alternatives we would have a large number of pairs to evaluate. For example, if there were four alternatives, A, B, C and D, we would have six pairs to analyse (AB, AC, AD, BC, BD and CD). A more serious reservation is that the significance level over all the alternatives is much higher than for a simple two-alternative comparison. This problem can be solved by reducing the pairwise significance level. However, a better technique is called **analysis of variance**, which allows all alternatives to be compared simultaneously.

Analysis of variance

Analysis of variance or ANOVA is a statistical procedure for comparing a number of alternatives. The null hypothesis is that all the alternatives have the same mean. The alternative hypothesis is that at least one of the means is different from the others.

In the case of the comparison of two alternatives, it was possible to either use different random numbers, in which case the data between alternatives are independent of each other, or the same random numbers can be used. This idea can be extended to more than two alternatives, and when common random numbers are used, the alternatives are said to be *matched*. The same reservations regarding the use of common random numbers apply in this case. That is, the same random events should occur in all alternatives at the same time. Since there were doubts as to whether this condition could be met in the paired case, there must be stronger doubts as to whether the technique is valid when there are several alternatives. Common random numbers should therefore be used with care.

Data between alternatives are independent

When the data are independent, we talk about a **completely randomised design**. The principle behind this design is that there is a variation both within and between alternatives. The variation between alternatives represents the variation due to the alternatives themselves, while the variation within the alternatives represents the unexplained variation or *error*. If this error is small compared to the variation between alternatives, this indicates that there is a real difference between the means.

The ratio between the two sources of variation has an **F-distribution** and the larger this value the more likely that there is a difference between the means. Tables are used to determine whether this value could have occurred by chance or whether a real difference exists.

The conventional way of setting out the calculations is in the form of an ANOVA table as shown in Table 12.7 In this table there are k alternatives (factors) and m observations. The sum of squares is the squared deviation from the mean while the mean sum of squares is the sum of squares divided by the degrees of freedom. The F value is the ratio of the mean sum of squares for the between factors to the mean sum of squares due to the error. This table is often referred to as a **one-way analysis of variance table**.

Table 12.7 ■ One-way ANOVA table for the completely randomised design

Source	Degrees of freedom	Sum of squares	Mean sum of squares	F
Factor	$k-1$			
Error	$m-k$			
Total	$m-1$			

The calculations involved in the ANOVA procedure are not difficult but are rather tedious so a statistical software package is normally used.

If ANOVA shows that there is a significant difference between means, it is natural to ask which pair or pairs of means are different. It could be that all combinations are significantly different, but it is more than likely that it is just one or two pairs that are different. There are several methods for deciding this question, such as **Scheffe's method** or **Tukey's honestly significant difference (HSD) test** (*see* Black, 1994), but the simplest is probably to look at the confidence intervals between each combination. MINITAB prints these confidence intervals by default.

▮ Whiteladies Health Centre

Since there is strong indication that an appointment system might reduce the mean waiting time, a further experiment was performed. For this experiment half the patients had an appointment while the other half turned up at random. The appointments were made in groups of five patients at ten-minute intervals. The results from the two experiments were compared with the original model. These results can be seen in Table 12.8.

Table 12.8 ▮ Table of results comparing three independent alternatives

	Mean waiting time to see a doctor (minutes)		
Replication	No appointments	All appointments	50% appointments
1	15.6	10.8	18.6
2	18.9	7.8	8.5
3	13.0	8.1	8.5
4	6.8	8.9	8.6
5	14.3	5.2	10.5
6	9.3	9.6	10.8
7	22.6	9.1	9.4
8	8.6	9.6	15.3
9	13.5	7.7	17.2
10	14.3	7.6	9.8
Mean	13.69	8.44	11.72
Standard deviation	4.762	1.534	3.831

To use MINITAB for ANOVA the data for the three experiments are put into a single column (Qtime) and the factor identifier is put into another column. The factors were given the value of one, two and three corresponding to the columns in Table 12.8. The output is shown below:

MTB > Oneway 'QTime' 'Factor'.

One-Way Analysis of Variance

Analysis of Variance on QTime

Source	DF	SS	MS	F	p
Factor	2	140.7	70.3	5.31	0.011
Error	27	357.3	13.2		
Total	29	498.0			

```
      Individual 95% CIs For Mean
      Based on Pooled StDev
  Level       N  Mean   StDev  ——+———+———+———
  1          10  13.690  4.762           (——*——)
  2          10  8.440   1.534  (    *    )
  3          10  11.720  3.831           (——*——)
                                ——+———+———+———
  Pooled StDev = 3.638                 9.0   12.0   15.0
```

These results suggest that there is a difference between means since the probability that the means are the same is only 0.011 or 1.1 per cent. This was expected since we have already shown that the mean queuing times for the 'no appointment' and 'appointment' models were significantly different. But is there also a significant difference between the mean for the 50 per cent appointment model and the means for the other two models? MINITAB also gives us a pictorial view of the confidence intervals and we can see that this model (factor 3) overlaps factors one and two and so suggests that the mean for the 50 per cent model is not different to the other two means. This is not a proof in itself but it does give an indication that no difference exists. For a more rigorous test Tukey's method can be used and the results from using this test are provided in the SPSS output below.

SPSS for MS WINDOWS Release 6.0
- - - - - O N E W A Y - - - - -

Variable QTIME waiting time
By Variable MODEL model number

   Analysis of Variance

Source	D.F.	Sum of Squares	Mean Squares	F Ratio	F Prob.
Between Groups	2	140.6727	70.3363	5.3147	.0113
Within Groups	27	357.3290	13.2344		
Total	29	498.0017			

Variable QTIME   waiting time
By Variable MODEL   model number

Multiple Range Tests: Tukey-HSD test with significance level .050

▶

The difference between two means is significant if
MEAN(J)-MEAN(I) >= 2.5724 * RANGE * SQRT(1/N(I) + 1/N(J))
with the following value(s) for RANGE: 3.50

(*) Indicates significant differences which are shown in the lower triangle

$$
\begin{array}{ccc}
G & G & G \\
r & r & r \\
p & p & p \\
2 & 3 & 1
\end{array}
$$

Mean	MODEL			
8.4400	Grp 2			
11.7200	Grp 3			
13.6900	Grp 1		*	

Homogeneous Subsets (highest and lowest means are not significantly different)

Subset 1

Group	Grp 2	Grp 3
Mean	8.4400	11.7200

- - - - - - - - - - - - - - - -

Subset 2

Group	Grp 3	Grp 1
Mean	11.7200	13.6900

- - - - - - - - - - - - - - - -

The abbreviation 'Grp' refers to the three different alternatives and it can be seen that only the means for the first two alternatives (Grp1 and Grp2) are significantly different.

Common random numbers used for all alternatives

We saw in the comparison of two alternatives that the use of common random numbers enabled real differences between alternatives to be more easily identified. This was because the variability caused by the random numbers is reduced. A similar idea can be used when we have three or more alternatives. The design in this case is called the **randomised block design**.

In general, the 'blocks' can refer to anything that is the same for each alternative. So in the case of a simulation experiment, the block is the random number stream used for a particular replication. The variation within an experiment now consists of:

■ that due to the different alternatives (factors)

■ that due to the blocks (different random number streams)

■ that due to error

Since the error should be reduced, it is more likely that a real difference between means will be identified. The ANOVA table is amended to take account of this additional variation and can be seen in Table 12.9. This table is usually referred to as a **two-way analysis of variance table**.

Table 12.9 ■ Two-way ANOVA table for the randomised block design

Source	Degrees of freedom	Sum of squares	Mean sum of squares	F
Factors	$m - 1$			
Blocks	$b - 1$			
Error	$(m - 1)(b - 1)$			
Total	$mb - 1$			

■ **Whiteladies Health Centre** *Scenario 12.9*

The experiment involving the 50 per cent appointment scenario was repeated using common random numbers. Since each source of variability has its own unique random number stream, we can be justified in the use of common random numbers. We will, though, need to interpret our results with care. The results can be seen in Table 12.10.

MINITAB will perform the randomised block design using the two-way analysis of variance command. Although MINITAB does not give the F-value, it does plot confidence intervals for each alternative and these will allow obvious differences in means to be spotted. Alternatively, the F-values can be easily calculated and compared with the critical F-value found in Appendix 2. To use the two-way procedure the waiting time data (QT crn) was entered in one column while the replication number (Replicat) and the model type (Factor) were entered in two separate columns. The sub-command 'additive' was included to indicate that we are not interested in any interaction effects. The output for the two-way model is shown below.

MTB > Twoway 'QT crn' 'Replicat' 'Factor';

SUBC> Additive;

SUBC> Means 'Factor'.

Two-way Analysis of Variance

Analysis of Variance for QT crn

Source	DF	SS	MS
Replicat	9	303.9	33.8

▶

Factor	*2*	*131.8*	*65.9*
Error	*18*	*214.0*	*11.9*
Total	*29*	*649.7*	

```
              Individual 95 per cent CI
Factor   Mean   ——+———+———+———+——
1        13.7                      (———*———)
2         8.8   (———*———)
3        12.6           (———*———)
              ——+———+———+———+——
              7.5    10.0   12.5   15.0
```

The confidence intervals indicate that there is a difference between the 'no appointment' (Factor 1) and 'all appointment' (Factor 2) alternatives, but not between the '50 per cent appointments' (Factor 3) and the first two alternatives. The F-value is found by dividing MS for the factor by the error MS. This gives a value of 5.54. The critical value on 2 and 18 degrees of freedom at 5 per cent significance level is 3.555, and this confirms that there is a significant difference between the means.

Table 12.10 ■ **Table of results comparing three alternatives using common random numbers**

	Mean waiting time to see a doctor (minutes)		
Replication	No appointments	All appointments	50% appointments
1	15.6	10.9	15.6
2	18.9	10.3	7.5
3	13.0	7.1	15.5
4	6.8	7.9	7.6
5	14.3	8.8	10.8
6	9.3	9.2	7.8
7	22.6	10.3	25.5
8	8.6	6.2	14.6
9	13.5	10.9	12.5
10	14.3	6.3	8.3
Mean	13.69	8.79	12.57
Standard deviation	4.762	1.831	5.613

Factorial design

So far we have only looked at situations where each alternative is a separate experiment. By analysing these experiments using analysis of variance we were able to decide whether there was a significant difference between any of the means. In statistical terminology these experiments are conducted by changing a *factor* in the model.

In reality, an **experimental design** for a simulation model could include many different factors and the different values that these factors can take are called *levels*. A particular combination of levels used in an experiment is called a *treatment* and the output variable we are interested in is called a *response*. So in a model of a production system we might be interested in changes in throughput as a result of changes to the speed of a machine and to some priority rule. We may have three different speeds to consider and two priority rules (say, first-in, first-out and shortest job first). Both speed and priority rules are factors and there are three levels for the speed factor and two levels for the priority factor. For each factor and level combination we would need to make at least two replications so that the mean response can be calculated. If we plotted the means of these responses we might get the graph shown in Figure 12.4. This indicates that priority rule A gives higher output than rule B for all levels of the speed factor. The fact that the two lines are parallel also indicates that there is no *interaction* between the two factors. An interaction effect occurs when the response to a factor depends on the levels of another factor. However, we could get the graph shown in Figure 12.5, which shows that priority rule A is better for high and low levels of the speed factor but is inferior for the medium-speed setting. It is not necessary for the lines to cross to indicate that there is an interaction effect as it is the slope of the lines that determine the strength of the interaction. Provided the lines diverge or converge

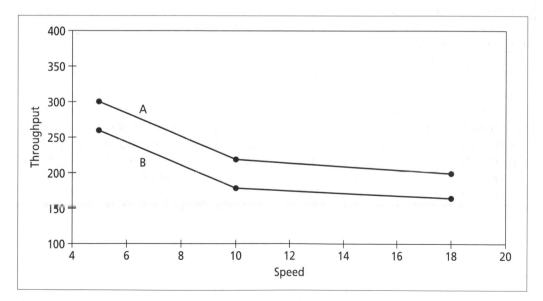

Figure 12.4 ▩ Graph of response for two independent factors

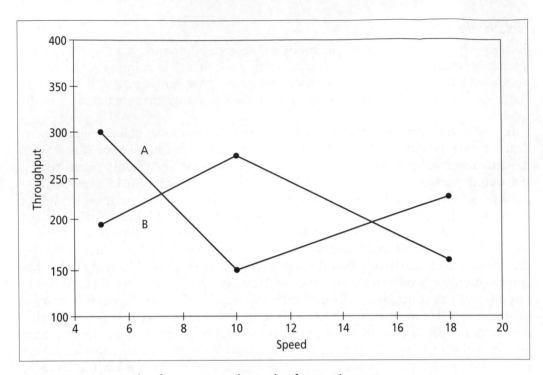

Figure 12.5 ■ Graph of response where the factors interact

over the range, we can conclude that the response to a factor is not constant but depends on the level of the other factor.

Unfortunately, when there are several factors and each factor has several levels, the number of combinations soon becomes very large. If, say, we have five factors and each factor has four levels, the number of combinations is $4^5 = 1024$!

To simplify matters we could restrict the number of levels to two, in which case for n factors we would have 2^n combinations. So, using our example above, we would have only 32 combinations, which is a little more manageable. However, the task now is to choose the two appropriate levels, which is not always easy. In addition, by restricting the number of levels to two we can miss important non-linear effects and interactions. This can be illustrated by looking at Figure 12.5 and noticing that if the middle speed is ignored, the graph would be approximately two parallel lines. We would conclude from this graph that there was no interaction between speed and priority rule.

■ Whiteladies Health Centre

The following factors were considered to influence the waiting time of patients:

- ■ number of doctors on duty
- ■ the interarrival time of patients
- ■ the mode of operation of the centre

Since the number of doctors on duty and the number of patients varies from day to day, it might be interesting to compare these factors together with the mode of operation of the centre and see if there is an interaction between them. Two levels were chosen for each factor. In the case of doctors these were four and six as these were the minimum and maximum number of doctors that are normally on duty. The interarrival times were chosen as 1.37 and 2.00 minutes as these represented the lower and upper limits that were observed. The modes of operation of the centre were taken as the appointment and no appointment alternatives.

Using these three factors, we have a 2^3 factorial experiment. This gives eight different combinations. The simulation was repeated three times for each of these combinations and the results can be seen in Table 12.11.

Table 12.11 ■ Results for the factorial experiment

Doctors	IAT	Appointment	Replication		
			1	2	3
6	1.37	no	15.6	18.9	13.0
6	1.37	yes	10.8	7.8	8.1
6	2.00	no	6.4	6.4	10.4
6	2.00	yes	6.2	7.2	7.6
4	1.37	no	14.5	33.1	37.8
4	1.37	yes	29.9	33.9	33.2
4	2.00	no	13.5	8.0	10.5
4	2.00	yes	5.5	3.3	3.5

This experiment was analysed by MINITAB using the ANOVA command. The three interaction effects (doctors/iat, doctors/app and app/iat) have to be specified in the model as well as the two main effects. (There is a three-way interaction effect, doctors/iat/app, which has been ignored.) The results from MINITAB can be seen below:

►

MTB > ANOVA 'Wait' = doctor iat app doctor*iat doctor*app app*iat;
SUBC> Means doctor iat app doctor*iat doctor*app iat*app.

Analysis of Variance (Balanced Designs)

Factor	Type	Levels	Values	
doctor	fixed	2	4	6
iat	fixed	2	1	2
app	fixed	2	0	1

Analysis of Variance for Wait

Source	DF	SS	MS	F	P
doctor	1	488.70	488.70	17.70	0.001
iat	1	1177.40	1177.40	42.65	0.000
app	1	40.30	40.30	1.46	0.243
doctor*iat	1	486.90	486.90	17.64	0.001
doctor*app	1	9.25	9.25	0.34	0.570
iat*app	1	6.72	6.72	0.24	0.628
Error	17	469.30	27.61		
Total	23	2678.58			

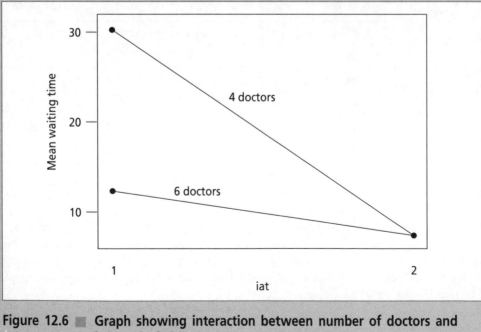

Figure 12.6 ■ Graph showing interaction between number of doctors and interarrival time

The results indicate that the effect on waiting time by the change in the number of doctors and the change in mean interarrival times are both significant. They also show that there is a significant interaction effect between the doctor and interarrival factors. A better way of observing this interaction is through a graph and this can be created with MINITAB using the %interact command (*see* Figure 12.6).

This graph shows that when there are more patients (the interarrival time is short), an additional doctor would have a big effect on the waiting time in the surgery. However, when the surgery is less busy the addition of another doctor will make very little difference.

■ Case study 4
THE GROWING NEED FOR RENAL SERVICES

This case study illustrates the use of simulation in health care. One of the technical difficulties of this simulation was that the entities must be able to take part in parallel activities that may interrupt each other. To overcome this problem a technique called patient-orientated simulation technique (POST) was used. The authors are Ruth Davies and Julian Flowers.

Renal replacement therapies save the lives of patients with end-stage renal failure but they are expensive. Moreover, the demand for treatment is growing and survival is improving. A simulation model has been developed that can help plan these services. Use of the simulation in East Norfolk Health Commission has shown that many more resources will be needed to meet the expected demand for services. The expense may be reduced, however, by increasing the transplantation rate. Simulation modelling is a flexible approach which has had the support of both the clinicians and the Health Commission, giving the results credibility as a basis for policy formulation.

Background

Renal replacement therapy (kidney dialysis and transplant) has been one of the great medical success stories. Prior to development of dialysis treatment in the 1960s, the average survival time from terminal renal failure was only a few months; now the median survival across Europe is around fifteen years.

Despite its undoubted efficacy, concerns have been raised about the resources required to maintain a renal replacement therapy programme. In the UK, the number of new patients entering renal replacement therapy per year was 40 per million population, on average, in the 1980s, rising to 65 per million in 1991. As the number of new patients increases and survival improves, the population of renal replacement therapy patients inevitably grows. The estimated number of new patients needing dialysis is 75–80 per million population per annum (Feest *et al.*, 1990).

Renal replacement therapy is not cheap, however. The average annual cost per patient is between £10,000 and £20,000 (this varies from unit to unit); thus the average lifetime cost of renal replacement therapy per patient will be in the region of £200,000. Between 1 per cent and 2 per cent of a Health Commission's acute services budget will be spent on dialysis and transplantation.

Health Commissions in the National Health Service (NHS) are charged with the responsibility of assessing the health care needs and of purchasing the appropriate services for their resident populations. If they are to meet the national target acceptance rate of 75–80 per million population per year, increased year-on-year funding will have to be found from cash-limited budgets. It is essential therefore that they understand the likely growth and cost implications of the renal service in both the short and medium term. Hence they need to be able to plan ahead and simulation modelling can aid this process.

Modelling patient flow through treatment

There are three main types of renal replacement therapies. These are as follows:

▓ *Haemodialysis*. The patient has to use a kidney machine two or three times a week for four to six hours a time. This may take place in a hospital unit, in an 'out-of-town' minimal care unit or at the patient's house, adapted for this purpose.

▓ *Continuous ambulatory peritoneal dialysis (CAPD)*. An exchange of fluids takes place within the patient's abdomen. A bag of sterile fluid is supported under the patient's clothing which needs changing every six to eight hours.

▓ *Kidney transplant*. Kidneys are normally obtained from cadavers but are sometimes donated by a live relative. The tissues have to be cross-matched with the patient's tissue to reduce the risk of rejection. Patients are given immuno-suppressive drugs to further reduce the risk of rejection.

When patients are accepted on to the programme, they are normally given haemodialysis or CAPD but a few are given immediate transplant operations. Many of the patients on dialysis are put on the transplant waiting list but continue to receive dialysis while they are waiting. Some patients are unable to continue haemodialysis for medical or social reasons and transfer to CAPD treatment. Others transfer from CAPD to haemodialysis. Those receiving a transplant generally experience a better quality of life but they may suffer a transplant rejection and return to dialysis. Some patients receive a second transplant. Patients may die at any stage.

The purpose of modelling the system is to predict the number of patients who may require treatment in the future, under different assumptions about demand and resource provision. The predicted workload can then be translated into costs. Discrete simulation modelling was chosen in preference to Markov modelling, time-slicing simulation or spreadsheet modelling (Davies and Davies 1994 and Davies 1985) because it can:

▓ include an independent source of transplants

▓ constrain the availability of resources, such as unit dialysis

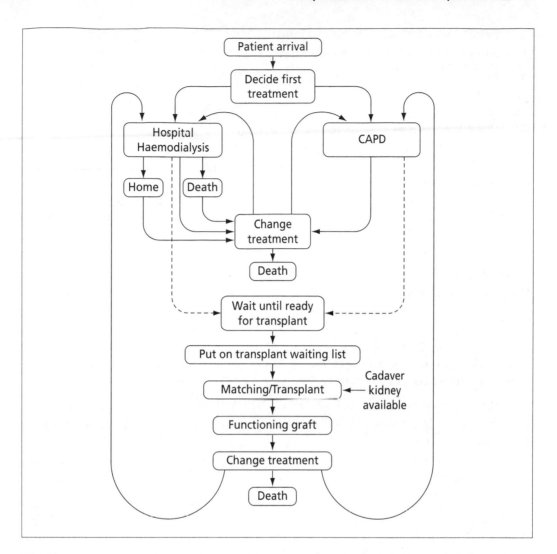

Figure 12.7 ■ Diagram showing the flow of patients through therapies

■ describe the attributes of patients that influence resource use

■ make realistic assumptions about the shape of the survival distributions

The simulation model used in East Norfolk was similar to that described by Bolger and Davies (1992). Patients (the simulation entities) take part in the different treatments (the activities), and move from one to another. Figure 12.7 shows the movement of patients through treatment. The arrival of new patients, the harvesting of kidneys for transplantation, the choice of initial treatment, the suitability of patients for transplantation and treatment survival are all sampled from probability distributions.

The simulation program is run on a microcomputer and has a 'front end' for the entry and editing of input data. There are separate data files for:

- patient risk factors (e.g. age groups)
- survival and transition probabilities
- patient and kidney arrival rates and resource constraints (e.g. unit dialysis places)
- the current number of patients on the different therapies and on the transplant waiting list

The output provides average predictions of numbers of patients on different treatments over several years, with means and 95 per cent confidence limits from the simulation replications. It also shows waiting lists, numbers of deaths and the use of resources such as the hospital dialysis unit. The results from each set of simulation replications are saved in two text files. One of these can be displayed by the simulation program and the other is designed for use in a spreadsheet so that further analysis and graphs may be produced.

Simulation software

The simulation software is written in Pascal, using an extension of Pascal SIM (Davies and O'Keefe, 1989). Davies and Davies (1994) have shown that spreadsheet modelling and commercial simulation packages are often inappropriate for patient flow models. In this system, for example, the point in time when the simulated patient starts haemodialysis the simulation program must:

- set the time of haemodialysis failure or death
- set the time when a patient goes to minimal care or home dialysis (if appropriate)
- set the time for a patient to go on a transplant waiting list (if the patient is suitable)

Thus the simulation must be able to hold a simulated patient's survival information, maintain the patient on a transplant waiting list and on a cycle of home dialysis with intermittent interruptions for periods of unit dialysis, all at the same time. In the event of death, going to CAPD or receiving a transplant, the patient must be removed from the other activities.

Conventional simulation software does not provide for individual entities in the simulation to take part in parallel activities which may interrupt each other. Davies and Davies (1994) have developed simulation software for describing patient flow in systems called the patient-orientated simulation technique (POST). The renal simulation program, which uses this software, is easy to use and may describe thousands of patients.

Use in East Norfolk Health Commission

The simulation model was used by East Norfolk Health Commission with the agreement and co-operation of the clinicians. Figure 12.8 shows the data collection process and the role of the simulation in the Health Commission.

The data concerning the numbers of patients on different treatments, the current arrival rate, the current transplant rate and the number of unit dialysis places in

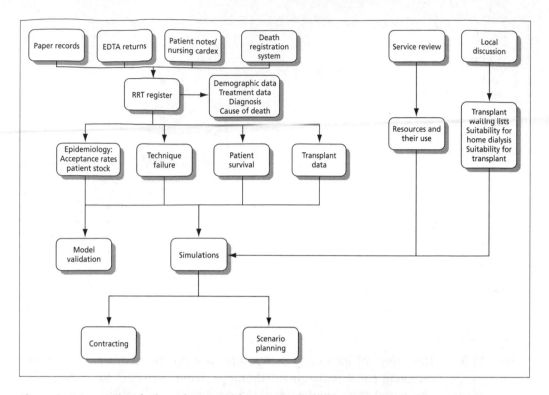

Figure 12.8 ■ Simulation data requirements and use in a purchasing Health Authority

Norwich and Yarmouth were all readily available. Patient records were not computerised, however, and so the survival and transfer probabilities were not so easy to obtain. Therefore, the first task was to collect information about treatment modes and treatment dates of all patients, past and present, and to put them on a database. The patient database was analysed to provide the treatment survival probabilities. As the total number of patients who had ever been treated in Norwich or Yarmouth District was less than 500, the patients were not analysed by risk groups (age or medical condition) because the numbers in each group were too small. The local renal physicians helped by advising on the quality of the data on the patient database and also on the other inputs to the model.

The simulation was validated by running it with past data to see whether it could predict the current number of patients. As the exact arrival and transplant rates were known, the validation was able to check whether the survival and transfer data and logic were sound. As might have been hoped, the predications were found to be quite accurate.

The simulation was then used for developing local strategies for renal replacement therapy. Each simulation run was done with 50 replications to provide means and confidence limits of results.

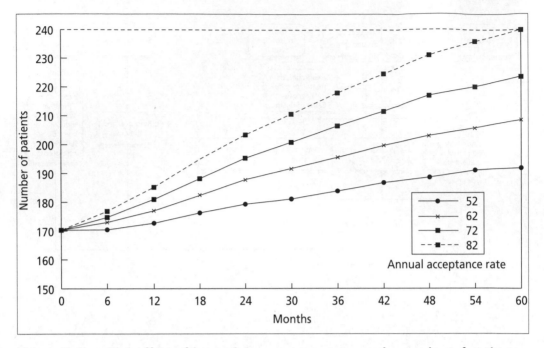

Figure 12.9 ■ **The effect of increasing acceptance rate on the number of patients receiving renal replacement therapy. (From mid-1993 to 1998. The initial start number was 171 patients.)**

Results from simulation runs

Increasing acceptance rates

Figure 12.9 shows the growth in the number of patients receiving renal replacement therapy over the next five years, as the number of new patients entering the programme varies. The current local acceptance rate is 75 per million population (pmp) which compares well with the national target rate. At this intake level, the renal units in Norwich and Yarmouth would expect to have to be able to treat 60 to 70 additional patients after five years – an average growth of about 8 per cent per year.

Resource implications

Figure 12.10 shows the impact of the growth in patient stock, as outlined above, on existing facilities. This assumes that dialysis is restricted to local residents only, that current clinical practice and use of dialysis places does not change, and that there is no change in the transplant rate. It shows that the hospital dialysis facilities would soon be swamped and patients whose first choice treatment was haemodialysis would have to have CAPD instead.

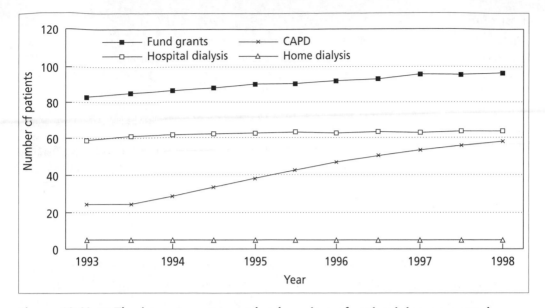

Figure 12.10 ▓ **The impact on current local services of maintaining an annual acceptance rate of 75 pmp**

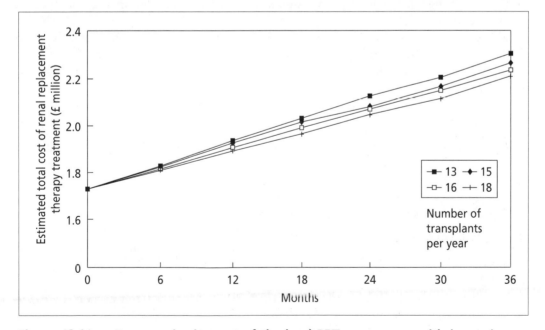

Figure 12.11 ▓ **Decrease in the cost of the local RRT programme with increasing transplant rate**

Cost-effectiveness

Figure 12.11 shows the effect of increasing the transplant rate on the likely future costs of the service. It can be seen that the higher the transplant rate, the lower the overall cost. These average costs are from Beech *et al.* (1994). A higher transplant rate will also reduce pressure on existing facilities.

Caution in using the simulation

As there are small numbers of patients on the different therapies, the confidence limits about the mean predictions are wide. If these means are used year on year to inform the annual purchasing cycle, there are likely to be substantial errors. However, accurate predictions are impossible because no-one knows how many patients will die or how many transplants will be made available in any one year. Clearly, in using the predictions in planning, attention must be paid to the confidence limits as well as the averages.

The simulation results are sensitive to changes in the availability of kidneys, arrival rates and survival rates. If these are consistently under- or over-estimated in the simulation, then there will be an error accumulating over time. If changes in any of these factors are expected to take place (for example, an increase in the arrival rate of new patients) then the simulation input can be adjusted accordingly.

Furthermore, the assumptions made in the original simulation model may change over time. A new treatment may be introduced or the policies with respect to providing long-term treatment on kidney machines at home rather than in a hospital unit may change. In these circumstances, some of the simulation logic may need to be recoded.

There is clearly a need to keep the patients' database up to date and to keep abreast of the policies and activities in the renal units so that the simulation data or logic can be changed, when necessary, and the output can be interpreted correctly.

Conclusion

One of the initial drawbacks in using the simulation was the need for detailed survival data which was not previously available. The data collection required the development of a register for the renal unit of all its patients, past and present, on the renal replacement therapy programme. This is now being kept up to date and provides a useful source of information for the renal consultants.

The results have been and will be used in the future for developing local strategies for the provision of renal replacement therapy. The involvement of local clinicians was very important in obtaining data to run the simulation and in gaining credibility for the results.

Simulation modelling has allowed East Norfolk Health Commission to make predictions of future need for a complex health care service and to develop purchasing policy.

They have shown that:

■ the current management of renal replacement therapy services is unsustainable

■ they need to find ways to increase the transplant rate to local residents as a matter of priority

■ there may be a need to expand the service – the effect of any options considered can be examined using the model

Simulation modelling has proved a flexible tool which has had the support of both clinicians and the Health Commission, giving the results credibility as a basis for policy formulation.

This case study was reproduced (with permission) from a paper by Davies, R. and Flowers, J. (1995), 'The growing need for renal services', *OR Insight*, April–June, Vol. 8, Issue 2.

Summary

This chapter has been concerned with the very important issue of the design and analysis of simulation experiments. There are several issues that need considering, such as whether absolute measures are required or whether comparisons should be made between two or more alternatives. When deciding on the correct statistical technique we have to make sure that the assumptions made by the technique are met by the data. If these assumptions are not valid we either need to use a different technique or control the way that the simulation has generated the data.

The advantage with experimenting with a simulation model is that we have full control of the experiment. When we use the same random number streams for each alternative, we are using a variance reduction method called common random numbers. This technique reduces the randomness between alternatives and therefore makes it easier to identify real differences. However, common random numbers should be used with care and ideally every source of variability within the model should have its own unique random number stream. Even then, there will be many situations where the use of this technique cannot be justified.

In many simulation studies, comparisons are made between two alternatives and the choice of test is usually between the two sample *t*-test and the paired *t*-test. These tests assume normality and if there are any doubts about this assumption a non-parametric test should be used. When several alternatives are being analysed together, a technique known as analysis of variance can be used. There are several different forms of this technique and the design used depends on whether common random numbers have been used and whether the identification of an interaction effect is important.

In statistical terminology, we use the term 'factor' to represent the variable that is going to be changed in the experiment. These factors may have several levels and the response from changing one factor may depend on the level of another factor. If this occurs we say that the factors interact and the identification of an interaction effect can be an important part of a simulation study.

Figure 12.12 summarises the techniques that can be used when comparing alternative models.

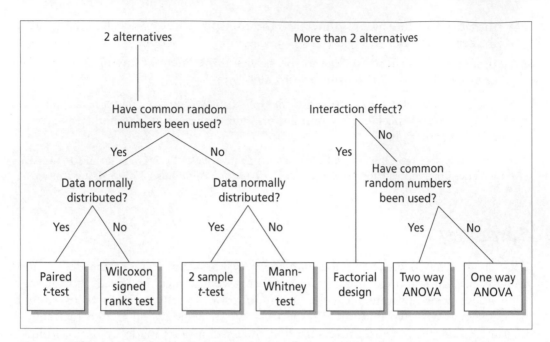

Figure 12.12 ■ Summary of statistical tests that can be used when comparing simulation experiments

■ Exercises

12.1 When would a paired *t*-test be the appropriate test for comparing the results from two alternative models?

12.2 Under what conditions would it be reasonable to use common random numbers as a method of reducing the variation between alternative models?

12.3 A simulation model of an airport was built in order to see the effect on turnaround times of aircraft if a new runway was built. What statistical test might be applicable for this type of experiment?

12.4 If a factorial experiment was to be performed on five factors and two levels with three replications for each experiment, how many runs of the simulation model would be needed?

12.5 Use a statistical software package to test whether the assumption of normality is reasonable for the 'appointment' data in Table 12.3.

12.6 When would it be necessary to use the Mann-Whitney test?

12.7 One use of a simulation model is to discover if there is an interaction effect between two or more factors. Why would this information be useful?

12.8 The Whiteladies Health Centre model was changed so that a relief doctor was called when the number of people waiting to see a doctor reached fifteen. Ten replications of the model were made using different streams of random numbers. The mean waiting time to see a doctor for each of the ten replications is provided in Table 12.12. Analyse this data and decide whether the relief doctor has made a significant impact on the waiting time.

Table 12.12 ▓

	Mean waiting time to see a doctor (minutes)	
Replication	Original model	Relief doctor
1	15.6	12.6
2	18.9	10.5
3	13.0	13.5
4	6.8	14.5
5	14.3	8.6
6	9.3	9.9
7	22.6	8.8
8	8.6	14.2
9	13.5	15.1
10	14.3	10.8

Exercises for students with access to simulation software:

12.9 It is required to see the effect of employing a nurse to treat the 10 per cent of minor cases. Repeat the simulation using this idea and see if this significantly changes the mean waiting time for all the patients.

12.10 Another experiment could be to consider the use of a nurse as a mode of operation of the surgery. Carry out a factorial experiment for:

▓ mode of operation (existing system and use of a nurse as in Exercise 12.9)
▓ doctors (five and six doctors)
▓ mean interarrival time (one minute and two minutes)

12.11 Use the model you developed in Exercise 11.5 (page 269) and try out the following experiments:

a An increase in the arrival rate by 20 per cent.
b An increase in the arrival rate by 20 per cent and an additional service window.
c Combining the ordering and service window into one.

References and further reading

Banks, J. and Carson, J. (1984) *Discrete-Event System Simulation* (Chapter 12), Prentice-Hall, New Jersey, USA.

Beech, R., Gulliford, M., Mays, N., Melia, J. and Roderick, P. (1994) *Health Care Needs Assessment*, Radcliffe Medical Press, London.

Black, K. (1994) *Business Statistics* (Chapters 10 and 11), West, Minneapolis, USA.

Bolger, P. G. and Davies, R. (1992) 'Simulation model for planning renal services in a district health authority', *British Medical Journal*, 305, pp. 605–8.

Box, G. E. P., Hunter, W. G. and Hunter, J. S. (1978) *Statistics for Experimenters*, Wiley, New York.

Davies, R. (1985) 'An assessment of models of a health system', *Journal of the Operational Research Society*, 36, pp. 679–87.

Davies, R. and Davies, H. T. O. (1994) 'Modelling patient flows and resource provision in health systems', *Omega*, 22, pp. 123–31.

Davies, R. and O'Keefe, R. M. (1989) *Simulation Modelling with Pascal*, Prentice Hall Int. (UK).

Feest, T. G., Mistry, C. D., Grimes, B. S. and Mallick, N. P. (1990) 'Incidence of advanced chronic renal failure and the need for end stage replacement therapy', *British Medical Journal*, 301, pp. 987–90.

Harrell, C. R., Bateman, R. E., Glogg, T. J. and Mott, J. R. A. (1992) *System Improvement Using Simulation* (Chapter 10), Promodel Corporation, Orem, Utah 84058, USA.

Kleijnen, J. and Groenendaal, W. (1992) *Simulation: A Statistical Perspective* (Chapter 9), Wiley, Chichester, England.

Law, A. M. (1983) 'Statistical analysis of simulation output data', *Operations Research*, November–December, Vol. 31, No. 6.

Law, A. M. and Kelton W. D. (1991) *Simulation Modelling and Analysis*, Second Edition (Chapters 10, 12), McGraw-Hill, Inc., USA.

Lindman, H. R. (1992) *Analysis of Variance in Experimental Design*, Springer-Verlag, New York, USA.

McHaney, R. (1991) *Computer Simulation: A Practical Perspective* (Chapter 6), Academic Press Limited, London.

Needlamkavil, F. (1987) *Computer Simulation and Modelling* (Chapter 10), Wiley, Chichester, England.

Sincich, T. (1995) *Business Statistics by Example*, Fifth Edition (Chapters 11, 12 and 19), Macmillan Publishing Company, Singapore.

13

A review of simulation software

Les Oakshott

Introduction

Simulation is a computer-modelling procedure, and this means that we have to have some way of telling the computer what to do. To achieve this communication, it is necessary to have a computer program that will translate the conceptual model into a form that the computer will understand. At one time there was little choice; an analyst would use his favourite programming language, such as FORTRAN or Pascal, to write the code. Nowadays the choice is bewildering. There are literally hundreds of different programming languages and simulation tools available, and each is advertised as being the best on the market. So is there a best choice and how do we know if the manufacturers claims are justified? Unfortunately, it would be very difficult, if not impossible, to find a 'best buy'. This is because different people have different requirements and not all products are designed for the same purpose. For some people, particularly where the cost is a major factor, or where the application is unusual, a programming language may still be the better option. For many other people, particularly those in business, time is money and a product is required that can allow simulation models to be built quickly. In these cases a simulation language or package may be preferred. There is also the problem that simulation development is not static, and new or upgraded products are appearing all the time. A product that is good today may look quite mediocre in a few years' time when compared with newer products. This chapter will therefore concentrate on looking at the different types of software currently available and give some guidelines on how to choose a product for a particular application.

Historical perspective

Until the 1970s, simulation models were developed using general-purpose programming languages such as FORTRAN. Use of these programming languages allowed great flexibility, but were time consuming to write and debug. It also restricted modelling to analysts who had a good knowledge of programming. Of course, in those days personal computers were unheard of and programming was carried out on mainframes or mini computers. There were also a few simulation languages available, such as GPSS, Simula and Hocus. These languages still required some programming ability, but they avoided an analyst having to develop the *executive* of the model each time. The executive would be some computer code that would schedule the events to occur at the right time and in the correct sequence. The precise way that the executive worked depended on the *world view* adopted (*see* Chapter 9 for an explanation of the different world views or approaches to simulation). These languages certainly reduced the time to build a simulation model, but there were still many analysts who preferred the total flexibility of writing their simulations in a familiar and trusted programming language. Many FORTRAN programmers even thought that using a modern programming language, such as Pascal, was cheating! Pascal was a *structured* programming language and was better suited to simulation, but was not liked by all analysts.

During the 1980s the personal computer (PC) became the big success story of the decade, and many applications that at one time needed the power of large computers could be transferred to PCs. All the main programming languages were rewritten to work in this new environment, and the move was started to use these 'office' computers to develop simulation models. At the beginning, PCs were rather slow and memory limitations prevented many large simulation models from working efficiently. However, this situation did not last long, and by the middle of the decade a number of new simulation languages had emerged, such as SIMAN. At the same time, software manufacturers had begun to see that the market for simulation could be opened up if the technique could be used by people not skilled in programming. This development took two forms. The first was the manufacture of simulators or simulation packages. These were products that were designed for specific purposes, and were generally manufacturing orientated. Two of the first, and most successful, were SIMFACTORY and WITNESS. The other development was the manufacture of visual interactive simulation software. This software would ride on top of the host language and *animate* the model. Probably one of the most well-known products is CINEMA, which can be used to animate a SIMAN model.

During the early 1990s, the Windows environment became the standard operating system for PCs and this encouraged the development of a graphical user interface or GUI. Essentially, this involved the use of graphical objects or icons to represent parts of the model. The model could then be developed by linking these icons together in a logical fashion. These new tools were more flexible than packages, yet they were easier to use than some of the programming languages. In addition, they often incorporated a range of functions to assist in data input and output analysis. Examples of this type are ARENA and SIMUL8.

Simulation tools

A simulation tool is *any mechanism that can assist in the development of a simulation model*. Simulation tools can therefore range from general-purpose programming languages, to the 'state-of-the-art' simulation packages. Programming languages have the advantage that they are freely available and flexible. Flexibility in this instance means making the program do exactly what you want it to do. Unfortunately, flexibility comes at the expense of ease of use, and in the case of programming languages you need to have programming skills. At the other extreme, we have very specific simulation packages that are very easy to use but lack the flexibility of programming languages. There are a number of in-between states, such as simulation languages and packages that make full use of the graphical capabilities of modern computers.

General-purpose languages

Perhaps the most familiar programming language is FORTRAN. Although it has undergone many changes in its long life, it is still fundamentally an example of an unstructured language. It does not contain any features that can help the simulation analyst, although there are sub-routine libraries containing codes for random variate distribution. An analyst using FORTRAN would need to write the executive for the event scheduling and time advance procedures, as well as the code for the main structure of the model. The problem with using FORTRAN for large programs is that they can be difficult to debug and are not very easy to amend at a later date.

An alternative to FORTRAN is a structured programming language, such as Pascal. Pascal allows a structure to be imposed on a program and this makes for more sound programming methods. The language has a more extensive range of operators than FORTRAN, and allows mixed data types and dynamic arrays.

During the late 1980s and early 1990s, a new range of programming languages have emerged. These include C++ and Smalltalk, as well as many others. These languages support a programming approach called **object orientated programming**, or OOP. This approach is supposed to be better for programs which include interacting objects. Object-orientation programming is not a new concept as it was first used in the writing of the SIMULA programming language in 1967! It is, however, a very powerful method of writing simulation programs, although it initially takes some time to learn and understand the ideas used. Most recent simulation languages and packages have been written in an object-orientated programming language.

Simulation languages

Simulation languages are languages that can be used to model a variety of systems. The most common are SIMAN, GPSS, SIMSCRIPT, SLAM and HOCUS. Each of these languages employs a particular world view, which in most cases is the **process interaction approach**. In the process interaction approach, the life cycle of an entity is described in terms of its creation, and the other components that it interacts with during its life cycle. This is an intuitive method of modelling, and is ideal for people with little programming experience. However, it is designed for queuing systems, and so is not so easy to use where the identification of an entity is difficult. Some languages, such as GASP, use the event scheduling approach, which is the most general method of simulation modelling but requires some knowledge of programming techniques. Many languages, such as SIMAN and SIMSCRIPT, allow models to be developed using both the process interaction and event scheduling approaches. The advantage of these types of programs is that parts of the model can be built using the easier process interaction approach, while other parts which need the flexibility can use the event scheduling approach. In SIMAN these event scheduling routines are written in a programming language called *C*. Using the process interaction approach allowed the program to be designed in blocks. These blocks often used an easily understandable terminology, such as the word 'SEIZE' to mean that an entity requires the service of a resource. The model could then be completely specified by the inclusion of the required blocks in the correct logical sequence. A language that is rather different to the ones already mentioned is HOCUS. This language has been around since 1967, and has many devotees. It is developed around the *activity cycle diagram* method (*see* Chapter 9), and users of this language are encouraged to develop a hand simulation of the model before running the computer version.

The SIMAN simulation language

SIMAN was developed by Systems Modelling Corporation in 1982, and since then there have been thirteen major releases, with Cinema being launched in 1986 and ARENA in 1993. Although SIMAN has changed over the years, the idea that a SIMAN model contains both model logic and data has not changed. This idea has been implemented through the use of a modelling framework that consists of the *model* and the *experiment*. The model contains the logical statements that are needed to represent the system being studied, while the experiment consists of the data needed to run the model. The model and experiment files are compiled, and a listing of the files are sent to the screen together with any error messages produced. If there are no errors, an object file is created, which is a file that has been coded in the form the computer can understand. If there are errors during the compile stage, these errors must be corrected before the files are re-compiled. Usually the compiler is able to specify the type of error and its location in the source file. When object files for both the model and experiment frames have been created, the two files are linked together into a *program* file. It is possible that further errors may appear at this stage, as a result of incompatibilities between the model and experiment files. If this occurs, the errors must be corrected and the offending file or files re-compiled. When the two files link successfully, the program file can be executed. It is possible that *run-time errors* could occur at this stage. Run-time errors are more difficult to isolate than other types of errors, but SIMAN contains a run controller that allows you to step through the execution of the model. Once the program is working correctly, output will be saved to a print file, as well as any data files specified. The sequence of operations needed to reach this output stage is summarised in Figure 13.1.

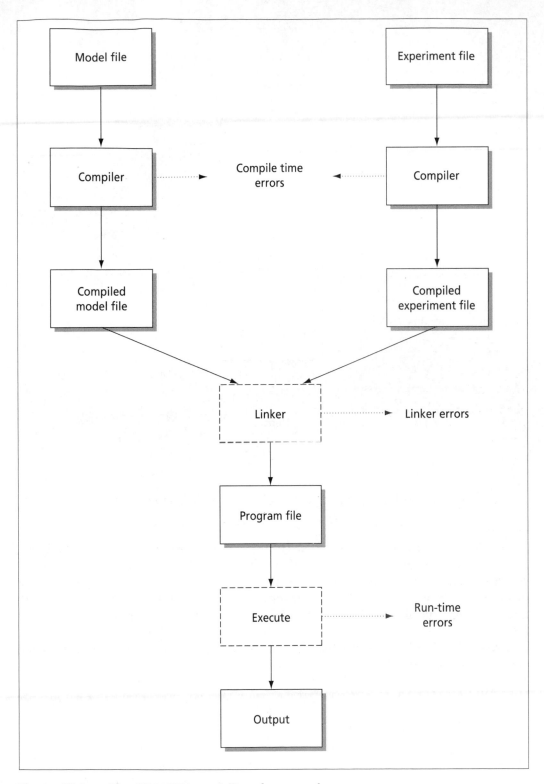

Figure 13.1 ■ The SIMAN V modelling framework

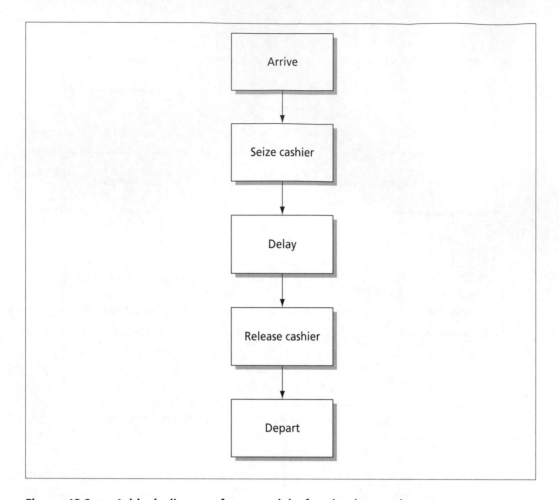

Figure 13.2 ■ A block diagram for a model of a simple queuing system

Processes in SIMAN are modelled using a block diagram approach. A block diagram has already been mentioned in Chapter 9, but essentially it represents the life cycle of an entity as it moves through the system. In a simple queuing example, such as a bank, where a customer arrives, obtains the required service, and then departs, the block diagram might look like the diagram shown in Figure 13.2.

SIMAN contains over 40 blocks, but these are categorised into ten basic block types and these are:

    HOLD
    TRANSFER
    OPERATION
    QUEUE
    BRANCH
    PICKQ
    QPICK

MATCH
SELECT
STATION

The first three blocks contain a sub-set of similar but distinct modelling functions. For example, the OPERATION block contains around twenty sub-blocks, such as CREATE, for creating an arriving entity, and DELAY, for delaying an entity for a period of time. (This delay could be a constant or a variable defined by some probability distribution.) The remaining seven blocks are single function blocks.

In terms of our bank example, the block names would be:

CREATE	Creates an arriving entity
QUEUE	Customer waits in a queue if cashier is busy
SEIZE	Customer seizes the cashier
DELAY	Customer is delayed while the required service is obtained
RELEASE	Customer releases the cashier, so that the next customer can be served
COUNT	A running total of the number of customers served is maintained
TALLY	Tally the time in the system
DISPOSE	The customer departs and the time in the system is recorded

This model file will contain details of the interarrival time distribution, and the distribution of the time taken to be served. Names are given to the queue and the resource that is to be seized, and comments can be added to each line. So, the final model might appear as:

```
CREATE,     1:expo(34.5):MARK(TimeIn);
QUEUE,      bankQ;
SEIZE,      1:cashier,1;
TALLY:      QueueT,Int(TimeIn),1;
DELAY:      cont(.17,25,.45,35,.7,45,.9,55,1.0,75);
RELEASE:    cashier,1;
COUNT:      bankC,1;
TALLY:      bankT,int(TimeIn),1;
DISPOSE;
```

The arrival customers are created by sampling from an exponential distribution, with a mean of 34.5 seconds. In order to record the time that a customer spends at any point in the system, a **mark attribute** is assigned to the customer. An attribute is a particular characteristic of the entity, but a mark attribute records the time that an entity was created. So in the bank example, we could imagine that an arriving customer is given a piece of paper with his arrival time on it. At any point in the system, the time that the customer has been in the system can be found by subtracting the arrival time from the clock time (called TNOW). The command for this is TALLY, and in this example the time that the customer has been in the queue and the time that he/she has been in the system is recorded.

If the cashier is busy, the arriving customer will have to wait in the queue called bankQ. When the cashier is free, the customer will seize the cashier (only one cashier required), and will be delayed by a time sampled from a continuous empirical probability distribution. This distribution is expressed in the *cumulative* distribution form, so the probabilities given in *cont(.17,25,.45,35,.7,45,.9,55,1.0,75)* are cumulative. The first number is the cumulative probability and the second is the value of the distribution at this point. The cashier is released when the customer has obtained his required service and the number of customers passing through the system is recorded by the COUNT command.

The experiment file for this model might contain the following *elements*:

PROJECT,	*Bank example,,,Yes;*
DISCRETE,	*100,1;*
ATTRIBUTES:	*TimeIn;*
QUEUES:	*bankQ,FIFO;*
RESOURCES:	*cashier,Capacity(1,);*
COUNTERS:	*bankC,,Replicate;*
TALLIES:	*QueueT:*
	BankT;
DSTATS:	*nq(BankQ);*
REPLICATE,	*1,0.0,3600,Yes,Yes,0.0;*

The PROJECT element can contain details of the title of the project, analyst and date, while the DISCRETE element specifies that the model is a discrete-event type (instead of continuous), and a maximum of 100 customers will be in the system at any one time. There will be an attribute called *TimeIn*, and there is one queue called *BankQ*, that operates on a first-in, first-out basis. The resource, called *cashier*, has a capacity of 1. The COUNTER is called *BankC*, and there are two TALLY blocks within the model file called *QueueT* and *BankT*. In addition to information on time in the system, the number in the queue is given by the DSTATS element. DSTATS stands for discrete statistics and will give statistical information on various parts of the system that are discrete in nature, such as numbers in the queue and utilisation of the resource. In this example, only statistics on the queue length have been specified. Finally, the REPLICATE element will specify run-time information, including the number of replications to be made and the length of each replication, which in this case is 1 and 3600 seconds respectively.

The output obtained after compiling, linking and executing the program file was as follows:

SIMAN
Systems Modeling Corporation

Summary for Replication 1 of 1

Project: Bank example	*Run execution date : 5/22/1996*
Analyst:	*Model revision date: 5/22/1996*

Replication ended at time : 3600.0

TALLY VARIABLES

Identifier	Average	Variation	Minimum	Maximum	Observations
QueueT	122.62	.66994	.00000	301.14	92
BankT	160.84	.50920	25.000	355.16	91

DISCRETE-CHANGE VARIABLES

Identifier	Average	Variation	Minimum	Maximum	Final Value
nq(BANKQ)	3.2336	.69824	.00000	9.0000	3.0000

COUNTERS

Identifier	Count	Limit
bankC	91	Infinite

This output shows that during the hour, 91 customers passed through the system. The average time in the queue was 122.62 seconds, although one customer spent 301.14 seconds in the queue. The number of customers in the queue varied from zero to nine and the average was 3.23 customers. We can also deduce from these results that there were three customers left in the queue and one being served when the simulation ended.

The model developed above is an extremely simple one, but it shows the general idea. SIMAN can be used to model most systems, and contains blocks for incorporating material-handling devices, such as conveyors, transporters and guided vehicles.

Simulation packages

Simulation languages free an analyst from having to write routines for the executive, but it still requires an ability to learn the syntax of a language and be able to understand the logical steps in program design. This problem has been recognised for some time, and it was also recognised that many applications were very similar. This was particularly the case in the manufacturing industry, where the process of manufacture is similar from company to company. The idea is that *a simulation package* should contain a small number of functions, and these functions can be linked together in an intuitive manner. These functions might be to drill a part, and the data on the speed of the drill or the reliability of the machine could be input by the user of the package. The package is really a data-driven device that requires little, if any, programming knowledge. Two packages that use this approach are SIMFACTORY and WITNESS. SIMFACTORY, from CACI Products Company, is a factory simulator written in the simulation language SIMSCRIPT. WITNESS, a product of AT&T ISTEL, was originally written for the motor industry, but is now used in other manufacturing organisations as well as business in general. It is a very popular package, particularly in the UK. Both SIMFACTORY and WITNESS contain excellent animation facilities.

ARENA

ARENA is a simulation product that has the flexibility of a simulation language and the ease of use of a simulation package. It was developed by the same company that developed SIMAN, and it is essentially a means of developing a SIMAN model using a graphical interface. ARENA, and products like it, are said to provide a modelling environment, as they include facilities for both input and output data analysis. Examples of the use of the input processor in ARENA have already been given in Chapter 10. The output processor allows post-simulation analysis to be conducted, such as confidence intervals and various statistical tests. Graphical output can be obtained, including histograms and moving average plots.

ARENA consists of a number of *templates*, which contain a set of *modules*. The highest level in the ARENA hierarchy is the COMMON template. Within the common template there are a number of commonly used modules, such as ARRIVE, SERVER and DEPART. For simple models, these are sufficient, but for more complicated models, it is usually necessary to go down to the SUPPORT template. Where the use of conveyors or transporters are required, it is also necessary to use the modules in the TRANSFER template. If further flexibility is required, it may be necessary to use the SIMAN commands found in the BLOCKS and ELEMENTS template. In all cases, the model is developed using a click and drop procedure, and the data is added to the dialogue box by double-clicking on the appropriate module. This avoids the need for the user to create both a model and experiment file as he would using SIMAN. Animation is added automatically to some modules, although additional animation can be obtained from the ANIMATE panel, and by incorporating icons from the picture libraries supplied with the package. These pictures include a set of people, office objects and transporters, as well as numerous manufacturing-orientated pictures. Other pictures can be generated by the user directly from the DRAW panel. To execute the program, the user simply clicks on the GO button after specifying the number and length of each replication. The speed of the animation can be controlled during the run, or animation can be disabled if required.

For the simple bank queuing model, the ARENA model would consist of an ARRIVE, a SERVER and a DEPART module. Within the ARENA environment, each of these modules is a *station* through which the entities pass. The time that an entity takes to pass from one station to another is added to the origin station, together with information pertinent to this station. For the ARRIVAL, information of the interarrival time distribution would have to be provided, while for the SERVER, information on the resource would be required. The SERVER dialogue box for the bank example is shown in Figure 13.3.

In this example, the station is called *cashier* and the resource is, by default, given the name *cashier_R*. When the customer leaves this station, he will go to the *depbank* station, which is where the customer departs. There are various other levels of detail that can be specified by clicking on the buttons. For example, by clicking on the QUEUE button, it is possible to change some of the defaults, such as the queue priority or the maximum size of the queue.

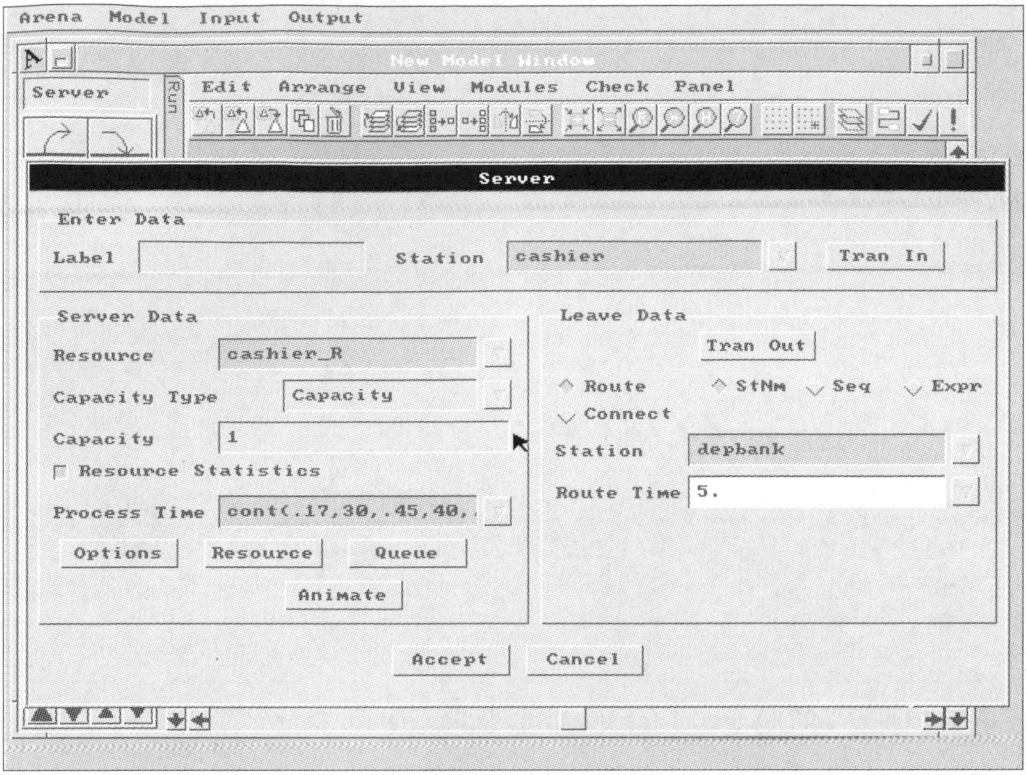

Figure 13.3 ■ SERVER dialogue box in ARENA

■ **Whiteladies Health Centre**   *Scenario 13.1*

The ARENA model for the Whiteladies Health Centre is shown in Figure 13.4. This model has used all ARENA modules except for the PICKSTATION, and the ROUTE modules, which were obtained from the SUPPORT and ANIMATE templates repectively. These modules were included so that the entities (patients) would be routed to the doctor with the shortest queue. The VARIABLES and EXPRESSIONS modules are static modules in the sense that they do not form part of the model logic. They are present to enable certain variables within the model to be updated at specific times.

Although the model is animated, the animation is rather crude and in need of enhancement. This can be done quite easily by making use of the picture libraries. Also, the DRAW template can be used to give the model some interest. The final animated version can be seen in Figure 13.5. Other refinements could also be added, such as graphical and statistical displays, which are updated as the simulation proceeds. These would be provided on separate screens, and *hotkeys* used to switch to the different views.

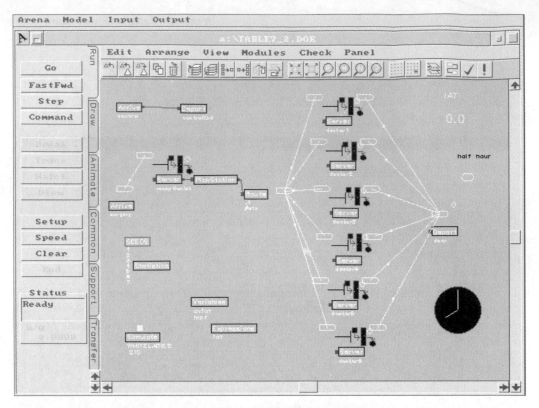

Figure 13.4 ■ ARENA model for the Whiteladies Health Centre

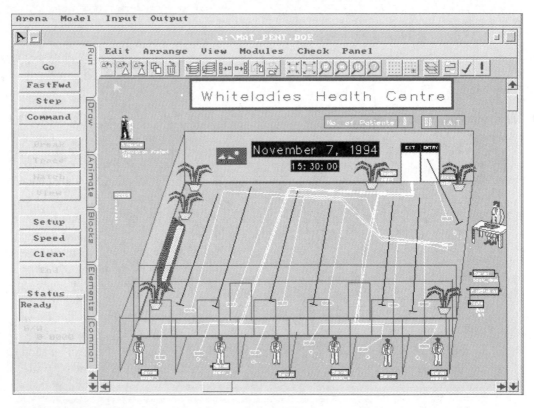

Figure 13.5 ■ ARENA model enhanced through the use of the Draw panel

SIMUL8

SIMUL8 is a package which was introduced in 1995, and the aim of the designers, Visual Thinking, is 'to put simulation on every desktop'. To achieve this they aimed to meet a number of objectives. These were:

- Easy to use for new users
- Fast model building
- Easy to use for experienced users
- Extendibility
- Different levels of complexity
- Common 'learnable' logic programming
- Low price

Certainly they have achieved the price objective, as the package is considerably cheaper than any other commercial simulation package. It may not have as many features as, say, ARENA, but many users will probably not need all these features anyway. The package is written in an object-orientated programming language, and can be extended using Visual Basic. There is also a link with the spreadsheet Excel.

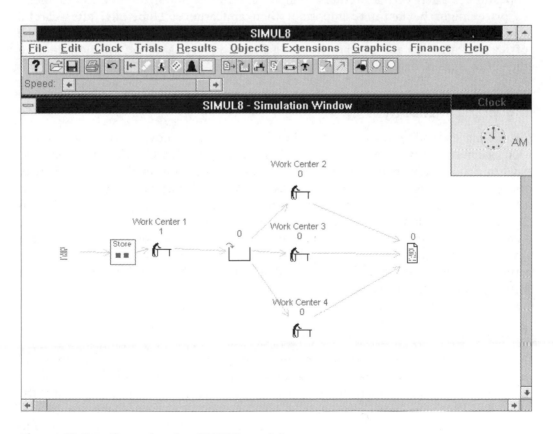

Figure 13.6 ■ Example of a SIMUL8 model

The package has been designed with new users in mind, with start-up hints, an on-line help facility and automatic defaults to many functions. A tool bar is positioned at the top of the screen, containing the commonly used functions. Figure 13.6 is a screen print of a simple model developed in a few minutes. Complex models can be developed by shrinking part or parts of a model into sub-windows. To do this, a box is dragged around part of the model and a click of the right-hand mouse button allows that part of the model to be represented by a single icon. There is no limit to the number of times that this can be done, so it is possible to display a complex model on a single screen. At the end of a run, results in the form of statistical output and graphs can be obtained with a click of the mouse.

Features required from a simulation tool

The selection of a simulation tool for a particular application is no different to the selection of any consumer product. In most cases we try and compare a range of products using a number of criteria, such as price, durability and cosmetic appearance. Each of these criteria will have some importance attached to them, so price might be far more important than appearance. Hopefully, after careful thought, we make a choice that best meets our requirements. There are a range of features that we might want from a simulation tool and we will now look at the most important ones.

Modelling flexibility

Modelling flexibility refers to the ability to use the software for any application. General-purpose languages would rate highly in this criteria, and might be favoured by a university department or research organisation that had staff with the required skills. The alternative to using a general-purpose language is to use a simulation language or a simulation package. These tools are not as flexible as general-purpose languages and their use may mean that certain aspects of the system cannot be modelled accurately. However, some simulation languages and packages allow the user to add his or her own program code to handle these situations. Of course, this is only a viable option if the organisation has people with programming skills.

Ease of use

Ease of use refers to being able to use a simulation tool with a minimum of learning time. This eliminates general-purpose languages and probably simulation languages, as these usually require users to be sent on a course to learn the language. Simulation packages with a good graphical user interface would rate highly here. Ease of use also means that the model can be built quickly and has good error-checking facilities. Error-checking facilities include being able to step through the simulation and the ability of the software to produce meaningful error messages. Unfortunately, there are still too many products on the market (not just simulation software) where the error messages are anything but meaningful. And often some errors will cause the program to crash without warning.

Animation

The recent increase in the popularity of simulation modelling is the result of the improvement in animation. Modellers and clients can now sit round a computer screen and watch the system being simulated in graphic detail. This provides an excellent means of communication between the different groups involved in a simulation project. It can also greatly assist the modeller in verifying that the model is working correctly. There is, of course, the danger that the animation will be used to solve the problem, by changing input parameters until some desired result is achieved. To conduct a proper simulation study, a thorough statistical analysis is required, and this requires multiple replications of a simulation model to be made. However, it is recognised that many simulation projects are simply vehicles for thinking about a particular problem and do not lead to any formal conclusions about system design. In these cases, being able to see immediately the possible effect of a change in an input parameter can be very useful for generating ideas about how a system could be improved.

The type and quality of the animation supported by a particular product varies considerably. Some animation can only be performed in *playback* mode, where the animation is displayed after the simulation has been completed. This is not as convenient as being able to see the animation as the simulation is proceeding. With some software, there is no choice in the form of the animation, while other products come supplied with picture libraries or facilities for importing graphics from other applications. Some packages, such as Taylor II, give three-dimensional animation. This can greatly add to the realism of the animation. The ease of use of the animation is also important. With some software, the model is animated automatically, while with others it is necessary to add the animation after the model has been built. Simulation software should also have facilities for allowing graphical and statistical information to be viewed and updated as the simulation is running. It should be possible to turn the animation off, so that multiple or long runs of the model can be performed.

General simulation functions

The simulation of a stochastic system requires the generation of random variates, so a simulation tool needs to be able to sample from a range of standard probability distributions. We also need to be able to specify the random seed used for each distribution, so that simulation results can be reproduced if necessary. In addition, we need to control the random numbers used in the comparison of simulation experiments (*see* Chapter 12). Other important functions include the ability to specify a *warm-up* period by making the program reset statistics to zero at some pre-determined point in time. We might also want to have some say in how the program handles multiple runs of a simulation. For example, is it possible to reset either or both the statistics and system status between replications? In the method of *independent replications*, we want to reset both, but in the method of *batch means*, we will probably only want to reset the statistics.

Statistical functions

Many users of simulation software are not statistical experts and need help with the analysis of the input data, as well as the results from simulation experiments. For these users, one of the comprehensive simulation packages, which support these facilities, is recommended. These packages allow the input data to be analysed, so that the correct probability distribution can be found, and they also allow the output data to be analysed statistically as well as graphically. Ease of use of these functions is very important, and the inclusion of 'help' screens to aid in the correct choice of statistical test is desirable. Banks (1996) has compared the statistical functions supplied with five software packages using the following catogories:

1. Single variable statistics
2. Multiple variable statistics
3. Statistical graphics
4. Business graphics
5. Data manager
6. Other (copy to clipboard)

Obviously, different people will have different needs regarding the features required, but this checklist could help with a comparison of the different products on the market.

Interface with other software

We have already mentioned that it is desirable to have the option of adding user-written code to a simulation package to increase the flexibility of the software. Although this is important for some modellers, it is probably more important to be able to interface the package with a spreadsheet. This is especially useful for the output of simulation results, as this will aid in the analysis of the results and in the preparation of the project report. Where there is no direct link with a spreadsheet, the ability to read and write data in text format would be helpful.

Product help and support

We have come to associate Windows programs with comprehensive on-line help menus. These usually contain a search facility for finding details about a particular command, and demonstrations and information about important parts of the software. Although we may find it annoying after a while, the start-up hints in packages such as Microsoft WORD can be useful to someone new to the program. However, no matter how comprehensive the on-line help, there should also be good user guides, written in plain English. These user guides should allow a new user to quickly build a simple model, and to obtain some results. Pre-loaded demonstration models can be useful too. Training facilities, either included with the price of the software, or as a separate deal, are often seen as essential by many companies.

In addition to helping the novice user, there should be product support in case of problems and difficulties. Unfortunately, no software is 'bug free' these days, and when users encounter these problems, they need to be able to speak to someone immediately. Information on known problems and upgrades should be sent to users when these occur, and this means that companies have to maintain an accurate register of users.

Price

Obviously, price is a key factor in determining the product to buy, but a cheap product that does not have the required facilities is of little use. Conversely, buying an expensive package that has features that are not needed is a waste of money. However, it is always difficult to know in advance whether a certain feature will be required at a later date. When comparing the price of a number of simulation products, remember to include all the additional expenditure that may be needed. Some companies may charge for upgrades, while others may charge an annual licence fee that includes upgrades and product support.

Expandability

Expandability can refer to being able to include user-written code to handle unusual situations, or the ability to purchase 'add-ons', such as statistical analysis routines or 3-D graphics. Simulation models that are written in a general-purpose programming language are by their nature easier to expand, although a poorly documented program may not be so easy. Simulation packages will be the most difficult to adapt to unusual situations, although many can be expanded by the inclusion of a user-written code. This code often needs to be written in a language such as C, although some packages now allow the use of Visual Basic.

Selection of simulation software

There have been some attempts by groups and individuals to find a 'best buy', but this is an exercise that is fraught with difficulties. The problem is that there are hundreds of simulation tools on the market, with new and upgraded products being produced all the time. There is also the problem that many products are designed for specific applications and may not perform so well in other areas. Breedam *et al.* (1990) attempted to use *cluster analysis* to categorise simulation products by eleven different characteristics. However, this study was criticised by some companies for ignoring their products. Probably the most thorough comparison of simulation software is published regularly in *EUROSIM – Simulation News Europe*. EUROSIM is the Federation of European Simulation Societies and the purpose of the newsletter is to promote the use of simulation in Europe by publishing information relating to the subject. The idea of the comparison is that institutions and companies developing or distributing simulation software are asked to use the software to simulate one (or more) of seven different problems. They then send in a one-page report that gives details of the software and results of the tasks carried out. The advantage with this type of comparison is that it allows companies to choose the comparison that best suits their type of software. So, a company that produces a general-purpose discrete-event package may chose comparison 6 (Emergency Department – Follow-up Treatment), while a company that produces a continuous simulation product might choose comparison 7 (Constrained Pendulum).

In order to choose the best product for a particular application and business, a company or organisation needs to research carefully the products currently on the market. The type of application should enable the list of potential candidates to be of a manageable size. This shopping list should then be used in conjunction with the features required to narrow the choice down to two or three products. The use of a decision package, such as HIVIEW for Windows, can help in this task. This package enables the user to model decision problems that involve multiple criteria using a technique known as Simple Multi-Attribute Rating Technique (SMART). Essentially, the SMART technique requires that users weight each criteria according to its importance, and the package then uses a weighted average score to assess which option is more 'attractive'. The final choice of software can often be made following demonstrations of the software or discussions with the vendor.

The future

The future is notoriously difficult to predict, but there are some areas where this can be attempted. The price of software should continue to fall as the market expands and competition intensifies. The current high prices are partly the result of the small customer base, and this is a self-perpetuating cycle. Visual Thinking are attempting to break this cycle with their SIMUL8 package, and hopefully this should set a trend that other companies will follow. However, this increase in competition will probably mean that the number of companies producing simulation software will decline.

As personal computers become ever more powerful, simulation models will be executed faster. However, increase in power also means that the animation capabilities of simulation software will improve. This is likely to result in the widespread use of 3-D graphics in simulation.

One development that should emerge from the research sector is the joining together of simulation and artificial intelligence, particularly in the area of statistical analysis of simulation results. Many users of simulation packages are not statistical experts, so a semi-automatic means of analysing the results would be helpful. This could take the form of the package deciding on the number of replications to make, whether any warm-up period is necessary, and the appropriate statistical test to apply to the results.

Summary

In order to apply simulation to a problem, we need to select software that will translate our conceptual model into a form suitable for a computer to solve. There are many simulation tools on the market, and each one has its merits and demerits. This chapter has attempted to describe the differences between the various tools, and to identify the criteria in selecting a package. Unfortunately, because of the large number of products on the market and the wide variety of problems that can be solved by simulation, it is very difficult to come up with a single product that will be suitable for all problems. For small companies and university departments, the product by Visual Thinking could be worthy of consideration, while companies who regularly develop large models may prefer to purchase an established product such as ARENA or WITNESS. However, there is no substitute for careful research into the software available and the requirements of the business.

References and further reading

Banks, J. (1993) 'Software for simulation', *Proceedings of the 1993 Winter Simulation Conference*.

Banks, J. (1996) 'Output analysis capabilities of simulation software', *Simulation*, January, Vol. 66, No. 1.

Banks, J. and Carson, J. (1984) *Discrete-Event System Simulation* (Chapters 4 and 5), Prentice-Hall, New Jersey, USA.

Breedam, A. V., Raes, J. and Van de Velde, K. (1990) 'Segmenting the simulation software market', *OR Insight*, April–June, Vol. 3, No. 2.

Law, A. M. and Kelton, W.D, (1991) *Simulation Modelling and Analysis*, Second Edition (Chapter 3), McGraw-Hill, Inc., USA.

Law, A. M. and McComas M. G. (1992) 'How to select simulation software for manufacturing applications', *Industrial Engineering*, July.

Pidd, M. (1992) *Computer Simulation in Management Science*, Third Edition (Chapters 6 and 10), Wiley, Chichester, England.

'Simulation Software Buyer's Guide' (1993) *Industrial Engineering*, July.

Watson, H. J. and Blackstone, J. H. (1989) *Computer Simulation*, Second Edition (Chapter 8), Wiley, Singapore.

Appendix 1

Scenario and case study information

Whiteladies Health Centre: Interarrival time (minutes)

Monday 07/11/94 Afternoon	Tuesday 08/11/94 Morning	Thursday 10/11/94 Morning	Friday 11/11/94 Afternoon
1.27	0.03	1.93	2.12
3.36	5.73	1.48	3.04
3.85	0.22	3.70	0.43
0.40	0.63	2.11	0.34
0.71	0.98	0.05	2.50
1.56	0.89	0.63	0.78
0.19	3.15	0.25	0.65
0.18	0.18	0.87	2.14
0.37	13.21	0.01	4.06
2.15	4.67	2.65	0.48
0.44	0.03	0.52	3.37
3.35	2.03	0.39	2.02
1.15	2.03	0.50	6.95
1.17	4.53	3.57	0.01
1.27	2.66	1.84	4.55
1.35	2.47	4.61	0.41
1.19	1.87	0.23	2.72
0.90	0.52	2.45	1.96
1.44	0.03	5.48	1.55
1.73	0.05	0.82	1.44
0.12	0.97	1.37	1.95
0.01	2.67	1.42	0.16
0.05	3.30	1.29	0.44
0.44	0.98	1.11	0.58
0.83	0.70	1.07	0.76
1.28	1.27	1.18	1.08
0.34	2.22	0.98	1.42
0.94	0.30	1.02	0.60
0.83	1.20	4.02	1.47
0.56	2.15	0.22	1.01
0.08	0.97	1.23	1.46
0.58	0.70	1.90	0.47
0.03	0.48	0.58	0.95
0.22	0.32	4.22	0.32
0.33	1.33	1.10	2.80
0.08	0.08	7.92	3.32
0.08	1.18	5.92	0.09
0.28	2.90	0.12	1.73
0.18	1.10	2.77	1.85
0.30	1.50	0.03	1.53
4.02	5.17	0.05	4.90
1.08	0.95	0.08	1.15
0.15	1.45	1.40	3.28

Monday 07/11/94 Afternoon	Tuesday 08/11/94 Morning	Thursday 10/11/94 Morning	Friday 11/11/94 Afternoon
0.30	1.33	4.17	2.33
0.22	0.35	1.13	4.15
0.22	2.57	4.92	0.68
1.28	2.47	1.93	1.53
2.13	0.97	6.07	0.72
0.98	1.68	2.05	0.87
0.45	0.65	0.25	0.02
1.40	0.65	0.08	0.07
5.37	1.78	0.95	0.35
0.27	1.30	0.07	11.48
1.23	5.85	5.62	0.03
1.33	0.98	3.12	10.46
0.98	3.53	3.25	3.75
1.78	1.37	3.97	4.20
0.18	0.23	2.43	3.15
1.03	4.13	0.78	6.77
2.85	0.17	0.48	1.10
1.20	0.82	1.57	9.70
3.68	0.85	0.58	
1.05	2.08	0.45	
0.47	0.28	2.25	
0.73	0.87	1.17	
4.95	0.47	4.65	
4.42	0.12	5.33	
3.32	4.12	6.42	
1.08	3.52		
0.27	2.82		
0.30	2.15		
0.90	5.65		
0.40	12.77		
1.18	1.93		
0.92			
1.57			
1.43			
2.05			
0.57			
0.02			
1.55			
1.60			
2.37			
0.03			
3.05			
4.25			
0.92			
0.07			
0.72			
0.25			
2.02			
9.17			
2.22			
6.37			
1.12			
0.25			
0.53			
3.18			
2.43			

Whiteladies Health Centre: Consultation time data (minutes)

	Monday 07/11/94 Afternoon	Tuesday 08/11/94 Morning	Thursday 10/11/94 Morning	Friday 11/11/94 Afternoon
Doctor Green				
	2.55	8.05	6.20	4.92
	3.28	1.82	5.58	3.88
	7.57	1.07	4.58	7.42
	4.87	0.00	7.25	2.95
	13.63	2.65	2.02	4.12
	10.28	3.82	5.37	2.82
	0.00	6.22	5.53	
	5.52	10.87	8.47	
	7.70	7.78	7.87	
	5.22	5.37	6.03	
	8.35	1.95		
	4.97	4.78		
	8.62	5.50		
	3.63	5.80		
	5.23	3.52		
	10.58			
	4.50			
Doctor Pink				
	3.78	9.88	7.82	5.30
	14.50	4.95	15.25	18.03
	3.53	8.18	4.13	8.75
	8.63	14.97	9.17	2.73
	0.50	4.27	5.57	4.78
	5.53	6.38	4.70	4.57
	2.73	5.02	6.90	5.82
	5.75	9.50	10.10	6.98
	6.70	4.28	17.82	4.62
	6.00	10.88	8.30	2.52
	10.50	7.90	11.05	10.43
	8.45	7.10	4.48	2.25
		7.73	12.62	2.30
		3.13		10.17
		6.75		9.75
		7.88		
Doctor Yellow				
	13.00		5.87	3.65
	6.85		9.55	2.37
	7.33		7.90	3.45
	4.75		2.55	7.42
	2.82		11.83	18.40
	11.35		4.08	3.15
	5.38		2.97	7.80
	5.93		6.48	6.65
	4.97		12.65	6.23
	6.15			4.70
	6.97			7.82
	17.95			2.50

Monday 07/11/94 Afternoon	Tuesday 08/11/94 Morning	Thursday 10/11/94 Morning	Friday 11/11/94 Afternoon
7.38			4.02
7.48			10.68
11.60			1.72
5.35			5.45
			9.90
			5.27
			3.70
			3.00
			3.18

Doctor Orange

Monday 07/11/94 Afternoon	Tuesday 08/11/94 Morning	Thursday 10/11/94 Morning	Friday 11/11/94 Afternoon
0.67	2.83	3.57	
16.08	15.62	1.93	
2.47	6.47	2.42	
2.07	3.40	9.30	
11.23	17.20	1.13	
2.97	8.90	1.45	
8.93	1.10	3.53	
4.40	4.55	7.43	
5.35	4.15	3.37	
6.37	5.23	3.38	
8.18	4.27	12.40	
1.95	11.02	8.13	
7.13	20.25		
16.78	4.50		
5.70			
2.30			
4.12			
1.93			
3.35			

Doctor Red

Monday 07/11/94 Afternoon	Tuesday 08/11/94 Morning	Thursday 10/11/94 Morning	Friday 11/11/94 Afternoon
4.67	4.33	13.18	
10.12	2.18	4.75	
5.43	2.52	3.42	
11.62	16.35	10.68	
5.33	17.13	14.12	
0.00	17.13	10.87	
4.22	8.27	3.00	
7.17	3.62	11.17	
9.30	6.62	7.58	
4.70	42.37	7.57	
4.48	9.03	5.97	
4.52	3.10	5.47	
4.88	5.88		
16.50	2.70		
23.72	2.23		
3.30	5.82		
5.33	4.33		
3.68			
6.78			

Monday 07/11/94 Afternoon	Tuesday 08/11/94 Morning	Thursday 10/11/94 Morning	Friday 11/11/94 Afternoon
Doctor Blue			
8.15	4.65	3.77	3.50
2.00	4.92	3.10	5.57
5.70	17.08	6.00	2.07
15.37	5.15	4.27	2.00
1.37	17.92	6.38	7.60
4.20	2.55	7.72	5.30
2.07	7.88	2.82	2.00
4.00	9.43	5.60	0.93
9.97	5.53	4.25	5.12
2.87	5.70	4.42	6.87
6.20	13.40	3.30	3.02
6.20	10.68	5.07	5.10
5.40	6.58		3.62
4.88			0.00
8.45			2.83
6.47			5.07
4.57			1.87
			8.77
			4.33
			4.33

Whiteladies reception service times

Twenty patients were timed at the reception desk, and the time (in seconds) taken by these patients were:

12, 29, 15, 24, 12, 10, 28, 50, 5, 20, 21, 13, 27, 11, 16, 26, 19, 5, 12, 25

Drive Thru Burger restaurant

I.A.T. secs	Service Time 1 secs	Service Time 2 secs	I.A.T. mins	Service Time 1 mins	Service Time 2 mins
20	23	18	0.3333	0.3833	0.3000
70	25	25	1.1667	0.4167	0.4167
25	27	63	0.4167	0.4500	1.0500
35	35	38	0.5833	0.5833	0.6333
131	74	26	2.1833	1.2333	0.4333
95	23	94	1.5833	0.3833	1.5667
17	18	92	0.2833	0.3000	1.5333
240	104	33	4.0000	1.7333	0.5500
51	56	51	0.8500	0.9333	0.8500
122	56	30	2.0333	0.9333	0.5000
35	40	48	0.5833	0.6667	0.8000
9	30	37	0.1500	0.5000	0.6167
20	40	70	0.3333	0.6667	1.1667
30	40	60	0.5000	0.6667	1.0000
15	50	25	0.2500	0.8333	0.4167
2	30	15	0.0333	0.5000	0.2500
193	75	105	3.2167	1.2500	1.7500
68	30	30	1.1333	0.5000	0.5000
22	72	30	0.3667	1.2000	0.5000
265	30	80	4.4167	0.5000	1.3333
319	26	124	5.3167	0.4333	2.0667
48	45	125	0.8000	0.7500	2.0833
208	28	133	3.4667	0.4667	2.2167
86	60	171	1.4333	1.0000	2.8500
467	29	161	7.7833	0.4833	2.6833
87	45	199	1.4500	0.7500	3.3167
80	46	60	1.3333	0.7667	1.0000
86	23	15	1.4333	0.3833	0.2500
13	69	65	0.2167	1.1500	1.0833
56	55	193	0.9333	0.9167	3.2167
45	25	113	0.7500	0.4167	1.8833
8	10	72	0.1333	0.1667	1.2000
92	40	52	1.5333	0.6667	0.8667
175	105	76	2.9167	1.7500	1.2667
42	39	124	0.7000	0.6500	2.0667
177	92	133	2.9500	1.5333	2.2167
81	49	111	1.3500	0.8167	1.8500
230	45	52	3.8333	0.7500	0.8667
50	54	113	0.8333	0.9000	1.8833
175	47	188	2.9167	0.7833	3.1333
34	51	130	0.5667	0.8500	2.1667
101	36	23	1.6833	0.6000	0.3833
100	50	53	1.6667	0.8333	0.8833
199	32	86	3.3167	0.5333	1.4333
124	93	304	2.0667	1.5500	5.0667
7	29	103	0.1167	0.4833	1.7167
73	23	65	1.2167	0.3833	1.0833
362	55	128	6.0333	0.9167	2.1333
320	30	120	5.3333	0.5000	2.0000

Validation data for the Drive Thru Burger restaurant

Enter time	Depart time	System time (seconds)	No. in queue
12:02:30	12:04:56	146	0
12:14:10	12:17:25	195	1
12:15:00	12:18:50	230	2
12:15:15	12:19:05	230	2
12:20:00	12:23:25	205	1
12:30:32	12:35:45	313	0
12:43:13	12:47:50	277	0
12:49:20	12:56:40	440	1
12:54:37	13:03:15	518	0
13:02:45	13:07:53	308	0
13:10:25	13:16:07	342	0
13:15:48	13:22:55	427	1
13:15:55	13:17:00	balked	
13:17:08	13:24:05	417	0
13:23:10	13:28:32	322	0

Ashburton model file coding
Jobbing Simulation

```
22$        CREATE,1,0:60,1000:MARK(mark_time);
21$        BRANCH,1:With,0.15,20$,Yes:
                With,0.85,19$,Yes;


19$        ASSIGN:      picture=mdf:
                        type=0:
                        batchsize=1:NEXT(1$);


20$        ASSIGN:      picture=hardwood:
                        type=1:
                        batchsize=1:NEXT(1$)
```

Batch Simulation

```
22$        CREATE,1,0:480,1000:MARK(mark_time);
21$         BRANCH,1:If,AMOD(day,7)==0,20$,Yes:
                   Else,19$,Yes;


19$        ASSIGN:      picture=mdf:
                        type=0:
                        batchsize=10:NEXT(1$)
20$        ASSIGN:      picture=hardwood:
                        type=1:
                        batchsize=8:NEXT(1$);
```

```
1$         COUNT:       WIP,1*batchsize;


26$        QUEUE,       cut_saw_plane_q;
30$        SEIZE,       1:cut_saw_plane,1;
29$        ROUTE:       5,cutter;


43$        STATION,     cutter;
876$       QUEUE,       cutter_R_Q;
875$       SEIZE,       1:cutter_R,1;
874$       DELAY:
           5+(type*5)+(5+type*5)*batchsize;
873$       RELEASE:     cutter_R,1;
868$       ROUTE:       5,saw;


41$        STATION,     saw;
772$       QUEUE,       saw_R_Q;
771$       SEIZE,       1:saw_R,1;
```

```
770$        DELAY:
            10+(type*5)+(20+type*10)*batchsize;
769$        RELEASE:        saw_R,1;
764$        ROUTE:          5,plane;


39$         STATION,        plane;
668$        QUEUE,          plane_R_Q;
667$        SEIZE,          1:plane_R,1;
666$        DELAY:
            10+(type*5)+(10+type*10)*batchsize;
665$        RELEASE:        plane_R,1;


28$         RELEASE:        cut_saw_plane,1;
27$         ROUTE:          5,router;


8$          STATION,        router;
148$        QUEUE,          router_R_Q;
147$        SEIZE,          1:router_R,1;
146$        DELAY:
            10+(type*5)+(20+type*10)*batchsize;
145$        RELEASE:        router_R,1;


12$         QUEUE,          bencher_q1;
13$         SEIZE,          1:bencher,1;
11$         ROUTE:          5,sub_assembly;


137$        STATION,        sub_assembly;
564$        QUEUE,          sub_assembly_R_Q;
563$        SEIZE,          1:sub_assembly_R,1;
562$        DELAY:
            10+(type*5)+(20+type*10)*batchsize;
561$        RELEASE:        sub_assembly_R,1;


10$         RELEASE:        bencher,1;
7$          ROUTE:          5,sub_rack;


35$         STATION,        sub_rack;
396$        STORE:          sub_rack_S1;
460$        QUEUE,          sub_rack_R_Q;
459$        SEIZE,          1:sub_rack_R,1;
458$        DELAY:          day*480-tnow;
457$        RELEASE:        sub_rack_R,1;
390$        UNSTORE:        ;


6$          QUEUE,          bencher_q2;
5$          SEIZE,          1:bencher,1;
4$          ROUTE:          5,main_assembly;
```

```
33$      STATION,        main_assembly;
356$     QUEUE,          main_assembly_R_Q;
355$     SEIZE,          1:main_assembly_R,1;
354$     DELAY:
         15+(type*5)+(45+type*10)*batchsize;
353$     RELEASE:        main_assembly_R,1;

3$       RELEASE:        bencher,1;
2$       ROUTE:          5,main_rack;

31$      STATION,        main_rack;
188$     STORE:          main_rack_S1;
252$     QUEUE,          main_rack_R_Q;
251$     SEIZE,          1:main_rack_R,1;
250$     DELAY:          day*480-tnow;
249$     RELEASE:        main_rack_R,1;

18$      BRANCH,1:If,type==0,17$,Yes:
                  Else,16$,Yes;

17$      TALLY:
    mdf_tally,INTERVAL(mark_time),batchsize;
15$      DISPOSE;

16$      TALLY:          hardwood_tally,INTERVAL(mark_time),batchsize;
14$      DISPOSE;
```

Ashburton experimental file coding

```
PROJECT,  Ashburton Simulation;

ATTRIBUTES:mark_time,0:
         type:
         batchsize,1;

STORAGES:  sub_rack_S1:
         main_rack_S1;

VARIABLES: day,0;

QUEUES:    cutter_R_Q,FIFO:
         saw_R_Q,FIFO:
         plane_R_Q,FIFO:
         sub_rack_R_Q,FIFO:
         main_rack_R_Q,FIFO:
         sub_assembly_R_Q,FIFO:
```

```
            main_assembly_R_Q,FIFO:
            cut_saw_plane_q,FIFO:
            router_R_Q,FIFO:
            bencher_q1,FIFO:
            bencher_q2,FIFO;


PICTURES:   hardwood:
            mdf;


RESOURCES:  cutter_R,Capacity(1,):
            saw_R,Capacity(1,):
            plane_R,Capacity(1,):
            sub_rack_R,Capacity(50,):
            main_rack_R,Capacity(50,):
            sub_assembly_R,Capacity(50,):
            main_assembly_R,Capacity(50,):
            bencher,Capacity(2,):
            cut_saw_plane,Capacity(2,):
            router_R,Capacity(1,);


STATIONS:   cutter:
            saw:
            plane:
            sub_rack:
            main_rack:
            sub_assembly:
            main_assembly:
            router;


COUNTERS:   WIP,,Replicate,"DERW1WIP.OUT";


TALLIES:    mdf_tally:
            hardwood_tally;


DSTATS:     NR(cutter_R),cutter_R Busy:
            NR(saw_R),saw_R Busy:
            NR(plane_R),plane_R Busy:
            NR(router_R),router_R Busy:
            NR(cut_saw_plane):
            NR(bencher),bencher Busy:
            NC(WIP);


REPLICATE,1,0.0,9600,Yes,Yes;
```

Appendix 2

Statistical tables

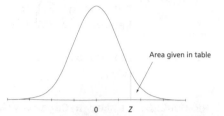

Figure A2.1 ■ The standard normal distribution

The normal tables

Z	0.00	0.01	0.02	0.03	0.04	0.05	0.06	0.07	0.08	0.09
0.0	0.5000	0.4960	0.4920	0.4880	0.4840	0.4801	0.4761	0.4721	0.4681	0.4641
0.1	0.4602	0.4562	0.4522	0.4483	0.4443	0.4404	0.4364	0.4325	0.4286	0.4247
0.2	0.4207	0.4168	0.4129	0.4090	0.4052	0.4013	0.3974	0.3936	0.3897	0.3859
0.3	0.3821	0.3783	0.3745	0.3707	0.3669	0.3632	0.3594	0.3557	0.3520	0.3483
0.4	0.3446	0.3409	0.3372	0.3336	0.3300	0.3264	0.3228	0.3192	0.3156	0.3121
0.5	0.3085	0.3050	0.3015	0.2981	0.2946	0.2912	0.2877	0.2843	0.2810	0.2776
0.6	0.2743	0.2709	0.2676	0.2643	0.2611	0.2578	0.2546	0.2514	0.2483	0.2451
0.7	0.2420	0.2389	0.2358	0.2327	0.2296	0.2266	0.2236	0.2206	0.2177	0.2148
0.8	0.2119	0.2090	0.2061	0.2033	0.2005	0.1977	0.1949	0.1922	0.1894	0.1867
0.9	0.1841	0.1814	0.1788	0.1762	0.1736	0.1711	0.1685	0.1660	0.1635	0.1611
1.0	0.1587	0.1562	0.1539	0.1515	0.1492	0.1469	0.1446	0.1423	0.1401	0.1379
1.1	0.1357	0.1335	0.1314	0.1292	0.1271	0.1251	0.1230	0.1210	0.1190	0.1170
1.2	0.1151	0.1131	0.1112	0.1093	0.1075	0.1056	0.1038	0.1020	0.1003	0.0985
1.3	0.0968	0.0951	0.0934	0.0918	0.0901	0.0885	0.0869	0.0853	0.0838	0.0823
1.4	0.0808	0.0793	0.0778	0.0764	0.0749	0.0735	0.0721	0.0708	0.0694	0.0681
1.5	0.0668	0.0655	0.0643	0.0630	0.0618	0.0606	0.0594	0.0582	0.0571	0.0559
1.6	0.0548	0.0537	0.0526	0.0516	0.0505	0.0495	0.0485	0.0475	0.0465	0.0455
1.7	0.0446	0.0436	0.0427	0.0418	0.0409	0.0401	0.0392	0.0384	0.0375	0.0367
1.8	0.0359	0.0351	0.0344	0.0336	0.0329	0.0322	0.0314	0.0307	0.0301	0.0294
1.9	0.0287	0.0281	0.0274	0.0268	0.0262	0.0256	0.0250	0.0244	0.0239	0.0233
2.0	0.0228	0.0222	0.0217	0.0212	0.0207	0.0202	0.0197	0.0192	0.0188	0.0183
2.1	0.0179	0.0174	0.0170	0.0166	0.0162	0.0158	0.0154	0.0150	0.0146	0.0143
2.2	0.0139	0.0136	0.0132	0.0129	0.0125	0.0122	0.0119	0.0116	0.0113	0.0110
2.3	0.0107	0.0104	0.0102	0.0099	0.0096	0.0094	0.0091	0.0089	0.0087	0.0084
2.4	0.0082	0.0080	0.0078	0.0075	0.0073	0.0071	0.0069	0.0068	0.0066	0.0064
2.5	0.0062	0.0060	0.0059	0.0057	0.0055	0.0054	0.0052	0.0051	0.0049	0.0048
2.6	0.0047	0.0045	0.0044	0.0043	0.0041	0.0040	0.0039	0.0038	0.0037	0.0036
2.7	0.0035	0.0034	0.0033	0.0032	0.0031	0.0030	0.0029	0.0028	0.0027	0.0026
2.8	0.0026	0.0025	0.0024	0.0023	0.0023	0.0022	0.0021	0.0021	0.0020	0.0019
2.9	0.0019	0.0018	0.0018	0.0017	0.0016	0.0016	0.0015	0.0015	0.0014	0.0014
	3.0	0.00135	3.1	0.000968	3.2	0.000687	3.3	0.000483	3.4	0.000337

Table of the *t*-distribution

The table gives the *t*-value for a range of probabilities in the upper tail. For a two-tail test the probability should be halved.

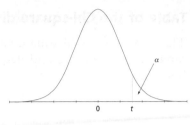

Figure A2.2 ▪ The *t*-distribution on *v* degrees of freedom

| df | \multicolumn{8}{c}{Probability} |
	0.2	0.1	0.05	0.025	0.01	0.0005	0.001	0.0001
1	1.376	3.078	6.314	12.706	31.821	63.656	318.3	3185.3
2	1.061	1.886	2.920	4.303	6.965	9.925	22.328	70.706
3	0.978	1.638	2.353	3.182	4.541	5.841	10.214	22.203
4	0.941	1.533	2.132	2.776	3.747	4.604	7.173	13.039
5	0.920	1.476	2.015	2.571	3.365	4.032	5.894	9.676
6	0.906	1.440	1.943	2.447	3.143	3.707	5.208	8.023
7	0.896	1.415	1.895	2.365	2.998	3.499	4.785	7.064
8	0.889	1.397	1.860	2.306	2.896	3.355	4.501	6.442
9	0.883	1.383	1.833	2.262	2.821	3.250	4.297	6.009
10	0.879	1.372	1.812	2.228	2.764	3.169	4.144	5.694
11	0.876	1.363	1.796	2.201	2.718	3.106	4.025	5.453
12	0.873	1.356	1.782	2.179	2.681	3.055	3.930	5.263
13	0.870	1.350	1.771	2.160	2.650	3.012	3.852	5.111
14	0.868	1.345	1.761	2.145	2.624	2.977	3.787	4.985
15	0.866	1.341	1.753	2.131	2.602	2.947	3.733	4.880
16	0.865	1.337	1.746	2.120	2.583	2.921	3.686	4.790
17	0.863	1.333	1.740	2.110	2.567	2.898	3.646	4.715
18	0.862	1.330	1.734	2.101	2.552	2.878	3.610	4.648
19	0.861	1.328	1.729	2.093	2.539	2.861	3.579	4.590
20	0.860	1.325	1.725	2.086	2.528	2.845	3.552	4.539
21	0.859	1.323	1.721	2.080	2.518	2.831	3.527	4.492
22	0.858	1.321	1.717	2.074	2.508	2.819	3.505	4.452
23	0.858	1.319	1.714	2.069	2.500	2.807	3.485	4.416
24	0.857	1.318	1.711	2.064	2.492	2.797	3.467	4.382
25	0.856	1.316	1.708	2.060	2.485	2.787	3.450	4.352
26	0.856	1.315	1.706	2.056	2.479	2.779	3.435	4.324
27	0.855	1.314	1.703	2.052	2.473	2.771	3.421	4.299
28	0.855	1.313	1.701	2.048	2.467	2.763	3.408	4.276
29	0.854	1.311	1.699	2.045	2.462	2.756	3.396	4.254
30	0.854	1.310	1.697	2.042	2.457	2.750	3.385	4.234
35	0.852	1.306	1.690	2.030	2.438	2.724	3.340	4.153
40	0.851	1.303	1.684	2.021	2.423	2.704	3.307	4.094
45	0.850	1.301	1.679	2.014	2.412	2.690	3.281	4.049
50	0.849	1.299	1.676	2.009	2.403	2.678	3.261	4.014
60	0.848	1.296	1.671	2.000	2.390	2.660	3.232	3.962
80	0.846	1.292	1.664	1.990	2.374	2.639	3.195	3.899
100	0.845	1.290	1.660	1.984	2.364	2.626	3.174	3.861
∞	0.842	1.282	1.645	1.960	2.327	2.576	3.091	3.720

Table of the Chi-square distribution

This table gives Chi-square values for a range of probabilities and degrees of freedom

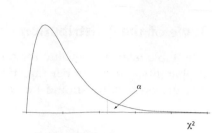

Figure A2.3 ■ The Chi-square distribution on v degrees of freedom

df	Probability								
	0.995	0.99	0.9	0.1	0.05	0.025	0.01	0.005	0.001
1	0.000	0.000	0.016	2.706	3.841	5.024	6.635	7.879	10.827
2	0.010	0.020	0.211	4.605	5.991	7.378	9.210	10.597	13.815
3	0.072	0.115	0.584	6.251	7.815	9.348	11.345	12.838	16.266
4	0.207	0.297	1.064	7.779	9.488	11.143	13.277	14.860	18.466
5	0.412	0.554	1.610	9.236	11.070	12.832	15.086	16.750	20.515
6	0.676	0.872	2.204	10.645	12.592	14.449	16.812	18.548	22.457
7	0.989	1.239	2.833	12.017	14.067	16.013	18.475	20.278	24.321
8	1.344	1.647	3.490	13.362	15.507	17.535	20.090	21.955	26.124
9	1.735	2.088	4.168	14.684	16.919	19.023	21.666	23.589	27.877
10	2.156	2.558	4.865	15.987	18.307	20.483	23.209	25.188	29.588
11	2.603	3.053	5.578	17.275	19.675	21.920	24.725	26.757	31.264
12	3.074	3.571	6.304	18.549	21.026	23.337	26.217	28.300	32.909
13	3.565	4.107	7.041	19.812	22.362	24.736	27.688	29.819	34.527
14	4.075	4.660	7.790	21.064	23.685	26.119	29.141	31.319	36.124
15	4.601	5.229	8.547	22.307	24.996	27.488	30.578	32.801	37.698
16	5.142	5.812	9.312	23.542	26.296	28.845	32.000	34.267	39.252
17	5.697	6.408	10.085	24.769	27.587	30.191	33.409	35.718	40.791
18	6.265	7.015	10.865	25.989	28.869	31.526	34.805	37.156	42.312
19	6.844	7.633	11.651	27.204	30.144	32.852	36.191	38.582	43.819
20	7.434	8.260	12.443	28.412	31.410	34.170	37.566	39.997	45.314
21	8.034	8.897	13.240	29.615	32.671	35.479	38.932	41.401	46.796
22	8.643	9.542	14.041	30.813	33.924	36.781	40.289	42.796	48.268
23	9.260	10.196	14.848	32.007	35.172	38.076	41.638	44.181	49.728
24	9.886	10.856	15.659	33.196	36.415	39.364	42.980	45.558	51.179
25	10.520	11.524	16.473	34.382	37.652	40.646	44.314	46.928	52.619
26	11.160	12.198	17.292	35.563	38.885	41.923	45.642	48.290	54.051
27	11.808	12.878	18.114	36.741	40.113	43.195	46.963	49.645	55.475
28	12.461	13.565	18.939	37.916	41.337	44.461	48.278	50.994	56.892
29	13.121	14.256	19.768	39.087	42.557	45.722	49.588	52.335	58.301
30	13.787	14.953	20.599	40.256	43.773	46.979	50.892	53.672	59.702
35	17.192	18.509	24.797	46.059	49.802	53.203	57.342	60.275	66.619
40	20.707	22.164	29.051	51.805	55.758	59.342	63.691	66.766	73.403

Table 1 of the *F*-distribution

This table gives values of the *F*-distribution for v_1 and v_2 degrees of freedom for $\alpha = 0.05$.

v_2	v_1 1	2	3	4	5	6	7	8	9	10
1	161.446	199.499	215.707	224.583	230.160	233.988	236.767	238.884	240.543	241.882
2	18.513	19.000	19.164	19.247	19.296	19.329	19.353	19.371	19.385	19.396
3	10.128	9.552	9.277	9.117	9.013	8.941	8.887	8.845	8.812	8.785
4	7.709	6.944	6.591	6.388	6.256	6.163	6.094	6.041	5.999	5.964
5	6.608	5.786	5.409	5.192	5.050	4.950	4.876	4.818	4.772	4.735
6	5.987	5.143	4.757	4.534	4.387	4.284	4.207	4.147	4.099	4.060
7	5.591	4.737	4.347	4.120	3.972	3.866	3.787	3.726	3.677	3.637
8	5.318	4.459	4.066	3.838	3.688	3.581	3.500	3.438	3.388	3.347
9	5.117	4.256	3.863	3.633	3.482	3.374	3.293	3.230	3.179	3.137
10	4.965	4.103	3.708	3.478	3.326	3.217	3.135	3.072	3.020	2.978
11	4.844	3.982	3.587	3.357	3.204	3.095	3.012	2.948	2.896	2.854
12	4.747	3.885	3.490	3.259	3.106	2.996	2.913	2.849	2.796	2.753
13	4.667	3.806	3.411	3.179	3.025	2.915	2.832	2.767	2.714	2.671
14	4.600	3.739	3.344	3.112	2.958	2.848	2.764	2.699	2.646	2.602
15	4.543	3.682	3.287	3.056	2.901	2.790	2.707	2.641	2.588	2.544
16	4.494	3.634	3.239	3.007	2.852	2.741	2.657	2.591	2.538	2.494
17	4.451	3.592	3.197	2.965	2.810	2.699	2.614	2.548	2.494	2.450
18	4.414	3.555	3.160	2.928	2.773	2.661	2.577	2.510	2.456	2.412
19	4.381	3.522	3.127	2.895	2.740	2.628	2.544	2.477	2.423	2.378
20	4.351	3.493	3.098	2.866	2.711	2.599	2.514	2.447	2.393	2.348
21	4.325	3.467	3.072	2.840	2.685	2.573	2.488	2.420	2.366	2.321
22	4.301	3.443	3.049	2.817	2.661	2.549	2.464	2.397	2.342	2.297
23	4.279	3.422	3.028	2.796	2.640	2.528	2.442	2.375	2.320	2.275
24	4.260	3.403	3.009	2.776	2.621	2.508	2.423	2.355	2.300	2.255
25	4.242	3.385	2.991	2.759	2.603	2.490	2.405	2.337	2.282	2.236
26	4.225	3.369	2.975	2.743	2.587	2.474	2.388	2.321	2.265	2.220
27	4.210	3.354	2.960	2.728	2.572	2.459	2.373	2.305	2.250	2.204
28	4.196	3.340	2.947	2.714	2.558	2.445	2.359	2.291	2.236	2.190
29	4.183	3.328	2.934	2.701	2.545	2.432	2.346	2.278	2.223	2.177
30	4.171	3.316	2.922	2.690	2.534	2.421	2.334	2.266	2.211	2.165
35	4.121	3.267	2.874	2.641	2.485	2.372	2.285	2.217	2.161	2.114
40	4.085	3.232	2.839	2.606	2.449	2.336	2.249	2.180	2.124	2.077
45	4.057	3.204	2.812	2.579	2.422	2.308	2.221	2.152	2.096	2.049
50	4.034	3.183	2.790	2.557	2.400	2.286	2.199	2.130	2.073	2.026
60	4.001	3.150	2.758	2.525	2.368	2.254	2.167	2.097	2.040	1.993
70	3.978	3.128	2.736	2.503	2.346	2.231	2.143	2.074	2.017	1.969
80	3.960	3.111	2.719	2.486	2.329	2.214	2.126	2.056	1.999	1.951
90	3.947	3.098	2.706	2.473	2.316	2.201	2.113	2.043	1.986	1.938
100	3.936	3.087	2.696	2.463	2.305	2.191	2.103	2.032	1.975	1.927

Table 2 of the F-distribution

v_2	10	12	14	16	18	20	25	30	50	100
1	241.882	243.905	245.363	246.466	247.324	248.016	249.260	250.096	251.774	253.043
2	19.396	19.412	19.424	19.433	19.440	19.446	19.456	19.463	19.476	19.486
3	8.785	8.745	8.715	8.692	8.675	8.660	8.634	8.617	8.581	8.554
4	5.964	5.912	5.873	5.844	5.821	5.803	5.769	5.746	5.699	5.664
5	4.735	4.678	4.636	4.604	4.579	4.558	4.521	4.496	4.444	4.405
6	4.060	4.000	3.956	3.922	3.896	3.874	3.835	3.808	3.754	3.712
7	3.637	3.575	3.529	3.494	3.467	3.445	3.404	3.376	3.319	3.275
8	3.347	3.284	3.237	3.202	3.173	3.150	3.108	3.079	3.020	2.975
9	3.137	3.073	3.025	2.989	2.960	2.936	2.893	2.864	2.803	2.756
10	2.978	2.913	2.865	2.828	2.798	2.774	2.730	2.700	2.637	2.588
11	2.854	2.788	2.739	2.701	2.671	2.646	2.601	2.570	2.507	2.457
12	2.753	2.687	2.637	2.599	2.568	2.544	2.498	2.466	2.401	2.350
13	2.671	2.604	2.554	2.515	2.484	2.459	2.412	2.380	2.314	2.261
14	2.602	2.534	2.484	2.445	2.413	2.388	2.341	2.308	2.241	2.187
15	2.544	2.475	2.424	2.385	2.353	2.328	2.280	2.247	2.178	2.123
16	2.494	2.425	2.373	2.333	2.302	2.276	2.227	2.194	2.124	2.068
17	2.450	2.381	2.329	2.289	2.257	2.230	2.181	2.148	2.077	2.020
18	2.412	2.342	2.290	2.250	2.217	2.191	2.141	2.107	2.035	1.978
19	2.378	2.308	2.256	2.215	2.182	2.155	2.106	2.071	1.999	1.940
20	2.348	2.278	2.225	2.184	2.151	2.124	2.074	2.039	1.966	1.907
21	2.321	2.250	2.197	2.156	2.123	2.096	2.045	2.010	1.936	1.876
22	2.297	2.226	2.173	2.131	2.098	2.071	2.020	1.984	1.909	1.849
23	2.275	2.204	2.150	2.109	2.075	2.048	1.996	1.961	1.885	1.823
24	2.255	2.183	2.130	2.088	2.054	2.027	1.975	1.939	1.863	1.800
25	2.236	2.165	2.111	2.069	2.035	2.007	1.955	1.919	1.842	1.779
26	2.220	2.148	2.094	2.052	2.018	1.990	1.938	1.901	1.823	1.760
27	2.204	2.132	2.078	2.036	2.002	1.974	1.921	1.884	1.806	1.742
28	2.190	2.118	2.064	2.021	1.987	1.959	1.906	1.869	1.790	1.725
29	2.177	2.104	2.050	2.007	1.973	1.945	1.891	1.854	1.775	1.710
30	2.165	2.092	2.037	1.995	1.960	1.932	1.878	1.841	1.761	1.695
35	2.114	2.041	1.986	1.942	1.907	1.878	1.824	1.786	1.703	1.635
40	2.077	2.003	1.948	1.904	1.868	1.839	1.783	1.744	1.660	1.589
45	2.049	1.974	1.918	1.874	1.838	1.808	1.752	1.713	1.626	1.554
50	2.026	1.952	1.895	1.850	1.814	1.784	1.727	1.687	1.599	1.525
60	1.993	1.917	1.860	1.815	1.778	1.748	1.690	1.649	1.559	1.481
70	1.969	1.893	1.836	1.790	1.753	1.722	1.664	1.622	1.530	1.450
80	1.951	1.875	1.817	1.772	1.734	1.703	1.644	1.602	1.508	1.426
90	1.938	1.861	1.803	1.757	1.720	1.688	1.629	1.586	1.491	1.407
100	1.927	1.850	1.792	1.746	1.708	1.676	1.616	1.573	1.477	1.392

Random numbers

1	11	14	5	42	40	37	42	56	58	26	4	84	81	81	66	96	55	42	62
36	75	42	21	22	80	62	96	38	66	85	54	43	10	99	52	21	8	87	78
46	26	47	54	22	15	40	58	81	31	37	54	95	72	6	25	22	35	95	32
45	91	7	50	7	58	98	77	69	98	98	77	66	39	9	24	81	7	4	66
86	43	12	9	34	92	46	15	48	59	100	65	78	28	51	77	90	30	32	3
15	83	50	44	45	49	90	49	40	92	89	94	89	97	61	13	46	11	68	48
5	98	95	100	74	7	82	63	66	92	47	98	98	7	11	45	56	88	12	81
41	35	87	10	46	69	12	47	78	16	4	55	43	81	9	87	51	43	38	6
47	83	90	14	67	47	21	35	24	69	69	97	31	19	58	11	62	15	84	25
43	2	22	35	88	45	93	52	33	89	30	35	28	62	64	46	66	54	19	50
100	71	2	5	29	33	36	20	45	76	29	73	12	15	87	7	27	25	96	4
91	88	73	66	71	48	29	19	90	65	86	2	16	20	45	27	38	26	80	89
6	4	62	9	89	47	51	83	64	38	11	30	44	46	85	17	42	15	60	26
21	94	30	19	45	6	12	55	24	95	23	33	70	93	93	52	10	21	33	80
72	58	51	71	66	47	3	52	16	62	52	31	28	81	30	14	27	75	94	64
65	75	80	38	19	80	3	54	11	93	50	66	90	66	43	44	64	79	54	3
1	7	68	19	6	47	46	20	94	11	25	73	9	95	65	4	91	73	43	58
29	76	66	15	77	90	40	95	60	46	58	54	53	5	55	24	55	6	27	83
33	85	78	12	90	50	79	41	7	60	22	31	36	82	52	75	17	19	5	84
16	16	5	9	65	74	82	78	2	54	84	21	40	88	5	9	49	25	79	65
58	73	42	56	80	14	11	17	57	38	68	89	25	32	36	20	16	91	88	67
87	33	96	37	12	45	72	62	87	21	65	19	64	58	72	74	25	34	61	81
99	82	27	74	42	5	10	46	14	8	11	39	64	32	34	26	17	43	22	64
35	33	36	41	56	96	1	75	13	69	52	50	47	19	12	56	70	65	3	29
39	59	8	95	22	57	72	88	25	93	70	45	88	71	21	92	1	17	17	79
54	76	39	47	4	82	83	76	65	40	14	12	33	98	5	88	75	54	13	88
89	5	30	78	45	12	54	87	74	74	59	3	25	65	44	72	3	71	24	52
18	38	77	2	20	87	56	2	46	90	27	66	30	83	34	12	63	66	89	37
50	41	14	91	82	75	72	52	30	91	67	81	27	32	37	53	13	98	82	59
87	90	19	46	36	93	3	52	45	67	3	35	84	58	88	88	30	44	56	82
74	12	50	57	94	76	98	53	38	71	24	95	59	60	75	28	63	66	63	34
82	66	70	15	81	30	27	33	69	22	29	54	79	64	87	52	96	8	21	12
3	33	77	50	28	66	9	22	21	60	84	85	100	22	13	71	95	38	57	47
96	38	4	35	46	84	65	93	60	80	46	46	18	74	46	23	72	97	38	71
16	61	89	6	9	22	4	49	17	52	37	23	8	87	70	49	82	75	34	58
3	47	47	77	44	68	88	74	74	87	2	99	87	55	2	62	90	7	61	47
23	73	42	89	92	92	27	70	14	27	19	19	8	24	9	98	16	52	81	100
9	56	75	2	48	52	1	71	38	46	99	44	12	75	84	70	42	25	20	19
97	41	88	4	61	79	44	51	57	6	27	80	20	73	6	36	26	42	63	59
5	81	84	52	93	25	73	61	94	8	13	7	4	4	57	76	15	57	36	93
89	24	41	59	91	29	23	39	53	97	68	85	63	52	35	49	99	58	9	41
88	14	31	96	35	84	76	42	80	69	43	41	5	90	12	76	35	51	84	75
65	99	21	28	95	84	2	82	9	14	93	41	24	66	97	31	85	34	15	100
74	5	81	93	74	26	32	97	59	5	87	54	84	91	10	74	39	90	78	2
97	83	43	4	92	5	89	60	43	84	22	63	52	10	40	32	78	87	97	47
19	68	90	38	40	9	26	62	19	54	62	92	51	37	92	18	75	22	44	63
95	93	18	22	55	51	85	78	72	83	77	94	54	7	82	50	48	18	57	92
38	13	65	94	87	89	57	14	29	48	72	92	57	73	17	23	61	24	9	24
47	18	80	11	42	65	57	57	80	49	86	33	24	26	29	39	16	74	75	68
7	92	74	12	18	77	86	35	100	47	34	13	24	37	97	99	37	21	84	87

Appendix 3

Answers to selected exercises

Chapter 2

2.1 All the systems are dynamic, except for (d).

   a This is a continuous system since gas flow is a continuous process.

   b This is discrete since there are various stages in the process, which occur at different stages in time.

   c Any queuing-type system is discrete.

   d The accounts represents a 'snap-shot' of the company at one instance in time, so could be classed as static.

   e The molten steel process is continuous, while the transportation part is discrete.

2.2 a The arrival process and 'service' process will both be variable, so this will need to modelled by a stochastic model.

   b Although some of the costs may not be known precisely, the calculation will be done on a purely deterministic basis.

   c Since the demand is variable, a stochastic model would be needed here.

2.3 Unless a model is validated, there will no evidence that the model adequately represents the real system. Any results from this model will therefore be suspect. It is difficult validating a model of a new system, because there will not be any data available from the system.

2.4 The Drive Thru Burger restaurant is a dynamic system, since the state of the system is changing with time. It is also a discrete system, since events are occurring at points in time. Simulation could be used to build a stochastic model of this system, since the system is sufficiently complex to make queuing theory difficult to apply.

The system of interest is from the time customers enter the approach road to the time they receive their meal and depart. Assumptions need to be made about the following parts of the system:

   ■ arrival rate (is it constant, or does it vary from hour to hour, or day to day?)

   ■ service time (depend on number in car?)

   ■ the servers are continuously available

   ■ cars do not balk from the system

The reason for studying the system could be to attempt to improve the service to the customer, in terms of speed of delivery. Also as a mechanism to see what might happen if more customers arrived, or to try out structural changes to the system such as having ordering and collection from the same window.

Validation could be achieved by comparing waiting times or time in the system with what was observed in the real system.

Chapter 3

3.1 c Overall sales have fallen although there is some evidence that they are beginning to pick up – the past two years have shown an increase. The south east have the largest sales, but they have seen the greatest fall and their sales are still falling in 1996. The Welsh region is the smallest, but their sales have remained static over the five-year period.

3.2 a Distribution has a slight positive skew.

b The mean is 4.72 minutes and the standard deviation is 1.48 minutes.

3.3 $\dfrac{4}{50} \times \dfrac{3}{49} = 0.00490$

3.4 The answer of 0.0361 could be found by either using tables, MINITAB or by adding the probabilities of zero customers, one customer and two customers and then subtracting this sum from zero.

3.5 An average rate of 43.8 minutes implies 0.73 arrivals per minute. This is the same type of problem used in Scenario 3.9, and the MINITAB printout can be used for parts a and b.

a $P(0) = 0.4819$

b $P(x \geqslant 3) = 1 - 0.9621$

$\qquad\qquad = 0.0379$

c Need to calculate the probability of no arrivals in two minutes. The average number of arrivals in two minutes is 1.46, so the probability of no arrivals is:

$$P(0) = \frac{1.46^0 \times e^{-1.46}}{0!} = 0.2322$$

3.6 a $Z = \dfrac{6-5}{1.5} = 0.667$

$P(Z > 1.667) = 0.2514$

b $P(4 < x < 6) = 1 - (P(x < 4) + P(x > 6))$

$\qquad\qquad = 1 - (0.2514 + 0.2514)$

$\qquad\qquad = 0.4972$

c $1.645 = \dfrac{x-5}{1.5}$

$x = 7.47$ minutes

3.7   Standard error of the mean is $\dfrac{13}{\sqrt{9}} = 4.333$

$$Z = \frac{40 - 45}{4.333} = 1.1539$$

$P(Z > 1.1539) = 0.1251$

3.8   Standard error of the mean is $1.22/\sqrt{50} = 0.1725$

$$\mu = 3.5 \pm 1.96 \times 0.1725$$

$$= \text{£}3.16 \text{ to £}3.84$$

3.9 H_0: $\mu = 3.65$ H_1: $\mu \neq 3.65$

Standard error of the mean is $1.34/\sqrt{12} = 0.3868$

$$Z = \frac{3.50 - 3.65}{0.3868} = 0.388$$

The t-value on 11 degrees of freedom at 5 per cent significance level is 1.796. The null hypothesis is therefore accepted; the mean amount spent has not changed.

Chapter 4

4.1   **a**   Three Ambassador and fourteen Baron cookers should be produced, giving a profit of £820.

   b   The tight constraints are the labour and clock constraints, since all these resources have been used at the optimum solution.

   c   The shadow price of the labour constraint is £7.50 an hour, and for the clock constraint it is £5 per clock.

   d   It would be worth obtaining an additional 36 clocks, giving a total profit of £1000.

4.2   This is an integer problem, but solved as a linear programming problem would give 3.43 doctors and 1.14 nurses. This results in a cost of £182.86 per session. A more sensible solution might be to employ one nurse and four doctors. This would satisfy all constraints, but the cost would increase to £210.

4.3   **a**   The optimal solution is to make 1500 batches of Vin Speciale and 1000 batches of Vin Ordinaire, which gives a profit of £130,000.

   b   The tight constraints are Somerset Pink and Wiltshire White grapes. 20,000 kilograms of Wiltshire White grapes should be grown, and the total profit would be £150,000.

4.7   **a** $\text{EOQ} = \sqrt{\dfrac{2 \times 20 \times 100}{0.05}} = 283$ bags

   The weekly cost of this policy would be

$$0.05 \times \frac{283}{2} + 20 \times \frac{100}{283} = \text{£14.14 per week}$$

and the time between orders is 20 days, on average.

b The standard deviation is 28.85 and the buffer stock is found from

$$\frac{x - 200}{28.85} = \text{£1.645.}$$

This gives the buffer stock as about 48 bags, and the cost will be £2.40 per week.

4.8 The EBQ $= \sqrt{\dfrac{2 \times 300 \times 1200}{0.026 \times (1 - 1200/2000)}} = 8321.$

The cost of this policy is

$$\frac{0.026 \times 8321}{2}\left(1 - \frac{1200}{2000}\right) + \frac{300 \times 1200}{8321} = \text{£86.53 per hour.}$$

4.9 The order quantity is $\sqrt{\dfrac{2 \times 50 \times 250}{1000}\left(\dfrac{1000 - 300}{300}\right)} = 10.41.$

So, ten cars should be ordered at a time. The number of planned backorders is

$$10 \times \left(\frac{1000}{1000 + 300}\right) = 7.7.$$

That is about eight backorders. The cost of this policy is

$$\frac{(10 - 8)^2 \times 1000}{2 \times 10} + \frac{50}{10} \times 250 + \frac{8^2}{2 \times 10} \times 300 = \text{£2410 per year.}$$

If the EOQ policy was adopted, the order quantity would be

$$\sqrt{\frac{2 \times 250 \times 50}{1000}} = 5$$

and the cost would be $1000 \times \dfrac{5}{2} + 250 \times \dfrac{50}{5} = \text{£5000.}$

4.10 The arrival rate $\lambda = 47$, and the service rate μ is 80 an hour. The mean number in the queue is

$$\frac{47^2}{80(80 - 47)} - 0.834$$

and the mean waiting time in the queue is

$$\frac{0.834}{47} \times 60 \times 60 = 6.4 \text{ seconds.}$$

4.13 $\lambda = 0.05$ per minute and $\mu = 0.0667$ per minute. $\lambda/\mu = 0.7496$.

The average number of lorries in the queue is

$$\frac{(0.05)^2 \times (3.6)^2 + (0.7496)^2}{2 \times (1 - 0.7496)} = 1.187.$$

The average time a lorry spends in the queue is $1.187/0.05 = 23.7$ minutes and time in the system is $23.7 + 15 = 38.7$ minutes.

4.14 The average number of lorries in the queue is now

$$\frac{(0.7496)^2}{2 \times (1 - 0.7496)} = 1.122$$

The average time a lorry spends in the queue is 22.44 minutes and the average time in the system will be 37.4 minutes.

Chapter 5

5.3 The average service time is about 44 seconds. We can amend Table 5.5 as follows:

Random No.	Iat	Clock time	No. in queue	Service time	Service starts	Service ends	Waiting time
08	15	15	0	44	15	44	0
87	75	90	0	44	90	134	0
15	15	105	1	44	134	178	29
04	15	120	2	44	178	222	58
52	15	135	2	44	222	266	87
46	15	150	3	44	266	310	116
95	105	255	2	44	310	354	55
10	15	270	2	44	354	398	84
02	15	285	3	44	398	442	113

The constant mean has reduced the mean time customers spend waiting for service from 72.2 seconds to 60.2 seconds. The standard deviation has also reduced from 50.4 seconds to 43.9 seconds.

Chapter 7

7.1

i	x_i	$17 \times x_i$	$17 \times x_i/13$	$U(0,1)$
0	6	102	91 r 11	0.4615
1	11	187	14 r 5	0.8462
2	5	85	6 r 7	0.3846
3	7	119	9 r 2	0.5385

7.4 7.3, 5.3, 4.2

7.5 2.5, 6.4, 10.4

7.6 The sampled Z value will be 0.927, so the normal variate will be $6.1 + 0.927 \times 1.8 = 7.77$.

7.7 The sum of the last twelve numbers is 5.2416, so $Z = 5.2416 - 6 = 0.7584$, giving a variate of value $6.1 - 0.7584 \times 1.8 = 4.73$.

7.8

r_1	Z	$f(x)$	r_2	h	Decision
0.0052	−4.948	0	0.3562	0.1425	reject
0.4550	−0.450	0.361	0.4485	0.1794	accept
0.8613	3.613	0.0006	0.1534	0.0614	reject
0.0547	0.470	0.357	0.4119	0.1648	accept

Two Z values have been accepted; these are −0.450 and 0.470. These can be converted into normal variates with a mean of 6.1 and a standard deviation of 1.8, to give values of 5.29 and 6.95.

7.9

n	r	x	cumulative x
1	0.0052	13.147	13.147
2	0.3562	2.581	15.728
3	0.4550	1.969	17.697
4	0.4485	2.005	19.701
5	0.8613	0.3733	20.07

There would be four arrivals in the first twenty-minute interval.

Chapter 8

8.1 b, c and e

8.2 **a** The values of *a* and *b* are given in the table below:

Relative frequency	Cumulative relative frequency	Demand ucb	gradient *a*	intercept *b*
0.0500	0.0000	5	22.73	5.00
0.2200	0.2200	10	33.33	2.67
0.3000	0.5200	20	66.67	−14.67
0.1500	0.6700	30	111.11	−44.44
0.1800	0.8500	50	333.33	−233.33
0.1500	1.0000	100	100.00	0.00

b The demand when the random number is 0.6514 is $66.67 \times 0.6514 - 14.67 = 28.8$.

Chapter 9

9.1 The entities are the items that are being produced. The activities are the creation of the items, the processes carried out by the machines, and the inspection at the end of the line. The system state variables might be the time taken to produce an item, the throughput of items, the time an item spends in queue or storage area, the number of items waiting to be processed, or the utilisation of the machines.

Chapter 10

10.1 (a) and (e) are deterministic and the others are stochastic.

10.2 Airport traffic is likely to be highly seasonal with higher levels in the summer than other times of the year. There might also be differences in days of the week and times of the day. The periods when the data should be collected will depend largely on the purpose of the simulation model. If the aim is to reduce congestion during busy periods, data will need to be collected for these periods and quieter periods ignored.

10.3 There are several examples. Some distributions, like the normal, *t*-distributions and uniform, are always symmetrical, while others can be symmetrical given the right parameters. Examples of the latter include the triangular, the beta, the binomial and gamma distribution.

10.4 Arrivals will turn up just before the start of the film, so the arrival rate will start off low, reach a peak just before the start of the film, and then quickly reduce to zero after the film has started. It is unlikely that arrivals of individuals will be random as most people come in groups of two or more, and in these cases the arrival of one member of the group is not independent of the arrival of the other members. However, the arrival of *groups* might be random over the short period before the film starts.

Chapter 11

11.1 (a) and (e) are terminating systems as they are operational for specific periods of time, and start in the empty state. b and c are obviously non-terminating as they do not close. (d) is non-terminating for the same reasons, although at certain times (during the night) a road junction will be effectively inactive. (f) is also non-terminating, even though a building society is a terminating system. This is because the system re-starts in the morning in the same state as it was left the day before.

11.2 Although five batches is a rather low number, this will be preferable to the second option. This is because five hours is a very short time, and autocorrelation could be a problem.

11.3 This is a non-terminating system (for the same reason as (f) in Exercise 11.1), and the time taken to reach steady state would need to be found. One long run of the simulation would then be made and the run divided into several batches. Each batch could then be analysed independently. The performance measures of interest would be the time to process claims, and the number of claims processed during a specific period. This information could be compared with actual figures from the existing system. This comparison could take the form of qualitative observations using graphical representations, and statistical comparisons using confidence intervals.

11.4 The mean and standard deviation of the data are 14.96 and 4.437. The standard error is $4.437/\sqrt{5} = 1.984$. The 95 per cent confidence interval will be: $14.96 \pm 2.132 \times 1.984$ $= 10.7, 16.9$. The value of eighteen minutes is outside this interval, and consequently the model cannot be validated. However, the value is only just outside and the model may be considered adequate, if other validation measures have proved satisfactory.

Chapter 12

12.1 A paired t-test is used when there is correlation between the two alternatives and the sampled population is normally distributed. Correlation occurs when the same random numbers have been used in both alternatives.

12.2 Common random numbers could be used when the two alternative models have essentially the same structure. Each source of variability within the model should have its own random number stream, and there should be a mechanism to discard a large number of random numbers between replications.

12.3 Since an additional runway means that a structural change has been made to the model, it might be wise to use different random number streams for each model and use a test for independent data, such as the two-sample t-test.

12.4 96.

12.6 The Mann-Whitney test is a non-parametric test, and may be necessary if there are doubts whether the data is normally distributed.

12.7 An interaction effect can provide important information on how the response to one factor is affected by the level of another factor. This could be important as it might reveal that a particular combination of factors could have a desirable or undesirable effect on the performance of the system.

12.8 The MINITAB output shown below indicates that there is no significant difference between the populations. That is, the use of a doctor does not appear to have improved the performance of the system.

> Twosample T for C1 vs C2
>
> | N | Mean | StDev | SE | Mean |
> |------|------|-------|------|------|
> | C1 | 10 | 13.69 | 4.76 | 1.5 |
> | C2 | 10 | 11.85 | 2.43 | 0.77 |
>
> 95% C.I. for mu C1 - mu C2: (–1.8, 5.49)
>
> T-Test mu C1 = mu C2 (vs >): T= 1.09 P=0.15 DF= 13

Appendix 4

Files available on the disk that accompanies the text

Whiteladies data file: WLAD.XLS   Whiteladies model file: WLAD.DOE

Drive Thru Burger data file: DTB.XLS   Drive Thru Burger file: DTB:DOE

Chapter 3

SCEN3_19.XLS   A spreadsheet file giving the Chi-square calculations for the doctor consultation time data.

SCEN3_20.XLS   A spreadsheet file giving the Kolmogorov-Smirnov test calculations for the doctor consultation time data.

Chapter 4

SCEN3_21.TXT   A text file giving details of the MINITAB commands for Scenario 3.21.

SCEN4_7.XLS   A spreadsheet file that uses the Solver routine to solve a linear programming problem.

SCEN4_17.XLS   A spreadsheet file to calculate the average service time for different values of the arrival rate.

CHAP4Q15.XLS   A spreadsheet file for solving the M/M/1 model where the population is finite.

Chapter 7

RANDOM.XLS   A spreadsheet file containing 1000 random numbers (an electronic copy of the table in Appendix 2).

RUNS.SPS   A SPSS syntax file for the 'runs' test on the 1000 random numbers.

AUTO.TXT   A MINITAB syntax file for the autocorrelation test on the 1000 random numbers.

Chapter 8

SCEN8_1.XLS	A spreadsheet file for a stock-control system. Constant delivery times.
SCEN8_2.XLS	As SCEN8_1 but order quantity increased to 300 tins.
SCEN8_3.XLS	Macro used to make multiple simulations.
SCEN8_4.XLS	As SCEN8_1 but variable delivery times.
SCEN8_5A.XLS	@RISK model A.
SCEN8_5B.XLS	@RISK model B.
SCEN8_5C.XLS	@RISK model C.
SCEN8_5D.XLS	@RISK model D.

Chapter 12

SCEN12_4.MTW	A MINITAB worksheet for Scenario 12.4.
SCEN12_5.SAV	A SPSS data file for Scenario 12.5.
SCEN12_6.MTW	A MINITAB worksheet for Scenario 12.6.
SCEN12_7.SAV	A SPSS data file for Scenario 12.7.
SCEN12_8.MTW	A MINITAB worksheet for Scenario 12.8.
SCEN12_8.SAV	A SPSS data file for Scenario 12.8
SCEN12_9.MTW	A MINITAB worksheet for Scenario 12.9.
SCE12_10.MTW	A MINITAB worksheet for Scenario 12.10.

Index